A RUMOUR OF GOD

A RUMOUR OF GOD

*Rekindling Belief
in an Age of Disenchantment*

Robert C. Sibley

NOVALIS

Cover design: Ingrid Paulson
Cover image: Alexey Popovsky/iStockphoto
Layout: Audrey Wells

Published by Novalis

Publishing Office
10 Lower Spadina Avenue, Suite 400
Toronto, Ontario, Canada
M5V 2Z2

Head Office
4475 Frontenac Street
Montréal, Québec, Canada
H2H 2S2

www.novalis.ca

Library and Archives Canada Cataloguing in Publication

Sibley, Robert C. (Robert Cameron)
    A rumour of God : rekindling belief in an age of disenchantment
/ Robert Sibley.

Includes bibliographical references and index.

ISBN 978-2-89646-231-5

    1. Spiritual life. I. Title.

BL624.S48 2010   204   C2010-905953-0

Printed in Canada.

We acknowledge the financial support of the Government of Canada through the
Canada Book Fund for business development activities.

5   4   3   2   1   14   13   12   11   10

Dedication

This book is dedicated to my mother, Diana Alice Sibley.
She made every house a home.

ACKNOWLEDGEMENTS

Every book has its origins, many of which become apparent only retrospectively and long years later. In this regard, I am grateful to Leon Logie, the high school English teacher who opened my eyes to the wonder of literature; Alan White, a former editor of the *Whitehorse Star*, who brought me into the craft of journalism; Tana Dineen and George Matheson for their friendship, encouragement and the solitude of the "attic"; and Kevin Burns, one of those rare editors with the imagination to see potential in a bare bones idea. I am also grateful to Carol Papworth, Carol Strobel, Nilla Brown, Carol Booth, Jolayne Dancey, Gillian Mailes and Susan Cavell for more "privileged moments" than any young man (or boy) has the right to expect.

I owe a great deal to the editors at the *Ottawa Citizen*, past and present – Neil Reynolds, Scott Anderson, Derek Shelly, Rob Warner, Christina Spencer, Lynn McAuley, Kurt Johnson and Susan Allan, in particular – who, in their various capacities, supported, edited or otherwise made some of these essays possible. More formally, I gratefully acknowledge the *Ottawa Citizen* and Postmedia News (formerly Canwest Publications) for permission to draw on essays, columns and features that have appeared in the newspaper. I must also thank the students who attended my lectures at the Ottawa School of Theology and Spirituality. Their comments and suggestions were most helpful.

My greatest debts, though, are, as always, to my wife and fellow writer, Margret Kopala, and my son, Daniel. Their love and support (and patience) keep my world enchanted.

CONTENTS

ONE

THE GLIMPSE OF UNDERGLIMMER
Introducing a Rumour

I can feel nothing but compassion for those who sincerely lament their doubt, who regard it as the ultimate misfortune, and who, sparing no effort to escape from it, make their search their principal and most serious business.
— Blaise Pascal, *Pensées*[1]

Absolute attention is prayer.
— Simone Weil[2]

One fine sunny morning, about a month after I began my pilgrimage trek along the Camino de Santiago, I walked out of the town of Sarria, following the pilgrim path as it entered the realm of *corredorias*, the narrow green pathways that lace Spain's Galician countryside like a maze. Eight hundred years ago, in the *Codex Calixtinus*, the French pilgrim Aimery Picaud described Galicia as the pilgrims' promised land. It's easy to understand why. After the mountains of the Pyrenees and the barren regions of Castile and Leon, it must have seemed a veritable paradise with its green valleys and lush vegetation. The route has not changed substantially in hundreds of years. The *corredorias* wind through woodlands of chestnut and oak, birch and pine, and, here and there, copses of tall, smooth-trunked eucalyptus trees. Sometimes the Camino is little more than a narrow twisting path, bordered by vine-covered stone walls or dense bramble hedges.

It had rained the night before and the air was fresh and clean as I set out in the early morning hours. I splashed through rivulets of water flowing down the middle of paths. Shafts of sunlight cut through gaps in the trees, dappling the path with shifting patterns of shade and light. An occasional breeze showered me with raindrops from the overhanging trees. I walked with the slightly disoriented sensation you sometimes get after waking from an afternoon nap and feeling out of kilter with the world. My sense of disorientation probably had something to do with having spent two days in a hotel in Sarria recovering from a bout of food poisoning. But it also had something to do with having finally settled into my role as a pilgrim.

For nearly a month – from the last week of March to the third week of April – I had been hiking the Camino de Santiago, an 800-kilometre pilgrimage route that crosses northern Spain from the Pyrenees mountains to the Galician city of Santiago de Compostela. The route is more than 1,000 years old, traversing the green valleys of Navarre and Rioja, the plains of Castile and Leon and the lush alpine mountains of Galicia until, finally, it reaches Santiago, where, according to tradition, the bones of St. James the Apostle are encased in a silver reliquary. Even today, in our avowedly secular age, the Camino de Santiago remains one of the most sacred pilgrimage routes in the Christian world.

By the time I reached Sarria, which is about 100 kilometres from Santiago, I had endured some rather nasty blisters that made walking excruciatingly painful, swollen tendons that left me limping, long hours that had me drooping with fatigue by the end of the day and, as I mentioned, a couple of days in a hotel bed flushing out the consequences of a bad meal. (I think it was a plate of *huevos con carne* – ham and eggs – that didn't smell right to begin with but that I ate nonetheless, not knowing enough Spanish to inform the waitress of my suspicions.) But despite these infirmities I talked to ghosts from my past, sang old songs from childhood, dreamed dreams of long-ago lovers that left me aching for what might have been, and remembered people and places that I had not even known to be in my memory. I also saw some splendid country, enjoyed great seafood, drank a lot of good wine and encountered an intriguing crew of modern-day pilgrims that even Geoffrey Chaucer would have appreciated. But most importantly I experienced moments of epiphany, moments of wonder, that even now, years later, continue to reverberate in my mind, telling me that my pilgrimage is ongoing and, perhaps, endless.

My morning walk out of Sarria offered one such moment. I would sometimes walk for ten or fifteen minutes at a stretch, aware of little more than the changing surface of the path beneath my feet – stony, muddy, leaf-thick – and the stretch and tension in my legs as I climbed or waded through a stream or stepped across a jumble of loose rock. I felt detached from my body. It was as though my mind floated above and behind my body like a balloon on a string. Light-headed, you might say.

This was as it should be. The pilgrim, like any serious traveller, undertakes an interior journey that parallels passage through the external world. Each sustains the other. There is a psychological benefit to the *feel* of the mud and stones and trees and rain and sun. The senses confront the natural world directly, no longer cocooned and cosseted by the machinery of a car or a train or a plane. The result is, or can be, a surprised awakening to the sheer presence of the world. Walking allows you to be in the world again in a way

10

that is impossible in a car or on a plane. After a month on the road, after the blisters and the pain, the encounters with land and sky, the kindnesses of strangers, and especially after the sickness of the last couple of days, I felt calm and quiet and, well, clean. For the first time in I don't know how long I was content to be doing what I was doing and being where I was without nagging myself with the thought that I should be doing something more worthwhile or be somewhere more exciting. I was happy to be where I was in the here and now. I enjoyed that rarest of satisfactions – contentment. I wanted to walk forever.

Early in the afternoon, I followed the path downhill through the village of Morgade, stopping to rest by a small fountain in a clearing at the western edge of town. The spigot on the fountain wasn't operating, but the basin still held a couple of feet of water. I dropped my pack against the fountain wall and undid the bandana around my neck and dipped it in the water to wash my face and neck. I sat against the fountain wall to let the sun dry my face. I was content to look at the swaying branches of the chestnut trees overhead and listen to the chatter of linnets and swallowtails and let the warmth of the sun saturate my body.

I might have enjoyed an afternoon nap, but a loud splash in the fountain at my back startled me. I stood and looked at the surface of the water, seeing circles of ripples. I was about to sit down again when the shiny green head of a lizard rose to the surface. I watched it paddle to the fountain wall and try to climb the slippery surface. It tried and failed four times. Each attempt to escape left it weaker. It was going to die, I thought.

Death is not uncommon on the Camino. Just as in the Middle Ages, pilgrims still die on the road to Santiago. You occasionally see flowers or small crosses beside the pilgrimage trail. One morning I sheltered from the rain beneath the portico of a graveyard outside Navarrete. A plaque on the wall commemorates a young Belgian woman, Alice de Graemer. She died when a car hit her as she cycled to Santiago in 1986. A sculpture of an iron bicycle commemorates a German cyclist who died of a heart attack in the mountains of El Bierzo. I'd read of a Dutchman who died of a heart attack a few miles outside Santiago, only hours before completing his pilgrimage. But death on the Camino takes other forms, too. You sometimes come across the skeletons or desiccated carcasses of animals. Hares, mostly, but I once saw the body of a dog beside the trail, its eyes obscured by a covering of flies. Another time I found a sheep carcass. It looked like dogs had ripped it apart. The pilgrim museum in Roncesvalles, a small town at the foot of the Pyrenees where the Spanish portion of the Camino begins, possesses a medieval wooden bas-relief of dogs devouring a pilgrim.

Watching the struggling lizard, I remembered stopping at a roadside well a couple of weeks earlier in the town of Najera. Looking into the well, I saw the pale bellies of half a dozen dead frogs floating on the surface. But there were still two others struggling to escape, trying repeatedly to gain a grip on the slick stone wall. I thought of leaning over the lip of the well to scoop them out with my baseball cap, but it was all too easy to imagine myself falling into the well. I left them to their fate.

I don't really understand why I did what I did, but on this afternoon, at the fountain in Morgade, I thought it important to save the lizard. I'd let the frogs die but I wasn't going to let this lizard die, not if I could help it. I took off my boots and socks and climbed into the fountain. The water came up to my knees. Judging by the lizard's reaction, it must have assumed I was some big bird looking for a midday snack. It thrashed madly away when I tried to scoop it up with my baseball cap. I lunged after it, water splashing up my legs.

I tried again, only to have my feet go out from under me on the slippery stone basin. I sat down with a splash. My pants were soaked now, along with most of the rest of me. I glanced around the clearing, glad nobody from the village was there to watch a stupid pilgrim taking a bath in his clothes. I looked for the lizard, afraid maybe I'd sat on it. But no, there it was on the far side of the fountain. I got to my feet and splashed across the fountain after the creature. Clearly, the lizard didn't know I wasn't going to eat it. It kept trying to paddle away. But its movements were increasingly feeble and sluggish. I finally scooped its six-inch length into the bowl of my cap and stepped out of the fountain.

I set my hat on the grass, tilting it so the lizard could escape. Instead of darting away, though, it lay on its side in my cap, exhausted, pale white belly heaving and tail unmoving. Its turquoise-green head was motionless. I watched the creature while I stripped off my shirt and draped it across a bush to dry. I wondered if I'd exhausted the lizard to the point of death. But then suddenly the tail twitched. It jerked upright on its feet and scuttled out of my cap and across the open ground into a gap in the bramble hedge. Just before it disappeared, the creature stopped, its head turned back in my direction, eyes blinking. "You're welcome," I said.

I stared into the green gap after the lizard. Maybe the fact that I hadn't eaten anything besides fruit juice for two days had left me light-headed; my thoughts spun off into silly anthropomorphic sentiments. The lizard would reappear with its doting family to hail me as a hero. Or maybe if I'd kissed the lizard it would have turned into a beautiful princess and she would have joined my pilgrimage. After all, if not for my fortuitous presence, the lizard would have died. I was the saviour of lizards. I laughed at the thought, but I did feel that I'd assuaged my guilt at having abandoned the frogs in Najera. Perhaps I'd even shaved a few points off my karmic debts.

Lost in madcap fantasy, I gazed into the hedge, hypnotized by the green wall, my imagination following the lizard
deeper into the bower where it had fled. The world seemed
to be closing in around me. I saw everything close up, tightly
focused, as though through a telephoto lens. Everything –
leaves and grass, trees and stone – acquired a sharp-edged
vividness. The air seemed to hum. I heard birdsong and the
rustle of wind-stirred leaves in the trees overhead. The rich
odour of rain-damp earth enveloped me. The warmth of the
sun washed over me. I imagined the photons of light sinking into me like weights, pulling me into the earth. I tried
to resist for a moment, feeling a sudden panic, a reluctance
to submit. And then, of a sudden, like cork popping to the
surface of the water, I seemed to pop free of the world. For
a moment I floated a few inches off the ground, away from
my own body. The sensation didn't last long, a few seconds
at most, and then I fell back into my body.

I want to be careful in accounting for this experience. I
hesitate to claim it as mystical. I've read enough about mysticism to be fairly sure of this. Yet, I don't want to dismiss
the possibility altogether. As the American psychologist
William James noted more than a century ago, the words
"mystical" and "mysticism" are often employed derisively
to describe someone indulging in fanciful sentiments or
self-delusion, someone who believes in spirit haunting and
contact with the dead. James, however, took mystical experience seriously, arguing that he'd accumulated enough
evidence to be convinced that it was real. His most famous
book, *The Varieties of Religious Experience*, offers a still widely
cited description of mystical experience. Mysticism, James
wrote, starts with an experience that satisfies four criteria:
it is ineffable; you "know" only through direct experience.
Secondly, the experience possesses a noetic quality in that
it reveals significant and important knowledge despite the

inability to articulate that knowledge. Thirdly and fourthly, the experience is transient, seldom lasting for more than an hour (and more likely for only a few seconds), and it is a passive state in the sense that you feel "grasped and held by a superior power."[3]

James mentions elsewhere in his book that a feeling of blissfulness and a sense of overarching cosmic unity are often other aspects of mystical experience. However, he also observes that some mystics' experiences have been anything but ineffable or transient. Some go on at great length, detailing their visions of other worlds, and assert a permanent alteration in their psychic structure. Nor do all mystics report feelings of bliss and unity; some have felt great horror at their visions.[4]

I don't think I came near anything like a sense of oneness or unity with the cosmos or self-dissolution that some claim to be the height of mystical experience. I certainly didn't feel like I'd acquired some great knowledge or indisputable Truth with a capital T. Nor did I intuit a divine presence or awareness of transcendent reality, as far as I can tell. But in at least one aspect, my experience fit James' criteria: its ineffability. The closest I can get in trying to convey what I felt is to say that I was utterly at ease. However brief the experience, I felt like I had just come back from some amazing vacation where I'd enjoyed absolute relaxation. Not only did I feel physically at ease, but also I was mentally – spiritually? – utterly and blessedly at peace. I looked out on the world with great calm, as though I had been vouchsafed a glimpse of "the Way Things Are," to borrow a phrase from sociologist and Catholic priest Andrew Greeley.[5] Does this constitute a mystical experience? I think the answer has to be a tentative "yes," if only because it meets another of James' criteria. Mystical states, he said, are never merely interruptive. They don't just happen, only to be forgotten. "Some memory of their content always remains, and a profound sense of their importance. They modify the inner life of the subject, between the times of their occurrence."[6] I sometimes think this book was conceived in that moment.

I don't know how long I sat there against the fountain, but by the time I put my boots back on, my nylon pants and shirt were mostly dry. I might have continued to sit there, happy in my little bower, feeling all right with the world, if my stomach hadn't started gurgling and complaining about its emptiness. For the first time in days, I was hungry. I had a couple of hours walking ahead of me to reach the town of Portomarin, where I planned to stay for the night. I stood and hauled my pack onto my back. I took a last look around my green oasis – the fountain, the trees, the green wall where my lizard had disappeared. I would remember this place as special. The lines of a favourite poem by the Japanese pilgrim-poet Bashō flitted across my mind: "In this bush profound,/ Into the very rocks it seeps/ The cicada sound./ Here, now, the glimpse of the underglimmer."[7] It seemed an appropriate sentiment for the occasion.

That was a decade ago, in the spring of 2000. It was my first pilgrimage. I begin these essays describing this experience for two reasons. First, even though my epiphany of the lizard, as I came to call that moment, was an out-of-the-blue surprise, such moments are not unusual, particularly when you're engaged in a long-distance trek such as a pilgrimage. One of the most common psychological consequences of pilgrimage is the way hours of walking alone can trigger unexpected thoughts, fantasies and recollections. I've undertaken other pilgrimages since the Camino and I've had similar experiences, some of which have been more intense, some less. I've come to think of them as my "glimpses of the underglimmer," moments when I feel I've crossed some kind of threshold of perception. In pursuit of these moments I have undertaken other long-distance walks, but I've also had similar epiphanic moments in the most commonplace of circumstances – standing on the edge of a highway, walking in a park, or even sitting in my backyard on a summer evening. I shall draw on some of these moments over the course of these essays. There are numerous labels for these kinds of experience. The psychologist Abraham Maslow referred to them as "peak experiences." The French mystic Romain Rolland described them as the "oceanic feeling." The English novelist Virginia Woolf called them "moments of being," or "moments of vision." In this regard, I can safely say my "glimpse of the underglimmer" was not unique, or, as I shall show, unusual.

2. That brings me to my second reason for beginning with such an experience. There is nothing esoteric or particularly exotic about these everyday epiphanies. (Nor are they harmful to your health, although you might get wet if you chase lizards.) A glimpse of the underglimmer is available to anyone – in the right circumstances and with the right frame of mind (or spirit). The qualification is important because while such experiences might be available to most everyone, it takes effort to cultivate the conditions and the state of mind that make these experiences – what I'm calling, borrowing from theologian Karl Rahner, "mysticism of the everyday" – more likely. Research suggests that many people have "mystical" experiences,[8] but there are no guarantees. The "underglimmer" is there for all to perceive, but the proper perspective is necessary to perceive it. That perspective is not easy to achieve in an era of disenchantment such as ours.

****

With this argument in mind, I perhaps need to define my terms and set the scene for my exercise in re-enchantment. Let me begin with the phrase "disenchantment of the world" and what has arguably been one of the main consequences of that disenchantment: nihilism. I do this because it is important to understand our contemporary condition and what is at stake when I argue for the necessity of the world's re-enchantment.

The German sociologist Max Weber coined the disenchantment phrase in the early twentieth century. "The fate of our times," he wrote in 1917, "is characterized by rationalization and intellectualization and, above all, by the 'disenchantment of the world.'"[9] I'll be discussing the notion of disenchantment in Chapter Five, so it is perhaps sufficient here to point out that the reasons for this disenchantment are numerous: the Reformation challenge to the Roman Catholic Church, the increasing capacity of science and technology to explain the workings of the natural world, the urbanization of Western societies following the Industrial Revolution, to name but a few. But this "rationalization" of the world has also involved the decline of a sense of the supernatural. Weber's phrase encapsulates the notion that the modern, post-Enlightenment world has resulted in the gradual waning of mystery. The pre-modern world was "enchanted" in that it provided people with a transcendent sense of ultimate meaning and purpose, as well as a sense of mystery regarding the world in all its unknowingness.

The modern world, however, with its scientific explanations of natural phenomena, has, little by little, whittled away at the unknown. Physics, in short, replaced metaphysics. Rainbows, as Descartes taught, are neither signs of the goddess Iris streaking across the sky nor reminders of a divine covenant, but the consequence of prismatic refraction. A solar eclipse is not a sign of divine wrath but merely the moon interposing itself between the sun and the earth. Chemical imbalances, not demonic possession, explain psychological maladies. According to Weber, scientific reasoning could someday explain everything, all natural phenomena. The rationalization and intellectualization of the world through science and technology means "there are in principle no mysterious, incalculable forces that come into play, but rather that one can, in principle, master all things by calculation. This means the world is disenchanted."[10]

In the age of belief, people assumed that the sense of meaning they derived from their social and political institutions – from family to monarchy – was anchored in a divine reality. In the modern era, however, this God-oriented structure gave way to a science-based, human-centric worldview. As moderns, we hoped science and technology would create heaven on earth. It was thought that notions of a transcendent world beyond this one would eventually disappear from our collective mind. Behind this utopian idea is science's claim that nature, including human nature, is nothing more than mindless matter functioning according to natural laws of cause and effect. In theory, science would someday be able to explain everything – matter and energy and space and time – according to natural laws, eliminating all possibility of (or need for) a divine order beyond or behind or above the material world. Indeed, scientism purports to show, according to some proponents, that the emergence of self-conscious creatures such as human beings was nothing more than a quirky happenstance of biological history, an accident of evolution with no ultimate purpose or meaning to the world other than ones humans themselves create.

Morris Berman sums up this worldview in an influential study of the "progressive" attitudes of Western intellectual elites in the 1960s and 1970s.

The view of nature which predominated in the West down to the eve of the Scientific Revolution was that of an enchanted world. Rocks, trees, rivers and clouds were all seen as wondrous, alive, and human beings felt at home in this environment ... The story of the modern epoch, at least on the level of the mind, is one of progressive disenchantment. From the sixteenth century on, mind has been progressively expunged from the phenomenal world.

So it seems. Weber's phrase – *die Entzauberung der Welt*, in the German – was preceded in the eighteenth century by Friedrich Schiller's more poetic precedent: *die Entgotterung der Natur* – the "disgodding of nature." The history of the modern West, according to both the poet and the scientist, has been all about "the progressive removal of mind, or spirit, from phenomenal appearances."[11] And that includes the mind of God.

Philosopher Hent de Vries sums up this "disgodding" effort in noting the ways in which Western intellectual elites have variously dismissed religion as

truth in the garment of a lie" (Schopenhauer), "anthropology disguised as theology" (Feuerbach), "ideology and false consciousness" (Marx), "infantile neurosis" (Freud), "the nonsensical expression of feeling diffused by metaphysicians without poetical or musical talent" (Carnap), "a category mistake" (Ryle), "a form of life" (Wittgenstein), and so on.[12]

Thus, our Enlightenment forebears bequeathed the notion that God is, in the words of philosopher Paul Brockelman, "a hypothetical inference rather than a directly encountered phenomenon ubiquitous to human experience." The scientific revolution disenchanted nature by draining it of a divine presence, rendering it as mere stuff available for our exclusive use. Any notion of nature's beauty and grandeur as the immanent manifestation of God is merely a psychological projection of man's infantile longings (or so

Freud argued), an attempt to compensate for our sense of insignificance in the face of the universe's vastness and apparent indifference.

In the wake of our "disgodding," many people nowadays, particularly in the West, are hesitant to acknowledge religious or spiritual leanings. But even those willing to interest themselves in the religious or spiritual find that in a culture where only "scientific" knowledge – knowledge based on provable, empirical evidence – is considered legitimate knowledge, it is difficult, and even embarrassing, to speak of mystery or mysticism or things of the spirit. Our disenchantment may have won us a certain type of freedom and material prosperity, but it has come at a price. "The more we assert our will to control [the world], the more we enter a dark night in which the holy and creative power-to-be is pushed out of existence and our need to appreciate life is simply shunted aside," writes Brockelman. "God and spiritual experience are not argued out of existence; they become invisible and we become simply indifferent to them. The cost of conquering Being in order to secure our lives has been an alienation from ourselves to such a degree that God and faith make no sense at all."[13] In other words, our disgodding led to nihilism.

The Russian novelist Ivan Turgenev offered one of the earliest references to nihilism in his 1861 book, *Fathers and Sons*. In the novel, a young revolutionary character, Bazarov, is described as a nihilist. Turgenev meant it as a criticism, but Russian anarchists and revolutionaries of the time adopted the idea and used it to justify their propensity for violence and political assassination. The word comes from the Latin *nihil*, which means "nothing." A nihilist is someone who believes in nothing. (In a sense, it's impossible to believe in nothing, because to believe in nothing is still to believe in something.) For a nihilist, all human constructions and institutions, all traditions and values, are meaningless. In the words of philosopher Robert Bartlett, "Nihilism holds, in brief, that all so-called objective truths, and in particular all judgments of right and wrong, have in the modern era finally been revealed to be what they have always been, namely man-made creations of the human will. They are not grounded in Nature or God or Truth and can find no support in anything outside of, or higher than, our own will."[14]

An ancient Greek such as Achilles genuinely believed in the gods' existence, Bartlett observes, and believed that what the gods declared to be right and true was unqualifiedly so, and that the causes for which Achilles fought and died were truly noble and worth dying for. By contrast, moderns think all "causes" and "meanings" to be historically conditioned and relative to their time. Unlike Achilles and all those other poor ignorant pre-moderns, we know there are no real and true foundations to life. We know that everything we believe is really a myth fostered by those in power to maintain their dominance. Where pre-moderns believe there is "something" of ultimate meaning, we believe "nothing" is ultimately meaningful. We believe in no beliefs. There is no Truth with a capital T, only temporary truths, truths suitable to a particular time and place. We cannot say the world really is a particular way; such an assertion is merely an expression of our will to power. Thus, there is no inherent or ultimate purpose or meaning to life and human existence. Such is the nihilist faith.[15]

We have, of course, applied our superior modern awareness to our personal lives, at both the individual and collective levels. As a result, says theologian Eugene Rose, nihilism "has become, in our time, so widespread and pervasive, has entered so thoroughly and so deeply into the minds and hearts of all men living today, that there is no longer any 'front' on which it may be fought."[16] Since nihilism is the disbelief in Absolute Truth, the result is a belief that all 'truths' are relative and all claims to truth merely an assertion of power on the part of some dominant group. Time-honoured political traditions and long-established cultural practices are merely the expression of the power of whatever particular group – say, white male heterosexuals – happens to dominate society at any given time. Where our forefathers might have spoken of "truth" and "justice," we fall back on "values."

This language of values, and the nihilistic thinking it reflects, comes straight out of Friedrich Nietzsche, the nineteenth-century German philosopher. To use the language of values, Nietzsche claimed more than 120 years ago, is to be a nihilist. Nietzsche arguably marked the crescendo of nihilistic disenchantment when, in the late nineteenth century, he pronounced that Western civilization had lost its Christian inheritance and stepped "beyond good and evil." In *Thus Spake Zarathustra* and *The Gay Science*, Nietzsche declared the death of God, and warned that when men realized the implications of that death, the knowledge might well drive them mad. "God is dead. God remains dead," he wrote. "And we have killed him. How shall we, murderers of all murderers, console ourselves?"[17]

This pronouncement was a metaphorical way of saying that the moral code of Christianity that had shaped European civilization for two millennia no longer claimed men's minds, and this presented a spiritual crisis of the first magnitude. If men and women no longer believed in transcendental justice or an absolute and universal morality derived from a divine source, how could they maintain a coherent moral order? Without God to provide divine sanction to human conduct, the door was open to nihilism, to the perception that life is without ultimate meaning and purpose. This, in turn, would promote a relativistic ethos that reduced all human relations to an equation of will and power. Nietzsche predicted men would succumb to a pessimistic nihilism that would drive them to great destruction in a desperate bid to recreate a meaningful world. The Age of Nihilism would see conflicts and violence on a scale never seen before as mankind tried to replace the lost God with another. Here's how Nietzsche put it with frightening prescience in the late 1880s: "What I relate is the history of the next two centuries. I describe what is coming, what can no longer come differently: the advent of nihilism ... For some time now, our whole European culture has been moving as toward a catastrophe, with a tortured tension that is growing from decade to decade: restlessly, violently, headlong, like a river that wants to reach the end."[18]

It is hard to deny Nietzsche's foresight. For all its bounty and benefits, the twentieth century was the bloodiest century in history, at least in terms of numbers killed – certainly worse than the Inquisition or Europe's religious wars in the sixteenth and seventeenth centuries. Perhaps we should worry more about this new century, since we have only just passed the halfway mark of Nietzsche's two centuries. If we do, we want to consider Nietzsche's warnings about the spiritual consequences of moral nihilism and the dangers of worshipping new idols.

One way to get a handle on the implications of nihilism is to join a long-dead Russian novelist, Fyodor Dostoyevsky, in an imaginative visit to the Kuntsmuseum in Basel, Switzerland. In 1867, nearly twenty years before Nietzsche pronounced the death of God, Dostoyevsky and his wife, Anna, toured the museum, where they saw Hans Holbein's sixteenth-century painting *The Body of the Dead Christ in the Tomb*. While Anna glanced at the painting, Dostoyevsky was transfixed. As literary scholar Mark Barna writes, Anna returned a quarter of an hour later to find her husband still staring at the painting. "His face was paler that usual. His gray-blue eyes had a frightened look. Gently taking his arm, Anna led away the subdued man."[19] What frightened Dostoyevsky? The painting is certainly grim. Where other painters have depicted Christ with a beauty that shines through even after the Crucifixion, Holbein portrays an emaciated corpse in a coffin. It is hard to imagine the Resurrection when you see the claw-like blackened fingers, the whites of the eyes rolled up, the skin slack and decaying. There is no peace in this death, no hint of glory to come.

Dostoyevsky used that image in his 1868 novel, *The Idiot*. "As one looks at the painting," says a character, "one conceives of nature in the form of some huge machine of the latest design which, deaf and unfeeling, has senselessly seized, crushed, and swallowed up a great and priceless Being, a Being worth all of nature and its laws." According to Barna, "Holbein's *Dead Christ* brought to the surface Dostoyevsky's lifelong dread: If Christ did not rise, there is no immortality." And if there is no immortality, if God does not exist, then, as Dostoyevsky wrote in his 1880 novel, *The Brothers Karamazov*, "there is no virtue ... everything is permitted."[20] At the core of nihilism lies not only the denial of a divine reality against which and by which men are judged, but also the corollary denial of man as a spiritual being. You don't get much more disenchanted than that.

For Dostoyevsky and his contemporaries, the death of spiritual man was a horrific thought. It meant there was no ultimate meaning or purpose to life, no life after death, no divine accounting or forgiveness for the horrors of this world. Man was utterly, unbearably alone, an alien lost in the cosmos. If everything was permitted, then nothing meant anything. There is no truth or justice or beauty; there are only subjective 'values,' and they are merely claims of power by those who wield social and political control, whether they are democrats or dictators, liberals or fascists. It's all relative.

Without God, might is right, however much sentimental humanists might wish otherwise.

Nietzsche wanted people to confront nihilism courageously. He comprehended the significance of Christianity's emergence, how it had utterly changed the way men and women think and feel and see the world, and so he understood the consequences of Christianity's decline. "Just as the Christian sensibility created a new sensibility by inverting many of the highest values of the pagan past," says theologian David Hart, "so the decline of Christianity ... portends another, perhaps equally catastrophic shift in moral and cultural consciousness."[21] But he rightly intuited that most would avoid confronting the full implications of the death of God. They would turn to new idols. Eventually, though, the new gods would prove false because nihilism is an emptiness that devours yet never finds satisfaction. Sooner or later, a pessimistic nihilism would take hold, and we would drive ourselves mad in our efforts to recreate a meaningful world, grasping at anything – ideologies, technological progress, nationalism, consumerism, entertainment, etc. – that might save us from the ultimate meaninglessness of materialism. It wouldn't work, though, Nietzsche warned. The Enlightenment dream of perpetual peace and unbounded progress would give way to a self-destructive and disenchanted world haunted by the spectre of its own futility.

You can see this devouring nihilism in what historian Jacques Barzun refers to as the "present decadence" of the West. Despite its technological prowess and prosperity, ours is a period of cultural decline, moral incoherence and waning intellectual rigour, he writes. He traces our decadence to the tensions and contradictions that have emerged by pushing the principles and ideals that are the chief glory of the West – individualism, freedom, self-consciousness and rationality, for example – to extremes that defy common sense. As a culture, Westerners perceive that much we once thought solid is melting away. Faith in the modern project of progress is faltering. The result is a spiritual crisis.[22]

"Spirit" is a rather vague and overused word, and it needs to be distinguished from the word "religion." "Religion" derives from the Latin *religare*, meaning to "bind fast" or "contain" or "tie back." Etymological dictionaries define religion as a means of establishing a relationship between the individual and whatever he or she regards as the ultimate nature of reality. The word "spirit" comes from the Latin *spiritus*. The Latin, in turn, is a translation of *pneuma*, the Greek word for "breath." *Pneuma* refers to the breath of life, that which gives life to the physical body. It also had connotations of courage and vigour.[23] The philosopher G.W.F. Hegel used the word "Spirit," or *Geist*, to refer to the highest mode of existence or the highest principle of life. Spirit, in this sense, has to do with that which animates or gives life its purpose.

Spirit and religion come together when our understanding of life's purpose and meaning is articulated – or contained – in institutionalized rituals, rules and conventions. You are being religious when you attempt to articulate, by whatever means – church rituals, pilgrimage, prayer, poetry, etc. – your understanding of the 'ultimate reality' that gives your life meaning and purpose. Religion, you might say, is the communal expression of individual spiritedness. The spirit of an individual, a community or a nation is a matter of self-understanding. That self-understanding is revealed through its institutional arrangements – religious institutions, political orders or cultural artifacts. Spirit struggles to find religious expression. Conversely, religious institutions (and other social institutions, too) cohere only so long as their rituals and practices reflect the 'spiritual' self-understanding of their members. When they don't, when institutional orders crumble, you have a spiritual crisis.

A spiritual crisis can be defined as that condition when the traditional concepts, metaphors and symbol systems by which we have previously made sense of our lives, and which gave meaning to our lives – truth and beauty, God and faith, nation and Christianity, for example – no longer readily fulfill that function, thus rendering our lives increasingly incoherent and, at the extreme, meaningless. When experience – political and social, intellectual and moral – ceases to be coherent or comprehensible, when old categories of understanding leave us unable to rely on the past as a guide to the future, when the centre no longer holds, well, that's a spiritual crisis. A culture is in spiritual crisis when the concepts by which it has understood itself and its purpose no longer help people make sense of the world, when their ways of thinking and feeling no longer satisfactorily account for the world they encounter every day.

The disintegration of the traditional family, the fragmenting of civil society, the corruption of politics, faltering faith in the post-Enlightenment assumption of historical progress, and, perhaps most significantly, the declining birth rate in many Western countries all suggest that the West is in spiritual crisis. But this crisis is paradoxical because it is rooted in the very principles that have made Western culture so materially successful. "What is special about our case is that we see the breakdown coming about in a particular way," writes philosopher Charles Taylor. "We see it coming through hypertrophy, through our becoming too much what we have been. This kind of fear is perhaps definitive of the modern age, the fear that the very things that define our break with earlier 'traditional' societies – our affirmation of freedom, equality, radical new beginnings, control over nature, democratic self-rule – will somehow be carried beyond feasible limits and will undo us."[24]

The idea of Western decadence is, of course, a favourite riff of intellectuals, and one that many dismiss as so much philosophic hyperventilation. Admittedly, if we are deep in an Age of Nihilism – and I think we are – it is a comfortable nihilism. "Today's nihilism is no angst and all play."[25] There is none of the existential nausea that Dostoyevsky experienced at the groundlessness of morality. Nowadays, the mad dance of pop culture, the glittering gizmos of technological novelty and the titillating diversions of the mass media mask the horror that Nietzsche and Dostoyevsky saw when they looked into the abyss. To be sure, the sense of life as ultimately meaningless has not gone unnoticed. Artists, poets, theologians, philosophers and even the occasional journalist have commented on the apparent vacuity of postmodern culture. But many, it seems, have grown indifferent. Either that or they are too numbed and exhausted by the mad dance to respond. If so, then we really are in crisis. Numbness and indifference are the consequence of a culture of damaged sensibilities. In Barzun's words, "When people accept futility and the absurd as normal, the culture is decadent."[26]

Consider the morality of, say, the film *Pulp Fiction* and the TV series *South Park*. Both the movie and the television show treat death as a joke. One of the movie's killers munches on a victim's fast food hamburger and quotes a passage from the Bible about vengeance – before he kills everyone in the room. An episode of *South Park* in which Santa Claus and Jesus engage in a bloody fight over which one reflects the true spirit of Christmas became a cult hit and prompted stories in *Newsweek* and *Rolling Stone*. In other words, everything is absurd; nothing is serious, much less sacred. The longing for meaning, order and coherence that characterized the nihilism and absurdity recognized by philosophers from Kierkegaard to Camus is lost. As scholar Eric Cohen says, "There is no tragedy, because there is no longing for something better; there is only darkness, and the futile laughter of a trivializing culture."[27] This nihilistic mentality has consequences beyond the movie screen, he says. How many times have we heard perpetrators of school shootings compare their gunplay to video games? The Littleton killers, Eric Harris and Dylan Klebold, "whooped and hollered like it was a game," according to one surviving witness. Is there not something wrong, says Cohen, when "the same nation that mourns over the mayhem at Littleton chuckles at the pop nihilism that comes out of Hollywood – and sees no contradiction?"[28]

Robert Bartlett finds a similar self-indulgent nihilism in the academic world. The scholar describes many university students as suffering from a deep-seated boredom that leaves them with "little direction or lasting desire and restricts their capacity to conceive of a noble and rewarding life." Much attention is paid to youthful hormones, but Bartlett is more often struck by the timidity of their concerns and their placidity in regard to almost all things. His own experiences with students have led him to a tentative conclusion: "The malaise in question is a fundamentally new and especially virulent strain of boredom."[29]

The word "boredom" is a relatively modern concept, Bartlett points out. Neither the Greeks nor the Romans had a word for boredom because they lacked the experience of it. The earliest recorded use of the word in the modern world was during the Enlightenment, in the latter half of the eighteenth century. And by the mid-1800s, according to French etymological dictionaries, the word *ennui*, which is the equivalent of "boredom," referred to a mental state of "moral lassitude" that "causes one to take no interest in or pleasure in anything." It is this kind of existential boredom that Bartlett detects in many students. He attributes this boredom, in part, to the postmodern education students receive at university. Such an education, with its denial of Truth and ultimate meaning, does not encourage or prepare people "to lead lives of noble aspiration and admirable accomplishment." Instead, they learn to accept technological imperatives – career-building over character-building and utilitarian efficiency over the life of the mind. They are pushed to accede to the mediocrity of career and consumerism as the height of life's purpose, and drilled to accept a moral code (or lack thereof) amenable to a rootless, hedonistic world: "Be tolerant." But to think this way, says Bartlett, is "to live within the embrace or stranglehold of a kind of nihilism."[30]

A culture devoted to the relativism of all values and the laissez-faire morality of tolerance can only exacerbate this condition of nihilism. Those who regard the world as merely an arena for the satisfaction of their desires, and all values as merely a matter of perspective and personal whim, may well find boredom to be their final fate. As the French philosopher Blaise Pascal once pointed out, without knowledge of or concern for ultimate truths and deeper realities, we tend to waver between desperate efforts at diversion that keep us from thinking about our existential condition and states of enervating boredom that bring us too close to the abyss for comfort. It is not that we are more prone to boredom than people in the past, but rather that the traditional means for fending off life-boredom (as distinct from the boredom of daily routines) is no longer available to us. Pre-modern cultures relied on religion and morality to keep boredom at bay.

Nietzsche hoped art and learning – he described books as "fly-swatters against boredom" – would provide a modern substitute for religious faith and help overcome nihilism. "It is only as an aesthetic phenomenon that existence and the world are eternally justified," he wrote.[31] That approach might work for a few – poets and painters, for example – but not for most. What do the rest do in this disenchanted world? The contemporary answer, the chief means by which modern Westerners fend off boredom, is conspicuous consumption. Shopping is the contemporary response to nihilism. We have come to equate instant gratification with meaningfulness. "A good deal of boredom can be buried underneath a heap of newly acquired gadgets," says political philosopher Leslie Paul Thiele. "Boredom's tendency to ooze through the cracks, however, necessitates an ever-growing heap."[32]

This is certainly not what the Enlightenment philosophers who inaugurated the modern world intended. They thought political emancipation, education, science – progress, in short – would produce a world of sufficient leisure and material comfort that would allow men and women to develop their best potential. Westerners certainly enjoy the benefits of technology, but as Thiele observes, "the question on the minds of many who remain secure in their leisured affluence ... is whether they have created a world where the guarantee of not dying from hunger is paid for by the certainty of dying from boredom."[33]

He has a point. When the Cold War came to an end in 1989, political theorist Francis Fukuyama speculated that with the triumph of liberalism, we had reached the "end of history" in terms of political evolution. At the same time, though, he wondered whether the courage and idealism that galvanized mankind's past struggles would be reduced to technical questions about efficiency and picayune lifestyle pursuits. The end of history might well be a sad time, he mused, with the prospect of an ever-deepening boredom.[34] Fukuyama's lament for history came before the War on Terror, so perhaps centuries of boredom will not be our fate. Yet, to the degree that boredom is a metaphor for a culture steeped in nihilism, and exposes our disaffected condition, you can't help but wonder – assuming you are not too numbed – if there are ways out of our present predicament of disenchantment, whether it is possible to re-enchant the world.

****

Can the world be re-enchanted? If so, how? These are questions I address in subsequent chapters, so I won't attempt to do so here. However, I should perhaps deal with another question now: Is the modern world really disenchanted? The question cuts to the core of my concerns: Re-enchantment presupposes disenchantment. If, however, the world is and always has been enchanted in one sense or another, then it is not a matter of re-enchanting the world but rather of rediscovering what has always been there. If that is the case – and I think it is – then addressing the third question effectively takes care of the first two. As religion scholar Patrick Sherry puts it, "What if the world always was enchanted and still is, if we but look and keep our sense of wonder?"[35]

Theologian Alistair McGrath picks up on this idea in his 2003 book, *The Re-enchantment of Nature*. Nature is already enchanted, he says. We need only learn to reappreciate it in that way. He describes the pre-modern era as a period in which nature possessed intrinsic and autonomous worth. Modernity reduced the physical world to a resource for the satisfaction of human needs and desires. This fostered the disenchantment of the world. Now, though, with our greater awareness of the environment, we are seeing a kind of return to nature and a re-evaluation of man's relationship to nature. But this re-evaluation points not only to a re-enchantment of the world, but also to an opening of the doors of perception to "a deeper level of existence." A re-enchanted world can still be open to scientific explanation, but explanation does not need to undercut our sense of wonder at the natural world.[36]

33

If this is the case, the question becomes how do we acquire (or recover) a sense of wonder? If the world is inherently enchanted, what can we do to perceive it that way? Theologian David Brown considers this issue in his 2004 study, *God and Enchantment of Place: Reclaiming Human Experience*. Brown argues that the world is, indeed, enchanted and that our difficulty in recognizing this reality – our disenchantment – is rooted in our lack of a sense of the sacramental. Brown agrees with Max Weber's notion that instrumental rationality – and the assumption that scientific knowledge is the only true form of knowledge – is responsible for the disenchantment of the world. For Weber, the world was losing its enchantment as a result of the rationalization of all areas of life, including religious life. In particular, he disliked the notion of a divine being beyond the access of reason, or, as Brown puts it, "a mysterious externality not subject to rational analysis." Weber saw the task of science as the elimination of mystery and its replacement with explanation. To explain something – rainbows, for example – is to shed its mystery and wonder. If the natural world is the realm for proving or disproving the existence of God, and science discovers that, according to its standards of evidence, no such proof exists, then religion's retreat was all but inevitable. The more science "explained" the world, the less enchanted the world became. Weber was somewhat ambivalent about this prospect, uncertain whether the "iron cage" of reason would be good for mankind. As Brown notes, Weber had no religious belief himself but, at the same time, regarded himself as "a cripple, a deformed human being."[37]

Responding to Weber's disenchantment thesis, Brown attempts to show that nature and culture continue to enchant the world if properly perceived. The rainbow can still evoke a sense of wonder despite its scientific explanation. Why, he asks, is "proof" or "disproof" of the divine presence in the world based solely on the assumptions of empirical evidence? Perhaps "a divine structure is already implicit in certain forms of experience of the natural world, whether these be of majesty, beauty or whatever." Perhaps God's presence is immanent to the world – rather than "beyond" the world – in a way not amenable to rational detection. Brown devotes most of his book to delineating those forms, places and experiences where the divine presence can appear – homes, gardens, churches, temples, theatre, poetry, painting, mountains, seashores and pilgrimages. According to the disenchantment mindset, such places and activities, or our response to them, can be "explained" in psychological, historical, sociological or political terms. They no longer possess a religious spirit. Brown, however, thinks these areas of human experience can provide a symbolic mediation of "the divine in and through the world." God, he says, "can come sacramentally close to his world and vouchsafe experiences of himself through the material." We need to engage in "a form of perception that has largely been lost in our utilitarian age, experiencing the natural world and human imitations of it not just as means to some further end but as themselves the vehicle that makes possible an encounter with God, discovering an enchantment, an absorption that like worship requires no further justification."[38] In effect, then, Brown argues that we can recover the enchantment of the world – or re-enchant it – by learning to perceive it in sacramental terms.

But isn't this how Catholics perceive the world? "Catholics live in an enchanted world, a world of statues, votive candles, saints, rosary beads and holy pictures," Andrew Greeley writes in the deliberately provocative first paragraph of his 2000 book, *The Catholic Imagination*. "But these Catholic paraphernalia are mere hints of a deeper and more persuasive religious sensibility which inclines Catholics to see the Holy lurking in creation. As Catholics, we find our houses and our world haunted by a sense that the objects, events and persons of daily life are revelations of grace." Less provocatively, Greeley goes on to explain that the paraphernalia of Catholicism is possessed of a sense of the sacramental; that is, it sees in the myriad objects and events of everyday reality the ongoing "revelation of the presence of God."[39]

Greeley is certainly aware of the notion of the disenchantment of the world. He asks how it is possible that a large group of people, such as Catholics, can perceive an enchanted cosmos when modern science has demystified and demythologized the world. Surely, in the modern era, disenchantment reigns. Is it possible that the Catholic imagination is postmodern? he asks, only to reject the idea. Concepts like modernity and post-modernity exist only in the imaginations of ivory tower intellectuals. True, there may be some "theoretical opposition" between science and enchantment, although considering the strange phenomena that science deals with – black holes, big bangs and great attractors, for example – scientists have their own enchantments. Nonetheless, Greeley finds "ample evidence that most humans (other than philosophers and theologians) see little inconsistency between science and religion in their ordinary lives." He goes on to explore various expressions of the Catholic sense of the sacramental in everything from architecture and opera to painting and poetry. The Catholic imagination, he says, tends to emphasize the metaphorical nature of God's presence. "The objects, events and persons of ordinary existence hint at the nature of God and indeed make God in some fashion present to us. God is sufficiently like creation that creation not only tells us something about God but, by doing so, also makes God present among us."[40]

Catholics aren't the only ones to try to retain an enchanted perspective on the world. Scholars point to the emergence of new religions and the "alternative spiritualities" of the New Age movement as evidence of efforts at re-enchantment. Some argue that these new religions amount to little more than the dying embers of the old faith, the desperate end-stage of the West's soon to be completed secularization. But I'm inclined to side with theologian Christopher Partridge on this issue. He understands that spiritual aspirations are intrinsic to the human condition, both psychologically and socially, and that religion or religious sentiment is unlikely to disappear. Even if older forms of religious expression fade, newer forms will arise to compensate, including what Partridge calls non-Christian re-enchantment. As an example, he points to the re-enchantment efforts of the eighteenth- and nineteenth-century Romantics, who were among the first to question the Enlightenment's disenchantment project.[41] (I'll have more to say on the Romantic sensibility in subsequent chapters.)

A similar neo-Romantic re-enchantment, challenging the modernist idea that scientistic reasoning alone is the source of truth and meaning, is evident in contemporary popular culture with its absorption in aliens and UFOs, vampires and werewolves, demons and angels, witches and warlocks. Television series such as *The X-Files*, *Buffy the Vampire Slayer*, *Touched by an Angel*, *Six Feet Under*, *Angels in America* and *True Blood*; movies like *Star Wars*, *The Matrix*, *The Lord of the Rings* series (based on J.R.R. Tolkien's books), and, more recently, *Avatar*; books such as the Harry Potter novels and C.S. Lewis' *The Chronicles of Narnia* — these all speak to a longing for re-enchantment, a desire to counterbalance the rationalization of the world and escape the iron cage of reason.[42]

All these books and movies and fashions also point to a significant cultural shift. The disenchantment of the world was the first step of a bigger process of freeing people from the debilitations and restraints of superstition and irrational fears. An unintended consequence was the de-spiriting and de-animation of the world. The world was reduced to mindless matter, raw material, available for human use according to the demands of instrumental reasoning and social engineering. The world no longer possessed intrinsic meaning independent of human will. This disenchanted mindset still characterizes much of Western society, as debates about the environment suggest, but many Westerners are turning to mysticism, the religions of the East, paganism and other forms of alternative spirituality.

This shift is more significant than supporters of secularization might like to acknowledge, says Partridge. "Re-enchantment is not a modern reconstruction of the enchanted landscape of the past, but a new growth in a secularized, globalized, technologically sophisticated, consumer-oriented landscape."[43] Reasonably or not, those who turn to neo-pagan rituals, claim a belief in angels or line up to buy the latest Harry Potter book are attempting to "re-enchant the world" and thereby halt, or perhaps reverse, the world's "disenchantment," understood "at least in part [as] the process whereby magic and mystery are driven from the world and nature is managed rather than enchanted."[44]

While many would no doubt endorse the desire for an enchanted world, we should be careful in lamenting the disenchantment of the world. In the pre-modern "enchanted" world, children often didn't make it to adulthood, and most adults didn't make it much beyond their thirtieth birthday. Poverty and disease, ignorance and superstition, famine and fear were an all too common fate. It would be perverse nostalgia to wish for the restoration of an "enchanted" world if it meant there would be no medicine to treat a cancer-stricken child and no food to feed a starving family. Thanks to science and technology, Western societies are better able than ever to feed, clothe, shelter, medicate and educate vast masses of people.

However, we do not judge society by material attainments alone. Our high-tech trinkets, medical marvels and supermarket cornucopia come at a cost. Essayist Eric Cohen sums up the predicament – and the paradox – of modernity this way:

> The modern age is tremendous for its accomplishments: wealth, comfort, more equal opportunity, scientific discovery. But despite its achievements, modernity lacks answers to man's fundamental questions; it lacks the transcendent vision that makes life joyful and death meaningful … And its very success often undermines its virtues. Wealth degenerates into indulgence; tolerance degenerates into unthinking relativism; science without philosophy reduces man to a laboratory study; technology without humility tempts him into dangerous projects … and the illusion of divinity and immortality.[45]

In other words, we remain "restless amidst abundance" (to borrow Alexis de Tocqueville's phrase). And that, I suggest, is a reflection of our existential disenchantment.

So, what do we do? I'm fond of biologist Rachel Carson's prescription for enchantment. "A child's world is fresh and new and beautiful, full of wonder and excitement," she once wrote. "It is our misfortune that for most of us that clear-eyed vision, that true instinct for what is beautiful and awe-inspiring, is dimmed and even lost before we reach adulthood … If I had influence with the good fairy who is supposed to preside over the christening of all children, I should ask that her gift to each child in the world would be a sense of wonder so indestructible that it would last throughout life, as an unfailing antidote against the boredom and disenchantment of later years."[46]

My brief consideration of nihilism and boredom illustrates some of the consequences when the gift of childhood enchantment lapses. But antidotes to disenchantment, responses to nihilism, are available to us as adults. We do not have to surrender to the debilitating boredom of consumerism and the ersatz spectacles of entertainment. That, in a nutshell, is the intent of these essays: to foster attentiveness to those activities and experiences that might help us re-enchant the world and even restore our sense of purpose and meaning, our *spiritus*. This book could just as easily be subtitled "Restoring Spirit in an Age of Disenchantment." However, the subtitle "Rekindling Belief in an Age of Disenchantment" is not inappropriate. In philosophical terms, "belief" is a weak mode of knowledge. In theological terms, however, belief has to do with people's willingness to put their trust in the Being toward whom they direct their faith. Such belief is not a matter of naivety or wishful thinking. Rather, it reflects the surmounting of disbelief after the engagements of doubt. In the words of etymologist Geddes MacGregor, "Belief, far from excluding doubt, implies both doubt and the transcending of the doubt. Claim to such belief is claim to a kind of knowledge."[47]

These essays are rooted in my own experiences of home, place, solitude, wonder, pilgrimage and "everyday mysticism," and, as such, constitute an extended exercise in restoring spirit even amidst doubt and uncertainty. It seems to me that these experiences point beyond themselves to the possibility of belief in something other than material existence. Moments of being, moments of enchantment, says theologian Robert Fuller, provide "an emotional experience that invites us to entertain belief in the existence and causal activity of an order of reality that lies beyond or behind sensory appearances."[48]

I am, of course, not the first to adopt an aesthetic approach to spiritual or religious experience. Theologians such as David Brown point out that many areas of human activity, including homemaking, painting, poetry and pilgrimages, have been experienced as "sites" where the divine has made its presence felt, where enchantment has been manifested. Our difficulty as postmodern Westerners is that we are no longer readily able to experience that enchantment. "Our own world is so different from the past that it is important to note how far we stand from the sacramental understanding that once prevailed," says Brown. "[F]ar from decrying such past attitudes, there is much of value worth retrieving. Seeing God in our midst in home and city need not imply idolatry but rather the complex mix of divine presence and human sin that is the reality of our world." Any and every place, he says, has "the potential to function sacramentally."[49]

Of course, you don't necessarily need to possess a particular religious belief to appreciate nature as a source of enchantment. Still, for those who see the world in sacramental terms, the experience of enchantment cannot help but draw your attention to, well, rumours of God. The main title of this book, A Rumour of God, encapsulates that possibility, literally and metaphorically. Which is to say, the title reflects the basic question to which these essays are a response: Where and how might you encounter those elements of everyday experience that foster and further a spiritual life, and, at the very least, leave you poised on the cusp between belief and disbelief? It is a question that has been with me for years, even though I have often done my best (worst?) to ignore it as I pursued more immediate inclinations. Yet, in retrospect, the question seems to have always been there. The books of my youth – I still have them on my shelves – betray a propensity for the spiritual: Herman Hesse's *Demian*, Carlos Castenada's *The Teachings of Don Juan*, Aldous Huxley's *The Doors of Perception*, Colin Wilson's *The Outsider*. During my university years I plowed through Gurdjieff and Ouspensky, Krishnamurti and Carl Jung, and read Alan Watts and D.T. Suzuki on Zen. Like many of my generation, I tried Transcendental Meditation, yoga and Eckankar. I dabbled with the I Ching and had Tarot reading sessions with a tall, gangly, bearded man by the name of Patches in a small candlelit room smelling of patchouli oil. (The only thing I took away from the sessions was an intense dislike of patchouli oil and a piece of advice: I should never throw out anything I write. I've been hauling boxes of notebooks and manuscripts ever since.)

All this spiritual stuff fell by the wayside as I got older and had to earn my own living. Yet, it never completely left me. I would sometimes find myself looking back through my old books, seeking whatever it was that first intrigued and excited me. So it was in researching this book of essays. The book as a whole is in some ways a kind of intellectual pilgrimage, a recovering and retracing of a path I once started to follow. Readers will find numerous references to and citations from artists, philosophers, theologians and scholars in these pages. As I did my research, I was surprised to find myself returning to sources I had not read for years, sometimes decades – from Morris Beja, Thomas Carlyle and Albert Camus to Thomas Merton, Tony Tanner, Ludwig Wittgenstein and, most surprising to me, Virginia Woolf. It was like that with many of the other sources on which I've drawn for these essays. Reading the poets and novelists and philosophers again over the past few months was a kind of rediscovery of my youthful spiritual enthusiasms. I was pleased, and somewhat surprised, to find that many of the ideas that once stirred me still did. My rediscovery of Virginia Woolf is a good example. I had to read her in university, but

I make no claim to having understood her then, much less to having identified with her characters. Yet, like so many other things in my youth to which I failed to pay proper attention, her work seems to have lodged in my mind, waiting for a time when I would be more receptive to it. (The return of the suppressed, you might say.) Encountering her "moments of being" again, and finally understanding what she was talking about, provided me with a revelation of sorts, a clue to reconciling epiphanic intuitions with the requirements of reason. I hope that sense of discovery comes across to readers, because I've drawn on Woolf and other artists for the simple reason that I see them as the proverbial canaries in the mineshaft of Western civilization. The artistic reaction, the aesthetic response, to "disenchantment" offers guidance in the midst of our spiritual crisis.

So, too, does the book from which I've taken my own title – sociologist Peter Berger's *A Rumor of Angels*. The book has sat on my shelves for years (along with many of the others I cite), unread since my undergraduate years. At one point, Berger recounts the story of a priest working in the slums of an unnamed European city. Someone asked the priest why he continued his efforts. He replied, "so the rumor of God may not disappear completely."[50] As soon as I read that phrase I felt a shiver of recognition – a minor epiphany – and knew I had my title, and my bedrock theme.

Indeed, the phrase aptly summarizes what I am attempting. I am "listening" for rumours about things in which many no longer believe in order that our disenchantment does not become total. In this effort I follow Berger's reading of our situation: Like it or not, we live in a time when "transcendence has been reduced to a rumor."[51] We cannot escape our circumstances by some magical jump into faith. Nor can we return to an earlier era of unquestioned belief. (Nor would we necessarily want to, if this meant abandoning modern medicine, abundant food, a longer lifespan, etc.) Yet, as Charles Taylor observes, there is today a widespread aspiration "to retrieve experience from the deadening, routinized, conventional forms of instrumental civilization"; many, he says, seek "contact with something where this contact either fosters and/or itself constitutes a spiritually significant fulfillment of wholeness."[52] Following Taylor, Berger and other "sources," including my own personal experience, I want to demonstrate that there are experiences that foster the restoration of our spiritedness and, perhaps, rekindle awareness of the transcendent.[53] My motives are those of Berger: "If the signals of transcendence have become rumors in our time, then we can set out to explore these rumors – and perhaps to follow them up to their source."[54] These essays, then, constitute a journalistic inquiry into the possibility that certain experiences provide the basis for the re-enchantment of the world.

****

Perhaps one of my own Rachel Carson–like moments of wonder on the Camino de Santiago hints at such a possibility. It was the beginning of my second week on the Camino. I had walked 170 kilometres in the first week, and then taken a day off in Logrono to play tourist. But I was glad to be back on the Camino. As I headed for Navarrete, I tried to recall where I had been three days, four days, even a week ago. It was all a blur; the days and the nights overlapped and melted into one another. It was as though the process of walking, of putting one foot in front of the other for mile after mile, had caused me to lose my ordinary sense of time. My memory seemed tied more to a sense of space than any division of time. And so it went that week. I was slightly out of my mind walking through the small towns along the Camino route – Navarrete, Najera, Azofra, Belorado,

San Juan de Ortega – toward Burgos. Each place provided something – the company of other pilgrims, a fine meal, some Romanesque or Gothic architecture to admire – but it was the Camino itself that worked its magic. After days of walking, the Camino was beginning to walk me.

Walking through the hills of La Rioja, with its roving herds of sheep and goats and the villages with their adobe-style houses and red pantile roofs, the days ran one into another, indistinguishable. Long-distance runners speak of a runner's high, a state of euphoria achieved after long effort. Something similar happened to me. The steady rhythm of footsteps and the metronomic tapping of my walking stick lulled my mind, nudging the doors of memory ajar. I found myself recalling old friends, many of whom I hadn't seen since childhood. I even found myself talking to the boy I had once been, asking if he liked what he'd become.

And then there were the golden oldies that played in my head – the Beatles and the Beach Boys, Elvis Presley and Roy Orbison. For some reason, though, like a needle skipping on a well-worn record, I was stuck on the songs of my childhood: "The Battle of New Orleans," "Tom Dooley," "Sink the Bismarck," "Moon River." It was as if I had walked into some psychic radio station where a gnomish DJ continued to spin the old 45s. Strolling beside some vineyard with gnarled vines thicker than my legs, I'd warble the tunes, surprised that I remembered the lyrics so well. One particular memory halted me in my tracks, it was so vivid. Stepping over fresh and pungent sheep dung, I suddenly saw myself as a boy leaning over the back of the front seat of our family's 1949 Chrysler Desoto, peering over my father's shoulder as the farm fields and telephone poles whipped by on our way from Red Deer to Drumheller. Bobby Vinton's "Blue Velvet" played on the radio. I hadn't thought of that road trip – or that song – for decades.

But it wasn't only songs I heard in my head. From some obscure storehouse in my mind, I pulled out poems that I had read years ago and didn't even know I still remembered – Wordsworth, Arnold, Eliot, Auden. And so it would go for hours, walking alone along the rough path of the Camino, jabbering lyrics and fragments of poems and watching my past scroll across the screen of memory. There was nothing unusual about this experience. One psychological by-product of pilgrimage is the way hours of walking can trigger unexpected thoughts and emotions and memories. "While journeying through this different time and place, pilgrims find that long-forgotten memories surface; memories of family members and friends, childhood places, secrets or painful circumstances," writes anthropologist Nancy Frey. "These new perceptions often take people to internal places not before visited."[55]

The mystic Richard Niebuhr once described pilgrims as "persons in motion – passing through territories not their own – seeking something we might call completion, or perhaps the word clarity will do as well, a goal to which only the spirit's compass points the way."[56] Admittedly, the motives for my pilgrimage had not been so clear, at least originally. The only completion I was concerned about was arriving in Santiago. Where my spiritual compass might be pointed, I had no idea. I had started out thinking of my trek as an adventure, an escape from the everyday, and it had certainly proven to be so. Yet, as the days passed and the miles clicked over, circumstance and serendipity recast the Camino, altering my understanding of my motives and goals. In part, this is the benefit of the constant presence of stones and trees and rain and sun. Add to that days of walking alone and the result is a charismatic effect on the mind that opens you to what Frey calls the Camino's out-of-time quality.

I had certainly grown more attentive to the world around me. I began noticing the different species of flowers and monitoring the sky for signs of rain. I grew aware of the changing nature of the Camino itself, the different mixtures of rock and pebble, the varying textures of mud, the variegated surfaces – hard or soft, bumpy or smooth. Walking on asphalt was different from walking on dirt or gravel. On asphalt, as your feet pound the unyielding hardness, the walking is monotonous. On the earthen pathways, there were constant surprises even in this flat land: a stream that required leaping from stone to stone, a lonely copse of stunted trees, an unexpected cluster of boulders covered with sun-blackened lichen, a sudden bright strip of poppies or wild lupins.

I became aware of the shift in my pilgrimage motives after one particular experience. A few kilometres outside Hontanos, just before the Garbanzuelo River, I came to a crossroads. There were no yellow arrows – *flechas amarillas* – painted on any boulders or tree trunks to tell me which direction to take. Uncertain which way to walk, I stood at the edge of the path and leaned on my walking stick, taking the strain off my legs. Gradually, I grew aware of how quiet it was. Normally, the crunch of my boots, the flapping of my poncho or the rasp of my backpack on my jacket filled my ears. Now, standing still, I was aware of how the wind had died and everything was utterly silent. I felt the thump of my heart. I was aware of the blood beating in my ears. But that, too, faded away. I waited, listening to the silence, watching the land. And then, out of nowhere, a memory filled my head: a summer long ago when I was a boy, maybe eight or nine years old. I was walking along a prairie road outside Hanna, Alberta, where I was born. The sun was hot on my shoulders. Grasshoppers and cicadas buzzed and chirped in the roadside ditches. More grasshoppers hopped around my legs. High overhead, like some colossal inverted bowl, a huge vacant sky hummed in the heat of the day.

The memory was so visually intense that for a moment I was conscious of being in two places at once: a small figure standing on the Alberta prairie and, at the same time, a much older figure standing in the silence of the Spanish *meseta*. It seemed to me that if I moved my eyes quickly enough, carefully enough, some hazy barrier at the periphery of vision would crack open and I could step back into that scene with my younger self. All I had to do was wait quietly and patiently and this other reality would open to me. And so I stood, waiting in silence, anticipating my disappearance.

It was a crazy thought, of course. I knew that even at the time. Nonetheless, I continued to wait, half lost to memory, wanting to disappear into the vision. But then, out of the blue again, this time literally, there was bird song. A flock of warblers, like a collection of question marks flying through the air, landed on a nearby hedge. The next moment, everything – the vast land, the lowering sky, the rain-puddled pathway, the pungent earth – shone with brilliant brightness as a gap in the clouds allowed a wide slab of sun to pass over the land. I could have sworn the land shimmered as the light moved across it.

The brightness lasted for maybe six or seven seconds and then began to fade, leaving me blinking and wondering what had happened. It was the most intense moment of enchantment I had known in years. Not that I thought the word "enchantment" at the time. I'm not sure what I thought, if anything. I was mostly dumbstruck, uncertain what to make of the experience. Whatever it was, it turned my pilgrimage from an adventure into a quest for more such moments.

TWO

THE LONG WAY HOME
Nourishing Neglected Roots

That people could come into the world in a place they could not at first even name and had never known before; and that out of a nameless and unknown place they could grow and move around in it until its name they knew and called with love, and call it HOME, and put roots there and love others there; so that whenever they left this place they would sing homesick songs about it and write poems of yearning for it ... and forever be returning to it or leaving it again!
    – William Goyen, *The House of Breath*[1]

Once there was a way to get back homeward ...
    – from the Beatles' *Abbey Road* album, 1969

I knelt beside the graves and ran my fingers across the names engraved in the headstones. Blackened flecks of lichen had settled into the chiselled letters. Tendrils of caragana crawled around the sides and over the crest of the tombstones. The inscriptions were still visible – "Magdeline Quast 1886–1963" and "Christian Edmund Quast 1881–1966" "Till we meet again" – but I could imagine the plant slowly covering the stone and obscuring the names. They were my grandparents.

I tugged at one of the creepers, peeling it away from the stone. "You want me to cut back the caragana?" I said, looking up at my mother standing on the other side of the two graves.

She nodded. "I guess they're not in too bad shape," she said, gesturing at the headstones. "I haven't been here for a few years. Nobody else has either, it looks like."

My grandfather's stone was slightly askew, leaning forward as though pushed by the caragana brush behind it. "No, not too bad," I said. "I've got some tools in the car and some spray stuff for cleaning. That'll get rid of the dirt, but you'll have to get the town to straighten the stone."

This was in the fall of 2003. My mother and I were spending a week together, visiting towns in Alberta where my family had lived when I was young boy. The tour included visits to the graves of my father, both sets of grandparents, and various aunts and uncles. Hanna was our last stop. It was my mother's hometown, and the place where I was born. We stayed for a couple of days, driving or walking around the town, dropping in on friends my mother knew from past years, and visiting the graveyard. We also wanted to find the farmstead where my mother, the youngest of eleven children, spent much of her childhood before the family moved into town when her father could no longer make a living as a farmer during the Great Depression of the 1930s. During the war years she went to school, got her first job, met my father, married, and, lucky for me, got pregnant.

I had parked under one of the tall poplars lining the narrow gravel lane that bisects the Hanna cemetery. Rows of headstones stretched away on both sides of the lane. It was a hot, sunny prairie day and the granite gleamed in the light. Walking back to the car to fetch a jackknife from the toolbox in the trunk, along with rags and window cleaner, and a couple bottles of water, I thought about how odd it was to be in Hanna again. The streets were familiar, but, at the same time, somehow strange, like a vaguely remembered dream. We left Hanna when I was two years old. My memories of the place were based on the three or four summers when I was a boy between, say, eight and eleven years old, when we would visit for a week or so on our family holidays, and one summer when we stayed with my grandparents for a couple of months while waiting to join my father in Inuvik, where he'd gotten a new job. That was in 1961, as I recall. I hadn't been back to Hanna since then. Yet it has always haunted me. For years, images of the place – a street, a house, a view down a road – regularly popped into my mind. Hanna also made regular, if distorted, appearances in my dreams (and, sometimes, nightmares), leaving me with an aching sense of nostalgia when I woke.

On the first day of our visit we walked around the familiar streets, from Centre Street to 7th Avenue. It took all of fifteen minutes. "I always thought it was much longer," my mother said.

"Me, too," I said, remembering that it was a big deal for my cousin David and me to be allowed to go the half-dozen blocks from my aunt's house on 7th Avenue to downtown on Main Street.

As we walked, my mother pointed to houses where friends of her youth – Wanda May Knot, Lillian Weiss – had lived. She showed me the small house where she and my father lived in the first months of their marriage – 209 7th Avenue West (the place where I must have been conceived, I thought to myself). I took my mother's picture on the stone steps of Hanna High School on 6th Avenue.

"My best friend and I were going to travel together after we finished school," she said as we stood on the sidewalk looking at the big stone building. "We were going to get jobs and save our money and go travelling." She paused, looking at me. "But then I met your father."

"Don't blame me," I said. "I wasn't there."

My mother laughed. "No, but you soon were."

"I'm not complaining."

"Neither am I. Like they say, life is what happens after you make plans."

We continued our walk, turning left on 2nd Street East toward the old family home on the corner of 7th Avenue East. Only it wasn't there any more. A condominium had replaced the house I remembered. I could see the house in my mind's eye. I tried to impose the image on the condominium in front of me, but it didn't work. Reality interfered with memory.

"When did they tear it down?" I asked.

"A few years ago. I'm not sure."

"I liked that house. I still remember the summer we spent with Grandma and Grandpa."

"Do you? It was a small house. We were very crowded."

"I sometimes think it was the best summer of my childhood. At least it's the one I remember most."

Thinking about that summer as I looked around the tree-shaded cemetery – the trees weren't there fifty years ago, were they? – I tried to picture the boy I had been. What did it feel like to be of an age before self-consciousness set in, when you were still confined to the chrysalis of childhood and had yet to break out in a world where you were a stranger even to yourself, a creature constantly watching yourself watch yourself. Back then, when my grandparents were alive, we visited Aunt Helen and Uncle Clarence in the summer – I can still see their house with its sunny kitchen and the shaded coolness beneath the extended roof at the back where we played on hot days and the terraced lawn and the barrels at the corners of the house below the gutters to catch any rain. Those barrels fascinated me. Somehow, in ways I didn't understand, there was always something swimming or floating in them, insects mostly, dead or alive. I would stare into the dark water – I could never see the bottom for some reason – watching insects struggling to escape. Sometimes I helped them. Sometimes I watched them die, wondering what that felt like.

Now, walking past the graves of various aunts and uncles – Helen and Clarence, Dorothy, Jack, a cousin who died in infancy – it struck me that my mother was the only one of her immediate family who was still alive. I could see her ahead of me at her parents' graves. She was on her knees, pulling up thistles and dandelions that had sprouted around the concrete apron encircling the plots.

"I think this'll do," I said as I reached the graveside. "You're OK? Not too hot? I've got some water if you want."

"I'm fine. I enjoy this. I don't do much gardening anymore." She removed her jacket and rolled up the sleeves of her blouse. I noticed the thinness of her arms. "If you want to clean the headstones, I'm going to get rid of the weeds." She paused. "When we drive back, I want to stop at the town office. They'll tell me if I can hire someone to fix the headstones."

We set to work. While my mother weeded the graves, I cut back the caragana bush and pulled the tendrils off the gravestones. I sprayed the headstones with window cleaner and used the rags to wipe away dirt and small patches of moss. With the jackknife I scraped the loosened lichen out of the engraved names and dates on the stone. I worked without paying much attention to my thoughts – a Zen meditation technique I'd once learned at a Buddhist retreat. You focus on the work at hand, letting go of any resentment-inducing thoughts or rather-be-elsewhere-doing-other-things sentiments. It was oddly soothing to work in the sun, hearing the somnolent buzz and chirp of cicadas and the susurration of wind in the trees, aware of my mother's movements nearby. An occasional breeze kept the heat of the sun bearable.

It was as I scraped some stubborn flecks of lichen from my grandfather's name that the image of my grandparents' house filled my head. The vision did not last long, thirty seconds perhaps, but it was enough for me to revisit the living room where I slept – the green couch with the white lace doilies pinned to the fat arms, the burgundy throw rugs in front of the two big chairs, and the photographs of stiff-faced men and women in high collars (unnamed and never-seen aunts and uncles and cousins from the old country) hanging in gilded oval frames on the brown walls. I saw the kitchen with its big black cast iron stove and the kitchen table covered with a green oilcloth, and took in the warmth of the room and the smell of burning coal and the rich odour of borscht. Then I was outside, hovering above the white-painted house with the green trim on the windows and the glass-enclosed porch where, inside, a boy of nine or ten was sprawled across one of the fat-armed chairs, reading – William Dixon Bell's *The Moon Colony*, Robert Louis Stevenson's *Kidnapped*, Mark Twain's *Tom Sawyer* and *Huckleberry Finn* were among the books I remembered[2] – and wondering if he could persuade his grandmother to give him another piece of coffee cake.

The house, built by my grandfather, claimed one corner of the property. A whitewashed slat fence surrounded the yard. At the other end of the yard there was a two-hole outhouse and, next to it, my grandfather's work shed. A wooden walkway, narrow and wobbly, cut through my grandmother's garden, connecting the house and the shed.

The garden was lush with rows of staked tomatoes, vines of drooping pea pods, aisles of thigh-high potato plants, lines of tall corn and, at the edge of the yard against the far fence, a phalanx of sunflowers taller than the other plants and stretching like sentinels the length of the property (they were huge to my child's eyes). When I walked from the house to the work shed, the massive seeded heads with their corona of yellow petals turned as I passed, watching me. Or I was convinced they did.

The garden always smelled of the dill that grew in the back corner. My grandmother used it to flavour her creamy potato borscht. When a breeze blew across the garden, the smell of dill wafted in through the windows and filled the house. Even today, a whiff of dill makes me think of my grandmother. Indeed, forty years after that summer, walking through the Spanish village of Burguete during a pilgrimage trek on the Camino de Santiago, I passed a house bordered by a tall hedge. The sharp tang of dill from a garden behind the hedge halted me in my tracks, sending me back to that summer in Hanna.

Cleaning my grandfather's grave, absorbed in a vision of that house and garden, I relived that summer in a matter of seconds – reading on the porch, making plaster-of-Paris animals at the town's summer camp for kids, paddling in the tepid waters of Fox Lake, the smell of hot creosote on railway ties at the train station. But mostly I remembered my grandfather's work shed. He went there each morning after breakfast. At my mother's insistence, he took me along. My memories of the shed are largely a collage of images – my grandfather in his baggy grey pants and red suspenders; his thick rough hand around mine as he showed me how to work a saw on a piece of lumber without pinching the blade; the hammers and hand drills and axes hanging on the walls; the dust-streaked window with a cracked pane above the workbench.

Working the jackknife on the headstone, I was seized by one particular moment. I was standing beside my grandfather in front of the workbench, watching as he planed the edge of a board, entranced by the long ribbons of shavings that curled out of the plane and spiralled to the packed-dirt floor. The sun poured in through the window. Dust motes danced and swirled in the shaft of light that fell on the shavings. And, suddenly, for the first time in my life, I was aware of myself looking at myself as I stared at the golden cluster of shavings on the floor.

Years later, during my undergraduate years, I came across the mystic George Gurdjieff's notion of self-remembering. "There are moments when you become aware not only of what you are doing but also of yourself doing it. You see both 'I' and the 'here' of 'I am here.'"[3] Such moments, he says, constitute brief periods when we are fully awake to the world and ourselves in the world. Most of the time as adults we live with a divided consciousness, either obsessed by the internal chatter in our heads or else lost to the tumult of the world around us. Gurdjieff believed we could recover a sense of wholeness by cultivating moments of "self-remembering," extending them as much as possible so that we live in the simultaneous perception of both our inner self and the external world.

Psychologists label what my younger self experienced as a moment of apperception, a moment when you are aware of yourself in the act of perception. Of course, I wasn't thinking anything so cerebral at the time of my sudden self-remembering. But I still remember that moment: the awareness of where I was and what I was seeing and smelling and hearing, and, at the same time, the equally intense awareness of myself in these acts of perception. What I perceived, or, rather, what I perceived myself perceiving, may have been ordinary, but it felt extraordinary.

I now know that this moment was both my first genuine experience of self-consciousness (for good and ill), and the first of those few brief moments of epiphany I have been lucky enough to have over the course of my life. I have other childhood memories, but I remember them without feeling part of them. After that summer, though, I started to feel myself as a presence in the world. And that knowledge, as any psychologist will tell you, marks the beginning of the end of childhood.

Half a century later, reliving that moment as I scrubbed my grandfather's headstone, I was for a few seconds back home in my childhood skin, back when the world was new and fresh and unquestioned. I recalled an interview that novelist Kurt Vonnegut Jr. gave a couple of years before he died. The interviewer asked him what one thing he would still like to do. Vonnegut, then in his eighties, said he'd like to be his nine-year-old self in his hometown of Indianapolis.[4] I knew exactly what Vonnegut was getting at. He wasn't being sentimental about wanting to start all over again. He just wanted one more experience of that time in his life when the world was whole because his consciousness was whole. He wanted to feel well and truly at home.

"Are you all right?"

"Sorry, what?" Temporarily lost to the present, I hadn't heard my mother.

"I said, are you all right? You were just sitting there, staring at nothing." I might have been a fifty-year-old man, but the concern in her voice was for a child. "Is the sun bothering you? Maybe you should have a hat?"

"I was just remembering that summer when we stayed with Grandma and Grandpa before we went up north to Inuvik," I said. But I was also thinking: You can leave home, but it never leaves you.

And that, to my mind, makes the experience of home a wonderfully odd and puzzling phenomenon. Even though I hadn't visited Hanna since that long-ago summer, the images

I have of the place remain psychic touchstones in my life. I am certainly not unique in this experience. In his autobiography, *Memories, Dreams, Reflections*, the Swiss psychiatrist Carl Jung recounts walking to school one day as a boy of twelve: "suddenly for a single moment I had the overwhelming impression of having just emerged from a dense cloud. I knew all at once: now I am myself! It was as if a wall of mist were at my back, and behind that wall there was not yet an 'I.' But at this moment I came upon myself. Previously I had existed, too, but everything had merely happened to me. Now I happened to myself. Now I knew: I am myself now, now I exist."[5]

My moment of self-remembrance in my grandfather's workshop was, I think, similar to Jung's experience. In the same way that he remembered the "long road" between home and school as the place where he emerged from the mists of childhood, I remember my own awakening at the sight of sun falling through a dust-coated window. Hanna was the place where I acquired my first sense of myself as a distinct individual, the first place of self-consciousness. And because of that experience it remains my spiritual home.

****

Childhood is that period when we begin to be aware of ourselves as distinct individuals. We tend to associate this time not only with other people, but also with places. Returning to those places in later life can produce strong emotions or, as in my case, modest epiphanies of remembrance. These memories often provide psychic touchstones to our lives, talismanic markers of who we are and from whence we came. As scholar Clare Cooper Marcus observes, we develop affective relationships with the places where we live from childhood through to old age. And not just with houses, apartments or rooms; we become attached to gardens, backyards, neighbourhood parks, the view out the front window. Over the course of our lives, the meaningfulness we derive from places changes as the circumstances of our lives change. Children, for example, often establish special or secret places as a way of asserting their own identity and their sense of autonomy, particularly in relation to their parents. Similarly, a grown man or woman will set aside a portion of the house for hobbies or create a garden. In both cases, these "special places" become an expression of self.[6]

Changing the décor of our homes can also reflect a shift in our sense of identity, while our refusal to throw old things out, our attachment to particular objects, reflects an attempt to maintain psychological stability amidst the flux and flow of events and circumstances. When we experience a significant change in our lives, we hold on to cherished objects that help us recall our feelings about particular events and places. Think, for example, of how people who have seen their homes destroyed by some natural disaster will break into tears of joy at finding a tattered photo album, or how the elderly take prized keepsakes that remind them of the past – and, no doubt, their sense of identity and self-worth – when they must move from the family home. "As we change and grow throughout our lives," says Marcus, "our psychological development is punctuated not only by meaningful emotional relationships with people, but also by those close affective ties with a number of significant physical environments, beginning in childhood."[7]

Home is one of those significant environments. In its most profound form, home reflects "an attachment to a particular setting, a particular environment in comparison with which all other associations with places have only a limited significance. It is the point of departure from which we orient ourselves and take possession of the world."[8] Philosopher Vincent Vycinus, drawing on the thought of another philosopher, Martin Heidegger, asserts that it is possible to experience home as "an overwhelming, inexchangeable something to which we were subordinate and from which our way of life was oriented and directed, even if we had left our home many years before."[9] Home, then, is not just the place where you happen to live. Nor is it a place easily located anywhere, a place readily exchanged for any other place. Rather, home is, in the words of geographer Edward Relph, "an irreplaceable centre of significance." While we are largely unaware of the psychological and, indeed, existential ties to our homes, past and present, they are no less important for that.[10] Leonard Woolf, a British writer and the husband of novelist Virginia Woolf, summed up the influences of home well: "In my experience what cuts the deepest channels in our lives are the different houses in which we live – deeper even than 'marriage and death and division,' so that perhaps the chapters of one's autobiography should be determined by the different periods in which one has lived in different houses."[11]

Carl Jung, the founder of analytical psychology, exemplifies this claim, both in his psychological theories and in his personal life. Our homes, he said, function as universal and archetypal symbols of the individual self. The house reveals how we see ourselves, or how we wish to see ourselves, as well as how we wish others to see us. Home constitutes both an inward and an outward projection of our sense of identity.[12] At one point in Jung's life, he dreamed of himself as a two-storey house with multiple levels, and interpreted the dream as a reflection of his own state of consciousness.[13] In later years, Jung regarded the house he built after the death of his wife – The Tower, as he called it – as the symbolic expression of his long quest for "psychic wholeness," the "concretization of the individuation process."[14] Jung's home was a symbol of self-creation.

To be sure, the experience of home is also one of the most common and ordinary experiences, one with which most people are familiar in one way or another. Most of us lay our heads somewhere at the end of the day, and, for the most part, we refer to that somewhere as home. For some, of course, the experience of home has not been a good one. We all know or know of abusive home environments, domestic situations gone bad, or, at the extreme, horror stories of murder and suicide that happen behind the bright façade of suburbia. But even those who have not enjoyed a positive home experience are likely to compare their situation to a pervasive ideal of home, even if only imaginatively. In this sense, we intuitively know the meaning of "home." After all, we know at some level of emotional intelligence – tacit knowledge or pre-knowledge, as philosophers call it – what it means when someone says they do not feel at home in a particular place, or when someone invites us to make ourselves at home, or when we feel homesick. So it is not unreasonable to assume that our sense of our home, with its walls, closets, furniture, pictures and ornaments, shapes us as inhabitants, and vice versa.[15] Home, in short, resides at the core of our inner lives.

Indeed, some argue that our homes provide the psychological anchors that keep us stable and capable as we venture forth into the cold, cruel public world. "Personalized and actively defended, the home becomes the one sure refuge for the individual who is compelled to venture beyond its confines on the regular basis," says geographer J. Douglas Porteous. Everyone, he says, has three essential "territorial satisfactions": identity, security and stimulation. Ideally, the home provides all three. In this way, the home becomes "a fixed point of reference around which the individual may personally structure his or her spatial reality," the "focus of psychic satisfactions."[16]

A wealth of clichés and common sentiments testifies to the "psychic satisfactions," the values and virtues, that we attach to and derive from home. "A man's home is his castle" suggests the home as a refuge from the world. "Be it ever so humble, there's no place like home" suggests that home is our source of being. "Home is where the heart abides" expresses the deep longing of our emotional lives. "You can't go home again" reminds us that, existentially speaking, we are all lost and alienated to some extent. "Make yourself at home" is, perhaps, the height of friendship.[17] Then, of course, there's the saying reserved for the needlepoint cushions of elderly aunts and grandmothers: "Home Sweet Home."

Culturally, too, the concept of home is ubiquitous. Many will remember the immortal phrase "E.T. phone home." When a wizened, doll-like creature uttered those words in the 1982 movie *E.T. – The Extraterrestrial*, it was a hard-hearted moviegoer who did not feel an emotional tug. But it is not just sentimentality that has given this phrase iconic status in pop culture. Economic recession gripped the North American economy, especially the industrial heartlands of the United States and Canada, when the movie first appeared. People were losing their jobs and, worse, their homes. *E.T.* captured the mood of the time with its expression of a perennial human longing: the desire to be enfolded in the secure and familiar, to find or return to that place where you truly belong, to be home safe and sound. "The leathery extraterrestrial was expressing a primal human emotion – the feeling of being lost, frightened, out of place, vulnerable, homeless," says interior designer Joan Kron. "The only antidote for those feelings is 'home.'"[18]

This emotional investment is amply demonstrated by all those glossy magazines at the grocery checkout counters that beguile us with advice on home decoration, interior design, renovation and the comforts of home. The writer

Bonnie Burnard captured the psychological importance we attach to homemaking in her 1999 book, *A Good House*: "It is your housekeeping that makes your home alive, that turns it into a small society in its own right, a vital place with its own ways and rhythms, the place where you can be more yourself than you can be anywhere else."[19] Rita Eng, in her 1960 novel, *Ruthie*, addressed the pervasive subterranean presence of home in our psyches: "Who can tell what a house is like unless one lives in it, knows its middle-of-the-night creaks, becomes familiar with the geometric patterns made by doors, window frames, light coming through the drawn bedroom shades."[20]

One of my favourite portraits of home comes from novelist Marilynne Robinson who made the experience of home a central theme in her now-classic 1980 novel, *Housekeeping*. Her descriptions of rooms and the things in them vibrate with a sense of home, turning the ordinary into something extraordinary. There is, for example, a scene of children exploring their grandmother's chest of drawers. "My grandmother had kept, in the bottom drawer of the chest of drawers, a collection of things, memorabilia, balls of twine, Christmas candles, and odd socks. Lucille and I used to delve in this drawer. Its contents were so randomly assorted, yet so neatly arranged, that we felt some large significance might be behind the collection as a whole."[21]

What adult doesn't feel a sense of home in remembering as a child being fascinated with things – photographs, notebooks, fountain pens, letters and cards from unknown places – found in boxes that parents or grandparents had stored in the basement or attic? It was wondrously disorienting, if a little hard to believe, to discover our parents had lives before us. That knowledge somehow expanded our own lives down mysterious corridors of time.

Robert Frost's poem "The Death of the Hired Hand" offers a particularly insightful understanding of how our notions of home can vary widely depending on circumstance and perspective. "It all depends on what you mean by home," says the farmer's wife, Mary, in an exchange with her husband, Warren. The poem tells the story of a farmhand who left the couple's employ in questionable circumstances, but returns when he is dying.

"Warren," she said, "he has come home to die / You needn't be afraid he'll leave you this time."

"'Home,' he mocked gently."

"Yes, what else but home? / It all depends on what you mean by home."

The husband responds with the famous line: "Home is the place where, when you have to go there, / They have to take you in."

The wife's rejoinder is equally celebrated: "I should have called it / Something you somehow haven't to deserve."

At first it may seem that we hear two differing notions of home, with the husband linking home to questions of one's responsibility to others in the household, while the wife uses the language of moral rights. But as scholar John Hollander notes, the two perspectives – rights and responsibilities – actually complement each other and work together, so that by the end of the poem the definition of home becomes "the human point of ultimate return."[22] Hollander's point is that our ideas of home cover a wide gamut of experience and circumstance. Home can be "the place where you lay your head, eat your supper, do your work, ignore your work, make love, experience being greeted exuberantly by one's dog, problematically by one's cat, or even more mutely by one's possessions, feel safe, feel well, instruct one's children."[23]

Hollander's observation underscores my earlier reference to Gurdjieff: Reflective thought, self-consciousness awareness, is necessary to bring the experience of home to the fullest possible understanding in order to make the most of that experience. It is not sufficient to live passively; we should live with greater awareness and, thereby, greater intention. A meaning-filled life requires thought-filled comprehension. In the context of this essay, that means it is not sufficient to occupy a house; we should want to live in a home. A life lived in the full self-conscious of "home" is itself a kind of homecoming.

I do not want to suggest home is all sweetness and light. We all know this is not the case. Home life can be abusive, oppressive and stifling.[24] Even the occasional male writer understands this. Bernard Shaw once wrote, "home is the girl's prison and the woman's workhouse."[25] In some cases – Mark Twain's *Tom Sawyer* and *Huckleberry Finn* come immediately to mind – home is the place from which we are at times desperate to flee. Home can also be a source of isolation, introversion and madness. In Edgar Allan Poe's "The Fall of the House of Usher," the house itself seems insane. Nathaniel Hawthorne compares a home to the human heart in *House of the Seven Gables*: "So much had been suffered, and something, too, enjoyed – that the very timbers were oozy, as with the moisture of a heart. It was itself like a great human heart with a life of its own, and full of rich and somber reminiscences." In the novels of F. Scott Fitzgerald, the homes of his characters, whether apartments or mansions, not only reveal their psychic state but also shape that state.[26] Artist Emily Carr regarded her father's attempt to recreate an English country garden in the wilds of nineteenth-century British Columbia as a debilitating nostalgia for a lost home. "It was as if Father had buried a tremendous homesickness in this new soil." At times this homesickness emotionally overwhelmed her parents. "It was extraordinary to see Canada suddenly spill out of their eyes as if a dam had burst and let the pent-up England behind drown Canada."[27]

Even when we escape home, it seems we still long for it in one fashion or another. We seem to carry an image or idea of home within us from which we cannot escape. Travellers, for example, often carry a small object from home as a talisman during their wanderings. We lug around photograph albums (and, more recently, CDs and DVDs) filled with photographs of loved ones as a reminder of whence we came and where we must return. And, like Emily Carr's parents, we may even try to reproduce in some fashion a home away from home. For instance, in Graham Greene's 1961 novel, *A Burnt-Out Case*, the protagonist, Querry, seeks an "empty place" that would be without any associations that might remind him of home. But after travelling deep into the African jungle, he finds that "in an unfamiliar region it is always necessary for the stranger to begin at once to reconstruct the familiar, with a photograph perhaps, or a row of books if they are all that he has brought with him from the past … It was a condition of survival."[28]

But then our lives are in a sense a constant journey homeward, even in the midst of wandering. The journey of life invariably takes us away from our original home, whatever or wherever it may be, and yet we sometimes think that if we could return to where we began, we would understand where we have been and where we have still to go. The ancient Greek philosopher Heraclitus said you never step into the same river twice. You long to return home, but you know you never really can. Regret laces our longing. The lyric from the Beatles song I quoted at the beginning of this essay reflects this emotional tug-of-war.[29]

Examples of the traveller's longing for home abound in ancient literature. There is Homer's *Odyssey*, in which the hero Ulysses overcomes all odds and every temptation "to reach my house and see the day of my return." In the Bible, the Israelites exodus from Egypt leads them eventually to a new tribal home. We also see both the attachment to a lost home and the longing for a new one in Virgil's *Aeneid*. In this epic poem the Trojan hero Aeneas carries both his father and the household gods, the Penates, from the burning ruins of Troy to seek a place where they can rebuild. That place, according to legend, was Rome. We also have Milton's *Paradise Lost*, in which Eve abandons the home of the Garden of Eden for a new definition of home, not as a shelter or a contained space, but as a relationship with another who has also been exiled from paradise. As they are about the leave the Garden with the world all before them, Eve says to Adam: "In me is no delay; with thee to go / Is to stay here; without thee here to stay, / Is to go hence unwilling."[30]

Numerous canonical works contain the theme of home, whether in terms of homecoming, longing for home, flight from home or homelessness – everything from *The Gilgamesh Epic* and Virgil's *Aeneid* to Dante's *Divine Comedy* and Tao-Chi's *Returning Home: Album of Landscapes and Flowers*. What all these works suggest is that regardless of frequent negative connotations and experiences attached to the concept of home, it nevertheless remains, in the words of religion scholar Huston Smith, an "enduring icon" of refuge, shelter and rest, "a haven of warmth where love and acceptance prevail."[31]

Clearly, then, home is much more than any particular arrangement of walls and doors and roof (or canvas or skins or palm leaves). It is those things but it is, as geographer J. Douglas Porteous observes, also a place of "emotional investment," a "preferred space" that "provides a fixed point of reference around which the individual may personally structure his or her spatial reality." Porteous sums up these variegated notions and purposes of home, as well as the contradictions in sensibility it generates, this way: "As the point of departure and return for journeys, home is a stable refuge for the individual. It provides the territorial satisfactions of security, stimulation, and identity to the most intense degree … Nevertheless, home may stultify the individual, and can be most fully appreciated by leaving it. As psychic space, home paradoxically involves journey, the result of which may be the loss of the original home image and an infinitude of regret."[32] In other words, you can leave home, but home never leaves you.

To say this, though, is to open up another puzzle. Why is our sense of home so important in our lives? What does it mean for us, psychologically and spiritually? Approaching those questions requires a brief history of "home," a look back at sources that go some way to accounting for our contemporary emotional investment in the home. This history is necessary because, like many "ordinary" things, we take for granted our contemporary experience of home as a permanent feature of being human, unaware that it is largely a modern idea, dating back only two to three hundred years.

****

One of the unremarked factors behind the economic upheaval of recent years – besides the greed and stupidity of so many financial geniuses – is our collective desire to be homeowners. As economist Mark Zandi puts it, "The roots of the subprime financial shock begin in the American psyche and run through the typical household's balance sheet."[33] That is to say, the recession was as much the result of psychology as of economics. We got into an economic mess in part because too many people with problematic credit histories were given loans – those notorious subprime mortgages – they could not afford so that they, too, could fulfill the great dream of owning a home. But let's not fault them too much. Generations of North Americans and Europeans since the Second World War believe that home ownership – the single-family detached house is the preferred shelter of North Americans – is inextricably tied to their economic, social and psychic well-being. This belief is comparatively new in history. Only in the modern age, and especially in the societies of the West, has owning your home become so highly valued. The occasionally utopian-minded communitarian society has existed, say scholars, whether in Europe or North America, but, by and large, Westerners have come to want their own "patch of space," whether it's a rectangular slice of property in suburbia or a tall and narrow condo in a gentrified city neighbourhood. These homeowners devote much attention and a great deal of money to those spaces, regarding them as pillars – physical, economic, psychological and (as I am trying to show) spiritual – of the good life. "The anthropologist who studies us in the future may wonder whether ... our yen to claim space and buildings is 'bred in the bone,' whether we have an almost genetic yearning, borne from centuries of ancestral serfdom, to claim and fence and demarcate our dwellings, physically and legally, from others."[34]

Maybe so, but this yearning has taken on a distinct form in modern times. Social scientists say that "owning" property is a modern concept. In many ancient cultures, land and buildings did not actually "belong" to anyone; they were communal property. The idea that an individual could "own" a building was foreign to ancient thought. However, our notions of property, like the idea of home, have undergone radical changes in the last two to three centuries. Premodern societies tended to think of "home" largely in terms of satisfying the basic human need for shelter: a place to eat, sleep and, perchance, reproduce. The modern idea of home shares these needs, but it also carries the additional burden of having to satisfy desires for comfort, attachment and self-fulfillment. The nobles and aristocrats of the pre-modern world may have enjoyed some extraordinary luxuries, but most everybody else lived in "homes" that were little more than hovel-like shelters.

Only in the late Middle Ages, and on through the sixteenth, seventeenth and eighteenth centuries, did "home" begin to take on its modern connotations. Improving economies and better technology fostered a new consciousness of family, domestic intimacy and comfort. Home became not just a place of physical protection, but also a place of psychological satisfaction.[35] This developing appreciation of the "home" experience is, it seems, rooted in a growing self-consciousness among Western Europeans. The typical medieval "home" reflected a consciousness that had little of our sense of comfort; that is, of convenience and well-being. A scarcity of furnishings characterized medieval dwellings, whether those of the rich or of the poor. What furniture they had was collapsible and portable, including beds, tables and benches. This was because the medieval house was much more of a public place. Work, entertainment and family life often took place in a single large room. Medieval households included the immediate family, as well as servants, employees and friends. Twenty-five people commonly shared one or two rooms. Beds, too, were large enough to accommodate half a dozen people. Even the largest and richest households had few rooms, if any, for purposes that we now regard as private. "People lived in general-purpose rooms," says historian Philippe Ariès. "In the same rooms where they ate, people slept, danced, worked and received visitors."[36]

The medieval room might be hung with rich tapestries and filled with benches, trestle tables, collapsible beds and large wooden tubs for bathing – contrary to the modern misconception, bathing was a regular ritual in the Middle

Ages – but they were not particularly built with comfort in mind.[37] The novelist Walter Scott captured this characteristic of the medieval dwelling in his novel *Ivanhoe*: "Magnificence there was, with some rude attempt at taste; but of comfort there was little, and, being unknown, it was unmissed."[38]

The key word is "unmissed." We should not misinterpret this lack of comfort as a symptom of crudity, or think that people of the Middle Ages took no pleasure in their surroundings. What they lacked, and what their dwellings reflected, was any self-conscious understanding of comfort as an objective concept. Medieval houses reflected a consciousness focused on externalities. Medieval men and women were concerned with where they fit on the Great Chain of Being, their station in life along a hierarchical order that descended from God to king to noble and on down to cleric, tradesman and peasant. And they lived according to rituals, rules and regulations that reflected their placement along that chain. Each station required conformity to certain rules of behaviour – everything from what kind of clothing you were allowed to wear to where you sat in church or at the dining table. A nobleman, for instance, could buy more new clothes each year than a lowly knight. Only aristocrats could wear ermine. Only some could wear coloured silk, with certain colours privileged to certain groups.[39]

Ritual even regulated "home" life. Simple functions such as washing hands and breaking bread at mealtime acquired ceremonial expression. This devotion to ceremony and ritual highlights what historian John Lukacs refers to as the external focus of the medieval consciousness.[40] Life in the Middle Ages was lived much more publicly than it is now. Most medieval homes did not provide individuals with their own rooms, their own personal space. This lack of privacy reflected their state of consciousness. "As the self-consciousness of medieval people was spare, the interiors of their homes were bare, including the halls of nobles and kings," says Lukacs. "The interior furniture of houses appeared together with the interior furniture of their minds."[41]

This situation changed with the development of the modern sensibility – what Lukacs calls the "bourgeois spirit" – from, say, 1450 onward. It is because of the rise of the bourgeois, those burghers and town dwellers of northern Europe who laid the foundations for the Renaissance with their emphasis on trade, commerce and craft, that we now have such concepts as individualism, rights and privacy. These concepts reflected a new way of thinking about the world, a new consciousness of the self. And it is out of this new psychology, this new self-understanding, that our notions of family life with its emphasis on privacy and intimacy, emerged.[42] Lukacs points out that words such as "self-esteem," "self-confidence," "self-knowledge," self-pity" and "self-love" – all of which are ubiquitous nowadays – appeared in English or in French with their modern connotations only two and three centuries ago. The same is true of words such as "ego," "conscience," "melancholy," "apathy" and "sentimental"; their arrival marked the emergence of something new in human consciousness: the appearance of the internal world of the individual, the self and the family. Where the medieval world reflected external concerns – the desire for a better world beyond this one, in particular – the arrival of "the bourgeois era" in fifteenth-century Europe promoted the internalization of consciousness, explains Lukacs. "As the exploration of the external world accelerated (in the sixteenth and seventeenth centuries), at the same time our ancestors became more and more aware of the interior landscape of their minds."[43]

The modern world emerged out of that inward awareness, and so, too, did the modern idea of home. Home became a place of private retreat from the public world, beginning with the bourgeoisie of eighteenth-century

France and England. This idea crossed the Atlantic in the early years of the nineteenth century to become the ideal of the urban middle-class families of North America. The development of the concept of home reflected the newly emergent character of the modern family as a private realm focused on the children, where men and women largely ascribed to respective public and domestic roles.[44] In turn, this new interior-oriented consciousness gave rise to the modern idea of home. Thus, the modern experience of home reflects a development in human consciousness. In the words of cultural historian Witold Rybczynski, "the appearance of the internal world of the individual, of the self, and of the family" reveals an appreciation of the house as a "setting for an emerging interior life."[45]

The early manifestations of this modern consciousness of home were evident at the beginning of the Enlightenment in the late seventeenth and early eighteenth centuries when the decoration of houses began to stir the imaginations of Europe's bourgeoisie. The richest burghers began to fill their townhouses with luxury goods – chairs, tables, beds, and so on – and divide those houses into separate rooms for eating, sleeping, work, sex, bathing and toiletries. More crucially, in terms of the development of the modern consciousness, this accumulation of things, as well as their arrangement in rooms, began to reveal something about the character of their owner; in other words, furnished rooms started to say something about self-identity. "Before the idea of the home as the seat of family life could enter the human conscious-ness, it required the experience of both privacy and intimacy, neither of which had been possible in the medieval hall," says Rybczynski. "The growing sense of intimacy was a hu-man invention as much as any technical device. Indeed, it may have been more important, for it affected not only our physical surroundings, but our consciousness as well."[46]

By the eighteenth century, there was an increasing awareness of the value and worth of family life, particularly in regard to children. Where medieval families tended to send all but the youngest children – those under age seven or eight – away to be servants or apprentices in other households, the bourgeois families of northern and western Europe began raising children to full adulthood. This practice encouraged a much greater sense of intimacy between parents and their children, which, in turn, fostered notions of privacy and the need for more individual living arrangements – rooms of their own. The household was no longer a combined work and living space, much less a public place. It became "a place for personal intimate behavior."[47] Nor was the house only a shelter against the elements, a place to lay your head. By the end of the eighteenth century, it was "the setting for a new, compact social unit: the family," in which the public was held at bay while a new private world that encouraged domesticity and intimacy came into being.[48]

Certainly, the house of the eighteenth and early nineteenth centuries remained very much a social place, but in a way much different from that of the Middle Ages. The English bourgeois home – such as those found in the novels of Jane Austen or Anthony Trollope – were unlike the big sociable houses of medieval times with their constant ebb and flow of people, including non-family members. The bourgeois house was, in Rybczynski's words, "an isolated world into which only the well-screened visitor was permitted; the world was kept at bay, and the privacy of the family and the individual, was disturbed as little as possible."[49]

This development of home consciousness is evident in literary history. For example, Jane Austen's nineteenth-century character Fanny Price, the heroine of *Mansfield Park*, lived in a house where she could retreat to the "best room" and enjoy an aspect "so favourable that even without a fire it was habitable in many an early spring and late autumn morning." In her "hours of leisure" she

> could go there after anything unpleasant below, and find immediate consolation in some pursuit, or some train of thought at hand. Her plants, her books – of which she had been a collector from the first hour of her commanding a shilling – her writing-desk, and her works of charity and ingenuity, were all within her reach; or if indisposed for employment, if nothing but musing would do, she could scarcely see an object in that room which had not an interesting remembrance connected with it. Everything was a friend, or bore her thoughts to a friend.[50]

Novelist Virginia Woolf, writing in the early twentieth century, often used the setting of the private home as a symbolic space for revealing the intimate inner life of her characters, as well as her own personal life. Woolf reveals her sense of release, her sense of freedom and newly obtained privacy, after the death of her father – a "transition from tyranny to freedom" – through the observation of physical details in which she compares the patterns of Morris wallpaper, red plush furnishings and black paint of her father's home with the white-and-green chintzes of the new home where she moved.

In a scene in Woolf's 1927 novel, *To the Lighthouse*, the focus on household objects reveals the emerging consciousness of a child.

> James Ramsay, sitting on the floor cutting out pictures from the illustrated catalogue of the Army and Navy stores, endowed the picture of a refrigerator as his mother spoke with heavenly bliss. It was fringed with joy. The wheelbarrow, the lawn-mower, the sound of poplar trees, leaves whitening before the rain, rooks

cawing, brooms knocking, dresses rustling – all these were so coloured and distinguished in his mind that he had already his private code, his secret language ....[51]

We follow James' mother, Mrs. Ramsay, as she climbs the stairs to her children's nursery, thinking about the couple she'd introduced to each other, Paul and Minta, and how they were now engaged. She notices various objects as she climbs. Each object evokes a memory of another person. In a revelatory moment – a moment of what I shall later refer to as "everyday mysticism" – Mrs. Ramsay wonders whether passing on household goods connects her across generations and thereby gives her a kind of immortality.

They would, she thought, going on again, however long they lived, come back to this night; this moon, this wind; this house; and so to her too. It flattered her, where she was most susceptible to flattery, to think how, wound about in their hearts, however long they lived, she would be woven, and this, and this, and this, she thought, going upstairs, laughing, but affection- ately, at the sofa on the landing (her mother's) at the rocking-chair (her father's) ... and she felt, with her hand on the nursery door, that community of feeling with other people which emotion gives as if the walls of partition had become so thin that practically (the feeling was one of relief and happiness) it was all one stream, and chairs, tables, maps, were hers, were theirs, it did not matter whose, and Paul and Minta would carry it on when she was dead.[52]

Another writer, Alfred Kazin, shows how one room – the kitchen, in this case – can contain the essence of home. He goes into exquisite detail, recalling the contents of the kitchen of his childhood and, thereby, revealing his con- sciousness of home.

The kitchen held our lives together. My mother worked in it all day long, we ate in it almost all meals except the Passover seder. I did my homework and first writing at the kitchen table, and in winter I often had a bed made up for me on three kitchen chairs near the stove. On the wall just over the table hung a long horizontal mirror that sloped to a ship's prow at each end and was lined in cherry wood. It took up the whole wall, and drew every object in the kitchen to itself. The walls were a fiercely stippled whitewash, so often rewhitened by my father in slack seasons that the paint looked as if it had been squeezed and cracked into the walls.[53]

What we see in these writers is the deployment of descriptions of home as a mirror of their characters' minds. Home, in this regard, is much more than a setting for the story. It also provides a symbolic structure of meaningfulness that represents the self-understanding of the characters, as well as their relationship to each other and to the world at large.[54] Thus, modern writers capture the meaningfulness that home holds for the modern consciousness. This meaningfulness represents a huge psychic shift from the sparseness of both the medieval room and the medieval mind. The medieval mind spared little thought for the "self." The modern mind, on the other hand, is dense with "self" obsessions, up to the rafters with the possessions of individuality, personal space, rights, self-esteem, self-expression and family sentiment. This consciousness is evident in our contemporary idea of home, with its emphasis on security, domesticity, privacy and comfort. In these examples we see the concept of home experienced as a place for privacy and security, a zone of retreat from the world, as well as that singular space where you can most be yourself, most fully the master of your life. Perhaps then we should not find too much fault with those who acquired mortgages they could ill afford. They, too, wanted a place of meaning, a place they could call home.

****

My brief history of home, along with the literary examples of the experience of home, highlights how our homes, or our attempts to create home, reflect our psychic state. I would now like to turn to a more philosophical consideration of home. I do this because we live more fully when we comprehend our everyday experience at the conceptual level. It's not enough merely to exist, to go with the flow; we need to reflect on that existence in order to be truly alive to all its possibilities. Admittedly, it might seem odd to attach so much existential import to the idea of home. For some, no doubt, a home is only a house, a physical space that shelters them from the elements and provides a place to eat and sleep. Yet, to confine our understanding and appreciation of home to such a prosaic level is to close off the experience of home as one of the most readily available and most fulfilling symbolic sources of meaning and purpose in our everyday experience, one of the best means to refresh our spirits and re-enchant our world.

Philosophers have certainly recognized that our homes structure and shape our psyches, both at the individual and the collective level. The experience of home is essential not only to the individual's sense of identity, they argue, but also to the coherence of society's self-understanding.[55] Thus, the experience of home can be much more than an expression of domesticity and shelter or our desire for companionship. The concept of home can serve as an all-encompassing metaphor for our lives. Home can be both particular *and* universal, concrete *and* abstract. Home offers an "image of the being of man and also an image of the world."[56] To reflect on the concept of home is to inquire into our deepest existential longings and concerns, including whether the world is truly a home for mankind.[57] As philosopher Derek Kelly says, "The nature of man's being-in-the-world may perhaps then be understood by reflecting on the notion of house."[58]

Philosopher Martin Heidegger, among others, offers a way to reflect on this deeper understanding of home. According to Heidegger, our sense of home, of what it means to be at home, and, conversely, what it feels like to feel "unhomed," informs and shapes our entire life. Home speaks to our sense of rootedness and belonging; unhomed, to our sense of uprootedness and alienation. In a famous essay entitled "Building, Dwelling, Thinking,"[59] Heidegger attempts to show that to build or create something genuinely meaningful amounts to an authentic "dwelling" in the world, a way of living that demonstrates care for the world. "To dwell properly is to be involved with the earth and to approach things in a respectful manner." The greatest joy, says Heidegger, is to be at home among those things that truly matter. "What distinguishes the person who is at home from him who is not is the relationship he has to the things of the world: he who exploits things cannot be at home anywhere." You become homeless when your relations with the things of the world, including other people, become manipulative. To recover a sense of home, to return home, "is to return to a non-manipulative, respectful relation to things."[60]

Heidegger's notion of authentic dwelling suggests that "home" is not a matter of a particular place, although it can be, but rather a question of relationships. To care for and be respectful of the things of the world is to be at home in the world. From this perspective, then, you can be homeless in your own house. As Derek Kelly puts it in summarizing Heidegger's views, "Without a sense of home, I am a stranger who must constantly practice the arts of duplicity and dissimulation for there is nowhere I can practice the arts of simplicity and naturalness that I can when I am at home."[61] To be home in the most meaningful sense is to be what you most truly are, your most authentic self. It is to have care for what is most important. It is to live among those things that truly matter. Home, then, is a quality of relationships, of connecting to the things of the world in a particular way.

We are at home – and here I am paraphrasing Kelly – depending on our intentions, our relation to the things around us. To be homeless, or unhomed, is not simply a matter of having no place to lay your head or to be missing a particular place or person, but rather to be "absent from a mode of relationship,"[62] to have failed in connecting properly with other things in the world. In this philosophic sense, then, home is not simply a place – the house or apartment where you happen to eat and sleep; rather, it is the bedrock of your identity as an individual, the dwelling place of your most essential being.

Clare Cooper Marcus, whom I cited earlier, picks up on this point, noting that a home fulfills many needs. It can be a place of self-expression, a vessel of memories and a refuge from the outside world, a cocoon where we can feel nurtured and drop our guard. But it is also a container and reflection of our psyches, and if we read it properly and honestly, we can gain valuable knowledge of ourselves. "We are all – throughout our lives – striving toward a state of wholeness, of being wholly ourselves. Whether we are conscious of it or not, every relationship, event, mishap, or good fortune in our lives can be perceived as a 'teaching,' guiding us toward being more and more fully who we are … (T)he places we live in are reflections of that process, and indeed the places themselves have a powerful effect on our journey toward wholeness."[63]

If we are concerned about spiritual growth, we need to pay attention to the "messages" implicit in our homes – their form and location, as well as their furnishings, decoration and condition. In saying this, it is well to remember that some of our homes are homes only in memory or dream. I figure I've had "homes" in numerous places in the world – from a fondly remembered bed-sitting room on Burdett Avenue in Victoria and a small room in a house on Ravensbourne Road in Bromley to a cave on Crete and a rickety clapboard shed on an Israeli kibbutz near the Golan. What they have in common is that I felt, well, at home in them. All of which suggests that our homes, with their basements, attics, bedrooms, kitchens, backyards, gardens, etc., reveal messages from the unconscious that, if we pay attention, we can learn to decipher in our quest for wholeness.[64] As the French philosopher Gaston Bachelard puts it, our homes can serve as "a tool for analysis of the human soul."[65]

All this might seem overly philosophical and obscurely abstract, but we need theories and concepts to help us make sense of lived reality. The trick is to translate theoretical understanding into everyday experience. I can think of no better way to illustrate an "analysis of the soul" than through the experience of home during Christmas. Scholars have long recognized the social and cultural significance of Christmas; whether as a religious or a secular festival, it is widely regarded as time set apart from the rest of the calendar. "The festival of Christmas is intimately linked to the attachment to places and the notion of home," says geographer Patrick McGreevy. "Almost any celebrant of this festival, if asked where it should take place, would respond that ideally Christmas should be celebrated at home. At no other time of year is absence from home considered more poignantly tragic than at Christmas."[66]

One of the more striking features of the Christmas season is the way we decorate our streets, stores and public buildings with lights, ornaments and religiously themed displays such as the nativity scene (unless, of course, the politicians and shopping malls cave in to the anti-Christian objections of politically correct ideologues and propagandists). That might seem an obvious observation, until you consider what those decorations imply. The familiar symbols of Santa Claus, Christmas trees and nativity scenes pull us into shared rituals and symbolic practices that reinforce our sense of and longing for community – or, put differently, our communal sense of home.

This ideal of being at home in the community finds various expressions. Charities appeal for donations to help the needy. Schools stage Christmas pageants. Local orchestras tune up for performances of Handel's *Messiah*. John Lennon's song "So This Is Christmas" saturates the airwaves, until even the curmudgeonly among us feel a touch of fondness for the human race. In this way, says McGreevy, "community identity is heightened ... [and] for a few weeks at least the community is defined inclusively."[67]

However, our closest Christmas attachment, our most deeply desired "place" for Christmas, remains the family home, whatever configuration – apartment, condo or suburban bungalow – it may take. Home, as I argued earlier, fulfills many needs: a refuge from the external world, a repository of memories, a shelter for self-expression, a realm of intimacy, the symbolic vessel of our values. These values are only intensified at Christmas. Students abandon dormitories and rented rooms for a few days of home cooking and family indulgence. Adults risk winter roads to spend time with aging parents. Grandparents endure cattle-pen airplanes to see grandchildren. Every year we transform our homes with strings of lights. Inside, we drape trees with beads and baubles and faux angels. And, somehow, the appearance of the house acquires a friendlier façade. The familiar space of a living room or dining room becomes a place of enchantment, a cozy realm of intimacy that fulfills, at least to some degree, our longing for a place where we truly belong. All of these external accoutrements of Christmas work a psychic alchemy on us; the transformation of the home transforms us spiritually, however modestly.

Christmas has not always been a popular festival. The festival's roots reside in pre-Christian pagan celebrations – ancient Romans and Germanic tribes staged mid-winter festivals to mark the winter solstice – but Christmas assumed official status only in the fourth century A.D., when the Bishop of Rome, Julius I, set December 25 as the Feast of the Nativity. The Christian celebration adapted many of the pagan practices, including charity to the poor and the display of lights and decorated evergreens. The festival continued through the Middle Ages, with an emphasis on feasting and drinking, and, no doubt, not a little lechery. Charity took the form of food and clothing for the poor. In the seventeenth century, however, the Protestant Reformation put a damper on Christmas. In fact, the English Puritans, acting much like the multicultural fundamentalists of today, banned Christmas. The Puritans extended their parsimonious purity to the New World when they settled New England. The suppression of Christmas largely held sway throughout the eighteenth century, and by the early 1800s the festival seemed set to fade away.[68]

Then along came Charles Dickens. His 1843 story, *A Christmas Carol*, is widely credited with renewing enthusiasm for Christmas, particularly among the rising middle class in Victorian-era Britain and North America. With his focus on children, Dickens reflected a growing social sentiment that Christmas was a time for family, as distinct from the pre-modern notion of Christmas as an adult celebration. But Dickens' story also had another theme: Christmas provided a retreat from the hurly-burly, get-and-spend public world.

In this manner, Christmas began to reflect the values that emerged among the middle class in response to the rapid industrialization, commercialization and urbanization of the West in the nineteenth century, values that idealized the private world of the family as a sanctuary from the clash and competition of the public arena. As Patrick McGreevy puts it, "The Christmas that emerged in the nineteenth century was an affirmation of the private home as a place of great worth: indeed, for the duration of the festival, the home became a sort of private paradise," an "ideal place."[69]

Of course, our Christmas place often falls short of the ideal – who hasn't witnessed a family blow-up over Christmas dinner, endured a holiday in hell with visiting relatives, or had a love affair die over the holidays? Nevertheless, the ideal of a few days in a private paradise remains. Beneath the tawdry and the tacky commercialism, behind the excesses of eating and drinking, outside the familial fights, there lingers the longing for "the sense of sublime equilibrium, a sublime stillness," to borrow John Lukacs' phrase, inherent to the ideal of Christmas. As Lukacs says, the cult of Christmas responds to some of our "deepest aspirations."[70]

G.K. Chesterton, the English essayist, novelist and Catholic apologist, underlines those aspirations in describing the family home as a vessel of genuine humanity. The Christmas retreat into the private realm offers a brief release from the strain and burden of the public world with its constant demands for conformity and structured behaviour. While he acknowledges that Christmas has its public dimension, its real spirit – "the spirit of the Child,"[71] as he puts it – is more readily available in the domestic realm. Indeed, Chesterton would like us to close the doors to the outside world at Christmas because it is, or should be, a time for inwardness, for partaking of the rich interior life of home and family. "Let there be one night when things grow luminous from within: and one day when men seek for all that is buried in themselves; and discover, where she is indeed hidden, behind locked gates and shuttered windows, and doors thrice barred and bolted, the spirit of liberty."[72]

Chesterton's notion of home as a place of luminousity, whether in dream, remembrance, imagination or reality, highlights the idea of home as a possible place of liminal experience. The word comes from the Latin *limin*, meaning a doorway or threshold. Liminality involves moments of spiritual awareness, however modest or profound, when you temporarily cross the threshold of the mundane world and experience a heightened sense of reality. Liminality marks a transformative period in which spiritual and psychological change can occur. In liminal experience we abandon old ways of perception, calling old mental concepts and categories into question, for new ways of perception. Liminal moments are a kind of pilgrimage of the psyche from one mindset to another. To experience the Christmas home as a liminal event is to step out of the strictures of the external world and into a more enchanted inner realm, however temporarily. Experienced this way, the festival of Christmas, with its rituals of decoration, the presence of family and friends, the exchange of gifts and the sharing of food and drink, can, for a short time, make the world a slightly different and, perhaps, slightly better place.

****

What about the rest of the year? The world, as the poet William Wordsworth once said, is too much with us, and there are times when it seems meaningless and purposeless. If we cannot attain a sense of meaningfulness through the experience of home – whether spiritual, psychological, emotional, cultural or geographical – then I doubt we can regain it anywhere. If we cannot achieve a sense of home in some place and at some time in our lives, then we really are homeless, aliens in the cosmos.[73]

Vaclav Havel, the one-time anti-Soviet dissident and eventual Czech president, alludes to this dark possibility in *Summer Meditations*, where he writes of "home" as a series of concentric circles experienced on different levels – from the house where you live, the family with which you share the house, and the streets of the town or city where the house is located, to the place you work, your professional milieu and the nation in which you have citizenship, the language through which you express your self and your identity, the culture and civilization that provide your heritage, and, ultimately, the planet and cosmos that shape and inform your very being. Havel allows how he came to regard his prison cell as a home, and how annoyed he was when he had to move to another. "The new cell may have been exactly the same as the old one, perhaps even better, but I always experienced it as alien and unfriendly. I felt uprooted and surrounded by strangeness, and it would take me some time to get used to it, to stop missing the previous cell, to make myself at home." Havel argues, "Every circle, every aspect of the human home, has to be given its due." This, he says, "is the only way that room can be made for people to realize themselves freely as human beings, to exercise their identities. All the circles of our home, indeed, our whole natural world, are an inalienable part of us, and an inseparable element of our human identity. Deprived of all the aspects of his home, man would be deprived of himself, of his humanity."[74] We would be homeless and, therefore, inhuman.

Our ancestors attempted to overcome the fear of homelessness by inviting the gods into their dwellings. Their "homes" possessed an alcove or shrine where the gods dwelled, religious rituals were performed and ancestors were honoured. These rituals helped unify symbolically the supernatural and natural worlds, god and man, society and the individual, the living and the dead, and thereby helped resolve conflicts among them. Or, put differently, the "homes" of the ancients provided a "space" where the occupants achieved a sense of wholeness and unity with the cosmos.[75] In this regard, the ancient "home" was genuinely liminal, in that it served as a threshold between the individual and the wider world (or cosmos), and helped orient the individual to this wider experience.

Political scientist Robert Rakoff argues that the modern-day home serves a remarkably similar symbolic function "despite the desanctification of houses and everyday life." The sense of significance we derive from our home comes, as it did in ancient times, from the sense of control over our lives that possession provides. Our ancestors maintained control through propitiation of the gods. Today, whether we worship a divine reality or pray at the altar of consumption, we still seek to establish some kind of control over our lives through the objects we possess. "The [modern] house is a dominant symbol of a variety of problematic and conflicting life experiences – personal success and family happiness, mobility and permanence, privacy and social involvement, personal control and escape." This is not necessarily a straightforward matter of power for power's sake, Rakoff says, or even the mundane power of being able to alter the structure of a house – adding decks and dens and basement bathrooms, for example. Rather, the home also symbolizes control in psychological and spiritual ways. "First, having control of one's own private space gave people a feeling of freedom from the control and intrusion of others. Second, and more importantly, people felt that by being in control of their own private space, they had the power and the opportunity to make something of themselves, to be 'more of an individual,' to achieve a kind of self-fulfillment."[76]

Rakoff concludes that this sense of control can be detected in people's statements of self-satisfaction regarding their homes: "'This is my little piece of ground! I can lay in bed at night or on a Sunday morning and just think and reflect and feel very good that I am in a house that's got a lot of wood and warmth.'" But what is most striking is how people perceive their control of private space in terms not only of escaping the control of others, but of helping "their development as humane, loving, potent individuals."[77] Thus, even in our secular, desanctified society, we link our psychic well-being to the possession of a home. Our claim of personal space in the home is both an assertion of identity and a means of spiritual satisfaction. We feel secure, in both a physical and a psychological sense, because we control the "spaces" that we call bedrooms, kitchens, bathrooms and basement dens. We derive a sense of value and meaningfulness from those spaces and the things in them. The novelist Henry James said it well: "Objects and places, coherently grouped, disposed for human use and addressed to it, must have a sense of their own, a mystic meaning proper to themselves, to give out."[78]

The challenge, then, it seems to me, is how we might foster "mystic meaning" in and through our homes. Perhaps it is possible to know home as a liminal experience, even if only occasionally, and thereby achieve a spiritual homecoming. Writer Tracy Cochran captures this spiritual dimension of home – how home life can sustain the spirit – in a short but elegant essay in which she recounts her attempt to deal with the shock of the terrorist attacks of September 11, 2001. "In the months after 9/11, I had taken to cooking, to lighting candles. Instinctively, I was returning to a role that women have filled since the dawn of time, keeping the home fires burning, and that the softest of things – love, the smell of banana bread – overcome the hardest."[79] Cochran rightly recognizes that it is in our everyday lives, our actions in the world, that we become conduits for those moments of transcendent awareness. In this case, her domestic instinct – "ordinary acts of nurturance," as she puts it – suggests that the meaning our lives acquire, our spiritual fulfillment, is intimately related to our success in making a house a home, in the degree of care and awareness we bring to our dwellings.

The novelist Rita Eng says something similar in describing a character who does not regard domesticity as a burden or a life of drudgery. Rather she uses domestic rituals – hanging the laundry, setting the table, picking up after the children, monitoring the condition of the house – as a means for comprehending and participating in the world around her, thereby demonstrating that for many women, "the domestic world of ordinary life holds as much significance as the world of extraordinary adventure."[80]

This devotion to home, and the domestic rituals that make up the home, are necessary for cultural survival, according to theologian Kathryn Allen Rabuzzi. She points out that housework undertaken and perceived as a ritual enactment "makes the individual a player in a scene far older and larger that her individual self. No longer does she participate in profane historical time; instead, she is participating in mythic time."[81] Moreover, as Cochran's experience and Eng's character intimate, such domestic rituals are the kind that most cultures rely on for their survival. In these everyday rituals, "the ideal life of the tribe's ancestors is 'ritually made present,'" thus maintaining "a continuity of belief and knowledge from one generation to the next."[82] Literary scholar Ann Romines, drawing on Rabuzzi's views, points out that for many women, particularly those who have invested their sense of identity in maintaining a home, "ritual is domestic, and it is a constant of everyday life." But even as daily work, housekeeping remains, at least potentially, "a sacramental activity that provides essential cultural continuity."[83] In other words, liminal experience of the home is possible through a proper attendance to everyday household duties.

The emphasis here is on "proper attendance." A proper frame of mind is necessary if work is to be more than drudgery. The task is cultivating that sacramental mindset. How might we become better homebodies, so to speak? My guide on this matter is French theorist Gaston Bachelard, who probes more deeply into the ideal experience of home than any other thinker I know. To think through his theories and then test them against our experience of home illustrates the possibility for regarding the home as a potential site of everyday mysticism.

Bachelard's book *The Poetics of Space*, first published in English in the early 1960s, looks at how our homes and the things in them – drawers and doorknobs, cellars and attics, closets and cupboards, figurines and furnishings – influence our self-understanding and our view of the world. A home, he says, is not only a place of shelter but also a place of dreams. It serves as a shelter but it also shapes our self-understanding. To properly attend to our homes, to pay attention to the rooms and the objects in them, is to understand how the physical influences the psychological and the spiritual. Our lived-in houses are more than just collections of boxes with a roof on top. A proper "topoanalysis" – an inquiry into "space we love" – reveals as much about our "intimate being" as it does about the objects examined.[84] For Bachelard, the various manifestations of the "oneiric house" – all those images of trunks, attics, closets and cupboards that we carry in our heads – "are interrelated in their common evocation of a relationship of intimacy and refuge."[85] Indeed, to apply the word "home" to a particular space is to recognize a relationship between it and ourselves, to foster what Heidegger might describe as a non-manipulative, reciprocal relationship of being. Or, put differently, the study of our homes is a study of ourselves (and vice versa).

Bachelard also maintains that our childhood memories of home, along with our daydreams and other imaginative reveries (including poetry), provide a link that connects home and psyche. Through these phenomena of consciousness we gain a deeper appreciation of the concept of home and its importance in our lives. The mind, our consciousness, needs to situate itself in a particular space. It needs both to find itself at home and, in the absence of a sense of home, to articulate its alienation. Equally, the mind needs to express its desire to escape home and, often at the same time, to express its longing and nostalgia for home. Thus, says Bachelard, "by remembering 'houses' and 'rooms,' we learn to abide within ourselves."[86] If any one statement encapsulates Bachelard's concept of home as a space of self-remembrance, a shelter for creative dreaming, it is this one:

> All really inhabited space bears the essence of the notion of home. In the course of this work, we shall see that the imagination functions in this direction whenever the human being has found the slightest shelter: we shall see the imagination build "walls" of impalpable shadows, comfort itself with the illusion of protection or, just the contrary, tremble behind thick walls, mistrust the staunchest ramparts ... Thus the house is not experienced from day to day only, on the thread of a narrative, or in the telling of our own story. Through dreams, the various dwelling places in our lives co-penetrate and retain the treasures of former days ... If I were asked to name the chief benefit of the house, I should say: the house shelters daydreaming, the house protects the dreamer, the house allows one to day dream in peace ... In the life of a man, the house thrusts aside contingencies, its councils of continuity

are unceasing. Without it, man would be a dispersed being. It maintains him through the storms of the heavens
and through those of life. It is body and soul."[87]

The home, in other words, constitutes an abode for
human consciousness. Bachelard's task – and ours, too, I
would argue – is to perceive the ways in which that space
accommodates consciousness, especially the half-dreaming
consciousness that he calls *reverie*. For Bachelard, we need a
home to dream, to imagine, if we are to be truly human. But
this is to say that a genuine appreciation of the concept of
home, of learning to "dwell" properly, is a kind of homecoming for the soul.

Bachelard attempts to show how, through the contemplation of or meditation on a particular object – a room with
a view (as in Virginia Woolf's experience) or the recollection
of my grandparents' home in Hanna, Alberta – we can foster
those epiphanic moments in which we achieve a sense of
connectedness between the self and the object, can achieve
what Gurdjieff called self-remembering. To put it in abstract
terms, the thing contemplated – the kitchen, the bookshelf,
the old chair – is no longer merely an object out there, but
becomes in the moment of epiphany (or self-remembering)
an object that calls on the subject (you) to enter into "a receptive [and] self-aware ... state of being."[88] Or, to use my
own terminology, Bachelard teaches that our meditations
on home and the things of the home can provide us with a
glimpse of the underglimmer.

Although Bachelard is not unaware of the dark side of
our dwelling places,[89] his self-declared purpose is idealistic.
He considers only those "felicitous images" of the house –
closets, cupboards, seashells, nests, etc. – that help us feel
more at home in the world. He is engaged in topophilia – the
study of loved places – and therefore brackets out consideration of the unloved aspects of home. In this fashion he seeks

to awaken our sense of "naïve wonder," the wonder we once may have experienced as children.[90]

Bachelard's meditations on the space in which people live and the things they love within that space cannot help but deepen our awareness of how we experience our houses: how we make the house (or condo, hut or tent) into a home. His study of the "phenomenon of dwelling" encourages us to reflect on the ways our dwelling places influence our consciousness. That reflection, it is to be hoped, deepens our awareness of the relationship between where and how we live and the state of our psyches, makes us more aware of the interrelationship between our inner place and our external space. In exploring that "felicitous space" of home, with its menagerie of closets, drawers, cubbyholes and cellars, Bachelard taps the psychological reality that the things we surround ourselves with resonate with deep emotional meaning. He teaches that there is a dynamic interrelationship between our consciousness and the world. In particular, he affirms what many children know when they dissolve the barrier between the inner and the outer words in creating magical caves behind the couch or embark on their first half-fearful exploration of the dark corners in the basement: Our homes are the place where the dream of life begins, "our first universe, a real cosmos in every sense of the word."[91] To experience our dwelling place this way again as adults is surely a kind of homecoming.

****

It was so for my mother and me. After we finished our work at the graveyard, we drove back into town. I dropped my mother at the town office so she could arrange to have the headstones reset. While she attended to that business, I walked around Main Street and along Railway Avenue, following the ghosts of my young self past stores and buildings that were both familiar and strange.

The streets were as wide as I remembered, but paved now, instead of oiled to keep the dust down. The National Hotel on 2nd Avenue West was closed, its windows boarded up. The butcher shop, Central Meats, had become a coffee shop with a cutesy name, Food for Thought. But Dick's Menswear was still across the street from the National Hotel. My father used to buy his suits and ties at the clothing store. I still have some of those ties. Next to the store was a bakery, which I remembered as the Liberty Café, with its chrome bar stools and booths where my older cousin Donna once parked me with a Coke float while she went shopping. Next to the café was Odell's shoe store and a candy store where I bought black jawbreakers and licorice sticks with the money I earned from collecting empty pop bottles.

I walked up 1st Street West, past the York Restaurant. The wooden slat-board walkways were long gone, of course, but I could still see David and me tromping on them to make the grasshoppers hiding in shade jump up through the slats. Gone, too, were the open stormwater ditches that once ran alongside the walkways and were full of frogs. Everything had disappeared under concrete and asphalt. But standing in the hot sun, conjuring the streets as they used to be, I could hear the frogs and cicadas that filled the streets with their croaking and chirruping on summer evenings.

I heard cicadas an hour later as we turned off Highway 36 and headed east along Highway 586 towards Spondin. Driving down the side roads off Highway 586, we eventually found my mother's childhood home just east of the intersection of Range Road 133 and Township Road 322.

"That's it," she said as we approached a crossroads. "I remember this corner. The four-way stop signs."

In my imagination, based on the stories my mother had told me about her Depression-era childhood, I'd expected a crumbled, abandoned farmhouse. What we saw was a prosperous-looking farm with a big modern house and a large barn surrounded by farm machinery. When we pulled into the yard in front of the house, a woman came out to greet us. My mother explained our quest. The woman's face lit up.

"I'm so pleased to meet you," she said, hugging my mother, explaining that she and her husband had been on the farm for only thirty years. "We've heard stories about the Depression and how hard it was. You know your old house is still standing."

My mother was surprised. "I don't see it," she said, looking around.

"You can't see it from here. It's behind the barn. We used it to store things for years, but not anymore. We've been thinking of knocking it down. Would you like to see it?"

The woman led us across the yard and around the barn and gestured for us to go ahead. "It's pretty run down," she said, looking at my mother.

So it was. The narrow one-storey frame house reminded me of an abandoned slum house waiting for the bulldozer. One of the front windows was broken. Bare wood showed on the roof where the shingles had disappeared. We stepped inside. Plaster had fallen away from the walls, exposing the lathing underneath. The linoleum in the kitchen had buckled and curled. I heard the rustle of birds in the rafters and smelled the damp wood. Mice droppings betrayed the current occupants.

"It was bigger," my mother said. "I always thought it was bigger."

"It was when you were smaller," I said.

"I guess so."

We wandered down the short hall that connected the kitchen and the living room. There were two bedrooms on one side. I couldn't believe how small they were. "Where did you sleep?" I said.

My mother explained that by the time she was born, her older brothers and sisters had left home. There was only my mother and three of her sisters, Dorothy, Ida and Helen, still at home. Mom was the youngest. The four girls shared a double bed in one bedroom while their parents had the other.

"I had to sleep in the middle because I was the youngest," my mother said as we peered into the shadowy room. "I thought it was much bigger. There was the bed and a chest of drawers. We kept the pee-pot in the closet."

I watched my mother as we picked our way around the house. I thought she might be upset at seeing the state of her childhood home, but if she was she didn't show it. I wandered outside, poking around what was once a garden at the back of the house. Now it was just a place for weeds and abandoned tools. When I came back to the house, my mother was standing in the kitchen, looking out a dirt-streaked window to a copse of trees about twenty or thirty yards from the house.

"You OK?" I asked.

"There used to be a well over there and my mother kept a big garden," she said, pointing to the trees. "The trees weren't there then. I was just remembering when I was little, carrying water from the well for my mother. I was so small I could only carry half a pail at a time."

As we stared out the window together, I wondered what else my mother might be seeing. I tried to imagine a little mop-haired girl in dungarees struggling across the field with a water pail.

We left a short time later, thanking the woman for her hospitality. "Come back any time," she said. I doubted we would.

Heading back to Highway 36, I drove slowly with the windows down, enjoying the warm air on my bare arm, the smell of crops in the field and the chirp of cicadas in the tall grass of the roadside ditches. My mother was silent, looking out the window at the passing farm fields. I wondered what she was seeing in her memory. I remembered how as a boy I used to crouch on the backseat of the car and lean forward against the front seat where my father sat behind the wheel and watch over his shoulder as he drove. His right arm was extended and his hand loosely gripped the big steering wheel of the Chrysler DeSoto, maneuvering the car effortlessly, while his left arm rested on the doorframe through the open window, shirtsleeves folded two turns of the cuff above his wrist so that the lower half of his forearm was always deeply tanned from being constantly exposed to the sun. I not only learned to drive watching my father from the backseat, but I picked up his sartorial habit of rolling my sleeves the same way. I laughed at the thought.

"What's so funny?" my mother said.

"I was just remembering how I used to lean behind Dad and watch him drive."

"Do you remember our Sunday drives?"

"Yes," I said, still seeing the image of myself in the backseat of the car when, if I wasn't watching my father at the wheel, I would stare out the side window and imagine myself as some kind of superhero running beside the car, leaping fence posts and telephone poles, hurdling over snow fences and clearing them in a single bound. "I always liked those drives."

I drove back to Hanna as night fell and the farm fields darkened and the land took on its strangely familiar enchantment. In the dim light I saw the vague shape of a young boy running beside me, performing incredible feats. I glanced at my mother. She was staring out the window. I liked to think she was seeing a young girl running across a farm field, her hair flying as she raced home.

THREE

THE SALVATION OF PLACE
Dwelling in the World

This is the most beautiful place on earth. There are many such places. Every man, every woman, carries in heart and mind, the image of the ideal place, the right place, the one true home, known or unknown, active or visionary.

— Edward Abbey, *Desert Solitaire*[1]

Like most of his countrymen, he is a migrant: somewhere along the lines traced on their personal maps of life they have encountered a place, in a certain time, which as they move on means more than any other.

— Paul Horgan, *Whitewater*[2]

The path descended through dripping cedars. It had rained during the night and I stepped carefully, following the slippery path to my favourite place on the planet. Coming around a curve in the trail, I found the red bench. It was faded and tilted to one side, but it was still there in a cavern of sumac on the edge of a cliff overlooking the Strait of Juan de Fuca. I stood gazing at it for a moment, remembering the last time I had been here – was it really thirty-three years ago? – before I continued along the twisting path, letting remnant memory guide me as the path dropped through the trees and bush until I came out on to a cliff edge overlooking the crescent beach. I scrambled down. The beach was empty. The tide was out, as I walked toward the shelter of the rocks on the far side of the beach, I looked back to see my bootprints following me in the sand.

Nothing had changed. The rocky outcrops at the top of the beach, smooth and rounded and marbled black, crouched at the base of the cliff like smooth-shouldered beasts huddled with their backs toward the sea. The fissured cliff face soared overhead, enclosing the beach in a curving embrace. Lines of salt rime had dried on exposed stones. There were tidal pools with their secret worlds and the blue sky streaked with feather-like cirrus clouds. But what struck me most powerfully was the smell of the sea. The odours – stranded kelp, seaweed, wet sand, cedar – were hauntingly familiar. It was the same sea smell that I had encountered for the first time in my life nearly thirty-five years earlier. It came rushing back now, surging into the subterranean caverns of my mind like an incoming tide, shifting treasure chests of memory. With every inhalation I sensed those chests creaking open, releasing memories to float slowly to the surface.

I found a familiar place out of the wind among the rocks and sat against them. I looked out at the water, squinting against the broken fragments of the sun. Anacortes Island stretched across the horizon, a blue and hazy bulk. A ship was in the strait. I watched as it moved westward toward the Pacific Ocean, remembering years ago watching other passing ships from this place. I lifted my face to the sun, enjoying its warmth, glad to be back at Point-No-Point, trying not to think, waiting for the rising tide of memory.

When I first discovered this place on the west coast of Vancouver Island in the fall of 1970, it was love at first sight. I was a student at the University of Victoria. One Sunday morning in late September, with nothing better to do, I went for a drive and ended up on Highway 14. Back then the highway was a winding, two-lane road connecting Victoria and Port Renfrew, a distance of about 120 kilometres. I'd never been on it before – I enjoyed its twists and turns between the tall walls of the rainforest that crowded in on the road. Through gaps in the trees I saw the strait shining in the sun. I rolled the driver's window down to enjoy the cool air and the smell of cedar. I drove through the little town of Sooke, thinking I might go as far as Port Renfrew. But twenty-five kilometres west of Sooke, I spotted a motel with a restaurant. A sign said Point-No-Point. For a name like that, I had to stop.

The motel consisted of a clapboard office-cum-living room and restaurant and half-a-dozen small cabins set on a cedar-thick bluff above the strait. Inside, beyond the reception desk area, was a large room with a big stone fireplace against one wall. Dark, fat-armed leather chairs and couches, the kind you see in old World War II movies about the Royal Air Force, occupied most of room. Framed black-and-white photos clustered on the walls. A moose head hung above the fireplace mantle, along with couple of stuffed and mounted fish. A bookshelf of dog-eared paperbacks took up a corner to one side of the fireplace. I readily imagined an evening in front of the fireplace reading Hammond Innes. You walked through the living room to get to the restaurant, which consisted of two rooms, one larger than the other, with maybe a dozen tables in total. Big windows provided a fine view of the strait and Anacortes Island.

The restaurant was empty when I arrived that first time. I took a table by the window in the smaller room. The waitress, an older woman, took my order – ham-and-cheese sandwich, soup and coffee. It was a good lunch: the bread fresh and the ham a thick slice that didn't come out of a package. The coffee was fresh brewed. It was pleasant to sit and eat in the sunny room and look at the view. Below me, I saw a trail winding through the trees. I asked the waitress about it and she explained that it was a private trail to a beach and was available to guests who stayed at the resort or those who took a meal in the restaurant. I decided on a short visit to the beach before I headed back to Victoria, then ended up spending the whole afternoon. Like I said, it was love at first sight. Until I wrecked my car the next year, I would go out to Point-No-Point at least once a month during the school year, either by myself or with a girl. We would enjoy a lunch at the restaurant and then go down the beach. Not every girl appreciated the place. Sometimes it was better alone.

The poet T.S. Eliot coined the phrase "objective correlative" to describe how a poet can express emotion by finding a set of objects, images or events that serve as the formula for the particular emotion he wants to evoke. Point-No-Point became my geographical correlative. It reflected a particular emotion or, more accurately, a particular state of being that I can only describe as a feeling of having arrived in a place where I belong. I've accumulated a few "sacred" places over the years – a cabin on Kootenay Lake in British Columbia, a house on Burdett Avenue in Victoria, Parc de Choisy in Paris, Primrose Hill in London, a tree-enclosed laneway off Hill View Road below the train station in Orpington – but Point-No-Point remains my holy of holies. For years after leaving after Victoria, I would dream of the place. The dreams were almost always exercises in frustration, some variation of scrambling along a maze of paths, the sea in sight through the trees, but somehow never being able to make it to the beach and the shelter of the rocks.

No doubt, there are biographical reasons, perhaps even genetic reasons, why certain places lodge in our memories. My places betray a certain predilection for heights and bodies of water with wide vistas and distant horizons. These are the kind of places where, for whatever reason – biographical, psychological or spiritual – I feel a deep sense of belonging, places where, if practical requirements allowed it, I can imagine myself abiding forever like some stone Buddha embedded in the ground.

Back now for the first time in more than three decades, I had that strange sense of timelessness as I sat huddled in my familiar shelter among the rocks at Point-No-Point, my back against the cliff, facing the sea. I watched the ship heading westward. A nonsense notion crossed my mind: Maybe it was the same ship I saw all those years ago, and maybe it was still that September afternoon in 1970 and all those years in between had been a dream and I was only now waking up. I was happy to see this landscape unchanged after such a long absence, but at the same time I felt disoriented.

I had returned to Point-No-Point because I was following through on a vision I had had several weeks earlier. I use the word "vision" advisedly, yet deliberately. Let me explain: Two months earlier, in April of 2004, I began walking the Shikoku no Michi, a 1,400-kilometre pilgrimage route that circles Shikoku, the smallest of Japan's four main islands. The route connects eighty-eight Buddhist temples like beads on a rosary. I was about three weeks into my trek, finally starting to sink into the walking after the usual spell of blisters and what-am-I-doing-here self-doubt. Walking twenty-five or sometimes thirty kilometres a day had worked its psychological magic, extracting me from my ordinary get-and-spend mentality and setting me into a kind of out-of-time mindset that accrues at some point in long-distance walking. At that point I had visited thirty-three temples and covered perhaps 300 kilometres.

One morning, walking through Kochi City, on the south coast of Shikoku, I came to Katsurahama Beach. The beach first appeared as I emerged from a copse of cedars on the top of a cliff. Below me lay a long, curving crescent of sand-and-pebble shoreline. To the west, on the far side of the beach, headlands thrust like fingers out into the blue water. A small, red-roofed pagoda sat on the top of the headland; beyond it, the Pacific Ocean stretched from horizon to horizon, the distinction between ocean and sky blurred by early-morning haze. The scene reminded me of one of those Oriental prints that show tiny figures walking through an overwhelming landscape. For the first time in a long time, gazing the length of the beach to the clifftop shrine, I fell in love with a place.

The Japanese have for centuries celebrated Katsurahama Beach as a place of singular beauty. Its deep-green pine forests, multi-hued pebble shore and the blue Pacific inspired the poet Keigetsu Omichi to write this haiku:

Watch the moon rise from the surface of the sea,
drawing the attention of all
on Katsurahama.

I decided to spend a few hours absorbing this place, or, rather, being absorbed by it. I found a path that led down to the strip of beach. This early in the morning there was no one else there. I walked along the shoreline, hearing only the grating surge and retreat of the ocean on the rocky shore. At the far end of the beach I found another path that climbed to the shrine. The shrine was set back only a few feet from the edge of the cliff. It was easy to give myself a cheap scare standing in front of the shrine and gazing at the ocean crashing against the rocks below. Fingers of black stone probed the sea. Isolated lumps of volcanic rock appeared and disappeared with the surging tide. Staring down at the black rocks and the white swirl of water, I felt a rush of vertigo. A sudden gust of strong wind might have blown me over the edge. There was no wind, but the image of such a mishap prompted me to step back from the edge. I could see why the southern coast of Shikoku was a favourite place for suicides, as well as the haunt of mystics and wandering holy men.

I pulled off my backpack and sat down against the shrine. I'd been walking for only about two hours that day, but it was so soothing to listen to the ebb and flow of the waves that I decided to give myself a break. Out in the bay, bulbs of small islands poked from the water. Solitary pines, bent and twisted by salt spray and wind, clutched the rocky ridges. A pair of kites rode the currents in the sky above me. A freighter moved slowly across the blue horizon. As I watched it, the image of another ship surged into my mind. For a moment I was looking through eyes that saw another time and another place – a fall afternoon nearly thirty-five years earlier on the clifftop of Point-No-Point as a ship churned through the Strait of Juan de Fuca towards the Pacific. The image was so sharp that if I didn't know better, I could just as easily have been on the west coast of Vancouver Island as on the east coast of the Japanese island of Shikoku. I imagined the long lines of curling waves rolling onto the shore one after the other, washing up before retreating to leave the damp sand shining in the sun. Seagulls whirled in the sky. On the horizon, a ship sailed away beneath a pale blue sky.

The vision didn't last long – a few seconds at most. But it was long enough to feel a stab of nostalgia for Point-No-Point. I was glad I'd taken a rest at the shrine. I might never have had my vision otherwise. Before I moved on I left an orange and thanked whatever gods presided over this shrine. Over the next month and a half of my Shikoku pilgrimage, the image of Point-No-Point would sometimes appear in my mind's eye like an omen. My old dream about Point-No-Point returned for the first time in years. It was much same dream I used to have: I was trying to find my way through a maze of paths, which got steeper and steeper. I had trouble staying on my feet. I grabbed at tree branches and tufts of grass and protruding stones to keep my balance. Somehow, I found the right path. But just as I neared the bottom of the cliff, with the open sea coming into view, I woke. Lying on the futon in my room, hearing the other pilgrims beginning to stir, I felt a sharp longing, sensed something meaningful withdrawing as the images of the dream receded from my mind.

Nostalgia is more than a longing for past times. It is also a longing for past places, for places where we can no longer live as we once did. A Swiss physician, Johannes Hofer, coined the term in 1688 to describe the melancholy of displaced Swiss citizens. The word "nostalgia," which comes from the Greek, literally means to feel pain at the inability to return home. Three hundred years ago, a diagnosis of nostalgia could sometimes get a Swiss soldier sent home.[3] Awake in my room, I diagnosed myself as suffering nostalgia. I decided that when I returned to Canada in June, I would detour to Victoria instead of going directly home to Ottawa.

I had left Victoria in the mid-1970s at the end of my undergraduate years, and had been back only twice for brief visits, once in 1989 and again in 1997, both times on assignment for my newspaper. But the place has always haunted me. I arrived in September of 1969 for my first year of university, flying into the small airport in Saanich and catching the bus to downtown Victoria. For someone who had grown up in northern Canada, that first sight from the air of all those green islands in the Strait of Georgia revealed the most beautiful place I had ever seen. The bus ride offered glimpses of landscape and seascape, the smell of cedar and salt water, oak trees and roses; I was entranced. But for force of circumstance I might never have left. The vision at Katsurahama made my return an act of retrieval, an attempt to reclaim a place that meant so much to me and, perhaps, to reclaim something of myself.

Returning from Japan in June, I got a hint of what I was retrieving almost the moment my plane landed at Victoria. It had rained earlier in the day; the smell of damp cedar hit me as I left the terminal. A shaft of sun fell through a gap in the clouds, making the trees and the wet pavement glow. I stopped in my tracks to take in the light and the fresh after-rain odours, suddenly flooded by the memory of my first arrival in Victoria. For a second or two I *lived* that encounter again. I don't mean that I had a specific image of my past self in my head. Rather, for a brief moment I recalled the feel of being a seventeen-year-old boy arriving from the Yukon in 1969, his nostrils filled for the first time in his life by the feel and smell of a place by the sea.

The recollection was a moment of sheer delight, and I had to laugh. The gods at Katsurahama had delivered. I was where I most truly belonged. Even after an absence of three decades, I was still in love with the place. I got the keys to my rented car and headed for Point-No-Point.

****

Many people, I imagine, have a favourite place – a lakeside cabin, a winding highway, a park bench or a room overlooking a garden – where by some inexplicable alchemy of circumstance, psychology and geography, they feel a greater sense of *belonging* than elsewhere. This is nothing new. Geographers have long understood that we "know" the world subjectively, through the emotional and psychological responses of lived experience. This is different from the scientific and empirically grounded approach to the world. Scientists try to understand the world as an "objective reality" whose laws can be known through detached observation. This scientific method of knowing has been very useful, allowing us to manipulate nature through technology to satisfy many of our needs and desires. But knowing the world in this detached observer manner is not the same as knowing it through lived experience. We might think we know a place after studying it on a map or spending a few days sightseeing, but that is not the same as living in that space, walking the streets, shopping in the stores, attending the schools or watching the kids in the park across the street from your front porch rocking chair. A place has to be lived (which, of course, includes both immediate sensory experience and reflective remembrance of that experience) to retain its placeness.

That notion might seem platitudinous until we consider what it means to "live" a place and why it is important to achieve a sense of place. Each of us is born with the need to identify with our surroundings and to establish a relationship to them. In this regard, a sense of place is necessary for a coherent life. "There is for virtually everyone a deep association with and consciousness of the places where we were born and grew up, where we live now, or where we have had particularly moving experiences," says geographer Edward Relph. "This association seems to constitute a vital source of both individual and cultural identity and security, a point of departure from which we orient ourselves in the world."[4] Writer Tony Hiss offers a succinct statement on why this is so: "Our ordinary surroundings, built and natural alike, have an immediate and continuing effect on the way we feel and act, and on our health and intelligence. These places have an impact on our sense of self, our sense of safety, the kind of work we get done, the ways we interact with other people, even our ability to function as citizens in a democracy. In short, the places where we spend our time affect the people we are and can become."[5]

Years after finding Point-No-Point, I came across a concept that seemed to capture my infatuation – the concept of topophilia (literally, "place-love"). Geographer Yi-Fu

Tuan, who coined the term, defined it as "the affective bond between people and place or setting."[6] These ties include emotional, psychological and even spiritual responses to a place, and can differ in terms of intensity, subtlety and mode of expression. Our response to our surroundings may be aesthetic; enjoying a pleasant view of a tree-lined street or the beauty of a mountain vista. A sense of bonding can come from a tactile response – anything from the feel of a cool breeze to the taste of water and the odour of fresh-cut grass. Moreover, topophilia can vary in scale from the furnishings in a small room to a house, a neighbourhood, a city, a region, a nation or a continent. Topophilia may not be the strongest of human emotions, Tuan says, but "when it is compelling we can be sure that the place or environment has become the carrier of emotionally charged events or perceived as a symbol."[7] To *live* in a place is "to be aware of it in the bones as well as with the head. Place, at all scales from the armchair to the nation, is a construct of experience; it is sustained not only by timber, concrete, and highways, but also by the quality of human awareness."[8]

What does it mean to live a place in your bones? Indeed, what is place, in the sense that Tuan uses the term? There are some who argue that Westerners suffer a "crisis of place." Some say we are "an increasingly exiled and uprooted people."[9] If this is true, and I think it is, we need to understand why. But even if we do feel the pull of place, *how* do we know a place in our bones? Surely it is not simply a matter of being born in one place and staying there all your life. That's not necessarily good for our psychic health, much less our intelligence. Places can be stifling and oppressive to the individuals stuck in them. Young men used to join the army just to get away from the small-town life into which they'd been born. So *why* is the possession of a sense of place important to us, psychologically and spiritually? Addressing these questions requires drawing on philosophers and theologians, as well as poets and scholars, who have devoted considerable attention to these kinds of questions.

Yi-Fu Tuan's thinking provides a good place to start. He argues that his notion of topophilia – the "affective bond between people and place" – highlights the idea of place as a "field of care" rather than simply a geographical location. To illustrate his point, Tuan contrasts place with space. The latter is an open arena for moving and acting. The former is about pausing and reflecting. Space is subject to scientific abstraction (Euclidean geometry, for instance) and economic rationalism (think of the real estate market); place is all about belonging and relating. In this regard, says Tuan, place can be "as small as the corner of a room or as large as the earth itself." Indeed, he notes that astronauts' wonder-filled observations of the planet from space drove home the message that earth is "our place in the universe."[10]

For most of us, our home is our primary place, Tuan observes. But home, he says, is more than a natural or physical setting or even a built place. Insofar as it is an intimately lived-in place, it possesses "moral meaning." We should think of home not solely in terms of its "material manifestation," but as "a unit of space organized mentally and materially to satisfy a people's real and perceived basic biosocial needs and, beyond that, their higher aesthetic-political aspirations."[11] Home, in short, is a symbolically created place. And what makes a home a place, more often not, are the things in the home that move us emotionally, the objects and accoutrements that possess us.

Tuan cites the example of novelist Wright Morris, who uses the word "holiness" to describe his regard for the ordinary things he finds in his home – from the odds and ends on the bureau and the pin cushion lid on a cigar box to faded Legion poppies and assorted bottles of medicine. Nothing was particularly beautiful, but for Morris they possessed a presence that evoked a sense of place. Tuan quotes Morris asking himself, "Was there, then, something holy about these things? If not, why had I used that word? For holy things they were ugly enough." What we are seeing in Morris' case, says Tuan, is home as an intimate place. "We *think* of the house as home and place, but enchanted images of the past are evoked not so much by the entire building, which can only be seen, as by its components and furnishings, which can be touched and smelled as well: the attic and the cellar, a stool, a gilded mirror, a chipped shell."[12] It is these kinds of small, mundane things that give our homes their sense of place.

Our experience of place can be equally intense outside the home, too. Tuan draws on a John Updike short story to illustrate how childhood experiences and the memory of those experiences can create a lifelong feeling of place. The sight of bare earth "smoothed and packed firm by the passage of human feet" affects Updike's character, David Kern. Such spots are found everywhere in small towns, Kern relates. You find them "in the furtive break in the playground fence," in the "trough of dust underneath each swing," and along "the blurred path worn across a wedge of grass." For Updike's character, these "unconsciously humanized intervals of day, too humble and common even to have a name," recall his childhood with melancholy intensity. Thus, says Tuan, we experience our places at different levels and on different scales. "At one extreme a favorite armchair is a place, at the other extreme the whole earth."[13]

Tuan's notions of place, like those of many humanistic geographers, draw on the thought of Martin Heidegger, the philosopher widely credited with reviving the concept of place.[14] Heidegger uses the word "dwelling" to describe an authentic way of living in the world, an attitude and a practice that allow the individual to "gather" the surrounding environment – his place – into a coherent whole. In a 1951 essay, "Building Dwelling Thinking," Heidegger offers a peasant-built, two-century-old farmhouse in the Black Forest of Germany as the embodiment of proper dwelling. Such a building reflects an organic harmony between the needs of the farmer and the necessities of the natural world. Invoking figures of myth and poetry to make his point, Heidegger writes, "Here the self-sufficiency of the power to let earth and heaven, divinities and mortals enter *in simple oneness* into things, order the house." The dwelling-mindedness of the peasants ensured that the house was set on a wind-sheltered, south-facing mountain slope. It was close to a spring. The roof was steep so it could bear the burden of snow, and it extended far out from the walls to provide shelter against cold winds. There was an altar behind the community table, and a place for both the children's bed and coffins for the dead. Thus, the ancient farmhouse naturally reflected under one roof the character of the different generations of occupants "in their journey through time."[15]

Such places possess the character of what Heidegger calls "sparing": that is, the willing acceptance of a thing without wanting to control, dominate or even necessarily change it. A "sparing" attitude towards a place is an attitude of care rather than control. Sparing lets places be what they are, accepts them in their essential character and cares for them even when subordinating them to human will through building on or cultivating them. "Sparing is a willingness to leave places alone and not to change them casually or arbitrarily, and not to exploit them."[16]

Heidegger was not, of course, suggesting modern Westerners go back to living as illiterate eighteenth-century peasants. He uses the farmhouse example because it captures the essence of proper dwelling; harmony between humans and the environment, how human beings can create a genuine *place* amidst the space in which they find themselves. As he puts it in his ponderous (if poetic) prose: "Dwelling is *the basic character of Being* in keeping with which mortals exist."[17] "Man's essential relationship to places … consists in dwelling [which is] the essential property of human existence."[18] In other words, if place *is* dwelling, then the acquiring of a sense of place is "a spiritual and philosophical endeavour that unites the natural and human worlds."[19] We achieve a sense of wholeness through the achievement of a sense of place.

For some scholars, the capacity to develop a sense of place is crucial, at both the individual and the collective level. If places are a fundamental aspect of human existence, sources of security and identity, then, as geographer Edward Relph argues, "it is important that the means of experiencing, creating, and maintaining significant places are not lost." Relph, like other geographers, worries that much of Western society, suffers from "placelessness." There are, he says, many signs that "'placelessness' – the weakening of distinct and diverse experiences and identities of place – is now a dominant force."[20] Such a shift – from place to placelessness – constitutes a major change in our understanding of the world, a change that is at the core of the modern project. To explain this idea, and why it is such a concern, requires some history and a bit of abstract theorizing. In a nutshell, the way we as moderns experience and thereby understand the world is rooted in the ancient quarrel between place and space.

We can go all the way back to the very beginning, biblically speaking, when, according to Augustine's reading of Genesis, God created the world *ex nihilo*, out of nothing. In this interpretation of creation, space precedes place. However, a more recent reading of Genesis argues that, in fact, God created the world out of *something*. "In the beginning, God created the heavens and the earth. The earth was without form and void, and darkness was upon the face of the deep, and the Spirit of God was moving over the face of the waters."[21] Philosopher Edward Casey points out that in referring to the Earth as "without form and void," Genesis is not saying that God created from a pre-existing abyss of nothingness, but rather that He created the world out of already existing material that needed only to be given form. "Things are already around when He begins to create – things in the guise of elemental masses, the watery Deep, darkness upon the face of the Deep, the pre-determinate earth."[22] God's creation was the imposition of order on disorder, or, put differently, the imposition of place on space. Interestingly, Casey's account of Genesis, and the priority given to place, is echoed in the thought of a pre-Socratic philosopher, Archytas of Tarentum, who maintained that place "is the first of all things since all existing things are either in place or without place," and that *"to be [at all] is to be in [some] place."*[23]

This biblical emphasis on place suggests a connection between the experience of place and religious experience, according to theologian Michael Northcott. The story of the ancient Israelites recounts the struggle of a people trying to find a place of their own under the guidance of Yahweh. The Talmud portrays their development from an often lost nomadic tribe to their settlement in the promised land. In this account, place is an essential aspect of their covenant with God. The prophets blame the Israelites' exile on their having forsaken their duty to God through greed and self-aggrandizement. They suffer slavery when they forget their place in God's order, literally and morally. In theoretical terms, the Israelites' story reflects the ongoing tension between space and place, along with a lesson about the downside of place. The Israelites were a much more devout and virtuous people when they lived nomadically and wandered in the desert. Only after they settled into the promised land did they grow corrupt. Finding your place brings moral dangers. This tension between place and space is resolved, in part, when Isaiah expands Israel's sense of place beyond that of a singular Hebrew tribe to the whole world. God's covenant now includes the whole world, not just the "place" of the Jews.

The ambiguity regarding place continued in Christianity, says Northcott. Jesus Christ was effectively placeless after he took up his ministry. He lived a nomadic existence, owning no land and rejecting possessions. He tried to clear the space of the temple of moneylenders. He taught in the desert spaces and marginal villages after his ejection from the temple at Capernaum. He prayed to God in the wide-open spaces of hilltops and wilderness. He rented a room for a farewell dinner with his disciples. But even then he left early for a wander in a nearby garden. The disciples borrowed a tomb for his body. There was, it seems, no place for the Son of God. As the Bible puts it, "Foxes have holes, birds have nests, but the Son of Man has nowhere to lay his head" (Matthew 8:20). Christianity attempted to settle the ambiguity of the relationship between space and place with the establishment of the Church in Rome in the third century, effectively linking place and religion. In Northcott's judgment, "The third-century movement of Christian worship from private house to purpose-built churches (basilicas) is one of the keys to this changed orientation to place."[24]

This connection of place and religion, and a largely balanced tension between place and space, held sway until the Enlightenment. On one hand, you can see the dominance of place in the religious orientation of medieval villages in which the church occupied the centre of the community. On the other hand, the popularity of pilgrimages, which saw hundreds of thousands of people during the Middle Ages – nobles and peasants, rich and poor – undertake long and arduous journeys to Rome, Santiago de Compostela or Canterbury, suggests a widespread longing to escape the claims of place for the freedoms of space. At the same time, though, pilgrimages are all about journeying to places where an encounter between the human and the divine has occurred. You travel through space to a holy place where, presumably, your religious roots are nourished. In this sense, argues theologian John Inge, "Christianity is not the religion of salvation *from* places, it is the religion of salvation *in* and *through* places."[25]

It would be a worthwhile project for some scholar to test the theory that the medieval longing for space was a catalyst for the Enlightenment. Surely the stories of strange and distant places that pilgrims brought back from their wanderings stirred the longing of many to escape their places. In any event, the balance between place and space began to tilt in favour of space – and toward the modern suppression of place – in the late thirteenth century, when the Bishop of Paris attempted to suppress doctrines that in his view claimed a limit to God's power. Aristotle's thought had been reintroduced to Europe by Thomas Aquinas, who devoted himself to reconciling Greek philosophy, particularly Aristotle, and Christian revelation. The archbishop, as Inge explains, wanted to suppress notions that went against the Church's claim regarding the infinite power of God, including the Aristotelian idea that there is only a finite amount of matter in the universe and thus a limit to divine power. The Church held that God is outside time and space and thus able to move the universe through space as He wills. Ironically, instead of suppressing Aristotelian ideas, the archbishop's condemnations ultimately proved harmful to Christianity's hold on the European mind, since it opened up the possibility of infinite space. As Casey explains, the condemnations "marked a decisive turning point in medieval thought concerning place and especially space."[26] In effect – and here I am paraphrasing Inge – the opening of infinite space altered the hitherto balanced relationship between space and place by allowing concepts that formed the basis of Newtonian physics, particularly the idea of the physical universe being infinite in space, to emerge.[27]

If God's power is limitless, then His presence in the universe must also be without limit. But this means that space must be infinite, too. With this idea you have one of the key ideas supporting Newtonian physics, which undermined the medieval Church's Ptolemaic notion of a geocentric universe that assured mankind of its cozy place in the cosmos under God's caring watch. "There can be little doubt that one of the most fateful things condemned by the [Archbishop's] Condemnations was the primacy of place," says Casey, "thereby making room for the apotheosis of space that occurred in the seventeenth century."[28] Newton's discoveries, along with those of Galileo – in particular, the latter's discovery that the earth revolved around the sun and not vice versa – lessened the importance of place.

We are living under this apotheosis of space today, Casey argues. The modern age reflects the reification of space. In the medieval world, people lived under the sway of a "sacred geography." Not only were they attached to the places where they lived, but also they regarded the world as replete with holy places to which they could go on pilgrimage. In fact, the world itself, as God's creation, was a holy place. This worldview began to fade in the centuries leading up to the Enlightenment. Between the fifteenth and eighteenth centuries, modern scientific theories and methods began to "disenchant" the world. To be sure, people remained attached to their places, but science opened the possibility of escaping the more oppressive requirements of those places, whether in body or in mind. The idea of vast spaces seemed to offer freedom. Thus, space came to dominate place. Here is how Casey sums up the modern situation:

> In the past three centuries in the West – the period of "modernity" – place has come to be not only neglected but actively suppressed. Owing to the triumph of the natural and social sciences in this same period, any serious talk of place has been regarded as regressive or trivial. A discourse has emerged whose exclusive cosmological foci are Time and Space. When the two were combined by twentieth century physicists into the amalgam "space-time" the overlooking of place was only continued by other means. For an entire epoch, place has been regarded as an impoverished second cousin of Time and Space, those two colossal cosmic partners towering over modernity.[29]

Recent centuries have been devoted to conquering Time and Space through technology. We have gone from sailing ships that took months to circumnavigate the globe and railway trains that required days to traverse a continent to jets that fly across the oceans in hours and Internet exchanges that circle the planet at near instantaneous speed. Electronic media effectively allow us to overcome time and space without even moving. We can sit on our couches in front of the television or at our desks with our computers and watch the latest bloodbath or riot thousands of miles away. Places become almost non-existent in the sense of one place being genuinely and abidingly distinct from another. When kids as far apart as Istanbul and Whitehorse affect the lupine swagger and jerky gestures of American rappers, you know that distinctions of place have been seriously diluted under the imperative of space-conquering technologies. Inge puts it well: "In conditions of modernity, places becomes increasingly *phantasmagoric*: that is to say, locales are thoroughly penetrated by and shaped in terms of social influences quite distant to them."[30]

****

The consequences of this diminishment of place are readily apparent. The technological imperatives of Western society, the demand for efficiency and speed, emphasize mobility and economic rationalization. This approach frames mobility as a cultural value, a freedom obtained through education and money. "The skyscrapers, airports, freeways and other stereotypical components of modern landscapes – are they not the sacred symbols of a civilization that had deified and derided home?"[31] Indeed, theologian Philip Sheldrake argues that a lack of mobility has come "to symbolize a lack of choice, an entrapment, which is the lot of the poor, the elderly and people with handicaps."[32] In a placeless culture, he says, your success depends on your ability and willingness to be a removable and replaceable unit readily transferred from one location to another without fuss.

This situation is made easier to bear, psychologically speaking, when every place looks the same, with the same stores, the same fast-food outlets and the same architectural appearance and consumer culture. Drawing on the work of anthropologist Marc Augé and his notion of "non-places," Sheldrake argues that a real place possesses an organic and deeply rooted social life and is full of historically meaningful buildings, institutions and monuments. A non-place, on the other hand, lacks this organic quality. People who live in non-places spend an inordinate amount of time in supermarkets, hotels and airports and on highways, connecting through their Internet servers, texting each other, watching television or playing games on computers, living virtual lives. They could be any place, or, rather, no place, and still function efficiently.

Living in non-places produces a fragmented awareness of the world that is ultimately incoherent and, arguably, fosters the breakdown of social order (or, conversely, the imposition of greater regulation and repression, to maintain order among citizens who lack a strong sense of communal identity). By contrast, a strong sense of place sustained by commonly shared symbols of identity – institutions, museums, monuments, etc. – provides, in Sheldrake's words, "a principle of meaning for those who live in it and a principle of intelligibility for those who observe it."[33] This need for meaning underscores the essential purpose of place: Deep ties to places, possessing a sense of belonging, are necessary for a truly meaningful and purposeful life. In the words of philosopher Simone Weil,

> To be rooted is perhaps the most important and least recognized need of the human soul. It is one of the hardest to define. A human being has roots by virtue of his real, active and natural participation in the life of a community which preserves in living shape certain particular expectations for the future. This participation is a natural one in the sense that it is automatically brought about by place, conditions of birth, profession and social surroundings. Every human being needs to have multiple roots. It is necessary for him to draw well-nigh the whole of his moral, intellectual and spiritual life by way of the environment of which he forms a natural part.[34]

This need for roots does not mean you should live in one place all your life. Being stuck in a place can be intellectually suffocating and emotionally deadening, as anyone who has wanted to escape small-town life but was unable to do so can testify. Roots can die for lack of nourishment. But living in a big city where you have few attachments besides the job is equally debilitating. We require, it seems, a balance between our need for place and our desire for space to explore. The former might provide the bedrock of our psychological well-being, but the latter leads us to other places that nourish our spirit and, so to speak, extend our root system. To say this, however, is to suggest that our experience of place is, in part at least, a matter of intentionality, "a focus where we experience the meaningful events of our lives."[35]

Geographer Edward Relph extends this line of thought in pointing out that our actions are significant only in the context of particular places, and acquire their meaningfulness in terms of the character of the place in which they occur. "Places are thus incorporated into the intentional structures of all human consciousness and experience," he says. Intentionality, as philosophers of phenomenology teach, reflects the notion that all consciousness is consciousness of something. Relph argues that our intentions should be understood not merely in terms of something deliberately chosen, but as a relationship between our surroundings and ourselves that provides meaning to our lives. The objects we encounter in the world – porches and patios, streets and buildings, mountains and oceans – "are experienced *in their meaning* and they cannot be separated from those meanings, for these are conferred by the very consciousness that we have of the objects." Moreover, we experience this sense of meaningfulness whether we consciously direct our attention toward the objects in a place or absorb them unconsciously. A rundown neighbourhood will likely register "danger" in your mind even if you aren't paying attention to it. A pink-painted room is emotionally soothing regardless of your noticing the colour, according to psychologists. But what makes that room or building a truly distinct "place" is the intentionality of our consciousness, says Relph. "Those aspects of the lived-world that we distinguish as places are differentiated because they involve a concentration of our intentions, our attitudes, purposes and experience. Because of its focusing they are set apart from the surrounding space while remaining a part of it. Places are thus basic elements in the ordering of our experiences of the world."[36]

Psychologists and sociologists have frequently noted that rapid changes to landscapes and neighbourhoods distort the lives of those who live there. The place we live sustains our sense of belonging and identity, but when it changes too rapidly, our sense of place takes a hit. The landmarks of our lives – our streets and parks, our shops and churches – serve to ground us, both as individuals and as a community. They are the symbolic objects through which we maintain coherence and order amidst changing circumstances and the ebb and flow of events. Our landscapes, our streets and our neighbourhoods – our places – are the markers of our daily lives, the objective reality that helps stabilize our often unstable everyday lives. The things by which we know our place, whether in memory or present-day living, provide at all three levels of being – physical, psychological and spiritual – a sense of belonging and coherence. When familiar streets change too rapidly, buildings suddenly disappear or established landmarks radically change, the world becomes less coherent and increasingly unstable.

To understand this point – and to know that a sense of place is integral to your self-understanding – you need only experience the dislocation of visiting the neigbhourhood where you grew up and seeing that it has become home to a different ethnic, racial or religious group. We feel forlorn when we visit a once-familiar place – our hometown or the street we grew up on – and find it no longer matches our memory. The buildings and parks may be much the same, but the *feel* of them is different. Our memoryscape has been disturbed, and with it our sense of attunement with the world. We feel displaced.

Geographers point out that as the greater mobility characteristic of modern society dilutes our sense of place, many people are no longer able to maintain affective ties with any particular place because they experience more places over a lifetime than their forefathers ever imagined. Moreover, places are losing much of the distinctiveness that once gave them their unique identities. To be sure, despite our increased mobility, there has been a resurgence in territorial loyalties on the part of ethnic groups in recent decades – everyone from French Canadians and Scots to Hispanics and Ukrainians. This geo-political topic goes beyond my concerns here; I will simply mention that the return to tribalism that we see in so many parts of the world (including the tribal enclaves now established in many Western cities) reflects a desperate desire to recover or establish a sense of place amidst the displacements of globalization.

Placelessness, in the sense I am using the concept, describes an environment – landscape, streetscape and even memoryscape – that not only lacks significant places, but, even worse, does not see a sense of place as significant. Relph describes the placeless mentality this way: "It reaches back into the deepest levels of place, cutting roots, eroding symbols, replacing diversity with uniformity."[37] It is not hard to find evidence illustrating Relph's point: Drive across Canada or the United States and you see the same big box stores, motel franchises and fast-food restaurants in each one. It's all very convenient and comfortable, but when every town looks like every other town, well, you are not really seeing these towns as distinct communities, because they no longer possess a unique sense of place. Gertrude Stein's famous remark about her childhood hometown of Oakland, California – "there isn't any there there"[38] – increasingly applies everywhere. Every place is becoming a no place. Anyone who has done some travelling can testify to this increasing homogeneity: If it wasn't for differences in signage, you couldn't tell whether you were in New York's Kennedy Airport, Tokyo's Narita Airport or London's Heathrow Airport. (Although, come to think of it, the Tokyo airport is much cleaner than Heathrow.)

But even when you leave the airport you find that every shopping mall looks similar, and contains pretty much the same stores and outlets. Tack on different anchor stores and you could be anywhere in the Western world. Multinational corporations with their same-shape-suits-all boxes of glass and steel only exaggerate the sense of placelessness. Just as bad, if not worse, are shopping malls that attempt to look like rustic Ye Olde Merrie England villages, casinos that masquerade as Egyptian pyramids, and hotels that imitate Arabic casbahs. This is place repackaged as a consumer commodity to produce a soulless no-place.

Heidegger once summed up the *zeitgeist*, or spirit, of the modern era, saying, "Homelessness is coming to be the destiny of the world."[39] He was referring not only to the millions who had lost their homes and their countries during World War II, but also to our "world alienation" at the hands of science and technology, our sense that we are no longer at home in the world. For Heidegger, one of the chief characteristics of our technological age is the systematic elimination of place – places where people can live deeply rooted lives – and the resulting global homelessness (or placelessness).

I suppose it is possible in an era of globalization that a future of placelessness is our collective fate. But I would like to think there is room for individuals to develop a sense of place. Where, though, do we start?

****

123

Our experience of place has a great deal to do with how we perceive the world. Another platitudinous statement, you might think, but learning to perceive a place properly is not that easy. Several years ago, I came across Tony Hiss' extraordinary two-part essay in *The New Yorker* entitled "Experiencing Places." Hiss recounted his efforts to discover what made particular places in New York – Grand Central Station, Prospect Park and even Times Square, for example – so appealing to him. The essay drew on a variety of intellectual disciplines, including geography, psychology and history, to show why we respond to certain places the way we do. Hiss argues, in essence, that our experiences of place reflect the perceptual habits we have acquired over the course of our lives, and says that if we want to better appreciate places, we need to change those habits and, thus, our perceptive state.

According to Hiss, there are two ways of experiencing the world: ordinary perception and "simultaneous perception." For the most part, we go about our lives in the mode of ordinary perception. We perceive the outside world only to the degree necessary for our daily survival, absorbed instead in the generally self-focused chatter in our heads. Simultaneous perception, on the other hand, "broadens and diffuses the beam of attention across all the senses, so we can take in whatever is there to be received." Hiss defines simultaneous perception as a state of mind that provides a more general awareness of the world, so that we are able to self-consciously experience more things at once: sights, sounds, smells and sensations of touch, as well as our thoughts and feelings regarding our sensory perceptions.[40]

Some places, says Hiss, seem to welcome our experiencing of them. They provide simultaneous perception with rich stimulation, and the opportunity "to intensify such perception by making it conscious." When this happens we need to choose whether to stay in our heads, absorbed in our own schemes and dreams, or let go, releasing ourselves to the full experience of the place and, as Heidegger might put it, dwelling there. That choice, whether made one or numerous times, "determines in the long run whether we get to know a place and whether we ever get the full benefit of the experiences it makes available."[41]

But *how* do we learn to perceive the world differently? Can we acquire the habit of simultaneous perception that leads to a better appreciation of place? Hiss offers this advice: "One part of experiencing places ... has to do with changing the way we look at things, diffusing our attention and also relaxing its intensity – a change that lets us start to see all the things round us at once and yet also look calmly and steadily at each one of them."[42] He also recommends reading or studying such subjects as aesthetics, wilderness, nature and art appreciation.

I want to take him up on that recommendation. My own reading over the years has certainly helped me learn to perceive places with greater devotion. I've come across the concept of place in writers as diverse as the nineteenth-century English novelist Thomas Hardy and mystery writer Ruth Rendell. Indeed, Rendell's series of psychological why-dunnits featuring Chief Inspector Wexford is deeply place-oriented. She regularly provides descriptions of landscapes and streetscapes, urban and rural settings, subdivisions and industrial parks that imbue her books with "a sophisticated sense of place."[43]

But if any novelist can claim to be a writer of place, it has to be Hardy. His novels are dense with images and descriptions that involve characters' relationships to places. Hardy, as one critic says, uses places to explore the psychological condition of his heroes and heroines, particularly their dislocation from the world around them.[44] Here, in the opening scene of *Jude the Obscure*, the young Jude Fawley is alone in a field. A newcomer to the region, he thinks the freshly harrowed field ugly and possessed of a utilitarian air. But as the narrator's subsequent description implies, Jude's reaction is that of a person who has no history, no roots, in the place.

> [T]o every clod and stone there really attached associations enough and to spare – echoes of songs from ancient harvest-days, of spoken words, and of sturdy deeds. Every inch of ground had been the site, first or last, of energy, gaiety, horseplay, bickerings, weariness. Groups of gleaners had squatted in the sun on every square yard. Love-matches that had populated the adjoining hamlet had been made up there between reaping and carrying. Under the hedge which divided the field from a distant plantation girls had given themselves to lovers who would not turn their heads to look at them by the next harvest; and in that ancient cornfield many a man had made love-promises to a woman at whose voice he had trembled by the next seed-time. But this neither Jude nor the rooks around him considered.[45]

Writers such as Hardy clearly display an abiding topophilia from which we can learn. Their descriptions reveal how consciousness is able to focus on place, and how imagination extracts meaning from place. Numerous other writers – Albert Camus, Virginia Woolf, Ernest Hemingway, the poet Philip Larkin, for example – also demonstrate a strong awareness of place. I'm particularly fond of the French existential novelist Camus, whose works I devoured during my undergraduate years, including the *Notebooks* he kept from 1935, when he was twenty-two, to his death in 1960. I liked best his earliest notebooks, from the years 1935 to 1937, when he was still living in Algeria and trying to write.

As I researched these essays, I recalled Camus' descriptions of and responses to place. It struck me that they fit with Hiss' argument that if we want to truly experience place, we need to learn how to better perceive it, psychologically and physiologically. Camus also lends credence to Yi-Fu Tuan's claim that a sense of place does not acquire a great deal of geography. Here, for example, is what Camus wrote in January 1936, describing a garden beyond his apartment window, and the epiphany he experienced in response to what he senses:

> Beyond the window there is a garden, but I can see only its walls. And a few branches flowing with light. A little higher, I see more branches, and higher still the sun. And of all the jubilation of the air that can be felt outdoors, of all the joy spread out over the world, I can see only shadows of branches playing on white curtains. There are also five rays of sunlight patiently pouring into the room the golden scent of dried grass. A breeze, and the shadows on the curtains come to life. If a cloud covers up the sun and then lets it through again, the bright yellow of the vase of mimosa leaps out of the shadow. The birth of this single flash of brightness is enough to fill me with a confused and whirling joy.[46]

In this example we get a direct experience of place that is close to ecstatic. Another person encountering those places might well feel indifference, but for Camus the place produced a deep sense of meaningful enchantment. This subjective quality of our experiences of place is important in the sense that the places we perceive as meaningful are, by and large, meaningful only to us.

Such experiences of place can also provide a deep sense of well-being, as well as serving as the catalyst for moments of mystical wonderment. William James, the turn-of-the-twentieth-century psychologist, pointed to this dimension of topophilia in his famous study of religion, *The Varieties of Religious Experience*. "Apart from anything acutely religious, we all have moments when the universal life seems to wrap around us with friendliness. In youth and health, in summer, in the woods or on the mountains, there come days when the weather seems all whispering with peace, hours when the goodness and beauty of existence, enfolds us like a dry, warm climate, or chime through us as if our inner ears were subtly ringing with the world's security."[47] Similarly, the mystic Evelyn Underhill reports that even an ugly London street can be conducive to moments of joy. "I still remember walking down the Notting Hill main road and observing the (extremely sordid) landscape with joy and astonishment. Even the movement of the traffic has something universal and sublime in it."[48]

Underhill's place-specific epiphany is very similar to the experience of topophilia recounted by Virginia Woolf in her novel *To the Lighthouse*. Woolf puts us in the mind of a woman who, pausing in the midst of cleaning a seaside cottage, experiences a near-transcendent auditory "vision" of place that intimates universal wholeness. The description is so detailed and evocative that you readily imagine the stillness and the sense of something humming just below the surface of things.

> And now as if the cleaning and the scrubbing and the scything and the moving had drowned it there rose that half-heard melody, that intermittent music which the ear half catches but lets fall, a bark, a bleat; irregular, intermittent, yet somehow related; the hum of an insect, the tremor of cut grass, dissevered yet somehow belonging; the dor-beetle, the squeak of a wheel, loud, low, but mysteriously related; which the ear strains to bring together and is always on the verge

of harmonizing, but they are never quite heard, never fully harmonized ...[49]

Ernest Hemingway, another of my favourite writers during my university years, reveals a deep feeling for place in his memoir of living in Paris in the 1920s, *A Moveable Feast*.

> When we came back to Paris it was clear and cold and lovely. The city had accommodated itself to winter, there was good wood for sale at the wood and coal place across our street, and there were braziers outside of many of the good cafés so that you could keep warm on the terraces. Our own apartment was warm and cheerful. We burned *boulets* which were molded, egg-shaped lumps of coal dust, on the wood fire, and on the streets the winter light was beautiful. Now you were accustomed to see the bare trees against the sky and you walked on the fresh-washed gravel paths through Luxembourg gardens in the clear sharp wind.[50]

My poetic example is Philip Larkin. The English poet is, perhaps, an odd choice to select as a poet of place. He is famous for mocking notions of "roots," once referring to the place where he was born, the city of Coventry, as "a forgotten boredom." For Larkin, it seems, place is a matter of happenstance, and it hardly matters where he is if basic needs are handled. "I don't really notice where I live: as long as a few simple wants are satisfied – peace, quiet, warmth – I don't mind where I am." Arguably, he was being deliberately disingenuous, at least judging by his poetry. Several of Larkin's poems reveal an abiding awareness of place, albeit indirectly through his lamentations for lost or disappearing "places." In the poem "Here," for instance, he describes an overnight drive through the English countryside that ends in "the surprise of a large town." Wherever Larkin has taken us, it is not, as one critic observes, a transfigured place like that seen in William Wordsworth's 1802 vision of London in "Lines Composed upon Westminster Bridge." Instead, Larkin describes a grey, stultifying post-war provincial town devoted to getting-and-spending, where "domes and statues, spires and cranes cluster / Beside grain-scattered streets" and the residents attempt to satisfy their inchoate longings by shopping for "cheap suits, red kitchenware [and] sharp shoes."[51] Yet Larkin's vision takes us out of the city, away from the "Tattoo-shops, consulates, grim head-scarfed wives," past the "mortgaged half-built edges" of suburbs, to the "isolated villages" and "fast-shadowed wheat-fields" of the countryside, where, down by the seaside, "loneliness clarifies" and "silence stands like heat," leading us to an "unfenced existence" that is, somehow, "untalkative, out of reach."[52] In other words, the narrator, and presumably the reader, is left staring out to sea, sensing some silent presence, something just beyond reach. Larkin's poem shows us a place where it is possible to envision a deeper reality.

Larkin's most religion-haunted poem, and one also redolent of "place," is "Church-Going." In this poem, the narrator, an ordinary desacralized, disbelieving and intellectually detached citizen, enters a church on some uncertain impulse. It's not hard to imagine this person. Like many of Larkin's poetic characters, he wanders without particular purpose, having no idea, quite literally, "what on earth they are doing,"[53] and no sense of significance regarding anything they do. He does his job, pays taxes, watches television (or, nowadays, the Internet), takes holidays, plays the lottery, and, well, that's about it. Work, consumption and entertainment fill up his (or her) life. Yet, he is also dissatisfied, but does not know why or for what.

Larkin's poetry, as one critic comments, often "celebrates the unexpressed, deeply felt longings for sacred time and sacred space." (And, I would add, sacred place.) The poet

might achieve this celebration negatively by offering characters that live passive, detached and seemingly indifferent
lives. Sometimes, though, he starts out negatively and ends
positively. This is the case with "Church-Going," where, as
one critic says, we witness "the confrontation between the
profane and the sacred."[54] Cynical, ironic and ill informed,
the visitor nevertheless finds himself strangely drawn to
the church, although unsure why. He takes in the mundane
trappings: "brass and stuff / Up at the holy end." He runs his
hand around the font, and mounts the lectern to peruse a
few verses (which he dismisses as "hectoring"). He wonders
who might be the last to worship in this place – "this special
shell," as he calls it – and what will happen to it when even
disbelief is gone. Yet, inexplicably, he is pleased "to stand
in silence here." Even in this desacralized and disenchanted
world there are places still occupied by mystery, perhaps
because they have witnessed so many moments of birth and
death that still remain a mystery despite all our scientific
explanations. Someone, the visitor thinks, "will forever be
surprising / A hunger in himself to be more serious," seeking
out a place where it is "proper to grow wise in."[55]

In this poem (and others), Larkin's narrator discovers a
longing in himself for a more serious life; that is, serious in
the sense of wanting "to see beyond the day-to-day life of a
modern city dweller towards something more mysterious."
The narrator's initial skepticism gives way to a sense of place
that awakens him, if only dimly, to the sacred. Thus, an ordinary place – a suburban church – acquires a "disconcerting
holiness."[56]

Clearly, Larkin's poetry, like the prose of my other selected writers, points up the importance of place, both psychologically and spiritually. Regardless of their differences,
their attention to place – a church, a beach, streets in Paris or
London, a garden in Algiers, or an English farm field – demon-

strates the intentionality of consciousness and the experience of meaning that results from this focus. But they also offer one more thing; the descriptions of place that come out of their sudden focus of attention provide a valuable lesson on how to foster a sense of place. Each of these writers serves as a guide on paying greater attention to our places, and thereby developing a meaningful sense of place.

This brings me back to Tony Hiss and his notion of "simultaneous perception." Like Hiss, I would argue that our experience of a place and the meaning we derive from that experience has much to do with how we look at things. Hiss, remember, says there are ways to encourage an expanded perception of place, including reading and the study of subjects conducive to fostering such perception. My poets and novelists, I suggest, underscore this point. Their vivid and detailed responses to place are prime examples of intentional consciousness,[57] of self-consciously focusing on the objects in our surroundings. This practice echoes Hiss' notion of "simultaneous perception." But he also recommends expanding our perceptions – acquiring the skill of simultaneous perception, in other words – by actively and self-consciously observing worthwhile local places with greater attention.

Perhaps the best way I can illustrate this claim is by drawing on my own experience of living in Ottawa, Canada's national capital.

****

Years ago, I memorized some lines from T.S. Eliot's poem "Little Gidding": "We shall not cease from exploration/ And the end of all our exploring / Will be to arrive where we started / And know the place for the first time."[58] The fragment has been with me ever since, but never more so than when I spent a good portion of one summer exploring the streets of Ottawa, searching out its monuments. Indeed, the words offer a summary and conclusion to my sojourn among the statuary. I've lived in Ottawa for nearly twenty-five years. Its streets and neighbourhoods, buildings and parks, and, of course, its monuments have become familiar to me – so much so that I stopped really noticing them. They became the visual equivalent of white noise.

Yet, as I made my daily walks to one monument or another – among others, the bronze Sir Galahad statue on Wellington Street dedicated to Henry Albert Harper, the young civil servant who drowned in his twenty-eighth year trying to save Miss Bessie Blair's life when the young woman fell through the ice on the Ottawa River on December 6, 1901; the soldiers on the National War Memorial in Confederation Square; Samuel de Champlain's statue on Nepean Point – long-familiar objects acquired the kind of sharp-edged quality of newness that you feel when you see a foreign city for the first time. The familiar shimmered with strangeness. Reacquainting myself with things that I was no longer really seeing – in this case, monuments – fostered sharper and greater awareness of the place where I live. I became a traveller in my own town, a pilgrim on my own streets.

I didn't feel that way at first. I was just out for some weekend walking. But somewhere along the way my walks took on a more personal resonance. Strolling familiar streets, pausing before memorials to the war dead, walking the pathways below Parliament Hill, meandering among the statuary of Canada's prime ministers, I started to rediscover – or, better, to remember – my own city. Walking around Major's Hill Park, for example, I recalled taking my mother through the park during one of her visits years ago, showing her the statue of Colonel John By and the cottage he built for his family. Contemplating the Sharpshooters' statue in front of the Cartier Square Drill Hall, I thought back to evenings watching my son go through his paces as an army cadet with the Cameron Highlanders regiment. Standing before the National War Memorial, I remembered my first time in Ottawa and how the sight of those splendid larger-than-life military figures left me with a lump-in-the-throat feeling. As the poet might put it, my walks took me back to where I'd started and helped me know the place for the first time.

Place, in the sense I'm using the word, is "an organized world of meaning," "a centre of felt value," to borrow Yi-Fu Tuan's phrases. A place, as he says, is something invested with meaning or created by human beings to fulfill their purposes. Churches and houses, parks and monuments, they all existed at one time only as ideas. But, once built, they reflect the "spirit" of those who create a *place* out of space. However, places do not remain places simply because they exist. A place must be lived to retain its placeness. This lived-in aspect makes a place, in Tuan's words, "an archive of fond memories and splendid achievements that inspire the present; place is permanent and hence reassuring to man, who sees frailty in himself and change and flux everywhere."[59]

This understanding of place as lived experience, as a sensibility that lends stability to our lives, readily applies to the streets and churches and monuments of our communities. The problem, though, as I've suggested, is that we become blasé about the things we live with and thus we lose their contribution to our sense of place. The recovery of our sense of place requires attending to those things that express the "spirit" of our places, our streets and cities. The concept of psycho-geography – coupled with an intentional conscious-ness – offers a way to foster the recovery of place.

Psycho-geography aims to know the world as a lived experience, not as a theoretical idea. Psycho-geography seeks a more intimate engagement with everyday life, for discovering how our streets, our community, our churches and monuments can become extensions of ourselves, a means for creating a sense of place. The practice emerged with the Situationist movement in the 1950s, an offshoot of French avant-garde cultural theories that have influenced everything from fine art to urban planning. Philosopher Guy Debord, the founder of the movement, defined psycho-geography as "the study of the precise laws and specific effects of the geographical environment, consciously organized or not, on the emotions and behavior of individuals."[60] Psycho-geography, then, is all about how places – streets and highways, buildings and parks, monuments and sculptures – affect us psychologically and, I dare say, spiritually.

I will have more to say about psycho-geography in Chapter Five, but offer a brief summary here to suggest how psycho-geography can contribute to a sense of place. In a nutshell, the practice of psycho-geography, as defined by Debord, requires considerable self-awareness: a constant attentiveness to where you are as well as an awareness of your feelings and thoughts regarding where you are. You must discipline your emotions to respond to the surrounding environment, following the route that "feels right." You want to be genuinely *in place*, and not displaced and diverted by the chatter in your head. Achieving this "placeness" is where the effort of intentional consciousness – or Hiss' simultaneous perception, if you prefer – comes in. I like to think of it as the practice of wide-awareness.

I tried to employ wide-awareness in my explorations of Ottawa. In paying attention to myself walking, I paid attention to the streetscape around me, to the point where I often saw things I hadn't seen before, or if I had seen them, hadn't previously deemed them worthy of attention.

The statue of the Jesuit priest Jean de Brébeuf in Parc Moussette in Gatineau had me sitting on the riverbank imagining the seventeenth-century *voyageurs* paddling their boats up the Ottawa River in search of a passage to China. I was tempted to wave. The statue of former prime minister John Diefenbaker on Parliament Hill reminded me of when I lived in Inuvik as a boy, and the family story of my father shaking hands with the prime minister when he visited the northern town in 1961. Major's Hill Park has always been one of my favourite places in Ottawa, but while I was familiar with the ruins of the old cottage that Colonel John By built for his wife and daughters in the 1820s during the construction of the Rideau Canal, I'd never paid much attention. This time, though, my attentiveness was a stimulus to imagination. The bronze reproductions of household items dug up by archeologists, including a teacup, had me conjuring the ghosts of Mrs. By and Francis Ramsay Simpson, the wife of the Hudson Bay Company governor George Simpson, having tea together on a sunny May morning in 1830 and taking a turn around the English-style country garden that once surrounded the cottage. Admittedly, I was indulging in a bit of historical extrapolation,[61] but my attention to those artifacts stirred my imagination and made my visit to the place more meaningful. And that, I suggest, is how psycho-geography encourages us to be travellers in our own town. Those who drift in wide-awareness become more aware of the space in which they live, and are likelier to acquire a more distinct sense of that space as a place.

I can attest to this finding, at least to some degree. One of my *dérives* took me along the river pathways on the Ontario and Quebec sides of the Ottawa River. Maybe it was the constant view of the copper roof of the Parliamentary Library, the silver spires of Notre Dame Basilica or the sight of Champlain's statue on the tip of Nepean Point, or maybe all of those things, but I found myself thinking that the whole panorama before me – legislature, church, explorer and, indeed, the city itself – was a monument writ large, a celebration of spirit amidst a daunting geography. And it occurred to me that in imagining Ottawa this way – an inspiring "archive of fond memories and splendid achievements," to again borrow Yi-Fu Tuan's phrase – it really had become my *place*, after twenty-five years of living there.

If so, then I like to think I gained a glimpse, however slight, into the soul of the place where I live. The word "soul" comes from the Greek *psyche*, and refers to that which animates a body, gives it its purpose in being what it is. The artifacts of a place – the museums and galleries, parks and churches, memorials and monuments – reveal the soul of a place, its self-understanding. They reflect the ideas that give meaning and purpose to a place and to those who live there. It might seem that twenty-five years is a long time to take to acquire some sense of the spirit of a place, its *genius loci*. Perhaps so, but I doubt I am the only one who takes so long. There are so many things nowadays militating against our experience of place, including the way we think and how we "know" the world.

This is something of puzzle when it comes to place. As philosopher Edward Casey observes, place surrounds us; we cannot live without it. "To be at all – to exist in any way – is to be somewhere, and to be somewhere is to be in some kind of place." Place, in other words, is as necessary as the air we breathe, the ground on which we walk and the body that provides our experience. We literally walk on, over, through, around and under places. How, Casey asks, could we fail to be aware of such a primal reality?[62]

Yet we are unaware of it. And the reason, according to Casey, is that modernity requires us to subordinate place to the universalizing imperatives of the time-and-space worldview. The career requires you to move to another city; well, off you go without question, uprooting family and saying goodbye to lifelong friends. A new roadway will be good for general prosperity; well, knock down a long-established neighbourhood. A small country wishes to remain isolated from the world; well, a few gunships will force it to open its doors to trade and commerce. This worldview is what academics call our dominant discourse or narrative. In the case of the West, the narrative we tell ourselves, as moderns, requires the conquest of space and time through science and technology. Historically, this narrative has translated into "the search for ideas, usually labeled 'essences', that obtain everywhere and for which a particular somewhere, a given place, is presumably irrelevant."[63] However, as John Inge observes, this worldview also translates into phenomena such as economic globalization that may bring considerable benefits, but also considerable cost. One of those costs, he says, "is the disappearance of a recognition of the importance of place not just from the world of ideas, but from the world which people inhabit."[64]

How might we recover a sense of place? Do we need to reclaim a sense of the sacred, a sense of mystery, to restore a sense of place? Theologian David Brown thinks so. He argues that at the heart of the modern scientific project is "the elimination of mystery and its substitution with explanation." Brown is certainly not advocating the abandonment of scientific reason, much less the adoption of new age irrationalism. What he is getting at is the notion that scientific epistemologies, or theories of knowledge, are insufficient to account for the full gamut of human experience, including religious experience. The West's "adoption of a particular model of rationality ... seemed to suggest that once something was 'explained' there was no further need to address religious questions," says Brown. Scientism examines nature, including human nature, and finds no evidence of God in all that matter. Thus, we "prove" God does not exist. But the question lingers: Why should phenomena we can prove empirically be the only valid way to experience manifestations of the divine?[65]

I am still struggling with that question. At best I can claim a few experiences over the course of a lifetime that have left me wondering, as the old Peggy Lee song goes, "Is that all there is?" And those experiences have often been grounded in geography. The modern disenchanted view of the world denies that such experiences have any inherent meaning beyond the merely subjective. I'm not so sure. As philosopher Erazim Kohak points out, our notion of "objective reality" as a process of "dead matter" driven by natural forces is a theoretical construct established on the basis of a highly abstracted worldview. It has been useful for improving the human condition, but it is still a construct.[66] Scientism, in effect, requires the suspension of *lived* experience. Some psychologist could attach electrodes to my skull and record the neurological responses when I remember my special places. But no matter how many measurements and oscillating charts she produced, she would never capture the lived experience.

I want to be careful here. I am not promoting New Age irrationalism or whatever-you-feel-must-be-real solipsism. But I am following the implication of Brown and Kohak's arguments that one possible way to recover a sense of place is through a renewed sense of the sacramental. The modern image of man alienated from and needing to master a disenchanted world is alien to the spirit of Western philosophy and theology. "Through its three recorded millennia, Western thought has been consistently personalistic and specifically *naturalistic*," says Kohak, "understanding humans as continuous with and at home in nature."[67]

Brown, arguing from a theological perspective, calls for a similar worldview, pointing out that "basic to Christian conviction is belief in a generous God. In his life, death and resurrection Jesus Christ revealed a loving and merciful God who, while calling human beings back from sin, none the less fully endorsed our material world by himself becoming part of it."[68] Brown takes from this the idea that it is possible to glimpse the divine presence in ways other than that of scriptural revelation. By valuing place in and for itself it is perhaps possible to draw closer)to the divine, whether in an immanent or a transcendent form.[69] Is it not possible, Brown asks, that the experience of the divine is inherent to our experience of the natural world through our sense of nature's beauty or awe at its majesty?[70]

****

I wasn't aware of any divine presence at Point-No-Point when I visited on my way home from Japan. I again enjoyed a soup-and-sandwich lunch in the restaurant – the view from the big glass windows was as stunning as ever, thank God – and then spent the afternoon climbing up and down the paths around the property, criss-crossing the beach and stretching out on the red bench in the small tree-cave. When I had tired myself out, I found my old place among the rocks and huddled out of the wind to watch the occasional ship plow westward through the Strait of Juan de Fuca and listen to the grating rattle of water on stone and breathe in the scents of cedar and sea and feel the warmth of the sun on my body. I tried not to think too much, or, rather, as Zen Buddhism teaches, I let my thoughts come and go like leaves caught in the wind.

Only some leaves kept snagging on mental fences. I kept seeing places from my just-completed pilgrimage in Japan, interspersed with images from other places and other pilgrimages. Some were images of places that had been with me for decades, etched into my memory like engravings on stone. They are a puzzle to me. Why, out of all the places I might remember, do certain images continue to haunt me with a kind of longing? A winding, grass-edged gravel path through Parc de Choisy, a table on the sidewalk outside Capisano's restaurant in Bromley, a kitchen alcove in an apartment on Richardson Street in Victoria, a view of an Alexandrian street from a window in the poet C.P. Cavafy's apartment – why do I remember these places and not others? It's not that anything spectacular happened when I was in these places, at least in an external sense. Their significance is strictly internal. In each of these places, as best I can surmise, I experienced one of those "queer, bright moments," to borrow a phrase from writer Alice Munro, when, for few seconds, I was caught up in what the mystic George Gurdjieff calls self-remembering: moments when I was suddenly aware not only of what I was doing, but of myself doing it. In those moments I was conscious of the "place" and of myself in that place.[71]

The Richardson Street moment I just mentioned is probably a good example. It was a few days before Christmas of 1971 and I was sitting in the kitchen alcove of the apartment where I lived in Victoria that year. It was a rainy night. I had just gotten off the phone with my girlfriend. Karen – as I will call her – had invited me to spend Christmas with her and her parents, and I was happy at the prospect. I poured myself a glass of wine and sat down at the table, where I'd been writing before the phone call. I lit a cigarette. Exhaling, I looked up from the table as a sudden gust of wind rattled the window with pebbles of rain. That was it: streaks of rain on the window, curling tendrils of cigarette smoke rising toward the ceiling light, sheets of paper on a red-checked tablecloth, a glass of wine, and the image of Karen in my head. The tableau has been freeze-framed in my memory for decades, like a picture taken with a flashbulb. No doubt I was looking forward to seeing my girlfriend; still, the persistence of the memory continues to puzzle me. But then so do other memories that seem to possess symbolic significance for me. Like bodies of water, they have depths of meaning that invite diving deep.

Someone once said the real pleasure of travel is not the arrival but the journey. But what is it about the journey that is most appealing? It is, I think, the mystery. You dwell for a brief time in the transit of anticipation between the place you left and the place you are going, looking forward to what might be, slightly anxious and uncertain, yet full of anticipation. I sometimes think I am happiest when I am between one place and another, living in the mystery of what is to come. If that is true, then my "places" are the touchstones of my transit through life, the place where I touched down, the points of meaning in a peripatetic existence.

Even so, I often wonder which of all the places I have touched down is the one where I most truly belong. Any of them? None? Did I miss it in passing? If I did, can I go back? Or is the place I'm supposed to be still somewhere ahead, down the road, on the horizon, over the next hill? And if it is, might I miss that one, too, in feeling nostalgic for some past place? After a lifetime of wandering, if only in imagination, would I even recognize where I am supposed to be? When I am in one place, I find myself thinking of some other place. But then I also find myself anticipating being in one place only to find that when I am there, I am comparing it to the place I imagined before I arrived. On the other hand, I often remember a place I've been with an intensity I didn't feel when I was there. Images of some place will suddenly flash on the screen of memory, often months after my visit. These images are, for the most part, scenes of utter ordinariness – a leaf-thick forest path, a sunlit stretch of highway, a table at a restaurant window, a bench at a bus stop – yet somehow they possess, in retrospect, a significance I did not feel at the time, or, at least, was unaware of feeling. It is as if I woke up to the true reality of the place, paid attention to it only after my mind had a chance to absorb my largely unconscious experience of the place. But that implies the meaning of a place is a matter of hindsight. We only *know* what we experience after reflection.

What, then, am I to make of my myriad places? They form a mosaic of streets and seascapes, cliffs and coves, fields and forest paths, a kind of private map of the scenes and settings encountered over a lifetime that, for some reason, mean more than others. The mystery, of course, is why these places rather than others. I study the mosaic in the hope of finding a meaningful pattern. It gets confusing.

One time when I was driving across Alberta on holiday with my son, Daniel, I remarked that the sight of one place reminded me of another place. He replied, "Dad, every place reminds you of some other place." He was being sardonic, a teenager commenting on the adult propensity for nostalgia. But he was also right. Every place I see does remind me of another place. Maybe that's inevitable if you live long enough to see a few places in the world. I hoard the places I've been like a magpie hoards bright baubles in a nest. Indeed, something innocuous — the smell of woodsmoke, the morning after a rainfall, an old song, a colourful doorway — sends me in memory to another place. A damp, still morning in Ottawa might return me to a winter morning in London. The cooing of a dove in a tree in my backyard loops me back to birdsong I heard in the forests of Shikoku. What is the meaning of these mnemonic moments? Do they signify anything beyond the haphazard firing of neurons? These flashes of remembered places last only a short time, but the mood they evoke, good or bad, happy or sad, can linger for hours, colouring the tone of the whole day. Therein, perhaps, resides their significance, and perhaps the significance of place in our lives. If, as the philosophers argue, a sense of place is necessary for our lives to have coherence, then reflecting on our experience of place is a search for that coherence.

Some scholars think we have an inherent preference for certain places, a preference that goes deeper than where we were born or grew up. Psychologists Stephen and Rachel Kaplan point out that we appear to have an inborn preference for landscapes that contain "mystery." Winding paths, for example, "give the impression that one could acquire new information if one were to travel deeper into the scene." They also offer the example of Japanese gardens, where the nature of the design, with its twisting paths and hidden alcoves, entices you to enter more and more deeply. Other places, too, possess the character of mystery, they say. We like open spaces, a preference that may well go back to our hominid ancestors on the savannas of Africa, who, in confronting a new place, had to decide whether it was worth exploring. That instinct remains, albeit in less savage form: We still like a bend in the road, an archway that leads to an open area, a clearing in a forest, a seascape glimpsed through a screen of foliage. They all have a hint of mystery. The trick, the psychologists imply, is learning to keep a sense of mystery even when you have grown familiar with a place.[72]

Was that why I came back to Point-No-Point? The philosopher Gabriel Marcel once said that "an individual is not distinct from his place; he is that place."[73] Looking out from my rocky hideaway, it occurred to me that Point-No-Point had been a reference point for my ideal self, a touchstone place where, with its open vistas and its passing ships hinting at the vast ocean just beyond the headlands, the mystery of life, mine and everybody's, had appeared to me as a young man. The thought surprised me. I had, in fact, known the place for only a few years when I was much younger. Yet, revisiting it after my return from Japan, looking out to sea, I could see it all like a flotilla of ships passing on the horizon:

the tree-lined streets of Fairfield, the long, curving beach at
Cadboro Bay, the green oasis of Beacon Hill Park, the sight
of the harbour from the bay window in my bed-sit on Burdett
Avenue. I thought of a girl who liked to go for long walks
along Beach Drive. I remembered a friend who took me in
when I was having a bad time.

Point-No-Point was a palimpsest of my past, the place
where I'd stored all the best and brightest memories of my
youth. Despite the passage of years, the many detours of
my life, all the other places, I had never been able to forget.
Yet, why that was so, why it haunted me, why I continued
to return to the place, even if only in dream and memory,
remained a mystery. Maybe, I thought, that was why I had
come back: to recover the sense of mystery.

But I was thinking too much. With Zen-like resolve, I let
the memories go and settled back against the rocks, releasing myself to the warmth of the sun and the susurration of
the sea. I closed my eyes and listened to the endless surging
of water along the shore and the long, sighing retreats back
down the sweep of sand. I imagined the tide rising and the
water lapping over my outstretched legs and the salt dis-
solving the flesh and the bones sinking into the sand and
the sea carrying me away until I returned to every place I
had ever been.

note 'palimpsest' is a word that I am seeing
more frequently; a few years ago I felt
it was almost my mine — Where's
Jung when one could use him?

FOUR

THE GIFT OF SOLITUDE
Learning to Be Alone

And when he had sent the multitudes away, he went up into a mountain apart to pray: and when the evening was come, he was there alone.
  – Matthew 14:23

Ours is certainly a time for solitaries ...
  – Thomas Merton, *The Wisdom of the Desert*[1]

In the late spring of 1976, I got a job with a firm of geologists doing surveying for mining companies in the mountains near the town of Ross River in the Yukon. The job basically involved walking up and down the sides of mountains hammering survey stakes into the ground. It was vigorous outdoor exercise, and good for me, health-wise. I ended the summer in great physical shape. I also benefited mentally, and, I would say, spiritually, although it certainly didn't feel that way at the beginning. In early June, a helicopter deposited me on a mountain plateau, where, I was told, I would be on my own for a few days until the rest of the crew arrived. All I had to do was make sure the tents didn't blow away and that animals, including bears, didn't get into the food stocks or start chewing on tarps. As it turned out, I was alone on that mountain for about two weeks.

Now you might think, no big deal – a two-week camping trip in the great outdoors with all that fresh air, mountain scenery and the stars (or in this case, the midnight sun) for companions. And so it proved in retrospect. When the rest of the crew did arrive, I was surprised to find I resented their presence. I had grown into my solitude. But between that time and those first days alone, there were a few moments of instability, including, as it seemed, imagining bears were after me.

One night about a week after I arrived in the camp, I woke to the slapping sound of canvas caught in the wind. I recognized the sound immediately, but I was also sure I'd heard something else: the snuffling grunts of a bear rooting for food. I lay still in my cot, heart racing, ears pricked for bear noises. In the half-light I could see the loose canvas of the tent flap moving in the wind, and beyond it a triangle of pale sky. At the foot of my cot, lying across my duffel bag on the plywood floor, I could make out the barrel of the Winchester rifle my employer had left with me. His words came back to me: "You probably won't need it, but keep it handy."

I tried to calm my thumping heart, listening, hoping the bear – if that's what I'd heard – would wander away after finding nothing to eat. I tried to recall what I knew about bears: their eyesight isn't good but they have acute hearing and a sharp sense of smell. Was that right? I couldn't remember. The thought struck me that my situation was absurd. I had to remind myself that I was no longer in the modern world.[2] I was in the Yukon wilderness and there was nobody else around, except, it seemed, this bear. Only I wasn't sure whether there really was a bear outside my sleeping quarters. Was it a dream?

There was only one way to find out. I pulled back the top of my sleeping bag and swung my legs over the side of the cot. Even today, more than thirty years later, I can still conjure the cold smoothness of the plywood on my feet and the sudden chill on my bare shoulders. I grabbed my jeans from the opposite bunk and pulled them on, then slipped my bare feet into my boots. I grabbed the rifle to check the chamber and extract the magazine. Both were empty. I found the ammunition box on the food shelf next to a row of Campbell's soup cans and loaded three rounds into the magazine. I slapped in the magazine and chambered a round. The click of the bolt sounded too loud in the silence. I stood for a moment listening intently, but heard only the quiet flap of canvas and the creak of the aluminum poles as the wind pressed against the tent's walls. I took a couple of deep breaths, untied the tent flaps and peered outside.

I was grateful not to see a bear, just the jagged silhouette of mountains against a glowing sky. I cautiously stepped out of the tent. Swinging the rifle — held in a proper shooting stance that my father taught me — I scanned the camp to the left and the right. Nothing. No bear.

The camp occupied a plateau about a hundred and fifty yards wide and half a football field in length, halfway up a mountainside. Half-a-dozen tent platforms were set in a line at the back of the plateau where it met the sloping face of the mountain. My tent was the last in the row at the far edge of the camp. Four unoccupied tents lay between my tent and the supply tent. Beyond the supply tent was a cache of a dozen or so 45-gallon drums of diesel fuel, a diesel generator and a few stacks of equipment covered by tarps weighed down by lengths of lumber.

I walked around all the tents. Except for mine, all the opening flaps were tied shut, as I'd left them on my last check before going to bed. Nor was there any torn canvas. No bear. I checked the supply tent and the area beyond. No bear. I scanned the thinly treed slope of the mountain above me. No bear. I crossed the width of plateau to look over the edge and down the spruce-covered slope to the valley below. There was enough light to catch the glint of the river winding through the dark mass of trees. Again there was no sign of a bear. All I heard was the snap of wind on canvas and creaking tent frames. I pointed the rifle into the sky and pulled the trigger.

Nothing happened. No bang. No recoil. I lowered the rifle, pulled back the bolt. The copper-jacketed bullet lay snug in its oiled chambered. What the hell? Only then did it dawn on me to check the safety. It was on. If there had been a bear, I'd be breakfast by now. I couldn't make up my mind whether to laugh or cry at my own ineptitude. I flicked the safety off, raised the rifle, pulled the trigger and listened to the gunshot echo across the valley. I jacked another round into the chamber and fired again, enjoying the brief obliteration of my own fear. When the silence settled again, I walked back to the tent to get a sweater and my cigarettes and returned to the edge of the plateau. I sat on a rock with the rifle across my knees and smoked one cigarette after another, watching the sky grow brighter behind the distant mountains and wondering what was happening to me.

I like to think my insecurities were warranted. You see, a week before being dropped on the mountain I had been living in England, working at a bar in a London suburb and dating a lovely English girl. I had returned unwillingly to Canada with the idea of earning a great whack of money and then going back England in the fall with a view to going to school. Things didn't work out that way. I never made it back to England and all my hopes turned to nothing. (I was in my mid-twenties, and at that age everything is rather intense.) In any case, I found myself in the Yukon wilderness a few short days after leaving the crowds and cacophony and pleasures of London.

I didn't count on how ill-prepared I would be for the geographical switch or the psychological shift that came with leaving London. Looking back on that summer of surveying, I realized that until then I had never spent such a long period of time alone. It wasn't just a matter of there being no other people around. There was also no music, traffic, radio, television, newspapers – none of the diversions that fill our daily lives, ensuring that while we sometimes feel lonely, we are seldom, if ever, truly alone.

Everything seemed fine for the first few days. I missed London and my girlfriend, but that was to be expected. I consoled myself by imagining my return to England. Still, it was hard to make the adjustment from the noise and crowded busyness of London to the silence and stillness of the Yukon wilderness. Call it a mild dose of culture shock. After more than two years wandering around Europe and Africa and living in England, I was in no shape, psychologically speaking, to be alone on a mountainside. It was utterly disorienting to be stuck in a wilderness survey camp when my head and heart were back in England. I kept imagining all the things I should be doing – traipsing off to a West End theatre, strolling around Regent's Park on a fine Sunday morning, enjoying an evening at the pub.

After a few days, the silence and my isolation started to get to me. Every little noise – the flap of a tarp or the creak of tent poles, for instance – had me thinking the bears were invading. I had to force myself to walk around the camp just to prove my fears were groundless. There were a few moments, particularly at night, when I felt on the edge of panic. I imagined that there had been a nuclear war and I had survived because of my isolation. Except I didn't know there had been a war and would realize something was wrong only when the rest of the crew didn't show up. What would I do then? How would I get back to whatever remained of civilization? As far as I knew, I was hundreds of miles from nowhere.

A few days alone can do strange things to your mind, but sometimes those strange things have unexpected benefits, at least in hindsight. Let me explain: My knapsack included several books by the American paleontologist and essayist Loren Eiseley. During his career, he produced a significant body of scientific work, but he is best known for literary essays that explore scientific topics – evolution, paleontology, and archaeology – from a personal perspective. Eiseley's writing is haunted, and haunting. His is the hauntedness of a man who felt the burden of solitude. A paragraph from his 1975 autobiography, *All the Strange Hours*, hints at the cast of his mind. Describing the conclusion to a traumatic field trip in Kansas, he wrote: "I have come to think I am moving in an endless extension of that single Kansas autumn. I am treading deeper and deeper into leaves and silence. I see more faces watching, non-human faces. Ironically, I who profess no religion find the whole of my life a religious pilgrimage."[3]

Eiseley's sense of solitude was rooted in his childhood. His mother was deaf, his father distant. As a young man during the Depression, he rode the rails. He eventually escaped the hobo life, got a Ph.D. and a teaching job, and spent the next thirty years, in his own words, as a bone hunter. But he never got over his sense of solitude, a solitude that was both psychological and metaphysical. In the 1950s, Eiseley started publishing essays. He had a remarkable talent for infusing his work with a spiritual sensibility. Embedded in his essays is constant meditation on questions of order and meaning and purpose. Like many moderns, Eiseley was unable to subscribe to a religious creed. Unlike many moderns, he had the honesty and courage to lament his lack of faith. "I have come to believe that in the world there is nothing to explain the world," he wrote. "Nothing to explain the necessity of life, explain the hunger of the elements to become life, nothing to explain why the stolid realm of rock and soil and mineral should diversify itself into beauty, terror, and uncertainty."[4] Yet, you also encounter a deep spiritual longing in Eiseley's thought. He is someone who, in the words of critic Richard Wentz, "has seen into the very heart of the universe and shares his healing vision with those who live in a world of feeble sight ...."[5] As a bone hunter, confronting the skulls of long-departed species, Eiseley comprehended the fragility of existence, and learned there just as easily could have been nothing instead of something.

Such thoughts don't recommend Eiseley as a cheery mountaintop companion, but it is to him that I owe my first significant lessons in learning to appreciate solitude. That night with the bear, real or imagined, was my initial lesson. Unable to find a bear, uncertain whether I'd actually heard one or whether I was the victim of my own fear and insecurity, and I wondered whether I was losing it.

At that time of year in the Yukon, early June, the sun barely dips below the horizon, and it never really gets dark. Instead, the world takes on a shadowless glow that makes everything – tents, rocks, trees – stand out in sharp relief. I looked at my watch. It was 3 a.m. but as light as dawn. The wind had died and I no longer heard the snap of tent canvas or tarps. Perched on my rock, I felt the silent world surrounding me, pressing down. I was aware of the slow thud of my heart and the pulse of blood in my ears. It occurred to me that I hadn't heard another voice, except the one in my head, which was full of Eiseley's thoughts, for several days. I looked around, as though expecting to see someone. But there was only the mountain and the silence and myself, seemingly cut off from the world. And with that awareness a rush of panic washed over me like a river breaching its banks. My heart raced. I felt light-headed, almost nauseous.

I was suddenly afraid – of what, I don't know. I gripped the rifle so tightly my knuckles were white. I stood up as if to run – anything to release the tension knotting my body. But there was no place to run to, and no lights or music or people to distract me.

An image from one of Eiseley's books blossomed in my mind: his description of crawling into a narrow sandstone crevice to encounter the fossilized skull of a long-extinct animal. Staring at it, Eiseley felt the skull was looking back. Only he recognized that what was looking back at him was himself. Somehow he was inside the skull peering out through its eye sockets at the strange creature that was himself looking at himself. That was the image in my head when I lifted out of my body and floated like a helium-filled balloon bouncing and tugging at the end of its tether. I looked down on the strange creature alone on the side of mountain, facing the darkness below.

Years later I would read about panic attacks and think maybe that's what I'd experienced. But it didn't quite feel that way. I don't know how long this bifurcation of consciousness lasted, twenty or thirty seconds maybe, but it came with a bolt of awareness, a sudden knowledge of reality. I may have had symptoms common to panic attacks, and I certainly felt frightened, but I also knew what Eiseley had experienced. It is difficult to put into words, but since I must, I will describe it as a sudden intuitive awareness of the mystery of human otherness, the ultimate solitude of self-consciousness, the knowledge that we are ultimately solitary, and that try as we might through all our imaginative constructions – language, art, politics, love, etc. – we remain wrapped in our skins, locked behind the bone of our skulls, an unsolvable mystery to others and to ourselves.

All of this – the ideas, the images, the sudden awareness – was in my head for only a short time, but even now, more than three decades later, I still remember that intense sense of knowledge, of grasping some fundamental truth about my own, and everyone else's, fundamental solitude. If not for those weeks of mountainside solitude, I might never have acquired that knowledge, frightening though it was at the time. In retrospect, I am grateful for the experience. It didn't stop me from feeling homesick for England, but at a certain level I also felt a sense of exhilaration, a sense of freedom and release at having confronted something in myself and no longer having to be afraid of it. I like to think of that lesson as the gift of solitude.

****

Our need for solitude is not widely recognized in contemporary Western society. There is a tendency to regard the desire to be alone as an aberrant attitude and even a symptom of social disorder. Togetherness, wanting to be with other people, is good; wanting to be alone is almost deviant. Parents fret about children who want to be by themselves. Social workers construct programs and outings to keep senior citizens from feeling lonely (and, presumably, dwelling morbidly on their mortality). Social scientists, psychologists, therapists and schoolteachers often regard the desire for solitude as a sign of social maladjustment or, at the extreme, symptomatic of pathological inclinations. The idea of being genuinely and willingly alone leaves many feeling uneasy, even fearful.[6]

This is puzzling. Many people have found solitude emotionally satisfying and, at the far end of the spiritual spectrum, revelatory. Being alone does not necessarily mean being lonely. You can be lonely in the midst of a crowded city. You may not possess the intimacy and companionship that you would like. You may miss an absent lover. You may have been rejected in love and therefore feel deeply alone.

Yet not all who are alone are lonely. Most famously, there are the examples of the great religious teachers. Moses, Jesus Christ, Zoroaster and Buddha experienced their visions and communion with the divine in places and circumstances where they could be solitary. Countless others over the ages – saints, mystics, sages, pilgrims, travellers, religious seekers, artists and poets – have attempted to repeat this experience. In the early centuries of Christianity, for example, an estimated 5,000 hermits sought solitude in the deserts of the Middle East.[7]

Even a cursory study of literature, philosophy and religion reinforces the point: Solitude can provide conditions that allow you to experience a sense of freedom, engage emotions and acquire experiential knowledge that are difficult to achieve when surrounded by others. Consider the philosophers. Some of the world's great thinkers – Descartes, Newton, Locke, Pascal, Spinoza, Kant, Leibniz, Schopenhauer, Nietzsche, Kierkegaard and Wittgenstein – lived alone for much of their lives. While some had relationships of one sort or another, none of them married.[8] Such behaviour contradicts our widespread assumption that social relations, particularly intimate relations, are the chief source of individual fulfillment. To be sure, no reasonable person wants to be utterly alone. Indeed, theologians have defined Hell as eternal aloneness. So, yes, we do need others. Psychologists and sociologists readily demonstrate that our desire for attachment and sociality is rooted in biological imperatives. But that doesn't mean we need to be "attached" all the time. Sometimes we need to detach. The example of the philosophers and the great religious teachers surely demonstrates that periods of solitude can have great consequence; solitaries have shaped or influenced numerous social, political and religious movements. "The mental experience of solitude is ineluctably as social as any other psychological experience."[9] Thus, solitude is not necessarily anti-social. It is itself a social phenomenon in the sense that it fosters our ability to reflect on our lives; this reflection can redound to the benefit of society.

Clearly, we confront a paradox. On one hand, we demand instant connection, constant hook-up, ever-ready wiredness and always on call functioning. We phone our spouse on the cellphone – never mind we're steering a ton of metal at 120 kilometres an hour on the highway – to tell her or him we'll be home in five minutes. We pack BlackBerrys everywhere, a technological succubus that drains our energy and attention by keeping us always on call. We constantly check our e-mail to see if anyone wants to hear from us, and, no doubt, feel a small sadness when there are no new messages. We blog and tweet every day even though few possess the ability to produce a daily supply of wisdom worth the world's attention. And so, desperate to stay connected, we live amidst an ever increasing cacophony of voices, few of which do more than reveal their own narcissism, effectively shouting to anyone who will listen, "I'm here, pay attention to me." If you don't respond within minutes to someone's e-mail you have committed a social *faux pas*. It's almost as if we can't accept any place or circumstance for disconnecting.

It certainly seems there are fewer and fewer places where you can enjoy solitude. Never mind the constant traffic, the airplanes flying overhead or the neighbour's blasting music. Video security cameras spread like spores in a petri dish. Muzak in the shopping malls, office towers and elevators provides a ubiquitous backdrop of mind-numbing white noise. Many seem unable to function without some sort of surrounding sound. In the office, the car, the home and even the bedroom, we seem to require steady auditory stimulation. How many households keep the TV or the radio constantly playing? Cell phones, the Internet, e-mail, Twitter, iPods, pagers, radio and television broadcasts: it sometimes seems well nigh impossible to find any significant time or place to be alone with your own thoughts. Perhaps we are afraid.

This is passing strange when you consider how much we supposedly value our autonomy. It is an odd kind of autonomy when you are afraid to be alone, afraid to be without a cell phone stuck to the side of your head or iPhone buds inserted into your ears. At the same time, though, we complain about the world being too much with us, lamenting our inability to get away from it all. (And even when we do, how many start to feel twitchy if they can't check the BlackBerry for messages every few minutes?) Perhaps the sweeping tide of technological society has drowned any awareness of the need for constructive solitude. Perhaps the idea of silence, of being genuinely and willingly alone, is lost to us. If so, then we are lost to ourselves. All that time, money and energy spent staying in touch masks our lostness and our deep and fundamental loneliness. Perhaps, as psychologist Ester Buchholz says, we are "terminally in touch."[10]

I am tempted to agree with French philosopher Blaise Pascal's notion that we hide our fear of solitude with *divertisse-ments*. "The sole cause of man's unhappiness is that he does not know how to stay quietly in his room," Pascal famously observed. He was not being cynical. Pascal understood that people are "unable to cure death, wretchedness, and ignorance," so they have decided that "in order to be happy, not to think about such things." And that is why "men are so fond of hustle and bustle," he says. "That is why prison is such a fearful punishment; that is why the pleasures of solitude are so incomprehensible." We desperately distract ourselves to avoid confronting our existential condition. This effort at *divertissement* or diversion is evident everywhere, including politics. The real pleasure of being a king, Pascal writes, is the potential for perpetual distraction, since everyone is always trying to keep the king's mind off his mortal limitations by providing him with endless pleasures.[11]

Nowadays, thanks to technology, we have more diversions available to us than any king in the pre-modern world could have imagined. But, like the king, we, too, seek distraction to sidestep anything that might cause us despair. The result is that we seldom seek those spiritual responses that have traditionally helped men and women face their deepest fears and concerns. Instead, we devote ourselves to the superficial distractions of careers, entertainment and various hedonistic satisfactions, including our technological trinkets.

Sadly, even religion seems increasingly devoted to diversion. Fewer and fewer churches provide a place for quiet retreat. Many are now mega-arenas for group entertainment and self-congratulation. Religious pilgrimages can disappoint those seeking a time and place for solitary meditation. Whether in Spain, England or Japan, I've encountered pilgrims – I use the word advisedly – nattering away on a cell phone to a spouse or friend back home, oblivious to the natural world around them or the interior of the church where they so rudely talk. There is nothing like the sudden jangle of a nearby cell phone inside a medieval church to destroy the accumulated quiet of a day's walking.

For Ester Buchholz, this devotion to diversion shows that we have become what she calls "intraviduals": people whose lives are internally fragmented rather than integrated. "Intraviduals" may well be deeply lonely despite – or, more properly, because of – being constantly connected. She questions whether this constant state of wiredness is good for us, psychologically or spiritually, and suggests that this state reveals our desperation to belong even as we assert our individuality. Technological connectedness produces spiritual disconnection. In Buchholz's words:

Computer life *is*, I believe, an attempt to solve the problem of alonetime and social needs. In a culture that no longer provides wilderness or stretches of solitary time, the computer is the one machine that seemingly offers it all: stimulation, knowledge, news, alonetime, relationships, and even sex. One might say it has universal appeal. However, if we are not aware of why computer technology is attracting us, we cannot use it to our best advantage.[12]

To me, this clinging to a computer (as cultural artifact) is a disguised attempt to balance needs for bonding and alonetime ... Are we just now becoming like trance societies, routinely using the computer and television to find alonetime without really realizing our unfulfilled alone need?[13]

More than ever, Buchholz argues, we need to rediscover how to be alone if we are to recover ourselves. All of us – children, teenagers, men and women – require reduced stimulation and more alonetime. Being alone provides a much needed rest.[14]

Peter Suedfeld agrees. The psychologist, who has devoted much of his career to studying the effects of isolation and sensory deprivation, points out that pioneers in the field of psychiatry long ago recognized that too much stimulation can be pathogenic. They often prescribed withdrawing patients from social intercourse as treatment for behavioural problems. Mentally ill patients were isolated to reduce sensory stimulus. This enforced solitude can certainly be unpleasant and stressful for some, producing negative feelings and fears that can lead to psychological dysfunction. Nevertheless, Suedfeld argues that our negative view of solitude is to a great extent due to cultural norms. Living in bustling, crowded, technologically determined cities and suburbs, constantly bombarded by auditory and visual stimuli, we have come to assume that isolation is bad, and we react accordingly. Only recently, he says, have we recognized that being terminally in touch creates social and sensory overload.[15]

The antidote to overload is "solitude, stillness and time out," according to Suedfeld. Sounding much like Pascal, the psychologist recommends "an environment with fewer frantic distractions (where) we can learn once again to appreciate the important things that we have been driven to ignore." Solitude is not an experience we should necessarily fear. Indeed, many people – from saints and sages to adventurers and spiritual seekers – have found solitude exciting and potentially enlightening. Even a brief look at the literature on solitude – which is considerable, I was surprised to find – suggests that being alone, imposing periods of solitude on ourselves, can open us to hitherto untapped emotions and previously unexplored imaginings and thoughts, whether hellish or joyful.[16]

I can testify to that judgment from my pilgrimage experience. The difference between a good and a bad pilgrimage is not only one of proper equipment and physical condition, but also one of psychological – spiritual? – conditioning. Do you as a pilgrim want to be alone and are you prepared for your aloneness? For many novice pilgrims, accustomed to being surrounded by others in their everyday lives – family, work colleagues, friends – venturing off alone on a pilgrimage may be the first time they are completely on their own, dependent on themselves, both physically and mentally. Not everybody can stand being alone. Loneliness is the most obvious psychological risk of a pilgrimage. The idea of solitude can stir childhood fears of abandonment and neglect, and cause some people to abandon the pilgrimage or, perhaps worse, turn it into an excuse for a lot of drinking and group conviviality.[17] But overcoming a fear of being alone is essential for a worthy pilgrimage. Solitude is necessary if the pilgrimage – or any long-distance trek, for that matter – is to be a journey of self-exploration and spiritual discovery. Let me offer this example, courtesy of Ester Buchholz. In 1993, Borge Ousland, a Norwegian explorer, pulled a 300-pound sled as he skied alone to the North Pole across about a thousand kilometres of drifting ice. He communicated with his base camp by radio at most twice a week. After finishing his fifty-two-day journey, he said, "I had feared I would be lonely; I had never spent so much as a single night alone in a tent before … But being alone proved to be one of the greatest experiences of the entire trek."[18]

While none of my pilgrimages – about which I'll have more to say in Chapters Six and Seven – have been as arduous as an Arctic trek, I can still attest to the benefits of being alone for significant periods of time. My point is that being alone is arguably a necessary pre-condition for most transcendent experiences, divine or otherwise.[19] For one thing, solitude can foster creative thinking. Novel ideas often emerge during periods of isolation. In these "positive" experiences of solitude "there seems to be no loneliness; rather the individual feels a freedom from distraction, from the usual restrictions imposed by social norms and the need to maintain face, and the benefits of reducing external stimulation to the point where the still, small internal voices can be heard."[20] To dwell in a place with fewer frantic distractions, even for a short time, opens us to the possibility of recovering those matters that our frenetic lives lead us to forget. It is those moments of solitude, when the small internal voices are most likely to be heard, that provide an introduction (or, better, a reintroduction) to a more meaning-filled world. Creative solutions require alone time. In Buchholz's words: "Alone-time is required for the unconscious to process and unravel problems. Others inspire us, information feeds us, practice improves our performance, but we need quiet time to figure things out, to emerge with new discoveries, to unearth the answers … Letting myself slide into reverie has proven far more productive when I'm stuck with a problem."[21]

In this light, then, the question becomes: How do we foster conditions of solitude that make it possible to hear those quiet internal voices or achieve some small insight? Perhaps the best way to approach that question is to consider the experiences of various creatively minded solitaries. Poets and philosophers, travellers and novelists, mystics and psychologists: all express an appreciation for solitude. We can draw on their experience for guidance in our own efforts to re-enchant the world.

****

Before I go any further, though, I need to clarify the concept of solitude. Surprisingly, perhaps, there are nuances to the concept. Generally speaking, there are two main aspects of solitude – physical separation from others and psychological detachment.[22] Philosopher Philip Koch covers both dimensions in defining the experience of solitude this way:

> Solitude is, most ultimately, simply an experiential world in which other people are absent; that is enough for solitude, that is constant through all solitudes. Other people may be physically present, provided that our minds are disengaged from them; and the full range of disengaged activities, from reflective withdrawal to complete immersion in the tumbling rush of sensations, find their places along the spectrum of solitudes.[23]

Thus, Koch proposed three necessary conditions to solitude: physical aloneness, disengagement from others, and the capacity for reflection. Other scholars reiterate these conditions to one degree or another. Solitude, say Christopher Long and James Averill, is "a state characterized by disengagement from the immediate demands of other people – a state of reduced social inhibition and increased freedom to select one's mental or physical activities."[24]

Such definitions are certainly comprehensive enough for my purposes. However, there are subtleties. Koch, for instance, observes that being physically alone doesn't mean you are unattached psychically to absent others. He refers to modes of solitude that involve "diminished engagement" with others, absent or not.[25] This leads him to conclude that social disengagement in one form or another is the most essential action in achieving solitude. That said, John Barbour, a professor of religion, points out that if we require the exclusion of thinking about others – children, lovers, spouses, etc. – as a condition of genuine solitude, few could legitimately be called solitaries. Solitude may involve physical distance from others, but the "geographical requirements for solitude are sometimes measured in inches."[26] In other words, you can be a solitary in a crowd.

What is important to note in all of this is that solitude, unlike loneliness, is a condition and not an emotional state. You can be in a solitary state and feel nothing in particular about it. This also implies, though, that solitude is not necessarily a matter of feeling isolated or alienated, both of which involve the awareness of being separated or different from others. Both alienation and isolation, says Barbour, "require a consciousness of others that solitude lacks." You can be so disengaged from others that you have neither a desire to be with them (as implied by someone who feels isolated) nor any sense of estrangement from them (as implied by alienation).[27] For this reason, we should not identify solitude with negative experiences such as alienation, isolation or loneliness. To associate solitude with negative emotions is to erroneously prejudge the solitary experience.[28]

At the same time, though, Barbour warns it would be equally wrong "to assume that solitude is necessarily a positive or affirmative experience, or that it is the only or most authentic kind of religious experience." Still, he concedes that solitude and spiritual endeavour go hand in hand, and being solitary is often a reflection of spiritual longing. Solitude and spirituality both seek to transcend those ordinary social roles and rituals that may bore, stifle or threaten to overwhelm you.[29] Put differently, solitude expresses our resistance to overbearing social pressures that threaten to crush our self-identity, and is, or can be, a self-chosen condition in pursuit of self-transformation.

Some have certainly made such a claim on behalf of solitude. The philosopher A.N. Whitehead, for example, regarded solitude as the essential condition for a religious sensibility: "Religion is what the individual does with his own solitariness ... [and] if you are never solitary, you are never religious."[30] Theologian Paul Tillich held that solitude is the route to God: "He wants us to penetrate to the boundaries of our being, where the mystery of life appears, and it can only appear in moments of solitude."[31] Similar notions of solitude as a pursuit of self-transcendence are evident in the lives of many solitaries – from St. Anthony and the Desert Fathers to Thomas Merton and Virginia Woolf.

The Desert Fathers' experience of solitude is probably too exotic for my purposes, at least in terms of the modern world, and thus lies beyond the "everyday" orientation of my inquiry. Nonetheless, a few observations about the Desert Fathers pertain to my purposes. First and foremost – and here I'm drawing on the work of two scholars, Helen Waddell and Peter France – we need to shed the notion that men and women such as St. Anthony and John Colobus and Theodora were half-crazed fanatics who imposed such severe ascetic austerities on themselves that they misinterpreted hallucinations as visions of the divine. Some, no doubt, were psy-chologically disturbed, but most of the thousands of monks and hermits who lived in the deserts of the Middle East after St. Anthony's example were, as France puts it, "on a spiritual quest of some kind which they felt they could not pursue in the society of their day." For the Desert Fathers, he says, the solitude of the desert was not so much an escape from society as a means for opening themselves to the presence of the divine without the distractions of others. "To remain silent and alone is to be open to influences that are crowded out of an occupied life." We may have responsibility to oth-ers, but our ability to fulfill those duties may well depend on our self-knowledge.[32] And the gaining of self-knowledge, as most every solitary since the Desert Fathers has taught, often requires solitude, even if only for brief periods.

In this light, the Desert Fathers have to have been emi-nently sane, perhaps more sane than those who stayed in the cities. In seeking to shed a life of distraction, they were trying to live "normal" lives, or, better put, the kind of lives that we wish were "normal." As Helen Waddell states, "Of the depth of their spiritual experience they had little to say: but their every action showed a standard of values that turns the world upside down. It was their humility, their gentle-ness, their heart-breaking courtesy that was the seal of their sanctity to their contemporaries, far beyond abstinence, or miracle, or sign."[33] The solitude of the Desert Fathers, while extreme to a modern technological world that regards safety and comfort as supreme values (and where it's hard to escape satellites and global positioning systems), produced moral and ethical views we would do well to subscribe to today. After twenty years, St. Anthony left the desert healthy, sane and more than willing to help other Christians. The Desert Fathers offer an example of the everyday benefits of solitude. In short, solitude can be the socially responsible thing to do.

This is exactly what one of the great modern solitaries discovered. Admiral Richard E. Byrd was famous for his explorations of the Arctic and Antarctic during the 1920s and '30s. His fame, however, imposed endless demands on his time, constant anxiety about his commitments, and what Byrd referred to as "a crowding confusion" in his life. He spoke of being "beset by the complexities of modern life," of being "caught up in the winds that blow every which way," and longing "desperately for some quiet place where [he could] reason undisturbed and take inventory."[34] In 1934, Byrd decided to spend a winter living alone at an isolated research station in the Antarctic. It was his experiment in solitude.

Byrd's official scientific job was to make meteorological observations, but his deeper inclinations were spiritual. He wanted "to know that kind of experience to the full," to be by himself for a time and to taste peace and quiet and solitude long enough to find out how good they really are. Wasn't a shack in the Antarctic winter a bit extreme? It's a question Byrd asked himself. But he felt he could not just sit in his apartment and rediscover his purpose in life. Genuine solitude was the only solution, as far as he was concerned. Like some desert hermit, Byrd sought solitude in an attempt at self-transcendence and consciousness-expansion through rigorous ascetic discipline, both physical and mental.

Byrd spent six winter months – April to August – in the discipline of solitude. He remained in radio contact with other members of his team at Little America, but otherwise was completely alone. He would remember those first days as among the best of his life. He felt he'd stripped himself of the superfluities of modern life; he was in direct contact with the cosmos. "A man had no need of the world here – certainly not the world of commonplace manners and security ... It occurred to me then that half the confusion in the world comes from not knowing how little we need," he wrote, sounding distinctly Pascalian. All Byrd seemed to need was food, shelter and clothing to sustain himself physically. The natural world sustained him spiritually. "All this was mine: the stars, the constellations, even the earth as it turned on its axis. If great inward peace can exist together, then this, I decided on my first night alone, was what should possess the senses."[35]

At other times, though, particularly in the last two months of his sojourn, the physical conditions were appalling – howling blizzards, months of darkness, and skin-freezing temperatures – and the sense of isolation and the lack of human contact became crushing. At times he felt that nature was a malevolent force focused on destroying him. The frigid temperatures blistered his face and sometimes froze his eyes temporarily shut. He tore the skin off his hands when he inadvertently touched metal surfaces. Psychologically, too, he felt himself eroded by the frightening thoughts, self-doubt and self-recrimination that accompanied him in his isolation.[36]

How did he stay sane? In part, by keeping busy at his work, by not brooding about things over which he had no control. Keeping busy helped him relax. He understood that "an orderly, harmonious routine was the only lasting defense" against his isolation. He set up a day-in-day-out routine of clearing his tunnels, keeping the snow from covering his shack, rearranging supplies, listening to his phonograph, building bookshelves, reading, and testing food recipes. When he found there wasn't enough time in the day to do everything, he left it for the next day. The result was a sense of peace, restfulness and self-control.[37]

Unfortunately, Byrd also suffered the worst danger of solitude – being sick with no one to care for you. The stove in his shack started to leak carbon monoxide. By the time he figured out what was wrong, it was nearly too late. Without its heat he would freeze, but the stove was also slowly poisoning him. Unable to stop the leak, he grew weaker and at times delirious. For two months he struggled to stay alive, refusing to let his crew in Little America know of his plight. Eventually, though, his increasingly erratic radio messages convinced them something was wrong. Disregarding Byrd's orders, they mounted a rescue effort.

Before the rescuers reached the weather station, Byrd underwent what can reasonably be labeled moments of revelation. His months of solitude taught him the value of others. As he later wrote, "To some men sickness brings a desire to crawl into a hole and lick the hurt. It used to be so with me ... [But] I discovered how alone I was; and the realization evoked an indescribable desire to have about me those who knew me best ... I realized how wrong my sense of values had been and how I had failed to see that the simple, homely, unpretentious things of life are the most important."[38]

Through his solitude and physical stress, Byrd discovered a renewed sense of meaning and a deeper appreciation for life. But more interesting, at least from my perspective, is the spiritual benefit Byrd derived from his months of solitude. Four years after his Antarctic ordeal, as he wrote a book recounting his experience, Byrd recalled those moments of wonder and harmony. Threaded through his narrative are moments of epiphany, moments of awe as he watched the light shows of the *aurora australis*, took in the brilliance of the star-painted sky, identified his own feeling of oneness with the world. His diary entry for April 9, 1934, recalls his encounter with the polar night. "These are the best times, the times when neglected senses expand to an exquisite sensitivity. You stand on the Barrier, and simply look and listen and feel ... The afternoon may be so clear that you dare not make a sound, lest it fall to pieces."[39] Five days later, after his "daily walk at 4 p.m. today in 89 degrees of frost," he wrote about the sense of harmony with the universe that he'd attained.

> In that instant I could feel no doubt of man's oneness with the universe. The conviction came that that rhythm was too orderly, too harmonious, too perfect to be a product of blind chance – that, therefore, there must be purpose in the whole and that man was part of that whole and not an accidental offshoot. It was a feeling that transcended reason; that went to the heart of man's despair and found it groundless. The universe was a cosmos, not a chaos; man was rightfully a part of that cosmos as were day and night.[40]

Byrd's experience of cosmic unity sounds similar to what the French writer Romain Rolland refers to as "oceanic feeling." [41] Rolland used the phrase in a letter he wrote on December 5, 1927 to Sigmund Freud. The father of psychoanalysis had written in his book *Civilization and Its Discontents* that feelings of transcendent or cosmic unity were little more than a psychological throwback to the narcissistic union of mother and child. Feelings of being one with the universe were "a first attempt at a religious consolation," or "another way of disclaiming the danger which the ego recognizes as threatening it from the external world."[42] In his letter, Rolland objected to Freud's dismissal of religious feeling as an illusion. "By religious feeling, what I mean – altogether independently of any dogma, any Credo, any organization of the Church, any Holy Scripture, any hope for personal salvation, etc. – is the simple and direct fact of a feeling of 'the eternal' ...

I may add that this 'oceanic' sentiment has nothing to do with my personal yearnings ... [T]he sentiment I experience is imposed on me as fact. It is *a contact*."[43]

Freud was right to be suspicious of "oceanic feelings." We are all subject to wishful illusions. But Freud too easily dismissed experiences like Rolland's and Byrd's. As psychologist Anthony Storr observes, delusions rooted in escapism or wishful thinking tend to be shallow and fleeting. What Byrd and Rolland experienced was far beyond escapist delusion. They experienced mind-altering moments that fundamentally changed their lives. Oceanic experiences, peak experiences, moments of being may be highly subjective – and possibly impossible to adequately measure in terms of their content in an empirical or objective, scientific manner – but to feel at one with the cosmos, even if only transiently, cannot, says Storr, be dismissed "as mere evasions or defences against unwelcome truths."[44] There is too much testimony from too many articulate and intelligent men and women to blithely dismiss these kinds of experience as merely infantile wishful thinking or the fantasy product of a psyche under strain from loneliness and hardship.[45]

So it was with Byrd. Despite his near-death experience – or, perhaps, because of it – Byrd was able to write: "Part of me remained forever at Latitude 80 degrees 08 minutes South: what survived of my youth, my vanity, and certainly my skepticism. On the other hand, I did take away something I had not fully possessed before: appreciation of the sheer beauty and miracle of being alive, and a humble set of values ... Civilization has not altered my ideas. I live more simply now, and with more peace."[46]

Acquiring simplicity is obviously a complicated task. Its achievement, as Byrd's account demonstrates, can be difficult. As Carl Jung once wrote, "How difficult it is to be simple."[47] Plato thought similarly. A life of philosophic contemplation was possible only if a man's wants "were reduced to a minimum."[48] But in a world devoted to *divertissement*, learning to perceive the minimal existence, knowing what constitutes simplicity, can be the work of a lifetime. Yet it seems that once you have acquired that sense of simplicity, it stays with you. Long after leaving the Antarctic, Byrd would remember those first months as moments when he was "conscious only of a mind utterly at peace." Six months of solitude, experiencing the extremes of loneliness, awe and deep peace, taught Byrd "to see and hear, and feel, and touch, and know the sheer beauty and miracle of being alive and being related."[49] Those moments of awe may have been few, but they were sufficient to sustain him spiritually for the rest of his life.

****

I am not, of course, advocating a winter on your own in Antarctica to discover the benefits of solitude. Nor is there a need to go far from home. William Wordsworth, the Romantic poet Byrd quoted, is an example of someone who reaped the benefits of solitude without undue physical hardship or long-distance efforts. Here is Wordsworth lying on his couch, recalling in tranquility his feelings at seeing a field of daffodils:

> For oft, when on my couch I lie
> In vacant or in pensive mood,
> They flash upon that inward eye
> Which is the bliss of solitude;
> And then my heart with pleasure fills,
> And dances with the daffodils.[50]

Like Byrd, Wordsworth regards solitude as the means by which he can uncover that part of himself that is submerged in a tide of worldly concerns.

When from our better selves we have too long
Been parted by the hurrying world, and droop,
Sick of its business, of its pleasures tired,
How gracious, how benign, is Solitude.[51]

Solitude was also necessary for Wordsworth's creative process. Solitude fosters those conditions of reverie and daydreaming that often result in inspirational ideas. Jung refers to these states of consciousness as "active imagination," a near-passive state in which the mind, unshackled from the restraints of daily concerns, relaxes sufficiently for the unconscious to allow ideas and images to emerge into conscious awareness.[52] Wordsworth describes such a state this way:

Musing in solitude, I oft perceive
Fair trains of imagery before me rise,
Accompanied by feelings of delight
Pure, or with not unpleasing sadness mixed;
And I am conscious of affecting thoughts
And dear remembrances …[53]

Furthermore, solitude was the pre-condition for Wordsworth's moments of epiphany, those brief periods when, like Byrd and Rolland, he experienced a sense of oneness with the cosmos. Recalling his youthful periods of being alone on the Cumbrian cliffs, Wordsworth describes a state in which the often-sundered aspects of his psyche came together in a moment of wholeness.

… Alone upon some jutting eminence,
At the first gleam of dawn-light, when the Vale,
Yet slumbering, lay in utter solitude.
How shall I seek the origin? where find
Faith in the marvelous things which then I felt?
Oft in these moments such a holy calm
Would overspread my soul, that bodily eyes

Were utterly forgotten, and what I saw
Appeared like something in myself, a dream,
A prospect in the mind ...
Evening and morning, sleep and waking, thought
From sources inexhaustible, poured forth
To feel the spirit of religious love
In which I walked with Nature.[54]

This is not solitude as consolation, but rather, as scholar George Watson remarks, solitude as "joy in the world of things." In these moments, Wordsworth was "surprised by joy, as if such moments were miraculously visited upon him. But they only come to him when alone, apparently, and his legacy to his century, and beyond, lay here, *in the first valuing of solitude as a condition of joy."*[55]

Wordsworth is not the only writer, of course, to relish solitude. "I only go out to get me a fresh appetite for being alone," Lord Byron wrote in his journal in 1813. John Ruskin recounted in his autobiography, *Praeterita*, published between 1885 and 1889, that as a child he especially enjoyed being alone. "My times of happiness had always been when nobody was thinking of me; and the main discomfort and drawback to all proceedings and designs, the attention and interference of the public, represented by my mother and the gardener. The garden was no waste place for me, because I did not suppose myself an object of interest to either the ants or the butterflies."[56] We see similar notions of solitude in W.B. Yeats' poetry. Here, for example, is Yeat's famous 1893 poem "Lake Isle of Innisfree" with its eremitical theme.

I will arise and go now, and go to Innisfree,
And a small cabin build there, of clay and wattles
    made;
Nine bean rows will I have there, a hive for the honey
    bee,

And live alone in the bee-loud glade.
And I shall have some peace there, for peace comes
  dropping slow,
Dropping from the veils of the morning to where the
  cricket sings;
There midnight's all a glimmer, and noon a purple
  glow,
And evening full of the linnet's wings.
I will arise and go now, for always night and day
I hear lake water lapping with low sounds by the
  shore;
While I stand on the roadway, or on the pavements
  gray,
I hear it in the deep heart's core.[57]

More recent writers share this longing for time alone. Novelist Katherine Mansfield admitted in her journal to great joy in occasionally being a solitary. "The amount of minute and delicate joy I get out of watching people and things when I am alone." Alone in Paris one time, she wrote: "When I see a little girl running by on her heels, like a fowl in the wet, and say 'My dear, there's a Gertie', I laugh and enjoy it as I never would with anybody." Such joy was only possible, it seems, when no others were imposing claims on her attention. "Other people," she declared, "won't stop and look at the things I want to look at."[58] Writer Elizabeth Bowen shared this affinity for solitariness. In her 1960 book, *A Time in Rome*, she wrote, "reprieve from talking is my idea of a holiday." It seems that her ideal company was herself. "At the risk of seeming unsociable, which I am, I admit that I love to be left in a beatific trance when I am in one."[59]

Such examples of solitary experience clearly suggest a link between solitude and creativity. But what are the psychological requirements that make one amenable to being alone in order to perform such work? Anthony Storr, in his study of the psychology of solitude, argues that the ability to be alone is "linked with self-discovery and self-realization; with becoming aware of one's deepest needs, feelings and impulses."[60] From where does this capacity to be alone come? Storr points out that the lives of creative thinkers – he lists Descartes, Newton, Pascal, Spinoza, Schopenhauer, Nietzsche, Kierkegaard, Wittgenstein, Rudyard Kipling and Henry James, among others – often demonstrate that contrary to the popular notion that psychological health depends in the main on our relations with others, many philosophers and writers derive greater satisfaction from their work than from their relationships. This finding fits Storr's thesis that our ability to engage in meaningful work is at least as important to our psychic health as is our ability to attach ourselves to others. No doubt some creative types become introspective and imaginative as a response to a childhood with emotionally detached parents. Nonetheless, Storr maintains that imaginative responses – from philosophic theories to novels – are a reasonable substitute for the love and affection of others. Perhaps nothing can entirely compensate for a lack of intimate attachments in early childhood, but what may have started as an effort to compensate for the deprival of attachments can become, ultimately, its own reward.[61]

Solitude is also a way to detach yourself from your normal social environment, stepping away from those places and circumstances and objects that tend to lock you into a particular role and identity. Those with whom you regularly associate, whether colleagues at work, the doctor and the dentist, even your family, have a particular conception of you that you tend to reinforce as part of ordinary let's-all-get-along social intercourse. Removing yourself from this situation provides the opportunity for examining that identity and, presumably, recasting it if you wish.[62]

But if you can't up and leave, if you don't have a cottage of clay and wattles at some bucolic lakeside, is there another way to foster the mindset of the solitary? Drawing on his research into sensory deprivation, psychologist Peter Suedfeld observes that by curtailing sources of social stimulation, you may begin "to generate (or perceive more sensitively) internal stimuli" – extended daydreams, vivid fantasies, emotional shifts, unusual thoughts or perceptions. Those who aren't prepared for this aspect of solitude may well react to such phenomena with fear – my own experience on the Yukon Mountain is one example – which may result in psychological breakdown. But for those with the internal resources to cope with the withdrawal of the stimulations that keep them locked into debilitating mental and social habits, this altered state of consciousness can be the beginning of genuine self-discovery.[63]

The poet May Sarton offers the example of someone who attempted the difficult task of creating conditions that would enhance her solitude, and thereby serve her creative purposes. Her *Journal of a Solitude* recounts the year she spent in the late 1950s living by herself in the small town of Nelson, New Hampshire, where she'd moved from Cambridge, Massachusetts after the death of her parents. She quickly found that Nelson was not only small in terms of population, but also in cultural and social stimulation. At times, Sarton lamented the lack of cultural sustenance and intellectual conversation. Even her home was unsettling. While it provided "order and beauty," Sarton feared she'd be inadequate to it. "What if I cannot find myself inside it?" she asked.[64]

Yet Sarton, who was prone to depression, also recognized that Nelson was exactly the environment she needed to do her work. "Solitude here is my life. I have chosen it and had better go on making as great riches as possible out of despair," she wrote. Much like Byrd – and, no doubt, for much the same reason – she kept herself busy. Her time was spent working in the garden, arranging flowers and, of course, writing poetry. "My need to be alone is balanced against my fear of what will happen when suddenly I enter the huge empty silence if I cannot find support there. I go up to Heaven and down to Hell in an hour, and keep alive only by imposing upon myself inexorable routines." Sarton even echoes Wordsworth in extolling moments of rest that produce periods of fruitful reverie: "It is then that images float up and then that I plan my work."[65]

She certainly tried to be a solitary, and there were moments when she achieved that condition and the deep awareness that goes with it. Her lyrical descriptions of rooms in the house and their spartan furnishings and the way the sunlight filled those rooms attest to a consciousness that has identified with its surroundings. There is a sense of peaceful and purposive solitude in this description of being inside while it storms outside. "Outside it is a milky world, snow driving past the windows incessantly in horizontal waves ... But I am truly in Heaven. There are charming 'February' daffodils out in a pale green pot on my desk, tulips on the mantel a subtle apricot color veined in yellow with dark purple hearts. I have lighted the fire in here because the wind creeps in and I feel the chill. I have Beethoven sonatas (*Pastoral* and *Les Adieux*) on the record player. And now to work!"[66]

At other times, though, there were too many visitors, too many poetry readings, too many letters to write. She was often exhausted at the effort of keeping others' lives from overwhelming her own. "There is no space for what wells up from the subconscious; those dreams and images live in deep still water and simply submerge when the day gets scattered."[67]

Sarton's journal is a literary work, like her many novels and poems, so we shouldn't assume everything she says is exactly what happened. Nevertheless, the journal retains an emotional honesty that speaks to the difficulty in achieving the kind of solitude Sarton thought she needed. Eventually the reader realizes that Sarton's insomnia and bouts of depression are rooted in an unworkable relationship, which is unsatisfactory because of her temperament and desire to be alone for the sake of her work. By the end of the book, with the decision to end the relationship made, Sarton had found herself. She had come home to her house. The last line in the journal reads: "Once more the house and I are alone."[68]

John Barbour regards Sarton as an example of the healing power of solitude. Her account of aloneness, he says, moves gradually to an act of self-acceptance that culminates in the recognition that there is nothing wrong with her wanting to be a solitary, and no need to apologize for it. Sarton understands that especially for a woman artist, solitude may be the only way to get her work done. Thus, her journal shows that solitude is "a constant challenge and an opportunity," as well as the necessary if insufficient condition for creative work.[69] For those like Sarton who want solitude so they can live as they wish, having others around can be a constraint on freedom and therefore on the quality of solitude. The mere presence of others requires us to adapt our actions with theirs, thereby disrupting our solitude and the creative work for which it is intended.

You can see this solitude-for-the-sake-of-creativity attitude in novelist Virginia Woolf and philosopher Ludwig Wittgenstein. While unlike each other in most ways, they share this desire for solitude. Woolf, like Sarton, wanted solitude for her writing, and saw her home as a realm of privacy where she could indulge in the daydreaming and reverie necessary to her craft. This point of view comes through in one of her most famous books, *A Room of One's Own*, with its theme of a woman's need to have a private place where she can be free of the demands of domesticity and express her own creative thoughts. Writing, she insists, depends on your physical surroundings. "A woman must have money and a room of her own if she is to write fiction," she writes, adding that imaginative works "are not spun in mid-air by incorporeal creatures, but are the works of suffering human beings, and are attached to grossly material things, like health and money and the houses we live in."[70]

But even when surrounded by others, Woolf's characters – and, presumably, herself – found ways to achieve solitude. Mrs. Ramsay, the main character in *To the Lighthouse*, disappeared into herself while knitting.

> For now she need not think of anybody. She could be by herself, by herself ... All the being and doing, expansive, vocal, evaporated; and one shrunk, with a sense of solemnity, to being oneself, a wedged-shaped core of darkness, something invisible to others. Although she continued to knit, and sat upright, it was thus that she felt herself; and this self, having shed its attachments was free for the strangest adventures. When life sank down for a moment, the range of experience seemed limitless.[71]

Wittgenstein, meanwhile, regularly isolated himself from society for long periods of time for the sake of his work. In 1913, while attending Cambridge University, he decided he needed some solitude. He headed for a tiny village on a Norwegian fjord that he had once visited. His friend and teacher, the philosopher Bertrand Russell, thought the isolation would drive him insane. Wittgenstein, however, survived two years in a little hut on a mountainside near Skjolden, a village on the end of the Lustrafjord in the Sogne Fjord district, about 250 kilometres northeast of Bergen. By all accounts, he enjoyed it immensely. He particularly liked the simplicity of the place, which contrasted sharply with the mountains-out-of-molehills narcissism of academic life in Cambridge. It was a place where, as biographer Ray Monk writes, "he could be himself without the strain of upsetting or offending people. It was a tremendous liberation. He could devote himself entirely to himself."[72]

Wittgenstein certainly thrived on seclusion. The peacefulness and beauty of the region were inspirational. He spent his days on long, solitary walks that sometimes resulted in moments of euphoria. He built himself a small hut. "It was perhaps the only time in his life when he had no doubts that he was in the right place, doing the right thing."[73] In fact, the time Wittgenstein spent in Norway was the most productive in his life. Alone, Wittgenstein produced the notes that would form the core of his most important works, including the *Tractatus Logico-Philosophicus*, *Notes on Logic*, *Philosophical Investigations*, *Remarks on the Foundation of Mathematics*, and *Culture and Value*.[74] Wittgenstein was not a complete solitary, to be sure. He came to know many of the villagers and learned to speak Norwegian. Nonetheless, as his biographer points out, he effectively abandoned the society of England, and thus escaped the social constraints and obligations imposed by that society. Most importantly, while he corresponded with colleagues in Cambridge, his distance from them allowed him to have "some thoughts that were entirely his own."[75]

When World War I began, Wittgenstein enlisted in the Austrian army. Some scholars have argued that while he may have been trying to become another kind of person, he also, strangely enough, looked to soldiering as a way to find solitude. The problem was that in the army he was seldom alone. Despite this situation, Wittgenstein "created private space by distancing himself from his military companions," psychiatrist Arnold Modell observes. Even when under fire, "he preferred to be in a solitary and dangerous position rather than in the company of his comrades, for whom he felt nothing but hatred and contempt." And he kept up his writing, at least making notes for the *Tractatus*.[76]

Trench life is probably not the ideal place for solitude, so what is most telling about Wittgenstein's situation is his effort to create a private space even in the worst possible conditions.[77] Like Woolf's character Mrs. Ramsay, Wittgenstein was able to create moments of solitude even when surrounded by others. This is an important lesson to learn. As philosopher Philip Koch says, solitude is possible even in the presence of others "provided that our minds are disengaged from them." Appropriately enough, he calls this capacity for psychologically detaching yourself from social situations "disengaged solitude."[78] Not everybody can escape to the Antarctic. Not everybody has a cabin on lake. Not everybody has a room of their own. But that does not mean the madding crowd will always surround you, or that you can never enjoy moments of solitude.

We all learn to put up psychological barriers when physical barriers no longer suffice. I can lose myself in my writing even in a crowded bar or café. It's as though the presence of others forces the mind to work harder to create a zone of disengagement to fulfill my purposes – getting words down on paper. A good example of this kind of disengaged solitude comes from novelist Ernest Hemingway in his autobiographical sketch, *A Moveable Feast*, where he describes himself trying to write in a Paris café on a cold winter's morning. At first he is fully aware of the café and the other patrons, including a pretty, fresh-faced girl who, he surmises, was waiting for her lover. He tries to focus on the writing, and soon "entered far into the story and was lost in it." It was almost as if the words were writing themselves, he says. "I did not look up nor know anything about the time nor think where I was nor order any more rum St. James." The next time Hemingway looks up – returns to café society – the story is done and he realizes with a small shock of sadness that the girl with the crow-black hair is gone and he'll never see her again (although he will always remember her).[79]

What these examples suggest is that disengagement is the essence of the experience of solitude. You don't have to be alone to be a solitary, but you do need to be able to disengage. There can be "deep" disengagement like Byrd's, or more "shallow" disengagement such as Hemingway's and Woolf's. In the former, it seems, you are more likely to open yourself to Rolland's "oceanic feelings." In the latter, you may enjoy fleeting moments of absorption in reverie.

I have had experiences of both the shallow and the deep (some of which are related in these essays). I have spent short periods at Zen Buddhist retreats where hours are devoted to meditating (or trying to). Once the body has adjusted to sitting cross-legged for long terms of time (a painful learning experience, I can tell you), the mind turns inward and sinks into itself. I was never sure I was meditating properly, but I still recall the sense of slow disappearance, as though I was moving down a long hallway, leaving the world behind at the far end. When the meditating was good, the hallway would stretch on for a long ways and the world would get farther and farther away. Yet I was never so far down that hallway that my awareness of the world – the presence of other meditators, the Zen master's slow pacing between the rows of practitioners, the quiet creak of the wooden floor, the pungent drift of incense – completely disappeared. I oscillated between shallower and deeper moments of disengagement. Sometimes, I went a long way down the hallway. At other times, I could barely make it across the threshold.

****

Thomas Merton, one of the great solitaries of the twentieth century, had similar difficulties. Merton sought solitude, but he also faced the demands and lures of the world. He spent twenty-seven years as a member of the Cistercians, a strictly enclosed order of Christian monks, but also became, as *Time* magazine put it, "'the most publicly visible Christian contemplative since Simon Stylites.'"[80]

Merton's predicament points up the contradictions faced by those who seek a spiritual life in a society devoted to material diversions. We may want solitude, yet we also want others in our lives. We want our autonomy, but we don't want to be alone. We need others to divert us from our existential solitude. If we don't have others available, modern technology makes it possible to enjoy the ersatz companionship offered by the entertainment industry. Television, the Internet, video games, social media: these allow us to feel socially attached even if we are physically isolated. Our *divertissements* ensure that we avoid active self-reflection, avoid being alone with our own thoughts.

Merton spent a lifetime struggling with these conundrums. He captured our largely unthinking devotion to diversion in a thirty-page essay entitled *Notes for a Philosophy of Solitude*. The purpose of all our diversionary ideologies and technologies is, he says,

> to anesthetize the individual as an individual, and to plunge him in the warm, apathetic stupor of a collectivity, which, like himself, wishes to remain, amused. The bread and circuses which fulfill this function may be blatant and absurd, or they may assume a hypocritical air of intense seriousness. Our own society prefers the absurd. But our absurdity is blended with a certain hardheaded, fully determined seriousness with which we devote ourselves to the acquisition of money, to the satisfaction of our appetite for status.[81]

Merton's observation highlights both the benefits and the ultimate purpose of solitude, a purpose that goes beyond notions of self-attunement or creativity even as it includes them. Merton's point is that we are all solitaries in a fundamental – or existential, as the philosophers say – sense. The everyday get-and-spend whirl of job and family and society distract us so completely that we are seldom conscious of this existential condition. Indeed, society seems deliberately designed to keep us from reflecting on fundamental realities. The world is literally too much with us (often out of necessity) and so we are alienated from ourselves, abstracted from those deeper structures of being that can, if we learn of them, provide us with a more substantive sense of meaning and purpose than what is offered by the superficial awards of society.

Ideally, Merton thought we needed solitude to transcend the claims of the world. But he also recognized that not everyone is able – or willing – to completely withdraw from society's "illusions and fictions," including himself. Besides, withdrawing from society merely for the sake of being alone "leads to a sick solitude, without meaning and without fruit."[82] Does that mean the benefits of solitude are not available to those who, for whatever reason, still have duties and obligations attached to their social role and continue to derive meaning and value from that function? Not necessarily. As Koch and others have argued, there are different kinds of solitude, and different styles of solitude, too. Solitude is not something to be dismissed as impractical, available only to those who want to be monks or hermits. Nor is it without its difficulties and moral hazards.

Merton was careful to point out that solitude is not a solution to life's cares and concerns. Solitude itself can be problematic. In the first place, you have to deal with "the disconcerting task of facing and accepting one's own absurdity."

When you acknowledge that much of the apparent meaning and purpose of your life is tied up with diversions of one sort or another, and then when you begin to consciously examine those distractions – or at least recognize them as distractions – you find yourself suddenly confronted with "an abyss of irrationality, confusion, pointlessness, and ... apparent chaos."[83] You may have felt vaguely dissatisfied with your life before, but now, in the full awareness of its *divertissements*, you are out there on the high wire without any delusory nets to catch you.

For Merton, this was a moment of great moral danger, but also the moment of great spiritual possibility. Solitude can foster greater self-knowledge, creativity and an appreciation of nature, but, ultimately, for Merton, "only the right understanding of solitude ... could save it from being simply a refined form of self-indulgence." For him, the ultimate purpose of solitude is the possibility it presents for opening yourself to God's grace.[84] Merton was particularly concerned with the motivation for seeking solitude. Was it egoism or an authentic call from God? The first difficulty facing any would-be solitary is being sure that the desire for solitude is not merely another form of illusion.

Merton distinguishes between those solitaries who genuinely seek transcendence and those who merely want to feel good about themselves. These latter "individualists," as Merton calls them, seek only "a heightened self-consciousness, a higher form of diversion." They have not so much turned away from the society of diversion but kept it as the horizon against which they measure their own spiritual achievement. Such individuals are not seeking a hidden metaphysical reality but "the smugness of self-congratulations." In effect, their solitude is a new illusion, "a more secret and more perfect diversion." What they undertake is not the hermit's struggle for truth "but the noisy self-congratulations and self-pity of the infant in the crate." They want the warmth of the womb, not chill winds of the desert night. Thus, Merton warns would-be solitaries against spiritual narcissism, the "world of private fictions and self-constructed delusions."[85]

How does a would-be solitary avoid falling into self-constructed delusions? First and foremost, I suggest, is being aware that our existential condition is fundamentally that of being solitary. This was the lesson I learned from Loren Eiseley. At the core of human experience is the mystery of our self-conscious mortality. Unlike animals, humans know they will someday die. Some, like theologian Paul Tillich, argue that the experience of death is the consummate demonstration of our ultimate aloneness. "We remain alone in the anticipation of our death. No communication with others can remove this loneliness, as no presence of others in the actual hour of our dying can hide the fact that it is *our* death, and *our* death *alone*, that we die ... We are deprived of all things in the encounter in which we forgot our being alone."[86] Who, Tillich asks, can stand this aloneness?

He answers his own question: "Loneliness can be conquered only by those who can bear solitude."[87] If we have courage, we learn that our solitude is, paradoxically, the source of life's juice and joy. It is because we know our aloneness, because we live in and with our solitude, that our lives can be so achingly meaningful. Consciousness of time and the transience of life separates mankind from the animals, giving us our self-awareness. The knowledge of our individual solitude makes us human. But as humans we cannot help but seek the satisfaction of our desires, including the desire for immortality and the mitigation of our solitude. Neither longing, however, can be satisfied as long as we remain human. I imagine that even if it were possible to eliminate aloneness by bringing two consciousnesses together, ridding ourselves of the physical separateness imposed by skin and bone, the results would be less than satisfying.[88] We should not regard solitude as a psychological symptom that needs to be overcome in order to live untroubled, stress-free lives. It is because we are solitaries that we are most human. While we are limited by our bodies, it is through our bodies that we know what it is to love another, whether our spouse, our children or our friends. How could you possibly love a child who was not separate from you? Could a man really love a woman (or vice versa) if she is not a solitary like himself? "The wonder of friendship and the magic of love depend on the separateness of friends and lovers," says philosopher Ilham Dilman. "Without it, where the other person becomes a mere shadow or extension of one, one only loves oneself in her ... For there to be real contact each person must have an independent identity ... Human separateness [is] the space in which personal bonds may be forged."[89]

Solitude, in other words, is the necessary prior condition for any togetherness. Only in perceiving and accepting your solitude do you learn genuine companionship. Solitude, thus, makes it possible to discover not only your deeper self, but also your deeper connections to others. Koch sums up the paradox well when he writes that we are all "touched by some dim sense of the nourishing and fulfilling power of solitary spiritual transcendence." This is the common human plight: the "human Way" of responding to that plight is neither to deny other people in your life nor to abandon the search for self-transcendence. Rather, it is to follow a path that traverses both landscapes.[90]

Such judgment brings me back to Merton. Scholars who have studied Merton's life and thought point out that he struggled throughout his monastic life to balance his longing for solitude and his need to connect with others. One evening in September 1938 when Merton was twenty-three, he sat alone in his New York home reading a biography of the poet Gerard Manley Hopkins. "Something began to stir within me, something began to push me, to prompt me. It was a movement that spoke like a voice. 'What are you waiting for?' it said. 'Why are you sitting here? Why do you still hesitate? You know what you ought to do, why don't you do it?'" Unable to sit quietly any longer, Merton grabbed his coat and went outside into the rainy evening. Walking on a sidewalk towards Broadway "everything inside me began to sing — to sing with peace, to sing with strength, and to sing with conviction."[91] Two months later, Merton was baptized in the Roman Catholic Church.

In his study of Merton, author Peter France points out that most of us regard that inner voice as little more than vague and ambiguous promptings rooted in emotional concerns and instinctive appetite. Merton, however, knew that the inner voice he heard was not his own, that it came from a source beyond himself, and that it spoke with an authority that overwhelmed his free will.[92] He understood in his moment of conversion that he was "not his own," that he belonged to something greater than his egocentric, rational self. And for the rest of his life he continually sought solitude in order to hear that voice again.

Merton's understanding of solitude is of crucial importance to those who might also wish to hear that voice. As various biographers point out, Merton's views on solitude changed over the years. In 1948, for example, seven years after he entered the Trappist monastery of Gethsemani in Kentucky, home to nearly 300 cloistered monks, he wrote about how he'd discovered that solitude was "not something you must hope for in the future. Rather, it is a deepening of the present and unless you look for it in the present you will never find it."[93]

He eventually found support for his hermitic inclinations in the writings of and about the fourth-century Desert

Fathers. They showed him that his longing for solitude was not an egocentric desire to escape the social realm, but rather a journey of self-discovery that allowed for a greater understanding of and compassion for the world. In this light, Merton could argue that the hermitic life had much to recommend it to the modern world:

> The Coptic hermits who left the world as though escaping from a wreck did not merely intend to save themselves. They knew that they were helpless to do any good for others so long as they floundered about in the wreckage … This is their paradoxical lesson for our time … Ours is certainly a time for solitaries and for hermits. But merely to reproduce the simplicity, austerity and prayer of these primitive souls is not a complete or satisfactory answer. We must transcend them, and all those who, since their time, have gone beyond the limits which they set. We must liberate ourselves, in our own way, from involvement in a world that is plunging to disaster.[94]

Merton lived a monastic life where prayer and contemplation are obviously the order of the day. Most of us, however, live in the get-and-spend world, raising families, paying bills and trying to do meaningful work. Does Merton really have anything to say to us in the everyday world? While his thought on solitude was not especially new, he reformulated ancient traditions of solitude, both Christian and non-Christian, in a way that made them relevant to the modern experience.[95] In doing so he showed that there is more to life than career-pathing and amusing ourselves to death. He shows that each of us needs to develop the reflective and spiritual side of our nature if our lives are to have more meaning than that of a statistical input for the consumer society. Through a period of solitude, our lives can take on new meaning.

Behind Merton's claim on behalf of solitude is his judgment that we constantly face the consequences of modern nihilism: "the inescapable specters of boredom, futility, and madness." In a healthy and well-organized society, we cope with the symptoms of nihilism through meaningful work, our love for others and the development of a substantive and integrated interior life. Someone who enjoys meaningful work and the satisfactions of meaningful relationships seldom feels bored or regards life as absurd. In a disordered society, a society in crisis, work is often absurd, love reduced to rivalries of power, and pathological boredom the product of pointless activity. In such circumstances we need to develop our inner life. This requires periods of solitude. "[W]e need to recognize that the gift of solitude is not ordered to the acquisition of strange contemplative powers," says Merton, "but first of all to the recovery of one's deep self, and to the renewal of an authenticity which is twisted out of shape by the pretentious routines of a disordered togetherness." In an age of disenchantment solitude helps us to realize "the ordinary values of life lived with a minimum of artificiality."[96]

The achievement of solitude, its genuine value, is that it helps you to disengage, intellectually, psychologically and spiritually, from the distorting diversions of society, and thereby discover (or perhaps recover) your truest nature.[97] That said, the discovery of the solitary life does not imply abandoning the active life or turning away from the world, according to Merton. The discovery of your essential solitude can make you a more worthy person. Karl Marx taught that the purpose of thought is to change the world, not simply understand it. For Merton, though, anyone attempting "to act and do things for others or for the world without deepening his own self-understanding, freedom, integrity and capacity to love, will not have anything to give others." Such a person will communicate little more than "the contagion of his own obsessions, his aggressiveness, his ego-centered ambitions, his delusions about ends and means, his doctrinaire prejudices and ideas."[98] In other words, solitude leads the solitary back to the social, but, unlike socially minded Marxists, solitaries are better able to cope with the world's disorder.

Indeed, as far as Merton was concerned, solitude is essential for society. Solitude provides men and women with the kind of detachment necessary for accurately perceiving society's myths and illusions. Such perception helps people seek the correction of social ills without succumbing to the illusion that there is some great fix that will create the just society. Solitude serves as a reminder against the superficial temptations of society and the diversions of its frenetic fantasies. "Withdrawal from other men can be a special form of love for them. It should never be a rejection of man or of his society. But it may well be a quiet and humble refusal to accept the myths and fictions with which social life cannot help but be full – especially today. To despair of the illusions and facades which man builds around himself is certainly not to despair of man. On the contrary, it may be a sign of love and of hope."[99] Thus, solitude reflects a quiet protest against and an alternative to the fictions to which so many devote their lives. The solitary is a witness against society's failings. He or she may well inspire others to protest those fictions by providing them with an alternative perspective on the world, but that is not the purpose of solitude.

While Merton was aware of the social benefits of solitude, he also knew its moral dangers. Solitude, he said, can reveal your own dishonesty, bring out your own "madnesses." Even if you prefer solitude, it can destroy you if you seek it only for yourself. Nor is solitude a way to escape yourself, a means for unburdening yourself of life's difficulties. You can flee the world in search of solitude, but you still take the world with you. For a man to lock himself up in his own selfishness is to put himself into "a position where the evil within him will either possess him like a devil or drive him out of his head."[100]

It is also dangerous to seek solitude simply because you want to be alone. Solitude is not a kind of rebellion against the world. Rather, it is "a matter of rigorous spirituality." Solitude is an interior exploration intended to heal the explorer. The danger lies in the solitary diverting himself with "a fiction worse than all the others," such that he becomes "a more insane and self-opinionated liar than the worst of them." Solitaries are well aware of the flaws and failures of others because they are aware of those flaws and failures in themselves. They know that each of us is alone in an existential sense, but most of us avoid awareness of this condition by grabbing at the world's *divertissements*. And the world is such that these diversions allow us to avoid our own solitary company most of the time. The real difference between the solitary and others is not that the solitary is unsocial while everyone else is social, but rather that the solitary recognizes his or her essential solitude while most everyone else tries to mask it with symbols of diversion.[101]

For Merton, there can be no genuine maturity, no potential for discovering the depths of the inner life without solitude. But he is nuanced on this point, too. Our deep self is not something to be possessed after a period of inner struggle. It is not ours to possess, like some thing or object. Certainly, the shallow 'I' of individuality that the modern world teaches us to worship can be possessed and pandered to – think, for example, of all those notions of self-esteem, self-fulfillment and self-realization (as distinct from self-awareness) promoted by the therapeutic industry. But in Merton's view, these efforts cannot reach the deeper self. "The deep 'I' of the spirit, of solitude and of love cannot be 'had', possessed, developed, perfected. It can only *be* and *act* according to the deep inner laws which are not of man's contriving but which come from God."[102] In short, solitaries learn that we are not our own.

Merton believed that the ultimate purpose of solitude and contemplation was the awareness of God. But even short of that awareness, he saw value in modest attempts at reflective solitude. When he spoke of the contemplative or solitary life, he did not necessarily mean the cloistered, monastic life, the institutionally organized life of prayer, although that was no doubt his ideal. Rather, he urged the seeking of "a special dimension of inner discipline and experience, a certain integrity and fullness of personal development, which are not compatible with a purely external, alienated, busy-busy existence." The fostering of solitary life does not have to be at odds or in conflict with our active life in the world, but unless we acquire a deeper understanding of ourselves through the exploration of our inner ground, we tend to live superficial and deceptive lives, lives given over to diversion. The discovery of the contemplative life through solitude is a matter of self-discovery.[103]

****

I could have used Merton's understanding of solitude that summer in the Yukon. Back then, in my twenties, I had not read any of his work (and probably wouldn't have paid attention if I had read it). Only in later years did I read *The Seven Storey Mountain*, his account of why and how he became a monk, and some of his more contemplative works. I started to read more deeply his views on solitude. (My favourite is *Contemplation in a World of Action*.) I am now old enough to better appreciate his appreciation of the gifts of solitude. Indeed, while I was researching this chapter I came across a moment of epiphany – a glimpse of the underglimmer – in one of his journals that provided me with what I have come to regard as a "retrospective epiphany," a topic I shall address in Chapter Five.

On the evening of September 6, 1965, looking out the window of his hermitage, Thomas Merton saw a red doe in the field. He watched the animal through his binoculars. A stag and a second doe joined her. "They were not afraid," Merton later wrote. "They looked at me from time to time. I watched their beautiful running, their grazing. Every movement was completely lovely." Then came Merton's epiphany. "The thing that struck me most – when you look at them directly and in movement, you see what the primitive cave painters saw. Something you never see in a photograph. It is most awe-inspiring. The *muntu* or the 'spirit' is shown in the running of the deer. The 'deerness' that sums up everything and is sacred and marvelous."[104]

When I read that passage I was jolted by the memory of my summer in the Yukon mountains. For a brief moment it was 1976 again and I relived my own encounter with the "spirit" of something other than myself.

About a week after my Night of the Bear (real or not), the rest of the crew arrived. Less than a dozen people, but I resented their presence. I had grown used to my solitude. They were noisy and distracting, an intrusion on my mountain. Luckily, I could sometimes flee their company. On weekends, I got the cook to fix me up with some sandwiches and a thermos of coffee. I packed a knapsack with a few survival necessities – rain poncho, hand axe, insect repellant, etc. – and grabbed the Winchester and headed off on a hike for the day.

I enjoyed my solitary days. I would walk hard for a couple of hours. Then I would take a half-hour break, enjoying a cigarette and a cup of coffee and maybe some of the apple pie the cook had baked. Then I'd hike for another hour or so. Most of the time I stuck to the alpine meadows or the upper slopes of the mountain foothills. The river valley was full of mosquitoes and, in late summer, blackflies, which can drive you mad as they cloud around your head. (You end up chewing on a few whenever you open your mouth.) By mid-afternoon I figured I'd done enough for the day, and would slowly head back to camp. If I was in no rush, I'd find a quiet spot somewhere along the way where I could sit out of the wind and read my book or write letters to England (things with my girlfriend hadn't fallen apart yet) or just watch the mountains and the sky and daydream. Sometimes I'd find a spot in a copse of aspen or against a boulder on some mountain slope where I could have a nap, covering myself with the rain poncho to keep off the mosquitoes.

On one weekend walk, I came down a mountainside to a foothills meadow with a creek running across it. The creek dropped into the valley to feed the river, but here on the meadow it ran slow and quiet with a cheerfully subdued gurgling. I found a copse of aspen that stretched along the creek where I could shelter and look down the sloping meadow to the jack pines and black spruce that formed a green wall at the edge of the valley. The meadow was thick with Arctic lupine and moss campion. I dropped my pack, spread the poncho on the ground at the base of a couple of trees, poured myself a final cup of still-warm coffee and enjoyed a cigarette.

It was a pleasant spot. The day had been hot and sunny. The trees provided welcome shade. I leaned back against a tree trunk, taking in the burbling creek, the somnolent buzz of insects in the still air, the smell of flowers. I stubbed out my cigarette butt on my boot, shredded the remnants of tobacco, and tucked the filter in my pant cuff for later disposal. I swallowed the last of the coffee, screwed the cup back on the thermos, stowed the thermos in my pack, and then lay the pack down to use as a pillow. I stretched out on the poncho, staring up through the fluttering leaves to the blue sky, waiting for sleep to claim me.

I woke to the nearby sounds of splashing. I immediately thought of bears, of course. I grabbed the rifle and rolled as quietly as I could onto my stomach, and peered over the edge of my pack through a gap between two tree trunks. No bears. But no more than fifty feet away were a moose and her calf at the edge of the creek, front legs bent and heads lowered as they drank. As silently as I could, I pulled my binoculars out of the knapsack and trained them on the animals: the coarse, tattered-looking coat of the cow, the slobber from her mouth, a raw-looking, partially healed gash, maybe two feet long, across her right flank. (Wolves? Grizzly?) By comparison, the calf looked beautiful, its coat glossy with newness, its legs spindly like a gawky teenage girl's.

I don't think I moved or made a noise, but the cow must have caught my scent, because she suddenly raised her head from the water, ears pricked as she stared in my direction. Her huge face filled the lenses of the binoculars. For the first time in my life I stared into the eyes of an alien creature. It was spooky. I kept still. The cow did, too, expect for the side-to-side sway of her shaggy head. We must have watched each other for half a minute. Then she made some kind of coughing sound. The calf stumbled to her side. I still didn't move. The cow shook her head, snorting, one of her front hooves pawing at the stony edge of the creek. I thought maybe she was going to charge. But then, still shaking her head, she backed away, nudging the calf up the slope above the creek towards the line of trees. The cow turned, keeping the calf on her far side. They trotted into the trees together and disappeared. I felt strangely sad to see them go.

I strolled over to where the cow and calf had stood, but there was nothing much to see besides their hoofprints in the mud at the creek edge. It was time for me to go, too.

I looked around. It somehow seemed important to remember the place as best I could. I felt gratitude, as though I'd been given the privilege of witnessing a rare event. Perhaps I had. If I hadn't been alone the cow would never have come so close, or, rather, allowed me to be so close. Solitude had granted me a close-up, unguarded glimpse of another species.

When, years later, I read Merton's story of his encounter with the deer, I understood what he meant: "The deer reveals to me something essential, not only in itself, but also in myself. Something beyond the trivialities of my everyday being, my individual existence. Something profound. That face of that which is in the deer and in myself."[105] A spirit, perhaps? A *muntu*? We may be solitaries, but we are not alone. I would like to think of that moment in the Yukon as another gift of solitude.

FIVE

THE REIGN OF WONDER
Re-enchanting the World

*Wonder ... is the basis of Worship: the reign of wonder is perennial,
indestructible in Man.*

   – Thomas Carlyle, *Sartor Resartus*[1]

*We need so to view the world as to combine an idea of wonder and an
idea of welcome. We need to be happy in this wonderland without being
merely comfortable.*

   – G.K. Chesteron, *Orthodoxy*[2]

O n impulse, I eased my foot off the accelerator,
popped the gearshift into neutral, and let the
pickup drift to the shoulder of the road. I was driving on the Klondike Highway just beyond Carcross, heading
for Whitehorse after a week's shift at the construction site
where I had a job in the summer of 1970. It was late August
and the sun was low in the western sky. As the truck slowed
to a stop I wound the window down and shut off the engine.
The crunch of tires on the gravel was strangely loud in the
twilight. I sat for a moment, left arm draped out the open
window, staring down the road through the bug-splattered
windshield. The shadows of black spruce trees fell in long,
spiky silhouettes across the highway. Shallow pools of water

left over from the rain earlier in the day shimmered on the road in the distance.

I opened the door, stepped out of the truck and walked across the road. My boots crunched on the gravel. On the other side lay a meadow patched with lupine and fireweed, sloping down to the broad rolling plain of the Watson River valley. Most of the valley was in shadow, but the higher knolls caught the sun in the crowns of the trees, creating scattered islands of light. On the far side of valley, the round-shouldered silhouette of the Grey Ridge Mountains bulked dark against a pale sky. Directly below me was Emerald Lake, the evening light playing across the lake's oblong surface.

Emerald Lake is famous in the Yukon. A geological anomaly gives it an iridescent glow of turquoise and green in certain angles of light. From the height of the road, in the half-light of a Yukon summer night, the lake shone and rippled like a multi-coloured veil stirring in the breeze. A green-roofed cabin occupied a clearing on a small rise. A light burned in the big window that looked out over the lake.

The sight was familiar. During my high school years in Whitehorse, we used to pile into one car or another on weekends and drive to Carcross, where we inevitably ended up at Carcross Hotel to shoot pool, play the jukebox in the small bar and try to persuade the hotel's most famous resident, Polly the Parrot, to have a beer and indulge in a few profanities.[3] We sometimes stopped on our way back to Whitehorse to admire the lake and envy the cabin's owner for living in such an idyllic setting. This particular summer I drove the road between Carcross and Whitehorse at least twice a week, going back and forth to the Venus Mine site south of Carcross, where I was working. I always noticed Emerald Lake as I drove by – and still felt a twinge of envy about the cabin – but until this Friday night I hadn't stopped.

I don't know what made me stop. I pulled a pack of cigarettes from my shirt pocket, extracted a cigarette and lit it, then watched the tendrils of exhaled smoke drift away and disappear. I toed the ground with my boot. What was I waiting for? Why wasn't I moving? I don't think I consciously asked myself those questions, but I remember feeling as if I was waiting for something to happen. I finished the cigarette, extinguished it on the sole of my boot, and let the wind carry the last shreds of tobacco away. And still I waited.

Studying the colours on the lake, I grew more aware of my surroundings – the ticking of the cooling engine, the chorus of cicadas, a breeze lifting the hair from my shoulders, the last warmth of the sun. But it wasn't simply a matter of heightened senses. It was as if I were discovering the world around me for the first time. The familiar was new and strange. I heard a birdcall coming from the meadow below me, startling in its singularity. A gust of wind shook the fireweed. And then, out of the blue, the damp air wrapped around me, compressing and pressing until, suddenly, the pressure released and everything was … wonder-filled.

Even now that's the only word I can use to describe that moment. One minute I was scraping meaningless patterns in the gravel, thinking nothing in particular. The next thing I knew, everything – lake, road, trees, flowers, mountains, sky – stood out in sharp relief, vivid, detailed, intense. The sky was brighter, the mountains bulkier, the fireweed a deeper purple, the rain-wet highway shinier. The cicadas' song reached a crescendo. And the lake shifted its colours like a gemstone catching the light. For a few seconds, the world shimmered as though something rippled beneath the surface. The ordinary world was unexpectedly extraordinary.

My words are no doubt inadequate. But then words can rarely convey the lived experience of wonder. I don't think that what I experienced was mystical revelation, at least as far as I understand such things. There was no soul-expanding, life-altering awareness of a divine presence. What I felt, though, was an intense and sudden spike of self-awareness. I was watching myself watching myself watch the world. The sensation lasted maybe ten or fifteen seconds at most. I could feel it going away, a kind of return of heaviness, a return to earth. Eventually, I was stranded in the familiar again.[4]

I've often wondered why I remember those few moments above Emerald Lake so vividly. As I said, the spell of wonder lasted for only a short time. The intensity of the Emerald Lake epiphany, as I've labelled it, is not there in memory, but the experience continues to ripple through my life like a stone thrown into a pond. In retrospect, I've come to think the experience subtly shifted the landscape of my life, sending me down a path I had not thought to take or had not even known existed until that moment. Looking back across the years, searching the past for patterns of meaning and coherence, I sometimes wonder if my life would have been different if I hadn't stopped that warm August night on the Klondike Highway.[5]

Of course, such thoughts occur only in hindsight. In the summer of 1970, not even out of my teens, I wasn't paying all that much attention to visionary experience. I was still focused on sensual experiences. When the shimmer subsided, when the strange became familiar again, I returned to the pickup and drove on to Whitehorse, more or less dismissing the incident with a metaphorical shake of my head as some kind of aberration, a minor psychic hiccup. Yet, the first ripple of Emerald Lake rolled over me that fall at the University of Victoria. I signed up for my first philosophy course. I remember in one lecture the professor quoting something from Martin Heidegger that included the phrase "The sheer Is-ness of Being." Those brief moments on the Carcross road came rushing back. Yes, I thought, that's it, that's what

I experienced – the sheer presence of being, the astonished awareness that there is anything rather than nothing.

There were other ripples, too, to remind me of my Emerald Lake epiphany. About a year later, researching an essay on the Irish novelist James Joyce, I found a copy of Morris Beja's study, *Epiphany in the Modern Novel*, on the shelves of the McPherson Library. Discussing Joyce's novel *Stephen Hero*, an early draft of *A Portrait of the Artist as a Young Man*, Beja relates how the book's main character, Stephen Hero, undergoes an experience of heightened awareness that he calls an epiphany – in Beja's words, "sudden illuminations produced by apparently trivial, even seemingly arbitrary, causes." Talking to another character, Stephen describes this "sudden spiritual manifestation" as the "most delicate and evanescent" of moments.[6]

As I stood in the stacks, skimming through Beja's book, the Emerald Lake moment returned again. Only this time I had a concept that allowed me to understand it. And once I had a concept on which to hang my wonder-filled moment, I knew that what I'd experienced wasn't an isolated psychic aberration, and wasn't unique to me. Traditionally, epiphanic experiences have been regarded from a religious perspective, and until recent centuries were often interpreted as having their source in divine grace. In modern times, though, as James Joyce tried to demonstrate, it is also possible to view epiphanic experiences as "spiritual" without being overtly "religious." Of course, an epiphanic experience can open the door to religious commitment. But you don't need to subscribe to a particular religious creed to have epiphanies.[7] That said, I do think you need to have some sort of spiritual orientation to appreciate moments of epiphany. I know that might sound pretentiously New Agey, but in my experience, while epiphanies of wonder are potentially available to anyone, not everyone recognizes them as such. (I didn't, at first.)

There are many reasons for this, I suppose – everything from the psychological to the biographical. The point I want to make here is that it is easy to let moments of possible wonder pass you by if you aren't prepared to recognize them or learn from them when (or if) they happen.

My own story, I suggest, provides anecdotal evidence to support this claim. I'd had other experiences before Emerald Lake that might qualify as epiphanies. However, sudden and intense epiphanies such as that at Emerald Lake have been rare – maybe half a dozen over the course of my life. On the other hand, I have had numerous minor epiphanies, situations of singular awareness or focus that rose above the horizon of the humdrum. But – and this, for me, is the lesson of Emerald Lake – it is only by learning to attend to the possibility of wonderment that such moments, minor or major, become possible. Emerald Lake prodded me, in Heidegger's words, to attend "to the presencing of things." Admittedly, I have often been inattentive, recognizing only afterwards that a particular circumstance – the solicitations of a lover, the sight of sleeping child, the smell of lilac, the quiet of a mountain path – might have stirred a sense of wonder if I had been focused on the moment, instead of preoccupied with the chatter in my head. I have learned that while you cannot induce wonder at will, you can prepare or ready yourself for its possibility. When, or if, moments of wonder happen, they seem to come out of the blue, occurring in ordinary circumstances, yet possessing the quality of extraordinariness.

****

I am not alone in detecting the apparent economy of wonder. "To feel wonder is to experience a sudden *decentering* of the self," says theologian Kelly Bulkeley. "Facing something surprisingly new and unexpectedly powerful, one's ordinary sense of personality is dramatically altered, leading to new knowledge and understanding that ultimately *recenter* the self." Such moments are "the fruit of the visionary capacity." These moments, he concludes, can be purely spontaneous or the culmination of a ritual. Either way they are initially characterized by a feeling of both surprise and disorientation.[8]

Religion scholar Robert Fuller echoes this judgment, pointing out that experiences of wonder often first arise in brief moments of high emotion. However, they have the potential to influence mood and personality over the long term. In this sense, says Fuller, it is not simply a matter of fostering those conditions that might prompt moments of wonder, but also of developing an "ongoing 'sense of wonder.'"[9]

Rachel Carson, a leading activist in the early environmental movement of the 1960s, offers an indirect way to understand the experience of wonder by noting its absence. Most of us, she writes in her most famous book, *Silent Spring*, "walk unseeing through the world, unaware alike of its beauties, its wonders, and the strange and sometimes terrible intensity of the lives that are being lived about us."[10] In another book, *The Sense of Wonder*, Carson issues a kind of baseline guide for fostering wonder-filled experiences: "For most of us, knowledge of our world comes largely through sight, yet we look about with such unseeing eyes that we are partially blind. One way to open your eyes to unnoticed beauty is to ask yourself, 'What if I had never seen this before? What if I knew I would never see it again?'" In other words, there is nothing like the thought of your own mortality, the awareness of how brief your time is on earth, to prod you toward the experience of wonder.

For Carson, our senses provide the avenue to wonder and meaning. Here's her evocative invocation of a day at the water's edge.

[S]enses other than sight can prove avenues of delight and discovery, storing up for us memories and impressions ... [T]he sharp, clean smell of wood smoke coming from the cottage chimney. Down on the shore we have savored the smell of low tide – that marvelous evocation combined of many separate odors, of the world of seaweeds and fishes and creatures of bizarre shape and habit, of tides rising and falling on their appointed schedule, of exposed mud flats and salt rime drying on rocks ... [T]he rush of remembered delight that comes with the first breath of that scent, drawn into one's nostrils as one returns to the sea after a long absence. For the sense of smell, almost more than any other, has the power to recall memories and it is a pity that we use it so little.[11]

These seaside experiences, and the wonder they induce, lift Carson out of the numbing routines of the quotidian world, assuring her that beneath the surface of appearances there is meaning, however elusive. "Contemplating the teeming life of the shore, we have an uneasy sense of the communication of some universal truth that lies just beyond our grasp."[12]

Philosopher Kenneth Schmitz offers a theoretical perspective to reinforce Carson's sensory concreteness. The key to wonder, he argues, is the recovery or development of a strong sense of the "things" of the world. Instead of seeing the natural world as a field of objects or data or material out there for us to exploit, we need to learn to regard nature as "a community of things in which we participate." We need to respond to the world "as a gift, and not simply as a given."[13] In making his case, Schmitz argues that because the scientistic view of the world shapes and informs the way we, as moderns, experience the world, we no longer really experience "things" in their everyday lived reality. Instead of seeing – and experiencing – a tree in all its colour and texture and shape, we learn to understand it in terms of its cellular structures and photosynthetic processes. There are particles, waves and processes, but no things in themselves. Things surround us, but we do not *sense* their living presence. As Schmitz puts it: "We are so surrounded by things that the effort to look at ordinary things closely is not unlike a fish trying to understand what is meant by water: for the fish, water; for us, *things*."[14]

The experience of wonder helps us recover the world of things for the simple reason that things are more often than not the source of wonder. Ideas and dreams, too, may spark inspiration and curiosity, but in my experience it has been the sudden "presence" of things, mundane, ordinary everyday things, that provides the most wonder. Certainly, there is something idiosyncratic about wonder: its meaning largely depends on the perspective of the individual undergoing the experience. The value of whatever object or event induces the epiphany is relative. Some feel wonder in the presence of a grove of ancient Douglas firs, while others see only timber and two-by-fours. But this example merely demonstrates that the thing or circumstance is important only insofar as it results in an epiphany. What might be unimportant to someone else, and even insignificant to you at some other time, assumes great worth in your mind at the moment of the epiphany.[15]

To better explain what I'm getting at, I shall resort to the exemplar of fictional wonder I discovered years ago in the stacks of the McPherson Library at the University of Victoria – James Joyce. According to Joyce, speaking through his character Stephen Hero, epiphanies arise out of encounters with the most mundane objects, in dreams, through the contemplation of works of art, in overheard conversations, in the sight of a particular scene or view of nature, or in some "memorable phase of the mind itself." Moreover, there appear to be two major types of epiphany: the sudden, out-of-the-blue revelation, and the epiphany where an event stirs no special impression at the time, but emerges later to "produce a sudden sensation of new awareness when it is recalled at some future time." Morris Beja refers to this moment of remembrance as a "retrospective epiphany."[16]

I regard my moment at Emerald Lake as an out-of-the-blue epiphany, but I have had retrospective ones, too. What intrigues me, though, is how both kinds seem to emerge out of seemingly inconsequential objects or events in everyday life.

Wonder is, or should be, available to everyone. Anyone who has children, or even remembers their own childhood, can testify to this truth. Things that adults no longer find astonishing – where do clouds come from? why is water wet? how does snow disappear? – fascinate children. Jacques Maritain, the Catholic philosopher, refers to what he calls "the gravity of the child's gaze," observing how children, in their focus on ordinary things, often seem "simply astonished to *be*."[17] Unfortunately, the wonderment of childhood gives way to ho-hum familiarity as we grow older and learn to rationalize our experience. What was once novel becomes repetitious. We grow habituated to the world, and no longer see it (or smell, taste, hear or touch it) with the innocent gravity of a child's encounter. We become more "realistic," more knowledgeable about how things really work, more utilitarian.

This shift is undoubtedly necessary for survival. We'd starve to death if we had to relearn everything with each encounter. Learning to regard some aspects of everyday life as a matter of problem solving is, thus, a lifesaver. Yet, there is also an element of regret at losing our capacity for wonderment. Our habituation to the world, our familiarity with its ways, leads to world-weariness. Caught up in the hectic pace of the workaday world, our lives tend to pass in a blur. I remember my teens and twenties vividly. My thirties and forties are in some ways a blur of busyness. We no longer attend to the mysterious presence of being, including our own. Indeed, we come to regard life as a problem in need of a solution rather than a mystery in which we participate. We are, in a sense, lost to ourselves, no longer able to see things as they appear. What once astonished us as children – being rather than not-being – becomes common, taken for granted. We grow bored with being. Life becomes dull and dutiful, drained of astonishment at its sheer presence. In this sense, it is the adult who suffers from delusion, not the child. As literary scholar Dennis Quinn puts it, "It is not the child who is deluded … by thinking the stars and snails extraordinary. It is rather the adult who is no longer conscious of his ignorance of these common things."[18]

Must it be this way? Is this the fate of adulthood? Heidegger argues that our Western understanding of wonder goes back at least to the Greeks, who, he says, were the first to be consciously astonished at the *being* of Being. They were wonderstruck at the very thought of *being*, when, as seemed equally possible, there could have been nothing. Thus, wonder nourished the root of Greek philosophy. Plato, for example, gives the following words to his character Socrates in the dialogue *Theaetetus*: "I see, my dear Theaetetus, that Theodorus had a true insight into your nature when he said that you were a philosopher, for wonder is the feeling of a philosopher, and philosophy begins in wonder."[19] Aristotle writes in the *Metaphysics*, "it is owing to their wonder that men both now begin and at first began to philosophize."[20] According to Heidegger, though, we no longer possess this Greek sensibility, no longer marvel at the mystery of existence, and, as a result, we no longer let *Being* be. Or, put more prosaically, we stop wondering.

I certainly haven't let *Being* be all the time. Like most others, I was educated to be rationalistic and regard nature as mere stuff, dead matter, available for our use as we see fit. In any case, it is difficult to maintain, must less recover, a child-like sense of wonderment about the world once you've been around the block a few times. (I'm ignoring those quasi-adults who try to live as perpetual adolescents well into their middle years; this is the narcissism of the pathetically immature, not the maintenance of a child-like region of the psyche.) Nor is it easy to make philosophizing a way of life when so much of your life is taken up with concerns about career, family and paying the bills. As adults, we overlook the mystery of our own existence. The get-and-spend life consumes us like the whale that ingested Jonah. And so we go through our adult lives without really noticing where we came from, or where we are going.

Still, I like to think that some of the ancient Greek attitude has taken hold, now and then reminding me to pay attention so that I have the occasional experience of wonder. Such moments, regardless of their intensity or brevity, have shown me it is possible to retain – or regain – something of the wonder we knew as children, and thereby restore a much needed dimension of meaning to our angst-ridden, hard-pressed adult lives. I have also discovered that others – poets and philosophers, artists and scientists – share my experience, and I turn to them as sources of inspiration and discipline.

I use the word "discipline" deliberately. Most adults need to relearn how to wonder again, or, rather, how to ready themselves for the experience of wonder should circumstances make it possible. Artists (and, sometimes, scientists) show us how. The fact is, after adolescence, most of us most of the time take our existence for granted. We spend a lot of time and energy (and money) trying to keep ourselves from being bored, indulging in everything from skydiving to whitewater rafting. Such activities can obviously provide a sensory thrill, but I suspect these experiences are mostly the product of adrenalin and endorphins rather than epiphanies of consciousness. They do not induce wonder.

Wonder is a state of mind, not a state of brain, although, of course, mind and brain are interrelated and mutually dependent and reinforcing.[21] Some physical activities do seem to foster moments of wonder. Long-distance walking, for example, forces you to slow down not only physically but also mentally. But in my experience, such moments come from the "outside," regardless of the effort made to induce them. As philosopher Juan De Pasquale puts it, "One slides into wonder, is surprised by wonder, is overtaken by wonder; but one cannot will to wonder."[22]

That said, you can discipline yourself to increase the possibility of moments of wonder, and of reaping its full benefits when (or if) it arrives. The wonder casts your world into high relief. You *see* the world rather than just look at it. You walk rather than drift. And if you pay attention to the experience, it prompts the kind of mindful awareness and reflective thought that leads to greater self-knowledge and a deeper appreciation of the fact that anything, including yourself, exists, rather than nothing. In saying this, I do not want to imply that wonder reveals some ideal vision of the world or even some vision of a world beyond this one. Perhaps experiences that engender wonder provide a first glimpse of the divine. Conversely, the desire for knowledge of the divine cannot help but induce wonder. In this sense, it seems that just as wonder is the beginning of philosophy, so, too, it can be the beginning of religious experience.

Nonetheless, I want to maintain a distinction between an epiphanic moment grounded in the everyday and a mystical experience that, as it seems, has it origins in divine order. My point, and my concern, is simply this: Wonder reveals the ordinary world – the *things* as they are – from an extraordinary perspective. Properly attended to, wonder can go a long way to re-enchanting your world. Robert Fuller sums it up nicely: It is true, he says, that we can go through life quite efficiently without ever experiencing wonder, and, no doubt, many do. "But it must also be emphasized that no other emotion so effectively induces us to pause, admire, and open our hearts and minds. No other emotion so readily kindles a reverence for life. And thus although you can surely go through life without a developed sense of wonder, it is equally true that a life shaped by wonder is attuned to the widest possible world of personal fulfillment."[23]

Indeed, philosopher and theologian Austin Farrer suggests that the divine is best known by "a sort of acquaintance … *in and through* finite things."[24] The possibility of the "beyond" is in the here and how. This happens, says Farrer, without our being fully conscious of it. The task is to make ourselves more fully conscious, more fully appreciative, of the finite things. We need to learn to pay attention to the world, to open ourselves to the possibility and potential of wonder. Farrer says it well.

> [T]he chief impediment to religion in this age, I often think, is that no one ever looks at anything at all: not so as to *contemplate it*, to apprehend what it is to be that thing, and plumb, if we can, the deep fact of its individual existence. The mind rises from the knowledge of creatures to the knowledge of their creator, but this does not happen through the sort of knowledge which can analyze things into factors or manipulate them with technical skill or classify them into groups. It comes

from the appreciation of things which we have when we love them and fill our minds and senses with them, and feel something of the silent force and great mystery of their existence.[25]

How do you foster this capacity? Is it really possible to attune yourself to wonderment? Few contemporary scientists show any interest in wonder. Fear and anger, sadness and joy, love and grief, desire and disgust: all are recognized and studied. But as Robert Fuller points out, "not one major western theorist in the past hundred years has explicitly listed wonder as one of the primary or secondary emotions."[26] This omission is telling when you consider that other eras regarded wonder as a primary human emotion. For this reason, it is necessary to understand the modern disregard of wonder before I consider my guides to wonderment.

****

The word "wonder" is something of mystery. The modern English word comes from the proto-Germanic verb *wundrian*, which means affected with astonishment. But wonder's "ultimate ancestry is unknown," says lexicographer John Ayto.[27] The *Oxford English Dictionary* defines wonder as "the emotion excited by the perception of something unexpected, unfamiliar, or inexplicable," something that strikes a person as "intensely powerful, real, true and/or beautiful." I won't quarrel with editors of the OED. The experience of wonder is usually unexpected and, as the dictionary says, strikes with considerable power. However, the testimony of those I have previously cited, as well as my own experience, suggests that the familiar and the well-known are also sources of wonder. Perhaps, then, there is something about wonder that calls us to a more comprehensive understanding. This call entails a brief foray into the history of wonder.

Philosophers have always wondered about wonder. "Philosophy begins in wonder," says Alfred North Whitehead. "And, at the end, when philosophy has done its best, the wonder remains."[28] Wonder, adds philosopher Jerome Miller, is the "hinge" on which we turn from the immediate world to begin our inquiries about the world.[29] Gabriel Marcel echoes the sentiment, albeit as a warning against losing a sense of wonder. "[A] philosopher remains a philosopher only so long as he retains his capacity for wonderment in the presence of certain fundamental situations, despite everything surrounding and even within him that tends to dispel it."[30] In his scholarly way, Marcel is referring to the demands of the daily grind, and all the little paranoias and perturbations that plague our minds like moths around a lightbulb. Marcel recognizes how difficult it is to genuinely experience the ordinary in all its extraordinariness.

Nevertheless, from the time of the ancient Greeks through to more recent centuries, philosophers have tended to see wonder as a cognitive passion available to everyone, at least to some degree. They believed wonder had as much to do with thinking as feeling. While late medieval and early Renaissance intellectuals debated whether wonder reflected one's ignorance or marked the beginning of rational thought, they generally accepted that "wonder was not simply a private emotional experience but rather, depending on context, a prelude to divine contemplation, a shaming admission of ignorance, a cowardly flight into fear of the unknown, or a plunge into energetic investigation."[31] This high regard for wonder comes from Greek philosophers who taught that it was not only the beginning of rational inquiry, but also the condition that sustains reasoning. For Plato and Aristotle, wonder was a continuous mode of consciousness in that it drew on new knowledge and experience to uncover (or recover) an ever-deeper comprehension of reality. To philosophize was to experience wonder as a state of mind, while moments of wonder are the crown of philosophic endeavour.

This high regard for wonder changed with the emergence of modern ways of thinking. For the last half-millennium, from the Renaissance and the Enlightenment through to contemporary times, various factors – religious, intellectual, cultural and psychological – have resulted in the decline of wonder.[32] In particular, the modern notion of methodological or pure mathematical reasoning, promulgated by the seventeenth-century philosopher René Descartes, is widely regarded as the main culprit in the weakening of wonder. Descartes sought a single indisputable principle that could provide an unshakeable foundation for philosophical knowledge. He began not with the traditional Aristotelian notion that the philosophic quest for truth begins with self-evident and unchanging first principles – the very existence of the world, for example – as the basis of all knowledge, but rather with universal doubt about everything, including the existence of the world. Descartes adopted a method of thinking that subjects everything – even the question of whether life is some vast demonic dream – to systematic doubt.[33] Through this method – Cartesian doubt, as it is known – everything is broken down to its simplest component parts. Descartes ultimately determined that the person doing the doubting is the one sure thing. In doubting you are thinking, and to be thinking is, obviously, to be alive. Thus, to think is to be. Or, as Descartes stated, *"Cogito ergo sum,"* – "I think, therefore I am." Descartes, it seems, found his one indubitable truth. This *a priori* truth – we think, therefore we exist – is the foundation stone of modern scientific knowledge. Which is to say that for moderns, doubt is the way to truth.

We have been living with the consequences of this idea ever since. It has unquestionably brought great benefits.

The doubting ways of modern science and its technological offspring, which lead to rigorous testing to confirm theories and approaches, have given many of us longer lives, better health, more abundant food and greater leisure. No rational person would want to surrender the benefits of modernity. Yet, we have paid a price, for science and technology have been abused in many ways, from the techniques for mass murder evolved by Nazi Germany and the Soviet Union to nuclear accidents and massive oil spills. Nevertheless, for good or ill, modern empirical science dominates not only our lives but also our ways of thinking. My concern, though, is whether Cartesian doubt corrodes our sense of and capacity for wonder. More to the point, is universal doubt responsible for the disenchantment of the world?

At first glance, it might not seem so. Descartes regarded wonder as one of the six main emotions (along with desire, love, joy, hatred and sadness), and declared it "a sudden surprise of the soul which makes it tend to consider attentively those objects which seem to it rare and extraordinary."[34] When you are surprised by an object on first encountering it, "this causes us to wonder," says Descartes. Since this happens before you know anything about the object, he claims wonder is "the first of all passions."[35]

Descartes' wonder, however, is more like curiosity. Wonder and curiosity may often go hand in hand, but they are not the same. Wonder can foster curiosity, but the former abides in admiration, whereas the latter is devoted to explanation. In Descartes' terms, the wonder a child experiences might prompt a desire to know more about the world, but for adults who actively seek knowledge of the world, the experience of wonder is no longer necessary, except perhaps as a spark to curiosity. This distinction comes through in Descartes' 1637 treatise on rainbows, in which he applied mathematical reasoning to explain this phenomenon. With various equations, he proves that anyone can produce a rainbow with a spray of water. Clearly, he concludes, a rainbow has nothing to do with God's promise to care for life, as the Bible teaches. In effect, then, Descartes' initial wonder at the rainbow turns to curiosity, and his scientific reasoning, his method of doubt, reduces rainbows to optical illusions. As Bulkeley observes, while Descartes might admit wonder as a primary emotion, his understanding of philosophy's purpose "leads in the end to the elimination of wonder, not its cultivation."[36]

For my purposes, what's important about Descartes is how his emphasis on skeptical thinking makes us dependent not on our lived or immediate experience of the world, but on our ideas about the world. As the philosophers might put it, the experience of *Being* becomes subordinate to thinking about the manifestations of *Being*. We think in order to master *Being*. Knowledge is all about control and domination. We use our minds to control the world by breaking it down like some kind of machine that we then set about to fix and put back together as we see fit through the application of the right methods and procedures. As Dennis Quinn remarks, "Today nearly everyone assumes that the highest mental functions are analyzing, arguing, comparing, synthesizing, deducing [and] inferring."[37]

It is this instrumental form of reasoning and the mechanistic understanding of the world that dominates the modern mind, according to Quinn. Whereas the ancients taught that the rational contemplation of the transcendental stature of the world provides the meaning and measure of human life, moderns hold that knowledge begins with the reasoning mind regarding the world skeptically, subjecting nature to an examination of its reasons for being what it is. In Quinn's view, though, this method of doubt effectively makes the human mind the measure of reality. And that, equally effectively, denies the world its own testimony independent of the human mind. The result is to regard the world and all that is in it as material subject to human will. This modern predilection became evident with the first modern man, Galileo, who declared that such things as colour, sound, taste, odour, texture and touch are "mere illusions of the mind."[38]

Does this mean the capacity for wonder is lost to the modern world? Philosopher Alfred North Whitehead thinks so. He describes the consequences of a disenchanted worldview this way:

> Nature gets credit which should in truth be reserved for ourselves; the rose for its scent; the nightingale for his song; and the sun for his radiance. The poets are entirely mistaken. They should address their lyrics to themselves, and should turn them into odes of self-congratulation on the excellency of the human mind. Nature is a dull affair, soundless, scentless, colourless; merely the hurrying of material, endlessly, meaninglessly.

> However you disguise it, this is the practical outcome of the characteristic scientific philosophy which closed the seventeenth century ... It has held its own as the guiding principle of scientific studies ever since. It is still reigning. Every university in the world organizes itself in accordance with it ... And yet – it is quite unbelievable. The conception of the universe is surely framed in terms of high abstractions, and the paradox only arises because we have mistaken our abstractions for concrete realities.[39]

In other words, the Cartesian mind allows that only those who use the proper method of knowing – the scientific mechanistic method – can legitimately claim to have knowledge of the world.

By contrast, pre-modern thinkers held that the highest thought included both the concrete and the abstract, and was both active and receptive. The capacity to analyze and argue was important, certainly, but for them discursive reasoning and intuitive understanding, *ratio* and *intellectus*, went hand in hand, with the former serving the latter. No one needs to reason to know that the world exists. From Plato and Aristotle to Augustine and Thomas Aquinas, says Quinn, the great thinkers taught that the world is knowable as a whole because the whole, all that is, is open to human intelligence. Thus, the world is intelligible to everyone, at least to some degree, because the fact of its existence, its truth, is there for all to experience. The truth is knowable because truth is an aspect of being itself. You do not need to be an intellectual or a scientific specialist or a technological master to know the world in its most vital being. Anyone can contemplate what is – starry heavens or arching rainbows – and, to one degree or another, can attune him or herself intuitively to the natural order of the world. As Quinn neatly notes, neither God nor the angels think; they know.[40] So, too, does a child in the grip of wonder. And so, too, do adults, if they are ready and able to experience wonder.

Philosopher Josef Pieper helps us understand why this is so by making a distinction between different kinds of knowledge. In his famous 1947 essays, in which he argued that the pursuit of leisure is the basis of culture, Pieper says that contrary to the modern Cartesian view, the gaining of knowledge does not necessarily require "activity": that is, lots of analyzing, deducing and inferring. Modern thinkers such as Immanuel Kant, however, regarded philosophy as work because they held knowing to be something active.[41]

Pieper argues on behalf of another type of knowing, one prasticed for thousands of years. From the Greeks through to the great medieval thinkers, it was thought that genuine knowledge of the world included not only physical and sensory perception, but also a capacity for receptive contemplation, for "listening to the essences of things," to borrow a phrase from Heraclitus.[42] Pre-modern thinkers, including Thomas Aquinas, distinguished between understanding as *ratio* and understanding as *intellectus*. Genuine knowledge combined *ratio* and *intellectus*, the discursive and the intuitive. "The mode of discursive thought is accompanied and impregnated by an effortless awareness, the contemplative vision of the *intellectus*, which is not active but passive, or rather receptive, the activity of the soul in which it conceives that which it sees."[43]

I do not want to imply that "activist," functional knowledge is necessarily wrong. We need to create a livable world. We cannot simply accept the world as we find it, or we would starve or freeze. A utilitarian approach to the world is essential if humans are to thrive rather than merely survive. However, knowledge used for strictly functional and utilitarian ends is not always benign. Everyone, I presume, is well aware of the perversions – political, social and environmental – to which science, technology and, yes, even philosophy were put in the last century (think Marxism, fascism, Nazism, etc.) There is no need for me to address them here. My point follows Pieper's argument: A utilitarian attitude to knowledge is too narrow an understanding of what it is to *know* the world. Such a worldview does not take into account the direct apprehension of the world experienced in moments of wonder.

For one thing, as Pieper argues, the narrowness of the rational-useful approach to knowledge weighs like a dead hand on our capacity to experience wonder in our daily lives. Most of us, he says, spend our lives in the daily effort to satisfy physical needs for food, clothing, warmth and shelter, with only a little time for leisure. But alongside this workaday struggle is the spiritual struggle for a sense of meaning and purpose in our lives. We go through life with a constant sense of strain and anxiety. We try to relieve this sense of strain through a variety of diversionary tactics or, as Pieper puts it, "breathless amusements or the brief pauses that punctuate its course: a newspaper, a cinema, a cigarette."[44]

Pieper's examples of diversions may need updating – the Internet, television, drugs, for example – but his idea is clear. Like Pascal, Pieper regards a devotion to diversion as a desperate effort to avoid coming face to face with reality, whether out of fear or sloth. To say this is not to hold the mundane world inferior or to assume some supposedly "higher" spiritual posture. I'm rather fond of movies and newspapers myself (not to mention well-aged Scotch and the occasional cigar). Nonetheless, sometimes in the midst of our daily routines we need to ask Rachel Carson's questions – "What if I had never seen this before? What if I knew I would never see it again?" – in order to transcend momentarily our quotidian numbness. Such questions ring out like a cathedral bell amidst the cacophony of traffic horns. You cannot help but pay attention. And to experience this "cry of wonder"[45] is to experience the ordinary as extraordinary.

Pieper offers the example of a rose. What happens, he asks, when we first look at a rose? What do we do in perceiving its colour and shape? Are we not, in a sense, passive and receptive, rather than active and analytical? Certainly, we are actively conscious in our awareness of the rose, but our attention is not straining in the act of perception. Rather, we simply look at the flower, contemplating it, rather than observing it. Observation, Pieper notes, is a "tense activity" in that it implies measuring, weighing up, judging. Looking, on the other hand, is "to open one's eyes to whatever offers itself to one's vision, and the things seen entered into, so to speak, without calling for any effort or strain on our part to possess them."[46] In this sense, then, our knowledge of the world includes not only the activist knowledge of discursive reason — *ratio* — but also the "purely receptive vision"[47] — *intellectus* — of non-activist comprehension.

Modern philosophy since Descartes largely rejects this receptive vision. Modern thinking is about changing the world rather than understanding it. Or, more precisely, understanding it just enough to change it to suit our often ill-conceived desires. Modern knowing is devoted to the physical and empirical. Anything pertaining to the "spiritual" or "metaphysical" is, if not beyond knowing, all too often dismissed as imaginary or even delusional. "Wonder has become a disreputable passion in workaday science, redolent of the popular, the amateurish, and the childish," say scholars Lorraine Daston and Katherine Park. Scientists might speak about a sense of wonder in their memoirs, but not in *Scientific American*. They may have been motivated to become scientists from an initial sense of wonder, but that experience is no longer regarded as integral to doing science.[48]

Thus, in the words of Dennis Quinn, "The introduction of Cartesian 'method' made wonder superfluous."[49] Or, put another way, modern philosophy and science promote the disenchantment of the world.

****

Is a disenchanted world devoid of wonder? It might seem so. Max Weber, the German sociologist to whom I referred in Chapter One as the source of the "disenchantment" thesis, thought our increasing technological mastery of the world was unlikely to provide a greater sense of meaningfulness. Disenchantment could force humans into an "iron cage of serfdom" and see traditional human values "suffocated by the almighty bureaucratic structures and by the tightly knit networks of formal-rational laws and regulations, against which the individual would no longer stand any chance at all."[50] Such a world leaves little space for wonder. A "rationalized" world is predominantly concerned with establishing predictability and order in an increasingly efficient manner. We must do everything faster and cheaper. Obviously, says theologian Christopher Partridge, religious beliefs – God's providence, divine intervention, the value of prayer, pilgrimages – are "at odds with a culture that values predictability, order, routine, and immediately quantifiable returns." Many Westerners, he says, even those with religious convictions, have come to believe there are more efficient ways of getting through life – as though life is something to endure – than those traditionally offered by religion. Add to this other forces – the impact of multiculturalism and pluralistic societies, the abandonment of traditional notions of family, the domination of morality by technology, and the acceptance of scientism as the only legitimate form of knowledge – and you have a situation where religion is less important.[51]

But matters are not that straightforward. To explain why, I rely on philosopher Charles Taylor and his monumental 2007 study, *A Secular Age*. Taylor asks one essential question: What does it mean, and how has it happened, that we, as Westerners, have shifted from being an "enchanted," God-centred civilization to being a "disenchanted" civilization in which belief in a divinely ordered world is no longer a given? "The process of disenchantment," Taylor says, "is the disappearance of this [enchanted] world, and the substitution of what we live today: a world in which the only locus of thoughts, feelings, spiritual élan is what we call minds." In the modern world all meaning and purpose resides "within the cranium." In the pre-modern, enchanted world, however, meaning and purpose are or can be beyond or outside the human mind. "[I]n the pre-modern world, means are not only in minds, but can reside in things, or in various kinds of extra-human but intra-cosmic subjects ... [I]n the enchanted world, the meaning exists already outside us, prior to contact; it can take us over, we can fall into its force field. It comes on us from the outside."[52]

As moderns, we live in an age of "secularity." For most of us, this refers to the decline in religious beliefs and practices and the retreat of religion from the public arena. At the political level it has translated into the separation of church and state. For Taylor, though, this understanding of secularization is insufficient. He distinguishes two theories about Western secularization. One regards scientific thinking as having resulted in a decline in individual faith. The consequence: religion as a social and political force is waning. Darwin's theory of evolution, for example, rendered it untenable to believe in a God-created world that was only a few thousand years old. A second theory flips the relationship to argue that the institutional changes – economic, political and educational – set in motion during the Reformation and Enlightenment increasingly marginalized the influence of religion. The Church became less influential as people turned to other institutional orders to satisfy their needs, both spiritual and material.

Taylor questions the adequacy of these theories. Copernicus, Galileo, Newton and Darwin blew big holes in the theological accounts of the world, but the popular idea that science defeated religion, that reason prevailed over irrationality because it "proved" God's non-existence, does not tell the whole story. The real clue to secularity is the moral appeal of science. The emergence of science allowed people to look to other things besides the Church to satisfy their highest aspirations.

On the basis of this claim, Taylor proposes a third theory of secularity. While not opposed to the first two, it goes beyond them to take into account the numerous "social imaginaries" that have emerged in the modern era. It is not so much that God was eliminated from the public space, or that God was no longer available to support prevailing political and social structures, but that there are other sources of moral and spiritual meaning available, thanks to the emergence of science. In an era of belief, people assumed God was the ultimate source of meaning. In a secular age, people believe they have alternatives to God for finding meaning in their lives.

For Taylor, science – or, more properly, scientism – is a moral perspective on the world, not simply a method for observing and analyzing the world. The fundamental purpose of science and philosophy since Descartes has been to acquire knowledge in order to gain rational control over the world and remake it according to our desires. Thinking, as Karl Marx more or less said, is not about understanding the world but changing it. Scientism, which holds that the empirical sciences are the only means to genuine worthwhile knowledge, maintains that in theory, the world is completely explicable in terms of science. This is the essence of the modern idea of progress, the concept at the core of technology.

Scientism, says Taylor, allowed people to find meaning in other things besides religion. Over the course of the last three centuries, a faith-based, God-dominated moral outlook has given way to a science-based, humanist perspective that "consists of new conditions of belief," including atheism, or, to use Taylor's phrase, "exclusive humanism." Secularity thus reflects a spiritual shift, not a rejection of spirituality. This shift produced a "titanic change in our Western civilization," says Taylor. "We have changed from a condition in which belief was the default option, not just for the naïve but also for those who knew, considered, talked about atheism; to a condition in which for more and more people unbelieving construals seem at first blush the only possible ones." Indeed, those who do not believe have great difficulty understanding those who do, so much so that they ascribe "gross error theories to explain religious belief: people are afraid of uncertainty, the unknown; they're weak in the head, crippled by guilt, etc."[53]

Taylor's difficulty with the secular humanist and atheistic worldview is that it rests on the unquestioned assumptions of scientism that only empirical knowledge born of instrumental reasoning is valid knowledge. Such an epistemological assumption is insufficient in explaining human behaviour, he says, because it cannot account for, much less provide for, the full panoply of human experience. (Including, I would suggest, the experience of wonder.) The "desire for eternity" is deeply embedded in the human psyche; it is this spiritual longing that has been the ultimate source for all our worldly efforts at transcendence – art, architecture, painting, poetry and, yes, even politics and science, insofar as those latter enterprises have devoted themselves to justice and truth.

With this point in mind, Taylor tries to articulate a perspective that takes into account both believers and disbelievers, attempting to weave his way between the boosters and the knockers of modernity. The boosters include those "exclusive humanists" who reject religion and insist on the diluted concepts of authenticity and autonomy precisely because there are no absolute horizons or moral standards for human conduct against which individuals must justify their desires and claims to power. The knockers include those who regard notions of individual freedom as little more than the promotion of a culture of narcissism, hedonism and nihilism, a society devoid of moral ideals. While Taylor resides in the camp of the faithful, he does not deny that secular humanism also seeks "human flourishing." Even atheists act out of a belief in the human good when they promote human rights.[54]

Still, Taylor cannot avoid touching the sore spot of the twenty-first century West – the spectre of meaninglessness. Despite the success of Western societies in the areas of economics, politics, science and technology, there is a sense of something missing. Not everybody, says Taylor, has "settled into comfortable disbelief." He recalls Peggy Lee's old torch song, "Is That All There Is?" in observing the growth in phenomena such as the human potential movement and New Age spiritualism as evidence of the "revolt from within unbelief" against the atheistic denial of humans' innate longing for contact with something of intrinsic meaning beyond the satisfactions of material life. The success of secularism depended on scientism's "disenchantment" of the world. But now there is widespread disenchantment with secular humanism. The narratives of modernity that replaced religion as the West's dominant "social imaginaries" – faith in rationalism, belief in progress, individual freedom, etc. – are now under attack. In a nutshell, the success of the Enlightenment's disenchantment of the world has boomeranged to the point where there is widespread disenchantment with the Enlightenment project. Religion has re-emerged, in part, because of dissatisfactions with secularism.[55]

It seems we require a spiritual dimension, an intimation of the sacred, if we are to flourish as more than creatures desperate to avoid violent death and live complacently in our material cocoons. We are unlikely to return to the all-encompassing religiosity of the past (short of the apocalyptic collapse or suicide of the West) or the kind of enchantment enjoyed (and suffered) by the pre-modern world. Nevertheless, we remain spiritual creatures in our most essential natures. The experience of wonder, I suggest, opens us to the recovery of this aspect of our nature. The question, then, is how might this recovery be achieved? That question brings me, finally, to my guides to wonderment.

****

One of my favourite fictional moments of wonder is a scene in Virginia Woolf's novel *The Waves*. Bernard, one of the characters in the novel, sits in a railway carriage on an overnight commuter train heading for London. Newly engaged, Bernard thinks about what marriage might mean for his life. But he also becomes increasingly aware of the world around him. It is one of the great epiphanic "moments of being" in a novel filled with such moments.

> "How fair, how strange," said Bernard, "glittering, many-pointed and many-domed London lies before me under mist. Guarded by gasometers, by factory chimneys, she lies sleeping as we approach ... All cries, all clamour, are softly enveloped in silence. Not Rome herself looks more majestic ... Ridges fledged with houses rise from the mist. Factories, cathedrals, glass domes, institutions and theatres erect themselves. The early train from the north is hurled at her like a missile. We draw a curtain as we rattle and flash through stations. Men clutch their newspapers a little tighter, as our wind sweeps them, envisaging death. Blank expectant faces stare at us as we pass. But we roar on ...."[56]

Standing at the train window, absorbing the images of London, aware of his fellow passengers with whom he has travelled all night, Bernard suddenly feels immensely happy. He knows his happiness is due in part to his forthcoming marriage. But there is also a sense of belonging to something larger than himself: "I am become part of this speed, this missile hurled at the city." For a moment he wishes the train would not arrive at Euston Station, that he and the other passengers in the car would go hurtling onward, a small community united in their common journey. The train does arrive, however, and the spell is broken. Yet, even as he passively follows his fellow passengers to the station exits, Bernard feels the afterglow of his epiphany and is aware of a subtle change in his psyche. And he longs for other moments of being when he can escape the get-and-spend world and "visit the profound depths; once in a while to exercise [his] prerogative not always to act, but to explore ...."[57]

Bernard's moment of wonderment is similar to the meditations of the narrator in William Wordsworth's poem "Composed upon Westminster Bridge," with its famous lines:

> Earth has not anything to show more fair:
> Dull would he be of soul who could pass by
> A sight so touching in its majesty;
> This City now doth, like a garment, wear
> The beauty of the morning; silent, bare,
> Ships, towers, domes, theatres, and temples lie
> Open unto the fields, and to the sky ...[58]

But Woolf's scene also finds an echo in the work of a more contemporary poet, Philip Larkin. In Larkin's "The Whitsun Weddings," a character experiences an epiphany while travelling on a train to London. Like Bernard, Larkin's narrator finds himself focusing on the concrete details of his journey. As the train pulls out of the station he notices "All the windows down, all cushions hot, all sense / Of being in a hurry gone." This sensory awareness continues to heighten as the trip progresses. The narrator notices the "backs of houses," smells the fish docks, sees the farms and canals of the English countryside, finds himself entranced by the rise and fall of the hedges that line the railway embankment, breathes in the whiff of fresh-cut grass as the train passes through the suburbs.

But then Larkin's character, like Bernard, starts to pay attention to what he sees on the station platforms. In Larkin's case, it is a series of wedding parties. Just as Bernard feels a sudden sense of wonder at and identity with his fellow passengers, so, too, is Larkin's poetic persona entranced by the newlyweds who join him on the London-bound train. They, too, watch the passing landscape of London, but, unlike the poet, they do not consciously realize "how their lives would all contain this hour." He thinks of "London spread out in the sun" as the train races into the city. And that's when the narrator's moment of epiphany arrives with a sharpened sense of identity with London. Like Bernard, he feels a sudden wonderment at the change in himself.[59]

Larkin and Woolf and Wordsworth not only demonstrate the experience of wonder, but also intimate the conditions necessary for that experience to happen. These writers are exemplars of wonder because they fulfill the best purpose of writing – finding the combination of words that replicates the experience being described to the reader.[60] In these examples, wonder is experienced only after a period of focusing on something – views of London, in these cases – and an absorption in the sensory world. This is knowledge before thought, Plato before Descartes.

The notion of attention leading (possibly) to epiphany is not unusual. Indeed, it is a common practice in most spiritual disciplines of which I'm aware. In Chapter Six, I discuss the Japanese poet Bashō and the way attention to ordinary, everyday things – "the chirp of a cicada, a leaf floating on water, moonlight on a temple roof, fog hanging in a forest" – provides him with the material for those moments of wonder that inform his poetry. A good haiku, like all worthwhile poetry, requires paying deep attention to the world, waiting for, without necessarily expecting, the sudden flash of insight that warrants poetic expression. It is not only a matter of accurately relating sensory experience, but also attending to the "presencing" of things of the world (as Heidegger would say). Out of this attention to the world in its ordinary and everyday moments, there perhaps comes an epiphanic moment that produces meaningful words.

This is what we get in Larkin, Woolf and Wordsworth. Their epiphanies constitute the mysticism of the mundane. They offer the key that sometimes unlocks wonder: our willingness and ability to attend to the world, to pay attention. This is the "trick" for transforming the ordinary into the extraordinary, the familiar into the strange. It may sound easy, even simplistic, but it isn't. Try sweeping the floor with absolute concentration on the sweeping, without your mind wandering. Try walking and attending just to the walking – the feel of the ground beneath your feet, the cracks in the sidewalk, a bit of litter in the gutter – without thinking about all the irritations in your life or your plans for the evening or your upcoming dental appointment. The reality is, we don't really pay attention to what is around us, including other people, because we are listening to the self-referential chatter in our heads. The experience of wonder transcends, however momentarily, this nagging, doubtful, unsettled self.

Some possess a greater capacity than others for experiencing wonder. This is not always a blessing. Virginia Woolf, for example, seems to have been preternaturally susceptible to "moments of being," but she also suffered bouts of deep depression and eventually committed suicide by drowning herself. Vincent Van Gogh's paintings reveal a man overwhelmed by wonder, to the point that he lived in a continuous state of emotional and mental exhaustion. He, too, eventually committed suicide. Paintings such as *Starry Night*, *The Bedroom at Arles*, *A Pair of Shoes*, or, my favourite, *The Café Terrace on the Place du Forum, Arles at Night*, display the perception of a world shimmering with wonder. Van Gogh perceived great beauty in the everyday, in the commonplace objects and scenes that most of us take for granted. He saw the transcendental in the actual.[61] He said as much himself: "It is true that you can see [such things] daily, but there are moments when the common everyday things make an extraordinary impression and have a deep significance and a different aspect."[62] Van Gogh's capacity for wonder allowed him to see heaven in a wild flower, to borrow William Blake's phrase. Considering the emotional and psychological difficulties that beset Van Gogh for much of his life, such intensity of perception is probably too much for the mind to sustain for any length of time and remain sane. We cannot survive as adults in the perpetual vision of childhood. Nonetheless, the fact that Van Gogh produced such magnificent paintings testifies to the potential of wonder-filled epiphanies.

For me, though, it has always been the wordsmiths who come closest to capturing the experience of wonder. They demonstrate that wonder can break through the seemingly bland and banal surface of the everyday. The familiar can be strange. The ordinary can be extraordinary. The dull can be numinous. Consider, for example, the seventeenth-century mystic and philosopher Thomas Traherne's recollection of his childhood. "The green trees when I saw them for the first time through one of the gates transported and ravished me, their sweetness and unusual beauty made my heart to leap, and almost made with ecstasy, they were such strange and wonderful things."[63] Traherne even wrote a poem entitled "Wonder." Here are a couple of stanzas:

> ... The streets were pav'd with golden stones,
> The boys and girls were mine,
> Oh how did all their lovely faces shine!
> The sons of men were holy ones,
> In joy and beauty they appear'd to me,

And every thing which here I found,
While like an angel I did see,
Adorn'd the ground ...
Proprieties themselves were mine,
And hedges ornaments;
Walls, boxes, coffers, and their rich contents
Did not divide my joys, but all combine.
Clothes, ribbons, jewels, laces, I esteem'd
My joys by others worn:
For me they all to wear them seem'd
When I was born.[64]

You have to envy a mind that perceives the ordinary things in the world – from walls and boxes to ribbons and lace – in such a luminous manner.

But when it comes to wonder, few exhibit the capacity to maintain a child-like enjoyment of the world into adulthood better than Wordsworth. To read his poems with imagination and sensitivity is to participate in his wonder.[65]

My heart leaps up when I behold
A rainbow in the sky;
So was it when my life began;
So is it now I am a man
So be it when I grow old ...[66]

At the same time, though, Wordsworth is well aware that our capacity for wonder can fade as we age. Our familiarity with the world induces a kind of perceptual numbness that leaves us unable to even appreciate the beauty of nature.

The world is too much with us; late and soon,
Getting and spending, we lay waste our powers:
Little we see in Nature that is ours;
We have given our hearts away, a sordid boon!
This Sea that bares her bosom to the moon;
The winds that will be howling for all hours,

And are up-gathered now like sleeping flowers;
For this, for every thing we are out of tune;
It moves us not ...[67]

You don't have to reach back to the Romantics, however, to find expressions of wonder at the everyday, although literary scholars argue that it was the early Romantics who first perceived and responded to "a particular form of experience, characterized by its brief duration and notable for its intense personal significance over time."[68] In an earlier chapter, I quoted W.B. Yeats' poem "The Lake Isle of Innisfree" as a symbolic expression of the longing for solitude. Part of the poem – "I hear lake water lapping with low sounds by the shore; / While I stand on the roadway, or on the pavements grey, / I hear it in the deep heart's core"[69] – testifies to moments of wonder that Yeats experienced in solitude. But Yeats also knew such moments in the most ordinary of circumstances. His poem "Vacillation" describes a fifty-year-old man sitting alone and reading a book in a London coffee shop. As the man leaves the shop, he is suddenly struck by the extraordinariness of the ordinary:

While on the shop and street I gazed
My body of a sudden blazed;
And twenty minutes more or less
It seemed, so great my happiness,
That I was blessed and could bless.[70]

Rupert Brooke, a contemporary of Yeats, goes to the heart of wonderment in a 1910 letter to a friend in which he describes his pleasure at "the things of ordinary life."

Half an hour's roaming about a street or village or railway station shows so much beauty that it's impossible to be anything but wild with suppressed exhilaration. And it's not only beauty and beautiful things. In a flicker of sunlight on a blank wall, or a reach of muddy pavement, or smoke from an engine at night, there's a sudden significance and importance and inspiration that makes the breath stop with a gulp of certainty and happiness. It's not that the wall or the smoke seem important for anything or suddenly reveal any general statement, or are suddenly seen to be good or beautiful in themselves – only that for you they are perfect and unique. It's like being in love with a person ...."[71]

In all of these poets, we see moments of wonder emerge from matter-of-fact situations. And that underscores my point: the value of an experience to the person undergoing it is often much greater than might appear to an outside observer. What might seem commonplace and boring to most of us, is, for the poets, a source of wonder. Yeats, for instance, talks of "luminous" moments, Wordsworth of "spots of time."[72] Ordinary experiences can be extraordinary without us deluding ourselves about their reality.

****

Nor do you need to be a poet to experience such transformations. Even hard-nosed "realists" like Mark Twain and Ernest Hemingway had moments of wonder. Twain, in *Life on the Mississippi*, is full of wonder at the variegated pattern of colours that play on the river's surface, the way its texture changes with the roil and swirl of its currents and eddies, the endless shifts of sun and shade and moonlight, the forested walls of trees that line the shore. "I stood like one bewitched. I drank it in, in a speechless rapture. The world was new to me, and I have never seen anything like this at home." To be sure, Twain also describes how he lost his sense of wonder after learning all the technical requirements of piloting a boat on the river. After awhile, he says, the river and its scenery became commonplace, and, as result, he "lost something" which "could never be restored to me while I lived."[73]

This is a puzzling statement. It is hard to believe Twain did not enjoy something of a "retrospective epiphany," to recall Morris Beja's phrase, in the act of remembrance, considering the detail with which he recalled the original experience of wonder. He obviously wrote the book long after the original experience, but his memories of the river remain sharp in their detail. He even recalled the sight of single leafy branch on an otherwise dead tree glowing like a flame as it caught the sun. You don't remember something like that so vividly without at least stirring the embers of wonder. It seems to me that in the act of writing Twain recovered something of his former experience.[74]

Hemingway's writing displays a similar attentiveness to the things of the world. And, as it does for Twain, the act of remembrance provides the recovery of wonder. For Hemingway, the best way to *know* the world is through our senses – touch, taste, smell and, most of all, sight – and not by classifying, analyzing or otherwise theorizing about it.[75] His stories and novels are replete with characters who remember mundane, everyday events or situations long after they have occurred. There may have been no immediate experience of wonder in the original event, but the remembrance of the event at a later date produced a sudden meaningful insight, a retrospective epiphany. For example, in Hemingway's famous short story "The Snows of Kilimanjaro," the main character, a dying writer, remembers all those things he wishes he'd written about, including a boyhood visit to his grandfather's cabin. "There was a long house, chinked white with mortar, on a hill above the lake. There was a bell on a pole by the door to call the people in to meals. Behind the house were fields and behind the fields was the timber. A line of lombardy poplars ran from the house to the dock. Other poplars ran along the point. A road went up to the hills along the edge of the timber and along that road he picked blackberries."[76] Such scenes constitute "Hemingway's wealth," says literary scholar Tony Tanner, his "meticulously retained sensations of the scattered munificence of the world."[77] Hemingway recalls the original experience and makes it as real as language allows.

His short stories and novels contain numerous other retrospective epiphanies, but there are also myriad epiphanic episodes in which his characters experience moments of wonderment in what appear to be the most mundane circumstances – anything from having a meal to going for a walk. I'm particularly fond of a scene in *The Sun Also Rises* where three of the characters, Jake, Bill and Robert, drive through the countryside of northern Spain.

> We came down out of the mountains and through an oak forest, and there were white cattle grazing in the forest. Down below there were grassy plains and clear streams, and then we crossed a stream and went through a gloomy little village, and started to climb ... After awhile we came out of the mountains, and there were trees along both sides of the road, and a stream and ripe fields of grain, and the road went on, very white and straight ahead, and then lifted to a little rise, and off on to the left was a hill with an old castle, with buildings close around it and a field of field of grain going right up to the walls and shifting in the wind. I was up in front with the driver and I turned around. Robert Cohn was asleep, but Bill looked and nodded his head.[78]

What we get here is two men given over to receptive contemplation of the world, apprehending the beauty of the whole in their focus on its particulars. That attention stirs a feeling of wonder in them, the knowledge of which they communicate to each other with a glance. That glance makes a telling judgment about wonder: Those who know how to see the world are awake to it; those who don't, like Robert Cohn, are asleep, figuratively and literally. Hemingway, of course, would probably never have made such an abstract claim. His prose, as Tanner says, "makes permanent the attentive wonder of the senses: it mimes out the whole process, impression by impression."[79] The meaning is in the lived experience, not in the conceptual afterthought.

An even more resonant episode of wonder, one reverberating with the poignancy of impending death, is found in *For Whom the Bell Tolls*. The main character, Robert Jordan, awaits death after being wounded while trying to escape with a guerrilla group from a troop of Spanish soldiers during the Spanish Civil War. Lying on a forest floor, recalling episodes of his life and thinking about his love for the woman he has just sent away, he offers what Tony Tanner describes as a "last act of communion" with the mundane world. "He was completely integrated now and he took a good long look at everything. Then he looked up at the sky. There were big white clouds in it. He touched the palm of his hand against the pine needles where he lay and he touched the bark of the pine trunk that he lay behind ... He could feel his heart beating against the pine needle floor of the forest."[80] Admittedly, the circumstances of Jordan's final moment of wonderment are far from ordinary. Yet, Hemingway sticks with the ordinary. He refuses to indulge in metaphysical speculation by having Jordan wonder about the meaning of life. Instead, Hemingway conveys the meaning of life, at least as he conceived it, by attending to the sensory experience of the world – pine needles, a tree trunk, clouds and sky. In Jordan's final action, says Tanner, we see "the senses taking their farewell from all the truth they have ever known; the wounded individual, his dignity unimpaired, preparing himself for the slide into nothingness with a final feel of the earth."[81] For Hemingway, "description is explanation,"[82] and that is cause enough for wonder.

Perhaps, though, the greatest literary exponent of wonder is the novelist Marcel Proust. After all, it is Proust who provides the most famous moment of wonderment – *moments bienheureux*, moments of well-being – in twentieth-century literature. In *Swann's Way*, the opening book in Proust's monumental *Remembrance of Things Past*, he describes returning home one day. His mother, seeing he is cold and tired, offers him a cup of tea and one of those small plump cakes known in France as *petites madeleines*. Dispirited by his day, he declines at first. But then, for no particular reason, he changes his mind. At the table, he breaks off a piece of the shell-shaped sponge cake, sets it on a spoon and dips the spoon into the tea. He raises the spoon to his mouth to take a sip.

> No sooner had the warm liquid mixed with the crumbs touched my palate than a shudder ran though me and I stopped, intent upon the extraordinary thing that was happening to me. An exquisite pleasure had invaded my senses, something isolated, detached, with no suggestion of its origin. And at once the vicissitudes of life had become indifferent to me, its disasters innocuous, its brevity illusory – this new sensation having had on me the effect which love has of filling me with a precious essence, or rather this essence was not in me, it *was* me. I had ceased now to feel mediocre, contingent, mortal ....[83]

Puzzled at what had come over him – "this all powerful joy," as he wrote – Proust takes several more mouthfuls of the tea-soaked *madeleine*, thinking he might feel the same surging of emotion. It doesn't work, and he realizes that the source of his moment of wonder resides within him, although it was the taste of the *madeleine* that called it into being. He puts down the cup and concentrates on the "indisputable evidence" of this "unremembered state," trying to work out what action on his part might have prompted this "exquisite pleasure." He tries to block out all distractions, stopping his ears against all noise, including the sounds of his mother in the next room. He feels his mind tiring, and surrenders to distraction for a moment of rest before making a final effort. He conjures that moment when he took the first sip and the taste of the *madeleine*, and he feels something start within him, a stirring of a near-forgotten memory, "something that leaves its resting-place and attempts to rise, something that has been embedded like an anchor at a great depth; I do not know yet what it is, but I can feel it mounting slowly."

Suddenly the memory rises to the surface. It is the taste, as Proust famously writes, of the little piece of *madeleine* that his aunt gave him on Sunday mornings when he lived with her as a child in the town of Combray. As soon as he remembers that taste, Proust's childhood comes rushing into his memory: the old grey house on the street, the garden, the sight of church towers from his window, the town square, the streets where he played. But it is not just the images that Proust recalls. It is the very *feel* of the past that he regains, the *experience* of his boyhood. For a few moments, Proust the weary adult is again that wonder-filled child. "The whole of Combray and its surroundings, taking shape and solidity, sprang into being, town and gardens alike, from my cup of tea."[84]

Remembrance of Things Past contains several epiphanic episodes – for example, in *Time Regained*, Proust stumbles on some paving stones and suddenly remembers with exquisite happiness the uneven paving stones of Venice. But the incident with the *madeleine* is the most famous. However, that's not the reason I've devoted so much space to it. Rather, it is because this particular "moment of well-being" exemplifies in the most concrete fashion the conditions for and the experience of wonder. These *moments bienheureux* arise out of seemingly mundane events and objects that become occasions for illumination. In such moments, Proust feels that he's gained a glimpse of something eternal in the human spirit.

What is most revealing about all these moments of wonder, whether those of the novelists or the poets, is both the transience of the experience – they seldom last more than a few minutes – and the significance attached to what otherwise appears to be trivial events or situations. This is in keeping with the nature of epiphanies. Yeats feels overjoyed at simply being on a Dublin street. Hemingway is close to sacramental in his regard for the natural world. Proust senses eternity in his memories. Such expressions of "worship" – to appropriate Thomas Carlyle's description of wonder – are not uncommon in a time when belief in a divine order "beyond" this world has faded, at least among the intelligentsia of the West. "Nowadays," says Morris Beja, "men modestly interpret their sensations any number of ways – emotionally, psychologically, physiologically – before they even think, and then usually with reluctance, of looking upon them as holy and consecrated."[85]

In a seemingly disenchanted world, epiphanic episodes offer a measure of enchantment, a means for extracting meaning from a world that, according to scientism, is without inherent meaning. Thanks to the artists, things of seeming insignificance take on much greater importance. Indeed, artists demonstrate that what we truly value most in this life, the things we most remember as important to us, are often the slight situations and the fleeting events, the glimpses and glimmers of that which is other to us. As Beja puts it, "Doubtful of immortality, they turned against it and cherished mortality; afraid of death, they worshipped life. Since they could endow nothing else with permanence, they began, paradoxically, to attribute it to whatever is most ephemeral, to value things *because* they are evanescent."[86] In other words, in a time of faded faith, the experience of wonder is an intelligible response to our existential anxieties, and, indeed, to the question Peggy Lee asked: Is that all there is?[87]

Virginia Woolf responded to that question with deep sensitivity. Her "moments of being" are a testament to the long duration of wonder. Her experiences of wonder – she called them "visions" – tend to appear out of the blue, arising from seemingly innocuous events or circumstance. Nonetheless, they take on immense meaning. For example, in one of her autobiographical writings, "A Sketch of the Past," Woolf relates several well-remembered "moments of being" from childhood, incidents that, as she herself admits, are utterly trivial, yet somehow retained a strong presence in her memory as an adult. One winter morning in 1894, Woolf, then twelve years old, encountered a rain puddle while walking along Hyde Park Gate near her home. "The moment of the puddle in the path," as she later described it, "when for no reason I could discover, everything suddenly became unreal; I was suspended; I could not step across the puddle; I tried to touch something ... the whole world became unreal." Woolf also offers one of the best impressionist sketches of the wonder of childhood as a whole. "Many bright colours; many distinct sounds; some human beings; caricatures; comic; several violent moments of being; always including a circle of the scene which they cut out; and all surrounded by a vast space – that is a rough visual description of childhood."[88]

Woolf's key memory from childhood, the base on which her life as a writer stands, might also be regarded as a retrospective epiphany. "It is of lying half asleep, half awake, in bed in the nursery at St. Ives. It is of hearing the waves breaking, one, two, one, two, and sending a splash of water over the beach, and then breaking, one, two, one, two, behind a yellow blind. It is of hearing the blind draw its little acorn across the floor as the wind blew the blind out. It is of lying and hearing this splash and seeing this light, and feeling, *it is almost impossible that I should be here;* of feeling the purest ecstasy I can conceive."[89]

Woolf's favourite word for her moments of being and what they mean to her is "it." In a diary entry, she asks: "Why is there not a discovery in life? Something one can lay hands on and say 'This is it'?" In a short story entitled "The New Dress," a character considers those "divine moments" when you cannot help but exclaim, "This is it!" Woolf often combines "it" with "reality" in trying to define her moments of being. The definition is always vague as to what she means by reality, but she has no trouble describing a sense of wonderment in her perception of reality.[90]

> What is meant by "reality"? *It* would seem to be something very erratic, very undependable – now to be found in a dusty road, now in a scrap of newspaper in the street, now a daffodil in the sun. *It* lights up a group in a room and stamps some casual saying. *It* overwhelms one walking home beneath the stars and makes the silent world more real than the world of speech – and then there *it* is again in an omnibus in the uproar of Piccadilly. Sometimes, too, *it* seems to dwell in shapes too far away for us to discern what their nature is. But whatever *it* touches, *it* fixes and makes permanent. That is what remains over when the skin of the day has been cast into the hedge; that is what is left of past time and of our loves and hates.[91]

These revelations of "it" occur for no particular reason, but they assume an "inexplicable significance" that echoes in the memory long after the event. "Such moments of vision are of an unaccountable nature; leave them alone and they persist for years; try to explain them and they disappear; write them down and they die beneath the pen."[92]

Woolf ascribed many of her epiphanic experiences to her characters. Almost invariably, her characters' moments of vision arise in the most ordinary settings and situations. For example, in the novel *To the Lighthouse*, the main character, Mrs. Ramsay, wakes in the middle of the night to watch the regular pulse of light from a nearby lighthouse pierce the bedroom window and bend across her bed and sweep along the floor. She stares in fascination, "hypnotized, as if it were stroking with its silver fingers some sealed vessel in her brain whose bursting would flood her with delight." Imagining the nearby sea and its rolling waves swelling and breaking endlessly on the shore, "the ecstasy burst in her eyes and waves of pure delight raced over the floor of her mind and she felt, it is enough! It is enough!"[93]

Ultimately, what we get in Woolf (and in Proust, Hemingway, Van Gogh, Larkin, Brooke, Wordsworth, and others) is wonderment at the presencing *Being*. They marvel at there being anything rather than nothing – from starry skies and mud puddles to streetlights and train stations. Here it is well to recall the distinction I made in Chapter One between "spirit" and "religion." Religion is an attempt to contain experiences that have such luminous significance that they seem to point to something greater than ourselves, something that some refer to as God. Understood this way, religion seeks to "bind" spiritual experiences in order to make them intelligible. It seems to me that the artists, philosophers and theologians I've drawn on are being religious in their attempts to articulate experiences that manifest the mystery of Being. They are saying to us, Look at this! Here it is: see it, hear it, taste it, smell it, feel it! Remember it! Wonder at it!

****

I like to think those exclamatory injunctions were behind my most recent epiphany. It was, in hindsight, one of those serendipitous conjunctions of psyche and circumstance that leave you wondering if Peggy Lee was on to something. In early June of 2008, I spent a few days in England before returning to Canada after completing a partial walk of the Camino de Santiago. One sunny day I decided to visit some of the places I knew when I lived in England in the mid-1970s.

Catching the 1:06 train on Platform 4 from Victoria Station, I fell into the well of memory almost immediately. Everything was familiar, yet strange. For a short time when I was in England, I had to commute each day between Bromley, a town on the southeastern fringe of Greater London, where I lived, and north London, where I worked at one of the several jobs I had during my time there. Each morning I took the train from Bromley South station into Victoria Station, and every evening I caught the train from Platform 4 back to Bromley. On Sundays, my girlfriend – I'll call her Jane – and I often took the train into London, where we'd spend the day walking around St. James's Park, Regent's Park or Primrose Hill, or go shopping at Harrod's (not that we could afford anything) or take in a film and a meal at the Swiss Centre before heading back to Orpington, where Jane lived. I unconsciously memorized the names of the stations along the way.

There's something about trains that leads to contemplation and, on this occasion at least, moments of wonder. As a passenger you can observe the world without participating in it. The car was nearly empty – a half-dozen seats in front of me, a man in a suit hid behind a copy of the *Telegraph*, and an elderly woman dozed in a nest of shopping bags – when we pulled clanking and swaying out of Victoria Station. The train picked up speed as it ran between the tall backs of highrise apartments, past the Battersea Cats and Dogs Home, across the muddy Thames, going faster and faster until I caught only flashing images – a wall of graffiti, a crowded high street, a field of slate roofs, a soccer field, a couple alone on a station platform, hedgerows rising and falling, narrow gardens at the backs of houses, a schoolyard full of uniform-clad girls (purple sweaters and grey skirts), walls of green and patches of Queen Anne's lace with a wedge of blue sky overhead. I found myself anticipating the stations. I think I got most of them: Herne Hill, West Dulwich, Syndenham Hill, Penge East, Kent House, Beckenham Junction, Short-lands, Bromley South, Bickley, Petts Wood. The incantation had me conjuring names of people I remembered from my sojourn in England – Sean and Kevin, David and Jack, Bob-bie and Beverly, Alison and Mary, Shane and Jennifer and, never to be forgotten, Jane. By the time the train rattled into Orpington Station, I was reliving a sunny afternoon in the summer of 1975.

I followed the ghosts of Jane and me as we got off the train. They walked along Platform 6 and across the small bridge over the tracks and through the waiting room and out on to Station Approach. Everything was familiar, achingly so. Sure, there were some differences – cash machines in the waiting room, security cameras above the doors, a bigger bus terminal – but otherwise the scene was unchanged. The two ghosts went ahead of me down the hill past Crown's Garage (Jane's dirndl skirt swaying around her fine legs) and turned through a gate and down a short lane onto Hillview Road and up Mayfield Avenue. They turned left on Lynwood Grove past the red brick church, admiring the big oak trees along the road and the steep-roofed homes with their leaded windows and the trim hedges and neat lawns. The traffic island in the middle of the road with its big oak in full foli-age surprised me. I had forgotten about it. Just beyond the oak tree, the ghostly couple came to a home with a small curving flagstone drive and half-moon patch of lawn. The whitewashed lions were still there on either side of the front steps. My ghostly younger self patted their stone heads – just like I used to do – before he went inside.

I followed them in my mind's eye, seeing the bright kitchen on the right just beyond the hallway, the living room and dining room with its round-edged teak furniture – Scandinavian Ercol, I was told – and bookshelves jammed with gardening and botany books and, here and there, Ian Fleming's James Bond books. The Lladró figurines in their elongated poses on the mantle fascinated me.

I looked up at the second-storey window on the left side of the house, seeing Jane's room with the bed, neatly made, in the corner against the wall, and the small desk and the monograph record player on a shelf and a collection of 45s, and her Tamara De Lempicka and Biba prints on the walls. As I stared up at the window, something gave way inside me like ice cracking on the surface of a lake at the end of a long winter. Something was trying to surface, a nearly forgotten memory. I concentrated, shutting out the distractions of a passing car, the buzz of a power tool somewhere up the street, a bird's cry, trying to lure the memory to the surface. The world grew quiet, muted, almost still. I could almost see it, something about the window. A breeze carried the smell of fresh-cut grass, and, barely detectable, the drift of lilac.

The lilac did it. As soon as I caught the scent of lilac the memory broke through the ice. It was a Sunday in August of 1975. I was standing at the window in Jane's room. It had rained but now the sun was out. The leaves on the trees, the sidewalk and the road below: everything glistened in the light. We'd returned from a day in London. We'd been to St. James's Park, feeding the ducks. Now I was watching for a cab to take me to Bromley, where I worked in a wine bar. Jane was curled up on the bed. A Led Zeppelin album was playing. I leaned out the window to inhale the rain-fresh air, and caught a whiff of lilac. A fragment of the lyric caught my attention: "Thinking how it used to be / Does she still remember times like these? / To think of us again? / And I do." Something about the situation – the combination of the lyric, the smell of lilac, Jane on the bed, the glistening street below – made me think, "You must remember this moment, this girl, this place, this afternoon for the rest of your life."

I remembered it all again as I stood outside the house on Lynwood Grove, looking up at the window at my younger self looking out. It was all there, *so close*: London, Orpington, Bromley Common, Primrose Hill, Cherry's Wine Bar; they all surged into being, and for a moment it seemed that all I had to do was step through the door between the lions and I would enter the still living past.

The shriek of an electric saw from a nearby house broke the spell. It was 2008 again, and I was merely looking up at an empty window. I told myself I was being a sentimental fool, but I also felt a strange gratitude. Proust once said something to the effect that the recovery of the past keeps life from being absurd. I'd never wanted to leave England and had only done so because I needed money. Now, all these years later, I was grateful to recover the memory of a particular moment and a particular place that meant so much to me.

On impulse I crossed the flagstones to the front steps and patted the lions. Then I walked back to the station and caught the train to London. I read a book and tried not to pay too much attention to the passing stations.

SIX

THE DEPTH OF WALKING
Pilgrimages of Enchantment

I have walked myself into my best thoughts, and I know of no thought so burdensome that one cannot walk away from it.
  — Søren Kierkegaard, *Letters and Documents*[1]

My God is the God of walkers. If you walk hard enough you probably don't need any other God.
  — Bruce Chatwin[2]

I was lost in Japan. I knew I was somewhere on Mount Yokomine, but after an hour of stumbling along a maze of paths that took me ever deeper into the forest, I finally had to admit I'd made a wrong turn somewhere. It was my own fault. I should have stuck with my fellow pilgrims — Yukuo Tanaka, Suji Niwano and his son Jun — when we left Yokomineji Temple. We had made the long climb to the temple from the valley town of Komatsu together in the morning, but I wanted to do the return hike on my own, thinking it would be pleasant to stroll through the cathedral-like silence of the forest. But I committed the cardinal sin of long-distance walking — not paying attention. I had been daydreaming instead of watching for the trail markers — the small signs of red silhouettes of a pilgrim with a walking

stave – that would have kept me on the right path back
to Komatsu. Instead, I was somewhere on the side of the
mountain, wandering around a criss-cross series of logging
trails and farmers' tracks, wondering what kind of idiot I
was for getting lost in Japan, of all places. Considering how
urbanized Japan is, you might not think it has any wilderness left. Yet there are still places where forests prevail. The
mountainous island of Shikoku, the smallest of Japan's four
main islands, is one of those places.

I looked at my watch: 1:44 p.m. I had plenty of daylight
left, lots of time to get off the mountain before nightfall.
I glanced up through the cedar canopy, grateful to see a
slit of cloudless blue sky. Sitting on a half-rotted log on
the edge of the trail, I studied the pilgrim map that for the
last six weeks had guided me two-thirds of the way along
the 1,400-kilometre Shikoku no Michi and its eighty-eight
temples, strung circle-like around the island. At 709 metres
above sea level, Yokomineji, Temple 60, is one of the most
difficult to reach. The hike up the mountain from Komatsu
had been a lung-aching thigh-burner; if I'd had to climb it at
the beginning of my pilgrimage, I might not have made it.
But after nearly two months of walking, I was in much better
shape physically than when I started. Judging by the unused
notches in my belt, I had lost at least twenty pounds. Sure,
I was huffing and puffing after the four-hour climb to the
temple, but it took only a few minutes' rest for my breathing
to return to normal. I was pleased with myself; I felt like the
Energizer bunny, ready to keep going and going.

Yokomineji was worth the climb. Hidden in the forest,
the 1,300-year-old temple possesses a haunting out-of-time
feel. It was pleasant to sit in the courtyard and eat lunch and
look out across the ridges of mountains and valleys in the
distance. I liked the swept courtyard, the hard-packed ground
showing the scratch marks of the twig brooms used by the

temple priests, and the curving lines of raked gravel swirling around the large boulders in the rock garden. I imagined the generations of priests who had spent the last millennium trying to maintain order and beauty in their small world.

The map showed two pilgrim trails leading from Komatsu to Yokomineji, but not the logging trails or farmers' tracks. I replayed the last hour's hike in my head, following the map to where it indicated a fork in the trail about a kilometre below the temple. One path – the shorter one – went almost due north down the face of the mountain directly into Komatsu; a second path turned west about three kilometres from the temple to descend another side of the mountain and loop around to the southern outskirts of the town. We had taken the shorter route on our climb, and I couldn't recall seeing the fork at that time. I could only assume I'd inadvertently turned onto the second longer path on the way down, and then drifted onto some side trail. I had two choices: Retrace my steps back to the fork in the trail, or go on. The prospect of climbing the mountain again had no appeal. I decided to stick with whatever trail I was on, figuring that sooner or later it would reach the valley floor and I'd find either the pilgrim route or a road back to Komatsu. On such vague decisiveness did I have the most memorable day of my Shikoku pilgrimage.

I had been trekking The Way of Shikoku for just over six weeks. In another week-and-a-half, I would reach Okuboji, Temple 88, the last on the Shikoku circuit. It was hard to believe the end was in sight. The pilgrimage had taken over my life. That was as it should be: Walking twenty to thirty kilometres a day over a long period produces more than physical consequences. Perceptions shift. Senses sharpen. The psyche does strange things. My sense of time had changed as the pace of walking literally forced my mind to slow down. The landscape of cedar forest and distant vistas, the downpour of sun and rain, the shower of birdsong and prayer had worked its enchantment. The world of highway traffic, television and radio, and the latest geo-political crisis were, well, a world away. I now paid attention to more important things – sunlight in the trees, flowers in a ditch, birds in the bush. So it was on this day, too. I might have been lost in the geographic sense, but I was also lost to the sensuous: Mountain air pungent with damp cedar; trails edged with blue wisteria, azaleas in pink and yellow and red, and purple iris; slabs of sunlight dropping through gaps in the trees; leaf-thick paths; nightingales chanting *ho-hokekyo, ho-hokekyo*.

But the day's real gift was the inward journey. I seemed to float above myself, watching as my body did the hard work of sweating up a slope or scrambling over rock while, at the same time, my mind made its own psychic sojourn. Images from the past six weeks replayed in my head: the green glow of a sunlit river; black-bellied clouds far out to sea; a parade of low-lying clouds floating through a mountain valley; a village street silent save for the rain gurgling in the gutters. My mind was a pilgrim mind now. I had not forgotten my "real" life back in Canada, but after weeks of walking that life seemed oddly unreal. Home was too distant, psychologically and chronologically, for me to start anticipating my return. There were even moments in the silence of some forest when I was willing to believe, as Buddhist tradition claims, that I was never alone, that Kōbō Daishi, the patron saint of Shikoku pilgrims, was my constant companions.

As it turned out, it was Jizō, the bald, toque-wearing Buddhist deity who protects children, the souls of the dead and, it seems, inattentive travellers, who restored me to the pilgrim path. I was following a farmer's trail that consisted of two rutted tracks and a line of grass running down the centre. High grass and bush edged the trail and a wall of trees loomed overhead. I didn't know where I was, only that I was heading north and, presumably, would reach civilization sooner or later. Rounding a corner, I came to an intersection with three trails leading off in different directions. I squatted in the middle of the intersection, looking up one path and then another. I had no idea which one to follow. Then, out of the corner of my eye, I caught a flash of colour. And there, at the edge of a track, poking above the grass like a child playing peek-a-boo, was a small statue of my pilgrim hero, Jizō. Bless his tiny red toque.

Always follow the Jizō, I told myself. Where there is one Jizō, there has to be more. I practically pranced down the trail, singing "Jizō loves me, this I know, because the Buddha tells me so." Jizō would surely lead me on the right path and set me on the road back to my hotel, where a fine evening meal would follow. I straightened Jizō's toque and splashed him with a generous share of water from my bottle. I was hot and thirsty after only a couple of hours of walking; a millennium of looking out for lost pilgrims must have left him parched. Two hundred metres down the track I came to another Jizō and another intersection. This one turned onto a two-lane asphalt road with a beautiful yellow stripe. I splashed more water on Jizō by way of thanks.

The god wasn't done with me yet, however. The road dropped steeply around a sharp turn. Trotting down the hill, I saw below me on the right side of the road, through a gap in the treetops, the roof of a temple set in a narrow gorge. I could hear a waterfall. At the bottom of the hill, a small gravel parking lot and a pathway disappeared into a copse of cedars. Something – Jizō, perhaps – told me not to pass this temple without offering a prayer. So I crunched across the gravel and down another tunnel of trees. There I found a peaceful place that, as it turned out, provided me with one of my more meaningful pilgrimage experiences.

I am in good company in linking walking and meaningful experience. Theologians, philosophers, poets and novelists all testify to having some of their most memorable experiences and profound thoughts while out walking. It's a psychological phenomenon that writer Rebecca Solnit rightly makes much of in her excellent "history of walking," *Wanderlust*. "The subject of walking is, in some sense, about how we invest universal acts with particular meanings," she writes. "Like eating or breathing, it can be invested with wildly different cultural meanings, from the erotic to the spiritual, from the revolutionary to the artistic."[3] She rattles off a list of philosophers – from the Sophists of ancient Greece and Aristotle's Peripatetics to Rousseau, Kant and Wittgenstein – who, to one degree or another, equated walking with thinking. Jean-Jacques Rousseau, for example, once confessed, "I can only meditate when I am walking. When I stop, I cease to think; my mind only works with my legs." Indeed, the eighteenth-century French philosopher claimed he was never able "to do anything with my pen in my hand, and my desk and paper before me; it is on my walks, among the rocks and trees" and at night in bed, lying awake, that "I compose in my head."[4]

To be sure, this linkage of walking and thinking was not new. Tradition holds that the ancient Greek thinkers, the Sophists, Plato and Aristotle, the Stoics, lectured to their students while walking to and fro along the colonnades – the *peripatos*, in Greek – of their schools.[5] Socrates, the godfather of Western philosophy, was known for walking the streets of Athens and asking inconvenient questions. Plato's *Republic*, with its theme of a search for justice, opens with Socrates walking from Athens to Piraeus to pay his respects to the goddess and observe a festival. In another Platonic dialogue, *Phaedrus*, Socrates takes a rare walk on the wild side, venturing outside the walls of Athens to stroll along the banks of the

Ilissus, where he not only reveals an unexpected appreciation of nature – he comments on the fragrance of flowers and the pleasant shade of a plane tree – but also suggests that it is in nature that we most readily glimpse the divine.[6] Virgil would not have produced the *Georgics* without his country walks. Chaucer and his pilgrims also spent much time on foot.

I mustn't forget the biblical walkers. Jesus Christ walked all over Galilee, trekked into the desert and high into the mountains. "Jesus of Nazareth spent forty days in the wilderness, and the three years of his ministry were, as we know, spent in unceasing wandering."[7] By one account he walked more than 4,800 kilometres during his three-year ministry. As a boy, he may well have walked the six hundred or so kilometres from Egypt when his family returned to His native land. Devout Jewish males attended religious festivals in Jerusalem three times a year. Nazareth is about two hundred kilometres from Jerusalem; if Jesus attended these festivals, he would have walked nearly thirty thousand kilometres in round trips between the ages of five and thirty, when he began his ministry. Baptized in the wilderness of Judea, Jesus walked to Galilee and then to Capernaum and Cana – a round trip of nearly four hundred kilometres. Add the various trips from Galilee to Jerusalem and back, and, well, the kilometres add up. And then there was the longest walk of all, the climb to Calvary through the streets of Jerusalem.[8]

Christ may be one of the greatest walkers in the Bible, but others did their share, too. Adam and Eve walked out of Paradise. "The world was all before them, where to choose / Their place of rest, and providence their guide: / They hand in hand with wandering steps and slow, / Through Eden took their solitary way."[9] Moses led his people across the Red Sea and into the Sinai, then climbed Mount Sinai, where he spent forty days alone before descending the mountain armed with the Decalogue. The Israelites walked the desert of Sinai for forty years. Jacob walked in the light of the Lord back to Canaan, and, along the way, had a vision of angels. The creed of the Desert Fathers included the practice of prayer walking. At the age of ninety, St. Anthony, one of the original Desert Fathers, walked for days in the desert to find Paul the Hermit after receiving a vision that the hermit was dying. And then there is Paul of Tarsus, who, as far as I can tell, did more walking than most anyone else. He may have been riding a horse on the road to Damascus when he received his vision of the resurrected Christ, but he certainly did a lot of travelling afterwards, much of it, no doubt, on foot. Paul is known to have visited at one time or another much of present-day Saudi Arabia, Israel, Syria and Turkey, as well as Corinth, Ephesus, Macedonia and, finally, Rome.

I am by no means in St. Paul's league when it comes to on-the-road conversion experiences. Still, there have been a few modest epiphanies over the years, some of which involved walking. I can even claim, like Rousseau, to do some of my best thinking (such as it is) either while I am walking or as a result of walking. Pilgrimage walks, in particular, have provided me with some of my most intense walking experiences. But I have fond memories of less arduous walks – a Sunday meander around St. James's Park in London; a day in Paris retracing the route Ernest Hemingway's characters in *The Sun Also Rises* (Jake Barnes and Bill Gorton) took on a drunken walk around the Left Bank; a long-ago afternoon in Victoria strolling along Dallas Road with a girl. For whatever reason, these "walks" are part of my memory palace.

The phrase "memory palace" refers to a mnemonic technique developed by the ancient Greeks and Romans. The technique relies on constructing imagined places in memory where things you want to remember – people, poetry, myths, speeches – are stored for future recollection. The idea is to build in the mind a series of *loci* or places in the palace –

bedrooms, dining rooms, living rooms, etc. – and then attach what you want to remember later to an object such as a lamp, a bed or a couch that you then place in the imagined room. When you need that speech or poem, you make a mental tour of the palace, checking for rooms that have a lamp or couch. The poem or speech returns to consciousness when you find the lamp or couch.[10]

The memory palace technique demonstrates that memory is largely sustained by references to place. Rebecca Solnit makes this point in *Wanderlust*, where she writes that if we imagine memory as a real space, whether a building or a landscape, then the act of remembrance constitutes a kind of mental walking in that building or landscape. And to walk the landscape of memory is, potentially, to recover something of the feel and thought attached to the original experience. "To walk the same route again can mean to think the same thoughts again, as though thoughts and ideas were indeed fixed objects in a landscape one need only know how to travel through."[11]

In my more fanciful moments, I imagine heaven as a great big memory palace. If God is kindly disposed to us, we spend eternity exploring the rooms where our best moments are stored. (Hell, I suppose, would be having to revisit your worst moments for eternity, or even to have no place at all in the cosmic memory palace, to be obliterated from all remembrance.) And why not? The mystic and poet William Blake once referred to seeing the world in a grain of sand. Perhaps you can also glimpse eternity in a moment of time. The closest I have come this side of the grave to even an opaque glimpse of the eternal has been by means of walking (or being in love, but that's another topic). I suspect in my heart of hearts that this is why I walk. The poet Philip Larkin once said he wrote poetry to preserve meaningful moments of experience from oblivion.[12] I feel much the same way about my walks, particularly my pilgrimage treks. Not only does walking help me retain and relive memories, but sometimes it helps me glimpse the meaning of those memories.

To be sure, I don't turn every Sunday stroll into a prayer walk. Most times I go to the corner store *just* to get milk and a newspaper. Glimpsing the underglimmer in sidewalk cracks would be rather distracting and time-consuming if it wasn't a rare experience (for which, I presume, my wife is grateful when I'm fetching a carton of milk for the morning coffee). Still, I have learned to regard walking as more than the mere ambulatory effort of getting from point A to point B. The best way I can demonstrate this idea is by recounting some of my walking experiences, as well as those of other serious walkers.

****

I am not sure my two philosophic examples – Jean Jacques Rousseau and Søren Kierkegaard – would have made good walking companions, but they were certainly good walkers. Scholars have long recognized that Rousseau's thought marks a shift in how we, as modern Westerners, regard the natural world. He launched the Romantic notion of nature that challenged earlier modern political philosophers such as Francis Bacon, Thomas Hobbes and John Locke, who saw nature as "a mere physical resource to be manipulated at will for human use." Rousseau argued that man and nature interconnect, and the good life is one lived according to "the simplest impulses of nature." Rousseau's views on this score informed his political thought and its fundamental claim that man is by nature good, and it is society that corrupts him. His *Second Discourse*, for example, praises man's original natural state so effusively that many have thought Rousseau to be advocating the abandonment of civilization and a return to nature. Even Voltaire thought this was what Rousseau meant.

He wrote to Rousseau, "Never has so much been used in an attempt to make us animals. The desire to walk on all fours seizes one when one reads your work."[13]

However, Rousseau explicitly denies the possibility of restoring mankind to its natural condition. There is no going back "to live in forests with bears." For modern man, "whose passions have forever destroyed their original simplicity," there can be no return to a state of nature.[14] Rousseau's political thought is, in essence, a response to this reality, and an attempt to work out how best to recreate a political society that would allow men and women to approximate and express their true natural goodness. He works this new society out most thoroughly in his book *The Social Contract*, which begins with the famous line "Man was born free, and everywhere he is in chains."[15]

Rousseau's political philosophy and his proposals for creating societies that foster natural goodness are beyond the scope of my concerns here. It is sufficient for my purposes to note Rousseau's view that he regards our estrangement from society and ourselves as part of our estrangement from nature as a whole. We need to find ways to ease our sense of estrangement if we are to recover some semblance of natural wholeness. To this end, Rousseau examined some variants on what it means to lead a "good life" – everything from the life of the savage who is at one with nature (or so he assumed) to the citizen who identifies with his city and the man educated to be his natural self in society. Rousseau's penultimate good life, however, was that of the solitary walker. It is this latter ideal with which I am concerned. For Rousseau, as Solnit observes, "walking functions as an emblem of the simple man and as, when the walk is solitary and rural, a means of being in nature and outside society."[16]

Walking was also freedom for Rousseau. One day, returning from a Sunday stroll outside his hometown of

Geneva, Rousseau returned to find he was too late. The city gates were locked. Acting on impulse, he decided to leave Switzerland completely, walking to France and Italy. In later years, writing *The Confessions*, he would recall his initial days of wandering as among the happiest in his life.

> To be travelling to Italy so young, to have seen so many countries already, to be following in Hannibal's footsteps across the mountains, seemed to me a glory beyond my years ... I do not remember every having had in all my life a spell of time so completely free from care and anxiety as those seven or eight days we spent on the road ... This memory has left me the strongest taste for everything associated with it, for mountains especially and for travelling on foot. I have never travelled so except in my prime, and it has always been a delight to me.[17]

In fact, when Rousseau was in Paris, he tried to persuade others to pool funds and join him for a year on a walking tour of Italy. The trip didn't happen, but throughout his life Rousseau regarded walking as a joyful experience and a source of inspiration. He believed he was most himself, his most real self, when he walked alone.

> Never did I think so much, exist so vividly, and experience so much, never have I been so much myself – if I may use that expression – as in the journeys I have taken alone and on foot. There is something about walking which stimulates and enlivens my thoughts. When I stay in one place I can hardly think at all; my body has to be on the move to set my mind going. The sight of the countryside, the succession of pleasant views, the open air, a sound appetite, and the good health I gain by walking, the easy atmosphere of an inn, the absence of everything that makes me feel my dependence, of everything that recalls me to my situation – all these

serve to free my spirit, to lend a greater boldness to my thinking, so that I can combine them, select them, and to make of them mine as I will, without fear or restraint.[18]

Rousseau's last book, written towards the end of his life, was *Reveries of a Solitary Walker*, published in 1782. In its ten short chapters we see a man who finds refuge in nature. Walking was a "mode of being" for Roussseau. In walking he was self-sufficient, alive to his own thoughts and memories. Indeed, reading Rousseau's walks provides a lesson in how the mind and the body work together; that is, how thinking and walking go hand in hand. Walking is conducive to what Solnit calls unstructured, associative thinking, the kind of thinking in which the mind literally rambles, shifting from the present to the past, projecting into the future, focusing on the near at hand, zooming out to look at the big picture. These kinds of free-flowing digressions reflect the way the mind works when it goes for a walk, and, as Solnit observes, may well be the literary source for the stream-of-consciousness techniques of writing developed by modernist writers such as James Joyce and Virginia Woolf.[19]

You certainly see Rousseau's mind in his *Reveries*. For example, Walk One opens with an admission of aloneness. "So now I am alone in the world, with no brother, neighbour or friend, nor any company left me but my own." The remainder of the walk is a reverie on how he has come to such a state. "Everything is finished for me on earth. Neither good nor evil can be done to me by any man. I have nothing left in the world to fear or hope for, and this leaves me in peace at the bottom of the abyss, a poor unfortunate mortal, but as unmoved as God himself." This is the mind of a man who was unquestionably persecuted and demonized during his lifetime and is seeking some final equanimity as he nears death. It is a situation he tries to appreciate, finding a sense of peace in just being able to walk and think. As he says in Walk Two, "These hours of solitude and meditation are the only ones in the day during which I am completely myself and my own master, with nothing to distract or hinder me, the only ones when I can truly say that I am what nature meant me to be." In Walk Three he realizes that he still longs to understand the meaning of his life. "Lonely meditation and the study of nature and the contemplation of the universe lead the solitary to aspire continually to the maker of all things and to seek with a pleasing disquiet for the purpose of all he sees and the cause of all he feels."[20]

Walk Five is perhaps the most famous one. He recalls the two months he spent living quietly on St. Peter's island in middle of the Lake of Bienne, Switzerland. "I could have spent two years, two centuries and all eternity there without a moment's boredom. I look upon those two months as the happiest time of my life." He did not have his books with him at the time, so he spent many hours walking in the forests and fields of the island, studying the local flora, idly drifting on the lake in a boat or just sitting on the lakeshore, lost in thought. It is clear he loved the place, with its greenery, meadows and shaded woodlands. It was a place suitable to those "solitary dreamers who love to drink deeply of the beauty of nature, and to meditate in silence which is unbroken but for the cry of eagles, the occasional song of birds and the roar of streams cascading down from the mountains."[21]

At one point, Rousseau remembers the island as the place where he came as close as humanly possible to experiencing a sense of timelessness, of knowing eternity in time. For most of us, most of the time, life is in constant flux, he writes. We are always looking longingly to the past or in anticipation to the future. We are seldom, if ever, fully in the moment. "Thus our earthly joys are almost without exception creatures of a moment." There can be no state of lasting happiness. Yet, if there were such a state in which our soul could find a resting place sufficiently secure to establish itself with no desire to recall the past or look to the future, where time is nothing and the present runs unnoticed, then, says Rousseau, "such is the state which I often experienced on the island of Saint-Pierre in my solitary reveries."[22]

Rousseau wonders we why cannot sustain this "mode of being," with its "precious feeling of peace and contentment," once we have experienced it. Sounding oddly like Pascal, he blames the diversions of our passions. "Most men being continually stirred by passion know little of this condition and having only enjoyed it fleetingly and incompletely they retrain no more than a dim and confused notion of it and are unaware of its true charm." For Rousseau, then, walking was a means of contemplation, an activity conducive to thoughtfulness. We see the interconnection between Rousseau's walking and thinking and his pleasure in the natural world in Walk Seven. His walks are a way to cleanse his spirit. "Bright flowers, adornment of the meadows, cool shades, streams, woods and green glades" serve to "purify my imagination."[23]

Kierkegaard, the nineteenth-century Danish philosopher, is another thinker who expounded on the connection between his thought and his habit of walking the streets of his hometown, Copenhagen. Yet he is very different from Rousseau. Where Rousseau was self-indulgent, and frequently amoral, Kierkegaard was rigorously ascetic and self-consciously moral. Where Rousseau travelled widely and had an eventful life, Kierkegaard's life was largely uneventful, at least on the surface, and he rarely travelled, going four times to Berlin and once to Sweden. What the two philosophers share – besides quarrels with the authorities – is an appreciation of walking. In an 1847 letter to his sister-in-law, Kierkegaard admonished her to walk.

> *Above all, do not lose your desire to walk: every day I walk myself into a state of well-being and walk away from every illness; I have walked myself into my best thoughts, and I know of no thought so burdensome that one cannot walk away from it.* Even if one were to walk for one's health and it were constantly one station ahead – *I would still say: Walk!* Besides, it is also apparent that in walking one constantly gets as close to well-being as possible, even if one does not quite reach it – *but by sitting still, and the more one sits still, the closer one comes to feeling ill.* Health and salvation can be found only in motion.[24]

Kierkegaard took his own advice. He was a "street philosopher," according to his most recent biographer, Joakim Garff. It was a role learned in childhood. "From his childhood on, Kierkegaard took pleasure in walking, and he loved to disappear into the crowd or wend his way through unfamiliar streets with no particular goal in mind." As an adult, Kierkegaard was known for his daily excursions in and around Copenhagen, during which he would talk – and walk – with anyone who caught his interest, from flower sellers to financiers. He cut an odd figure on the street, his form readily recognizable with its "'high shoulders, the restless hopping gait.'" He walked with a "'little thin cane with which he flicked off the tips of the plants and blades of grass along the edge of the path' when he got excited during his walks along the lakes." He sometimes stood still in the street, gesticulating and laughing aloud.[25]

Kierkegaard saw himself following in the footsteps of Socrates. Just as the ancient Greek philosopher walked the streets of Athens engaging in conversation anyone he met, tanners or tailors, sophists or statesmen, so, too, did the

Danish thinker. "I regard the whole of Copenhagen as one great social gathering," he wrote in his journal. "On one day I regard myself as the host who goes about conversing with all the many cherished guests whom I have invited; on another day I assume that some important man has given the party and that I am a guest. I dress differently, greet people differently, et cetera, all according to the varying circumstances."

Even inside his large apartment in downtown Copenhagen, Kierkegaard continued to walk. People on the street often saw him through the windows pacing from room to room, where there was ink, pen and paper always ready for use. On one occasion, a friend who was passing by noticed the whole apartment illuminated. He decided to stop and say hello. Kierkegaard, answering the door dressed in formal evening wear, invited his friend in for a chat. He explained the lighted rooms by saying he was giving an imaginary party. "I never have parties, but once in a while it occurs to me to pretend that I am having one, so I walk to and fro through the rooms, mentally entertaining my imagined guests."[26]

We might think this a bit odd, but we must remember that over the course of a writing career that spanned less than twenty years Kierkegaard produced works on philosophy, theology, psychology and literary criticism, as well as writing fiction and even devotional literature. While best known today as the father of existentialist philosophy, he saw himself as engaged in renewing the Christian faith. He certainly wrote with the fervour of a religious poet, including representing biblical figures in a manner that made them relevant to moderns. Walking was Kierkegaard's means for stimulating thought. "In order to bear mental tension such as mine, I need diversion, the diversion of chance contacts on the streets and alleys, because association with a few exclusive individuals is actually no diversion." The diversions of the street weren't distractions; rather, they kept him grounded and real. He did not want his thinking to float in a realm of abstraction. As he said in his journal, "This very moment there is an organ-grinder down in the street playing and singing – it is wonderful, it is the accidental and insignificant things in life which are significant."[27]

Kierkegaard often composed his works while walking, only writing his thoughts down after returning home. In this regard, argues Joakim Garff, "it was scarcely an exaggeration for Kierkegaard to say that he walked his way to his 'best ideas,' for what he wrote he wrote *currente calamo*, that is, as quickly as the pen could move, which was only possible, he explained, because he 'put everything into final form while walking.' His walks were therefore carefully calibrated to match his volume of ideas." Kierkegaard would break off a conversation or a walk and hurry home to write. He wrote for a certain number of hours each day, and those hours were set to correspond to the ideas that would come to him as he walked. He would often walk in the door and go straight to his desk, where he would stand with his hat and cane and write for a long time.[28]

Because Kierkegaard rarely left Copenhagen, the city became a metaphor for Kierkegaard's writing career. "When Kierkegaard moved about in the streets of Copenhagen, his strutting was connected with his writing, he was every where and nowhere, walking this way and that, conversing intimately with everyone, but at the same time distant and alien." He was at home in both the elegant plazas and the dark alleys. What began in childhood as a cheerful stroll on the streets became in adulthood "a demonstrative act in which Kierkegaard opposed the snobbish aloofness from the concrete and ordinary world he noted among the intellectuals of his day."[29]

Kierkegaard even developed a moral code for street philosophers. "Yes, of course, I am an aristocrat (and so is everyone who is truly conscious of willing the Good, because they are always few in number)," he wrote, "but I want to stand right on the street, in the midst of the people, where there is danger and opposition. I do not want ... to live in cowardly and prissy fashion at an aristocratic remove, in select circles protected by an illusion (that the masses seldom see them and therefore imagine them to be Somebody)." Such a code, Garff notes, is reminiscent of both Socrates and Christ, both of whom challenged the institutions of their day and adopted the streets as their platform. Socrates fought the Sophists. Christ challenged the Pharisees. Kierkegaard's fellow citizens, particularly those in positions of power, frequently vilified him, too. Still, he stuck to this walker's code: "Quite literally to make ordinary daily life into one's stage, to go out and teach in the streets."[30]

And he did. One regular walking companion recounted how Kierkegaard carried out his psychological examinations of those he met as he walked.

His smile and his eyes were indescribably expressive. He had his own way of giving a greeting at a distance with just a glance. It was only a small movement of the eye, and yet it expressed so much. There could be something infinitely gentle and loving in his look, but also something stimulating and exasperating. With just a glance at a passerby he could irresistibly "establish a rapport" with him, as he expressed it. The person who received the look became attracted or repelled, embarrassed, uncertain, or exasperated. I have walked the whole length of a street with him while he explained how it was possible to carry out psychological studies by establishing such a rapport with passersby. And while he expanded on the theory he realized it in practice with nearly everyone we met. There was no one upon whom his gaze did not make a visible impression.[31]

This account suggests, obviously, that Kierkegaard's "people bath," as he called his daily excursions on the streets of Copenhagen, provided him with the sights, sounds and smells that he wove into the tapestries that decorated the memory palace on which he drew for his philosophizing.

As Rebecca Solnit points out, Rousseau and Kierkegaard, unlike many philosophers, tried to understand lived experience – bright flowers and organ-grinders – rather than engage in purely abstract theorizing. They saw an intimate connection between walking and thinking and writing. "Perhaps it is because walking is itself a way of grounding one's thoughts in a personal and embodied experience of the world that it lends itself to this kind of writing,"[32] she concludes.

Of the twentieth-century philosophers who understood this point and took it seriously, only Edmund Husserl and Guy Debord come readily to mind. In a 1931 essay, Husserl argues that the experience of walking can illuminate the mystery of how out of the fragmentary, kaleidoscopic appearances of the world we create a coherent and meaningful world. Through walking we perceive the relationship between our body and the world. As Husserl put it, "[In walking] my organism constitutes itself."[33] More simply stated, the body in motion creates a unified experience out of the various sensory fragments – sight, sound, touch, etc. – that it perceives, a unity that tells us we are in the world and the world is intelligible. As one interpreter, Edward Casey, explains: "I cannot walk at all if I am utterly disjoint; to walk is to draw my body together, at least provisionally; and to do so is to constitute myself as one coherent organism."[34] What makes Husserl's idea different from previous thinking on how we experience the world is its emphasis on the act of walking rather than the senses and the mind. In short, the act of walking *embodies* us and establishes our relationship to the world. Perhaps the poet Wallace Stevens said it best: "I am the world in which I walk."[35]

Guy Debord says something similar in elaborating on the practice of psycho-geography. I referred to this practice earlier, in my discussion of place in Chapter Three; to recall, I quoted Debord's definition of psycho-geography as the study of the laws and effects of the geographical environment on our emotions and behaviour. Psycho-geography, he says, involves surrendering habitual walking habits and letting the streets pull you along where they will. This view makes psycho-geography not only a theory, but also a psychological practice. Indeed, Debord and his fellow Situationists, as they called themselves, employed what they called the *dérive* ("drift" in English) to explore urban Paris. The Situationists defined *dérive* as a "technique for locomotion without a goal," an attitude for moving around an urban environment on the basis of your emotional responses to what you encounter. They walked the streets of Paris, deciding which direction to go, which road to cross or corner to turn, on the basis of feelings evoked by the landmarks, buildings, pathways, etc. In a *dérive*, "one or more persons during a certain period drop their usual motives for movement and action, their relations, their work and leisure activities, and let themselves be drawn by the attractions of the terrain and the encounters they find there." To engage in a *dérive* was to become aware of how certain areas – streets, buildings or parks – foster particular states of mind and emotional responses. Thus, the *dérive* provides a model for the "playful creation" of human relationships, including those involving your environment.[36]

This might appear to be a rather self-conscious and intellectualized approach to something as seemingly simple as a

Sunday walk, and it is. And that's the point: The practice of psycho-geography, if taken seriously, requires considerable self-awareness, a constant attentiveness to where you are as well as an awareness of your feelings and thoughts regarding where you are. You have to train your emotions to respond to the surrounding environment, following the route that feels right. The practice of psycho-geography aims to *know* the world as a lived reality. It is a practice for more intimately engaging with everyday life, for discovering how our streets, neighbourhoods and cities can become an intimate part of our lives. In paying attention to yourself as you pay attention to the streetscape around you, you find yourself becoming deeply involved with those streets, attending to things that you hadn't necessarily seen before, or that hadn't seemed worth attention. The result, if you're lucky, is that something as simple as a Sunday stroll can become more of a journey than an eyes-to-the-ground shuffle to the cornerstore. To put it in perhaps overly poetic terms, the street passes through you rather than you passing through the street. The sidewalk takes on a quality of liveliness rather than being merely a route from one point to another. To rephrase Wallace Stevens, you become the world in which you walk.

Among the various practitioners of psycho-geography I've read is British novelist and journalist Will Self. A few years ago he began long-distance walking around London and, more recently, did a twenty-six-mile walk from New York's John F. Kennedy International Airport to Manhattan. In these walks he discovered a sense of meaningfulness that was no longer available to him in travelling by plane, train or automobile. His encounter with geography, cultural and natural, stirred an imaginative response that gave his local walks a deeper sense of meaning than going to famous tourist places. "The contemporary world warps the relationship between psyche and place," he writes. "People don't know where they are anymore. In our post-industrial age, [walking] is the only form of real exploration left. Anyone can go and see the Ituri pygmy, but how many people have walked all the way from the airport to the city?" Walking, he says, "blows back the years, especially in urban contexts. The solitary walker is, himself, an insurgent against the contemporary world."[37]

Psycho-geography is by no means an objective science. Rather, it is, in the words of scholar John Davies, "a strategy for engaging with ordinary life in ways which subvert the alienation most of us experience." Debord, as Davies notes, regarded alienation as one of the social consequences of market capitalism. We experience the world, our streets and cities, through a lens shaped by the priorities of capital and market forces. Debord referred to these "priorities of capital" as "the spectacle."[38] Modern society is a spectacle in which people's lives are largely controlled and directed by economic imperatives – work, consumption, entertainment. The result is that people find it more and more difficult to experience the deeper realities of the world. Debord's *dérive* is an attempt to restore the tradition of the Parisian *flaneur*, the solitary walker who ambles through the city, experiencing its multifaceted diversity while freed from the chains of consumption.

The socio-economic (or political) aspects of psycho-geographical practice are unrelated to my concerns in this book, so I shall leave them aside. Where I find psycho-geography theory useful is in comprehending my own walking experiences and those of others. Debord focused his concept on urban experience, but I think it also applies to pilgrimage. Indeed, Debord himself seems to allow for pilgrimage to be a form of psycho-geographical practice in promoting a kind of self-aware walking – the *dérive* – that entails shedding unthought walking habits (or non-walking habits, as the case may be) in favour of an acute awareness of the walking environment. I can't think of circumstances that better allow for the abandonment of our established walking habits than pilgrimage. The atmosphere and ambience of places I've trekked certainly affected me. So, too, clearly, did their walks affect Kierkegaard and Rousseau. In his daily walks through the streets of Copenhagen, self-consciously absorbing the places and people that became the grist of his philosophic mill, Kierkegaard engaged in the deepest kind of *dérive*, the kind of drift that, paradoxically, both lifts you beyond yourself even as it drives you deeper into yourself. Likewise, Rousseau's walks, while largely devoted to the beauty of nature, highlight a practice that helped him to occasionally transcend himself even as he discovered a deeper self in the contemplation of that beauty. The two men became the world they walked. Something similar happened to me on my pilgrimage walks.

****

By tradition, the pilgrim walking the Shikoku no Michi in Japan (a trek I did in 2004) follows the footsteps of Kōbō Daishi, the ninth-century ascetic and founder of the Shingon Buddhist sect. He established many of the eighty-eight temples that compose the pilgrim route, and, according to legend, continues to accompany all pilgrims on their journey. The Shikoku pilgrimage – or the Shikoku Henro – is one of a hundred or so pilgrimage routes in Japan, but is unquestionably the most famous and most popular. During the late 1980s, about 46,000 pilgrims traversed the route each year. Today, various estimates put that number at 100,000. The pilgrimage, with its white-robed *henro* (pilgrims) and picturesque temples, is certainly popular with the Japanese media. Television reports, newspaper articles and magazine features, as well as documentaries and plays, have embedded the pilgrimage in Japan's popular culture. Yet I think this popularity reflects something deeper.

During my walk, I heard many reasons for enduring the route's hardships. Some people regarded the pilgrimage, in its evocation of ancient traditions, as a means to affirm their sense of being Japanese. Others saw the route as a zone of meditation, a spiritual space that allowed them the time and place for reflection, a chance to slow down and enjoy nature's beauty. Initially, I tended to put myself in this second category. I hesitated to ascribe spiritual motives to myself. But after two months of walking, I wasn't so sure. Undertaking a pilgrimage, or any form of deep walking, has psychological consequences – some good and some discomfiting. As Nancy Frey, an anthropologist who studies pilgrimages, writes, "The journey of a pilgrimage can reveal wounds – loss, failure, fear, shame, addiction – left festering from daily life. Experiences along the way often act as the catalyst that allows them to be exposed. It has been, and appears to continue to be, a road for hopes and miracles of fulfillment of a different order."[39] I claim no miracles or grand illuminations of different orders. Nonetheless, as I said previously, walking twenty or thirty kilometers a day does things to your mind as well as your body.

I had decided even before the journey that, since I was undertaking a religious pilgrimage, I would participate as best I could in the formalities even if I didn't understand their meaning. But in going through the motions – visiting the sacred sites, trying to recite the *sutras*, following the paths that millions of others have taken for a thousand years – I couldn't help but become absorbed in the spirit of the pilgrimage. I discovered, as one traditional Japanese saying goes, that "the form makes the heart."

It takes between forty-five and sixty days to perform the Shikoku Henro. It took me fifty-four days, from the last days of March to late May, most of which I walked. Trekking through Shikoku's four prefectures, or provinces, I saw too much asphalt and urban sprawl and inhaled more exhaust fumes than was good for me. I hiked six to eight hours a day with an always too heavy pack, enduring blistered feet that hobbled me and leg muscles so sore I whimpered by day's end. Not to mention the occasional days slopping ankle-deep in mud, wading through streams that filled my boots with water, staggering soaked through downpours or panting through humidity that made me wish for rain. There were even times as I clawed my way up some rock-strewn slope that I thought I was going to blow a heart valve.

But I also had a wonder-filled time. I met friendly, helpful people – from hairdressers to postal clerks – who, surprised at the idea of a foreign henro, treated me with great generosity, tolerating my fractured Japanese phrases and my ignorance of their customs. I acquired friends who shared much of my journey and made it more enjoyable – and, indeed, doable. I wandered deep into Shikoku's verdant valleys, trod paths cut deep by the feet of past millions, stood on mountain ridges that offered a timeless panorama of sea and sky and land. The solitude and silence of sun-laced bamboo forests entranced me. I trundled across farm fields rich with rice and lotus, lounged on sandy beaches that seemed to stretch forever, and scaled windswept headlands that left me swaying with vertigo at the sight of foam-streaked rocks far below. I strolled through thatch-roofed villages that hadn't changed in their essentials for centuries. I fell in love with things Japanese – *sashimi*, or raw fish, so fresh it melted in my mouth, and *ryokans*, the traditional inns, with their *tatami* floors and sliding wood-and-paper *shōji* panels that opened on to gardens of sculptured trees and burbling ponds.

These physical experiences eventually reinforced what became one of my most meaning-filled walking experiences, producing occasional moments of enchantment – epiphanies – that I can only describe, borrowing from Wordsworth (and C.S. Lewis), as joyful surprises. I started out thinking of the pilgrimage as an adventure, a secular sojourn among sacred places. But there were too many serendipitous situations, odd circumstances and synchronistic events for me not to at least wonder if someone, or something, was watching over me. I set out on one kind of journey and ended up on a very different one. By the end of my trek, I was no longer able to dismiss the presence of Kōbō Daishi as a nonsensical folk superstition or, for that matter, deny the companionship of the seventeenth-century Japanese poet Matsuo Bashō. In particular, I came to feel an affinity for the long-dead poet, whose travel journal, *Narrow Road to the Interior*, was one of the few books I carried with me and dipped into most nights before sleep. By the end of my pilgrimage, I was reciting Bashō's haiku with mantra-like devotion as I walked. My affinity for Bashō offers a way to explore more deeply the relationship between walking and thinking, and the consequences, psychological and spiritual, of that relationship. I can do this best by setting Bashō's walk side-by-side with mine.

Bashō is Japan's most famous *haikai* master. But he may also be Japan's most famous travel writer.[40] In 1684, at the age of forty, Bashō embarked on the first of his extensive journeys. That autumn, he travelled from Edo (or Tokyo, as it is now called) around much of Japan's main island, visiting Yoshino, Nara, Kyoto, Ogaki and Nagoya. He returned home to Edo through Kiso and Kai the following spring. Two years later, in the autumn of 1687, he travelled to Kashima in the eastern provinces. Over the next seven years, until his death in 1694, he undertook several other journeys, from his hometown of Ueno in Kansai to Matsushima and Sado in the north. Bashō, as scholar Steven Carter observes, "literally spent half of his last years on the road."[41] These journeys produced travel journals. *Exposure in the Fields* (1685) is an account of his first walk. Others followed, including *A Journey to Kashima* (1687), *Backpack Notes* (1688), *A Journey to Sarashina* (1689), the slim *Saga Diary* (1691), and finally *The Narrow Road to the Interior* (1694). The latter is undoubtedly Bashō's most famous journal, combining short prose passages with haiku to provide an account of his arduous 2,400-kilometre, five-month journey across the Shirakawa Barrier to the mountainous regions of northern Honshu that began in the spring of 1689. However, it is more than a poetic travelogue. It is also an account of deep walking, an experiment in psycho-geography. Bashō journeyed to the interior of northern Japan but also to the interior of himself. In the words of one commentator, *Narrow Road* is "a vision quest," a walk into "the geography of the soul."[42]

Scholars argue that Bashō sought a way of writing poetry that could capture and express the effervescent essence of reality. He believed that occasions for "visionary" moments that might result in poetic expression were available in everyday activities, particularly the everyday activity of walking. Scholar Thomas Heyd highlights this aspect of Bashō's poetry in arguing that his poetic practice reflects the "aesthetics of wandering"; that is, Bashō's travels constituted an aesthetic practice that made him aware of "the real diversity of places" and revealed his life "within the larger context of nature."[43]

Consider how Bashō opens *Narrow Road to the Interior*: "I have always been drawn by windblown clouds into dreams of a lifetime of wandering. Coming home from a year's walking tour of the coast last autumn, I swept the cobwebs from my hut on the banks of the Sumida just in time for New Year, but by the time spring mists began to rise from the fields, I longed to cross the Shirakawa Barrier into the Northern Interior. Drawn by the wanderer-spirit Dōsōjin, I couldn't concentrate on things."[44] After placing his home in the care of another, Bashō set out "under the cherry blossoms of Ueno and Yanaka." By the time he got off the boat at Senju, he "felt three thousand miles rushing through my heart, the whole world only a dream."[45]

Clearly, Bashō regarded walking as a way to break out of the stultifying routines of habitual life, a way to feel more alive. But as Steven Carter explains, Bashō also saw walking as a way to foster his poetic craft. He travelled to famous places that allowed him to exercise his talents and acquire new students and patrons. But the travel was also inspirational in a spiritual sense. His poetry reveals his response to the stimulation provided by his walking. As Carter writes, "For Bashō, then, travel itself ... needs to be seen as an arena in which he was constantly called upon to test his mettle against the demands of the landscape and the poets of the pasts."[46]

This idea of travel, or walking, as a way of fostering the poetic sensibility, of opening the mind to those epiphanic moments that might produce poetry, is clearly evident in a *haibun* that Bashō wrote describing the island of Sado.

> While on a walking tour of the Northern Road I stopped at a place called Isumo Point in Echigo. And there was Sado, eighteen li over the blue waves, stretching sideways, thirty-five li from east to west. I felt I could reach out and touch it, so clear was my view of the place, even down to the crevasses and steep cliffs of the peaks and the deepest corners of its valleys.[47]

This vision of landscape produces a deep emotional response.

> The sun had already sunk into the sea and the moon was a dim blur, but the Silver Stream was there, suspended in the heavens, its stars twinkling in the cold as I listened to the sound of waves carried from the

offing, my soul as if torn from its body, my bowels wrenched, my heart suddenly so full of sadness that I could not think of sleep, but stood there, weeping so hard that I could have wrung the tears from my ink-black sleeves.[48]

That last bit about squeezing tears from his sleeves is a bit over the top for our modern tastes. Still, there's no denying Bashō's psychological response to the landscape, a response that produced this haiku encapsulating both the landscape and the poet's response to that landscape.

Across rough seas,
it arches toward the Sado Isle –
the River of Heaven.[49]

With his poetry, says Carter, Bashō "inscribes himself in a larger world, with a response that displays knowledge and the proper sensibility but is also personal – the record of a personal encounter with a place that in important ways he is well prepared to appreciate."[50] This is pure psycho-geography, or, what is the same thing to my mind, pure deep-walking psychology. Bashō imaginatively inserts himself into the landscape even as he observes the landscape. In responding to the outer world, he is fostering an inner world of meaning. The poetry is the distillation of this meeting of inner and outer worlds. Bashō is not only describing what he sees and responding to it, but also demonstrating how you should walk as an aesthetically aware walker. This psychology of epiphany is evident in his description of the mountain temple of Ryushakuji.

We arrived before sundown, reserved accommodations in the pilgrim's hostel at the foot of the hill, and climbed to the halls above. The mountain consists of piles of massive rocks. Its pines and evergreens bear the marks of many long years; its moss lies like velvet on

the ancient rocks and soil. Not a sound emanated from
the temple buildings at the summit … We skirted the
cliffs and clambered over the rocks to view the halls.
The quiet, lonely beauty of the environs purified the
heart.[51]

One of Bashō's most famous haiku – and one of my favourites
– emerged from this epiphanic moment.

Ah, tranquility!
penetrating the very rocks,
a cicada's voice.[52]

Not all of Bashō's walking experiences were pleasant.
On his trek into the north country, he nearly succumbed to
freezing temperatures on Mount Gassan.

I walked through mists and clouds, breathing the thin
air of high altitudes and stepping on slippery ice and
snow, till at last through a gateway of clouds, as it
seemed, to the very paths of the sun and the moon,
I reached the summit, completely out of breath and
nearly frozen to death.[53]

He risked drowning in a boat ride down the rain-swollen
Mogami River.[54] He endured sleepless nights in some truly
awful places that exacerbated his physical ailments. Consider,
for example, this description of a night's lodging at Iizuka:

Thunder rumbled during the night, and rain fell in tor-
rents. What with the roof leaking right over my head
and the fleas and mosquitoes biting, I got no sleep at
all. To make matters [worse], my old complaint flared
up, causing me such agony that I almost fainted."[55]

Still, he made every effort to stay poetically attuned, experiencing things that translated into poetry, such as the
following:

Cherry blossom guardians –
their white heads
bumping together.[56]

"The breathtaking views of rivers and mountains, lands and seas" left him in awe, but even little things, including lousy accommodations, that perhaps only a wide-awake walker would notice, produced moments of epiphany.

Eaten alive by
lice and fleas – now the horse
beside my pillow pees.[57]

This is only fitting, as far Bashō is concerned. The essence of his haiku is to be found in everyday experience – the chirp of a cicada, a leaf floating on water, moonlight on a temple roof, fog hanging in a forest. Good haiku depends on paying constant attention to the world, waiting for, without necessarily expecting, that sudden flash of insight. But, again, this is in tune with Bashō's intention to extract a meaning from everyday experience. As he writes in *The Records of a Travel-Worn Satchel*, the litmus test of art – and, I would argue, spiritual fulfillment – is "the poetic spirit, the spirit that leads one to follow the ways of the universe and to become a friend with things of the season. For a person who has the spirit, everything he sees becomes a flower, and everything he imagines turns into a moon."[58] His advice to his students reflected this view. "Go to the pine tree if you want to learn about the pine, or to the bamboo if you want to learn about the bamboo." The point, though, is not simply to ascertain the accuracy of your observations, to get your facts right, but, equally important, to involve yourself in these things of the world. For Bashō, learning requires entering into the object, perceiving its life. Out of this perception there perhaps comes the epiphanic moment that produces meaningful poetry. For Bashō, the two are the same thing.[59]

Just as walking and thinking are in lockstep for Kierke-gaard and Rousseau, so do poetry and walking go hand in hand for Bashõ. Each serves the other in a symbiotic fashion. Poetry teaches a deeper appreciation of the everyday things of life, while walking forces us to be attentive to these things that can be the subject matter of poetry. Walking fosters moments of epiphany. Poetry captures those moments. Thus, says Heyd, Bashõ's poetry reflects his "metaphorical jour-neys."[60] They contain the distillation of epiphanic moments that he experienced in his journeys. Moreover, Bashõ's poetry also reveals the rightly attuned psychology of walking, the mindset of a pilgrim given over to his pilgrimage. Bashõ's haiku are "an invitation to visit those depths of being, those metaphorical spaces, as he has done."[61] The reader is of-fered an "aesthetics of wandering"[62] by which he, too, might achieve those moments of epiphany that lend everyday life a purposeful, meaning-filled resonance. Bashõ teaches us how to walk, how to be pilgrims in this life.

****

These examples of "converting the experience of land-scape into poetry,"[63] to borrow Carter's phrase, should serve to illustrate my claim that there is a strong link between walking and epiphanic experience. In Bashõ's case, these epiphanies resulted in some beautiful haiku. In my case, as we shall see, there was only one poetic moment. Nevertheless, there are some commonalities in our respective travel experi-ences that allow me to claim a modest identity with Bashõ, moments when I came as close to mystical experience as I've ever been. For example, Bashõ's exhaustion after a hard day's climb on Mount Gassan parallels my own heart-thumping, leg-twitching climb to Shosanji, the twelfth of Shikoku's eighty-eight temples, on the third day of my pilgrimage.

I walked – staggered is a better word – for nearly nine hours, covering fourteen kilometres along a trail that climbs and descends three mountain ranges. By late afternoon, when I reached the final steep staircase that climbs to the temple, I was trembling with exhaustion. My leg muscles burned and my back ached from the load of my pack. I saw spots in front of my eyes. Worse, the worm of uncertainty crawled around my mind: The prospect of two months on the road was suddenly daunting.

Shōsanji is one of the six *nanshos*, or perilous temples, that Shikoku pilgrims find most difficult to reach. You climb from an elevation of 40 metres at Temple 11 to about 700 metres just before Temple 12 – the second-highest elevation on the entire route – following a path that is near perpendicular in places. No wonder locals call it *henro korogashi*, or "pilgrim falling." You see the gravestones of fallen pilgrims scattered along the route. The trail was a tease. It began with a slight incline that led gently into the shade of a cedar forest. The air was cool and damp and pungent. Nightingales noted my passing. But suddenly a set of stairs cut into the ground appeared and the trail climbed steeply into the trees. And kept climbing. And climbing. Until it reached a plateau that offered a view of the Yoshino River valley. I was huffing and puffing too much to appreciate the panorama. I dropped my pack and collapsed. I pulled out my map and looked at my watch. It had taken thirty minutes to climb one kilometre. I knew I was in for a long day.

And it was long. The trail followed a seemingly endless series of peaks and valleys. I'd reach the summit of one mountain only to drop to a valley floor and have to climb all over again. I filed along ridges that fell away in vertiginous drops. It was easy to imagine plummeting over the edge and disappearing in some tangle of dark wood. The path, slippery and soggy from spring rain, was so steep in places I

practically climbed on hands and knees, my face only inches
from the root-tangled earth. My boots were soon heavy with
mud. I had to clamber and leap over boulders – no easy task
with a 14-kilogram pack. I was grateful for Kōbō Daishi, my
walking staff, which saved me from twisting an ankle, or
worse. After a few hours, my leg muscles screamed and my
heart hammered like a bass drum. I envisioned a blood vessel
bursting and my body lying at the edge of the trail.

It took four hours to cover about eight kilometres. By
the time I reached the small temple of Yanagi-no-mizu-an,
nearly halfway to Shōsanji, I was wet, weary and wondering
if I would make it. I did, eventually. But what I most remember is not so much the hardship but the first inklings of a
psychological shift, the slow opening of the doors of perception, to borrow Aldous Huxley's phrase, the first hint of my
mind being changed by the movement of feet. After a rest,
I continued to climb and, no surprise, I was soon wondering
again if my heart would hold out. But I received encouragement from an unexpected source. I had earlier noticed little
statues of Jizō, the bald-pated deity of travellers, every few
hundred metres along the trail.

Stone Jizō statues are everywhere in Japan – at roadside
shrines and temples, on the edges of farm fields, at intersec-
tions, in cemeteries and, as I discovered, along mountain
trails. During those last kilometres to Shōsanji, I adopted Jizō
as my personal protector, the guardian of out-of-condition
gaijin, or foreign pilgrims. Or maybe, as I thought later, it
was Jizō who adopted me.

That day I took up the practice of marking my progress
on especially hard days by the number of Jizō statues I passed.
I would force myself to count three, four, five or however
many seemed necessary before taking a break. Each break
lasted only long enough to let me catch my breath and allow my heart to return to a less hysterical beat. I refused to

look at my watch or calculate the remaining distance. You get there when you get there, I told myself, remembering what my father said on Sunday drives. It didn't help to see occasional grave markers – short, pillar-like stones on the side of the trail, often huddled around a Jizõ statute. Covered with lichen and half sunk into the earth, they were nameless except for the word *henro*, pilgrim, carved into the stone. There would be times when I was desperate for the sight of one of the little statues peeping out from behind a tree or bush or hanging out on some wet trail corner. I'd stab the trail with my stick, put one foot in front of the other, until, coming around a bend or at the top of a slope, I'd spot one. Counting my Jizõs kept me going.

So it was on that day climbing to Shõsanji, early in my trek. When I faced a similarly difficult climb a few weeks later, I was in much better shape, physically and mentally. The conditioning of the mind is probably the hardest thing for a would-be pilgrim to grasp. In my case, I was into my second week before I realized I was gradually learning to walk like a pilgrim.

The hike from Temple 18 to Temple 23 is about 55 kilometres – no great distance. But the trail crosses two mountain ranges and requires arduous walking for two or three days. The greatest challenge, however, is psychological. By the time you reach Temple 18, you've been walking for nearly a week and the strains on your body – blisters, aching legs and strained back, for starters – begin to take their toll. You become aware of what it really means to walk the Henro Michi: That you still have seventy temples and 1,300 kilometres to go, it can rain for days on end and there is always another mountain to climb.

Suddenly you slam up against a mental barrier, asking yourself, "Why am I doing this?" and "What's the point?" Your mind scurries for an escape. What you imagined would be a stroll along country lanes, an intoxication of cherry trees in blossom and panoramic vistas of misty mountains to inspire the spirit has instead become a wearying, purposeless march of physical pain and soggy clothes. And it only promises to get worse. When – or if – you reach Temple 23 in the coastal town of Hiwasa, you face a three-day, seventy-five-kilometre trek to Temple 24. I had read that many walking pilgrims decide to pack it in by the time they reach Temple 23. I knew enough about long-distance hiking to expect this psychological barrier at some point. Still, it was depressing. Rain became the enemy, mud a hateful presence and the mountains a curse. I was no longer on a pilgrimage but on an endurance course. I was angry, resentful toward the Shikoku no Michi and the suffering it imposes. But I also knew you can't walk for two months filled with resentment. You can't rise at dawn every day and walk twenty or thirty kilometres if it fills you with loathing.

The secret is to walk the pilgrimage in your head rather than with your legs. You let the pilgrimage walk you. Stop seeing it as something to endure, a confrontation between ego and world. The Henro Michi has existed for more than a thousand years, and it will exist long after you've disappeared. Your ego, that fantasy of yourself as the centre of the universe, must humble itself before that which it cannot control. No excuses. No complaints. Just walk. You learn to leave the ego behind. So I did, gradually. I put one foot in front of the other, swung my walking stick with reasonable rhythm, let the rain slither down my back, let the blisters blister, and counted my Jizōs. And, after a time, there were brief moments – sometimes lasting a few minutes – where I felt no pain at all, almost no physical sensations, as if I wasn't there, although, strangely, I was often intensely aware of my surroundings – the flap of my poncho in the wind, the tap of my walking stick, the call of a nightingale, the wind-laden smell of cherry blossoms or ocean spray.

Even now, I still recall many of those mindful moments – the peacefulness of a sun-splashed forest path, the empty early morning streets of villages, the far horizon of the Pacific Ocean from some vertiginous cliff. But what I most remember are those rare moments when, after my body – and my mind – had grown accustomed to the walking, a deep sense of peace and detachment settled upon me, coupled with a sharp and often intense responsiveness to the landscape around me. I was intensely attached to the here-and-now of a given place, whether a forest path or an ordinary street corner. In hindsight, I like to think I was approaching that attentive state of mind Bashō demonstrated in his wanderings:

> In fields of blossoming
> rapeseed, they come flower viewing –
> a flock of sparrows.[64]

Several similar moments of attention – epiphanies, as I like to call them – come to mind. One morning I crossed the Naka River and began the climb to the Great Dragon Temple, Temple 21, one of the most beautiful on the Shikoku route. I walked in green-tinted sunlight along narrow country lanes that wind above ravines rushing with spring runoff. The air was cool and sweet with cedar. As I climbed, the lane became a path cutting into a valley with treed slopes closing in on the trail. Buttercups, violets and wild iris lined the edges of the path. The valley narrowed into a gorge that gradually sank into the ground until I was traversing a trench so deep in places I could brush my hands along the wet, mossy rocks and bulking roots that protruded from the earthen walls. If I had not been able to see the rectangle of sky above me, it would have been easy to believe I was walking underground. I thought of the millions of pilgrims who had walked here before me, each generation digging the trench a little deeper with their passing.

Then there was an afternoon at Yakuoji, a hillside temple overlooking the harbour town of Hiwasa along the coastline toward Cape Muroto. Sitting beneath a cherry tree in the terraced courtyard, I gazed across the red-and-grey tiled roofs, following the river as it emptied into the harbour and the Pacific Ocean. Green-hulled fishing boats moored along the seawall. The breeze carried the smell of salt and kelp. It was a pretty, if ordinary, view. Yet it felt extraordinary. But then the entire day had had an out-of-the-ordinary feel. Not that anything spectacular happened, but on a pilgrimage mundane occurrences, serendipitous situations and banal circumstances are brushed with a patina of meaning and portent.

Such a sensibility is a common psychological tic of pilgrims. They tend to perceive special significance in the most ordinary events. In my case, a man I'd met on the trail earlier that day insisted on taking me to a shoe store where I was able to by a pair of Nikes that allowed me to abandon my blister-producing boots. (I had been resisting such an idea, insisting to myself that my feet would eventually adjust to my $400 boots. What I hadn't reconciled was that your feet swell when you walk, and my boots were too damn small for my swollen feet and would always be too damn small. Pride goeth before blisters.) Also on that day, a grandfather approached me at a temple to ask me to bless his granddaughter. (He'd told the child I was the reincarnation of Kōbō Daishi, the patron saint of the Shikoku pilgrimage.) In the context of the pilgrimage, these moments seemed out of the ordinary. Catching a train in the nick of time, feeling minor aches suddenly disappear, unexpectedly meeting someone who takes care of a particular need: such banal occurrences can seem almost miraculous, encouraging you to imagine that someone is watching out for you.

Sitting beneath the cherry tree at Yakuoji, pondering my Nikes for spiritual significance, I thought of how Bashō visited not only temples, but also historical monuments and places of local fame. He played tourist because even touristy things can be extraordinary. He prayed at the temples, but he also enjoyed – and complained about – ordinary things. He was frustrated at not finding a certain species of iris in the hills of Asaka. He complained that his "bony shoulders were sore" because of the load he carried. He objected to a "filthy" inn. He cursed the lice crawling in his clothes. He was annoyed when mosquitoes disturbed his sleep. Still, he continued to find everything extraordinary. Bashō recounts receiving two pairs of sandals as a gift. The sandals had dark blue laces. He was inspired to write this haiku: "It looks as if / Iris flowers had bloomed / On my feet." I studied my ugly Nikes and their grey laces. I saw nothing to inspire a poem. But I could wiggle my toes and flex my feet, and when I took a step there was no squeeze of pain. I remembered a line from Bashō: "The body walks while the mind wanders."[65] I realized that I needed to take Bashō's example to heart. I needed to grasp the extraordinariness of the ordinary, including my ugly new shoes.

The Shikoku pilgrimage changed for me after that. I began to live up to an injunction attributed to the Buddha: "You cannot travel on the path before you have become the path itself." By the time I reached Kiyotakiji, Temple 35, during the third week of my walk my feet were free of blisters, my legs were stronger and, best of all, my mind had slipped into the rhythms and requirements of the pilgrimage. Sitting on a bench in the dappled shade of a maple tree in the courtyard at Kiyotakiji, looking at the rice fields and the Pacific Ocean below me, I was suddenly and self-consciously aware of just how much I was enjoying myself.

There's an old Buddhist saying that I like: "There is no happiness for the man who does not travel." The strange thing is that when I undertake long walks, whether as a pilgrim or a tourist, I soon begin to find that, like Bashō noticed, it is the everyday things — a curbside kiosk, the smell of cut wood, a sunlit path, rain thrumming on asphalt – that provide the journey with its moments of being. The deepest pleasures of walking seldom involve dramatic situations, extraordinary sights or epic efforts. Rather, commonplace situations and uneventful stretches of time can be the true gifts of walking. A ten-minute rest on a curb outside a Tosa City postal station sticks vividly in my mind. It was a narrow street largely empty of traffic. The only other people there were two middle-aged women who nodded and said "*Konnichi wa,*" (good afternoon) as they walked by. And yet, there was poetry – the green No. 32 bus rumbling past, with children in their dark-blue school uniforms leaning out of the windows; the yellow curb lines bright under the sun, a spider's web of electrical wiring silhouetted against the pale sky, shining tile roofs and tidy shrub gardens, a woman's lilting voice from the dark interior of a nearby house. It all seemed to hum and glow with significance.

Then there was a morning in the pouring rain, with me standing in the shelter of a roadside rest area overlooking the Bay of Tosa. I was suddenly aware of being utterly alone, without another pilgrim in sight. There was only me and the rain and the pungent smell of wet cedar, the heaving water below and the grey-bellied clouds shredding themselves on the tops of the surrounding hills. The sheer reality of being alone in the rain on a hill overlooking the ocean in an obscure corner of a Japanese island was, somehow, extraordinary. A quick, sharp, sweeping sense of *thereness*, a humming awareness of the moment, filled me. It was as if the barrier of the body had given way and I was part of what I was seeing and hearing and smelling, as if there was no veil of self-consciousness separating my awareness from the experience.

But it was during the long walk along the Ashizuri coast in southwestern Shikoku that I really felt a greater affinity for Bashō, felt that he was with me on those mountain paths. The area is one of the last remnants of natural Japan, with steep-sided mountains that hug the coastline, the slopes thick with cedar and cypress. It's easy to understand why the Japanese once believed the material world in all its manifestation is, as Shinto teaches, a living entity, and that *kami*, or spirits, populate the natural world. By the fourth week of my walk, I was beginning to wonder.

Standing on a mountain ridge, looking across a dense green valley, it took little effort to imagine the land populated with *kami* – if only my Enlightenment-scientific heritage did not preclude such fanciful notions. Surrounded by the haunting forests of Shikoku I might imagine a re-enchanted world, although in all honesty I could not sidestep a skeptical counteraction to such romanticism. I might feel nostalgia for our lost enchanted world, but I could no more believe in *kami* than I could recover a childhood belief in Santa Claus. At the same time, though, I knew that a world devoid of *kami* is a world where humans cannot feel at home, at least in any deep sense.

Maybe I had been reading too many of Bashō's poems, or maybe the mountain air was over-stimulating my endorphins, but there were times – wandering through some copse of swaying bamboo or looking down some steep-sided cliff to the crashing water – when I was near to convincing myself of the poet's presence, maybe a step or so behind me, a shadow at the periphery of my vision. I thought if I turned my head fast enough I would catch a glimpse of him.

This sensation was especially strong as I hiked through gorges so narrow that the rock face on each side seemed ready to fall on me. I would suddenly be aware of the echo created by the tapping of my walking stick, yet the sound seemed slightly unsynchronized, not quite matching the swing-and-step rhythm of my walking. I swear there were times when, after I lifted up my walking stick, I heard another pilgrim staff. It was spooky. I imagined that only a diaphanous barrier separated past and present, one universe from another, and that, for the briefest of moments, Bashō's universe and mine were so close that, like some *kami* wandering the cosmos, he had joined my pilgrimage, haunting my heels, he in his blue-laced sandals and me in my Nikes.

****

In retrospect, I think it was the forests of Ashizuri – all those *kami* – that prepared me for my most meaningful experience on Shikoku. I started to hear the whispers of the gods. My descent from Mount Yokomine was a prime example. When Jizō led me out of the mountain maze, I felt obliged to offer a prayer when I came across the temple on the road to Komatsu. I looked at my watch. It was nearly 3:30. I hesitated to stop, uncertain how far I was from the town. Yet, it doesn't pay to brush off the gods, especially after they've been good to you. And so, as I said earlier, I followed the tunnel of trees onto the grounds of the strange and lovely temple.

Kōōnji Temple is a *bangai*, an unnumbered temple, and is not included in the eighty-eight temples that make up the official Shikoku pilgrimage circuit. Buddhist ascetics use it to perform *suigyō*, a meditative technique that involves standing under waterfalls or dousing yourself with buckets of icy water as a form of spiritual discipline. *Suigyō* has a long tradition in

Japan, and reflects the belief that rigorous ascetic discipline is a means to greater spiritual awareness. The essential idea of *suigyō* is to push the body to its limits in order to break down the barriers of reason and logic and interrupt the incessant chatter of everyday consciousness. The hope, ultimately, is "to achieve the 'dropping off of body and mind.'"[66]

I had no such expectations as I followed the footpath toward a *shōrō*, or bell tower. A wooden building sat next to the bell tower. The door was unlocked, so I peeked in. There were rows of benches and neat lines of plastic flip-flops on a slat floor. There was a small courtyard extending beyond the bell tower. High cliffs enclosed the whole compound. A gurgling creek ran through the courtyard on the right. Benches, statuary, incense urns and candleholders were set against the rock face on the left. A waterfall graced the far end of the courtyard, guarded by three statues, green with age.

The place was empty and silent save for the cascade of water dropping into a pool beneath the falls. The cedars on the cliffs formed a canopy overhead, filtering the sunlight to give the courtyard a green glow. Shafts of sun falling through gaps in the trees formed pillars of light on the grounds. Mist floated over the pool like a gathering of new-minted souls. I thought I'd stumbled into some secret retreat of the gods. I rang the tower bell to announce my presence. I couldn't find fresh candles or incense sticks, so I lit several remnant stubs, along with a couple of the longer pieces of incense I extracted from the ashes in one of the urns near the bell tower. Then I sat on a nearby bench to listen to the waterfall and absorb the green peacefulness. The waterfall was hypnotic. I could easily have fallen asleep.

I shook off my fatigue and crunched across the courtyard to study the statues above the pool. I recognized Fudō Myōō, the fierce-faced protector of the Buddhist faith, sitting on a cairn at the top of the waterfall. Below him, set in an alcove on either side of the waterfall, were his child servants, Kongara and Seitaka. A line of stepping stones crossed the pool from the edge of the courtyard to a large, flat rectangular rock shelf under the waterfall. According to legend, Fudō Myōō once appeared to a ninth-century priest named So-o, a Grand Patriarch of the Tendai sect of Buddhism, as he stood under a waterfall. The shock inspired So-o to establish Tendai Buddhism's main temple on Mount Hiei, near Kyoto, and begin an ascetic discipline known as *kaihōgyō* – "the practice of circling the mountain" – in which practitioners try to transform themselves into the living embodiment of Fudō Myōō. These disciplines are extreme. After years of initiation, a would-be Tendai monk is required to complete the *byaku-nichi*, in which he runs forty kilometres a day for one hundred consecutive days, repeatedly circling Mount Hiei. He sleeps maybe two hours a day, and eats little more than a couple of rice balls and a bowl of misō soup. With only straw sandals on his feet, even in winter, he runs at night on the mountain's rough trails, enduring blisters, frostbite and fever. The point is to die to this world and become a living god. The *kaihōgyō* symbolizes the monk's willingness to withdraw from the community of the living and recast himself as a wanderer in the land of the dead.[67]

The hundred-day practice is mere basic training, however. There are more rigorous seven-hundred-day and thousand-day practices. The few monks who have undertaken thousand-day marathons and survived are "considered to be a symbol of a living Fudō Myōō," according to one scholar, Robert Rhodes, who has studied the sect. They also acquire amazing perceptual powers. I had read about Gyosho Uehara, a senior monk at Mount Hiei Temple – one of only fifty or so monks who have successfully completed the thousand-day *kaihōgyō* in the last four centuries – who claims that "some marathon monks are able to hear the sound of ash falling from an incense stick."[68]

Staring at Fudō Myōō, I envied those Tendai priests their self-discipline. How did they go beyond their physical limits? Did they enter a kind of suspended animation, a kind of sleepwalking existence, in which their metabolism slowed to such an extent that their bodies needed little sustenance? Compared to the Tendai priests, I was a spiritual dilettante. Beyond my pilgrimage walks, I had not imposed many austerities on myself. If pilgrimage is a symbolic act of death, I'd chosen to party hearty. I took advantage of vending machines and convenience stores to indulge in bottles of Pocari Sweat and cans of Georgia Café au Lait. And don't forget the beer and *shōchu*. I had gorged on *sashimi* and *udon*. True, everybody else did much the same, but that's hardly an excuse. Was I on a religious pilgrimage or a gastronomic holiday? Isn't a pilgrim supposed to die, at least a little?

My guilty questions might explain what I did next. Hustling to the bathhouse, I stripped off my clothes, borrowed the biggest pair of blue flip-flops I could find, I tied a towel around my waist and toddled across the courtyard. I crossed the pool's stone path gingerly, trying not to lose the too-small flip-flops in the water. I slipped once, but Kōbō Daishi – my walking stick – saved me from an embarrassing plunge.

There's probably a technique, a mental discipline, for plunging into ice water, but I didn't know what it was. As I stepped forward, I could hear my doctor back home saying, "You idiot, you'll give yourself a heart attack." I avoided heart seizure, but not shock. The icy water drilling into the top of my head and chest not only stripped the towel away, but ripped the breath out of my lungs. I lasted all of a nanosecond before I leaped, gasping and grunting, out of the waterfall. What kind of wussy pilgrim was I? I gritted my teeth and plunged under the waterfall again. I counted to twelve before leaping away. I tried a third time, stretching the count to nearly thirty. Not bad, I told myself, trying to ignore my chattering teeth and shaking body. So I did it again. This time I stayed in the icy shower until my body felt numb, stepping away only when I could no longer catch my breath and I started seeing spots.

Fudō Myōō didn't reward my short *suigyō* with his presence. There was only a jeering nightingale to witness my spiritual struggle. I was probably being an idiot – catching pneumonia on pilgrimage is not a good idea. I made my way back across the courtyard to the bathhouse, towel in hand, wincing at the sharp gravel on my bare feet after my flip-flops fell off. I was shivering and shaking like a scarecrow in a winter field. I used three towels to scrub myself dry and restore circulation. Walking back across the courtyard, I felt light-headed and unsteady. I sat on the bench near the candle stand again, leaning forward until the wooziness passed. In terms of spiritual conditioning, I was seriously out of shape.

I looked at my watch. It was just after 5:30. The sky had turned overcast. Yet, I remained, waiting, listening to the waterfall, to the faint stir of the trees. Without the sun filtering through the treetops, the courtyard took on a twilight luminescence, as if the light was rising from the earth instead of falling from the sky. The maples and cedars on the cliffs lost their distinctiveness in the absence of light, blurring into a solid grey-green canopy that seemed to descend toward the ground. The sound of the waterfall faded into the background. And through some alchemy of solitude, silence and the day's exertions, stillness settled over me like a blanket. The world fell away and I found myself remembering an incident from my childhood when I fell off a swing and knocked myself out. The memory surfaced like a iceberg lifting out of the water.

I was seven or eight years old again, at a playground in northwest Calgary, where my family lived, with a neighbourhood girl named Carol. We were standing on separate swings, pumping with our legs to see how high we could go. Carol's blonde hair flew like a flag. The swing's metal links screeched as we sailed back and forth. I bent my legs to obtain the maximum speed. As the swing reached its apogee, I felt a mix of fear and thrill as I leaned back, pulling on the metal links, to enjoy the fall backwards and the momentary weightlessness. Only that day my grip wasn't strong enough or my foot slipped on the seat. Suddenly, I was no longer holding on to anything.

I never recalled hitting the ground, so I must have lost consciousness for a few moments, because the next thing I remember was looking up at Carol crouched beside me, her eyes wide and scared. It was odd, though, because I wasn't seeing her from the perspective of where I lay on the ground. I was looking down on the scene, floating above it all. I heard the metal-on-metal squeak of the swaying swings and felt the grit of sand in my hands. But I also saw myself lying on the ground, and felt a sudden swoop of sheer terror at being split in two: the boy on the ground and the boy floating overhead.

My psychic bifurcation lasted for a few seconds at most, and as I stared at Fudō Myōō I was near to feeling it again – that feeling of dislocation and the frightening notion that like a kite lost to an unexpected tug of wind I could drift away, never to return. I remembered the relief that flooded me when the floating boy and the boy on the ground slammed together again like a pair of clapping hands. I was back in my body, whooping for air and crying. And for a moment, here in Japan, locked on the gaze of the god, I could almost feel myself as that floating boy again, sharply aware of the strangeness of my existence, aware that I was connected only tenuously and temporarily to this place.

Japanese Zen practitioners describe that point in their meditations where they experience hallucinations, resurgent memories or other unusual mental phenomena – anything from talking statues and marching Buddhas to ghostly apparitions and feelings of disembodiment – as *makyō*. According to Zen teachings, the experience of *makyō* indicates the emergence of the mind's unconscious elements. *Makyō* is not enlightenment, but it is generally a good sign, because it suggests the hard effort of *zazen*, or sitting meditation, has finally broken the mind of its obsession with logic and instrumental reason and opened it to unconscious life. But *makyō* can also produce psychosis – Zen madness – if a master teacher does not properly direct it. Had nearly two months of walking up and down mountains, reciting sutras and trying to sit *zazen* in my hotel room at night driven me around the bend? My periodic chats with Jizõ or bathing with Fudõ Myõõ might suggest a suspension of normal behaviour. On the other hand, I could not deny the tide of peacefulness that had washed over me in recent days, the sense that I had received balm for the soul. The visitation of my childhood self seemed to me to be a gift despite the momentary fright I felt.

I gazed around the temple. In the twilight, the courtyard had retreated into shadow. Still I waited, absorbed in the quiet. I didn't hear ash falling, but I smelled the sweet tang of burning incense and heard the rustle of leaves on an overhanging branch. I caught the grate of gravel beneath my shoes, felt the thudding metronome of my heart. Slowly, the world returned. Or maybe, as I sometimes think, it was my floating self returning to the world.

I stood to leave. I returned the flip-flops to the bathhouse. I hung up the wet towels to dry. I dropped a 1,000-yen bill – about $12 – in the offertory bin. I lit as many candle stubs and incense sticks as I could find, and I imagined them burning long after I was gone. Then I shouldered my pack and grabbed my walking stick. At the courtyard entrance I turned for a last look, committing the place to memory. Fudō Myōō cracked a smile, or maybe it was just bit of *makyō*.

An hour later I was sitting at the window of my room in the Komatsu Business Hotel, wrapped in a warm *yukata* and staring at the dark bulk of Mount Yokomine silhouetted against the evening sky. I thought about when I started my pilgrimage six weeks earlier and how I'd assumed it would be an adventure in cultural exoticism. But as the days and weeks passed and the miles marched by, a combination of geography and circumstance had produced a much different journey, one that I could not have imagined at the beginning. I had another two dozen temples to visit, but if the real purpose of my pilgrimage had been to arrive at some still point within myself, cross some liminal threshold, then Kōōnji Temple had provided it. Jizō had guided me there, and Fudō Myōō had shown me what was necessary to *be* there. And between them they made it possible for me to disappear into the walking.

In fact, those final weeks on the Henro Michi were deeply satisfying. The pilgrim path took me across a series of mountains and valleys in southwestern Shikoku that are as remote and wild as you'll likely find in modern Japan. Now that the physical demands of the pilgrimage had stopped being a preoccupation – a thirty-kilometre hike up and down mountains no longer left me prostrated in exhaustion at the end of the day – I felt myself letting go, absorbed in the walking, sinking into the landscape. In the mornings I was eager to return to the road, eager to disappear into the walking. The cherry blossoms were in bloom in the mountains. The rice fields in the valleys had their first blush of green shoots. There were moments when my "real" life – family, job, mortgage – seemed unreal. I had crossed into that psychic landscape where walking had become my reality. I was too far from completing my journey to start thinking of home again; at the same time, I was too far from home, both in time and space, to feel its immediate claims. I was, in other words, absorbed in the pilgrimage. I was no longer walking the pilgrimage. It was walking me. I disappeared into the rhythm of footfalls and the steady tapping of my walking stick.

There is an old Zen Buddhist saying, often attributed to Bashõ: "When you sweep the floor, just sweep; when you eat, just eat; when you walk, just walk." For a few weeks in Japan I walked with Bashõ.

SEVEN

THE MYSTICISM OF EVERYDAY
An Iterative Conclusion

What is the meaning of life? That was all — a simple question, one that tended to close in on one with years. The great revelation had never come. The great revelation perhaps never did come. Instead, there were little daily miracles, illuminations, matches struck unexpectedly in the dark.

—Virginia Woolf, *To the Lighthouse*[1]

Mysticism keeps men sane.

—G.K. Chesterton, *Orthodoxy*[2]

I was struggling to pick up a piece of octopus when Tanaka-san leaned across the table and whacked the back of my hand with his chopsticks.

"*Chotto matte*, Robert-san," he said. "Wait a minute, Mr. Robert."

It was a startling gesture from such a gentle man. I paused with my chopsticks hovering above the stubborn morsel. "*Nan desu ka?*" "What?" I said, setting my *hashi* down on the *hashi-oki*, the little porcelain chopstick holder next to my plate. I thought perhaps I had shown bad manners, forgetting to wipe my hands with the *oshibori*, the hot, damp cloth Japanese restaurants provide for customers. More likely

I had forgotten to offer the ritual thank you Japanese utter before each meal. I bowed and said, *"Dewa, itadakimasu."* "I humbly receive."

Tanaka-san waved his chopsticks. "No, no," he said, "look at the food. See the arrangement. Japanese people eat first with their eyes."

I had noticed that he and my other pilgrimage companions, Suji Niwano and his son Jun, paused for a brief moment to gaze at their food before eating. I assumed they were offering a silent Buddhist version of grace before a meal. But Tanaka-san was drawing my attention to something else: the Japanese notion that you shouldn't begin eating your food as soon as it is set before you. Instead, you let your eyes enjoy the food before gratifying your taste buds. This idea of pausing to enjoy even the most ordinary everyday things with the eyes, including food, is an essential part of Japanese culture.[3] Even a simple *bentō* box lunch deserves a moment's perusal when you lift the lid. As Tanaka-san put it, "Every different kind of food has its own plate and is arranged to please the eye. This is very Japanese."

I've come to think of that meal at the Nisiya Restaurant in Imabari, a city on the northern tip of Shikoku, the smallest of Japan's four main islands, as an early lesson in everyday mysticism. It was a lesson I learned well because I was ready for it, and one I have never forgotten. During the seven weeks I'd spent trekking the 1,400-kilometre Shikoku Henro pilgrimage route, I had walked much of it with Suji, Jun and Yukuo Tanaka. By the time we reached Imabari, we had about thirty-five temples and a week's walking ahead of us. It was mostly easy walking. Along this part of the Shikoku no Michi, the pilgrim path hugs the northern coastline of Shikoku, cutting through suburban areas and across flat stretches of farmland and rice fields. Many of the temples are close together, separated by only a few kilometres, which meant we often visited several in one day.

I remember the days as a cluster of images: The children's shrine at Emmeiji, Temple 54, stuffed with toys and candy and bottles of juice at the feet of the Buddha statue; the packed field of *haka*, or family graves, and the war memorial outside Imabari; old men playing *shōgi*, Japanese chess, in a park; the green spread of the Imabari valley and the Inland Sea blue and bright below us as we climbed to Senyuji; a group of white-vested bus pilgrims sitting in a line along a wall in the parking lot at Kokubunji, eating their *bentō* lunches. I remember an elderly woman on her knees at Hojuji, Temple 62, weeping as she rocked back and forth in front of the statue of Kōbō Daishi. I wondered what she was praying for, what sorrow caused such tears. After so long on the road, I had fallen into the pilgrim mindset where even the simplest and most ordinary things – wind in the trees, the early morning quiet of a temple courtyard, the warmth of the sun on your back – take on an out-of-the-ordinary quality. Perhaps that's why Tanaka's lesson in food etiquette had such resonance for me.

The Nisiya Restaurant occupies a small room on the second floor of a building near the Imabari train station: a half-dozen tables, a gleaming zinc-topped bar on one side of the room, polished wood walls and a wraparound picture window overlooking the street. We'd found it as we wandered through the streets, looking for a place to eat after our end-of-day baths at the Miyako Ryokan, where we were staying for the night. We stopped outside several other restaurants to study the plastic models of the food they offered – sushi, tonkatsu, donburi, soba, shabu-shabu – in their window displays. Looking at them made me hungry. Tanaka-san spotted the Nisiya, a *koryōriya* establishment specializing in a "small dish" menu.

There were six other diners in the place: a middle-aged couple and a foursome, two men and two women. The women were stylish and pretty and I liked how they covered their mouths with their hands when they laughed. Jazz played on the stereo – Chet Baker, John Coltrane and, to my great delight, Ben Webster. After several tumblers of *sake* I was close to dining *satori*.

Our food came on a series of brass platters. When we finished one, another would arrive. Jun supplied me with the Japanese words for the different items on each platter: morsels of fresh raw *ika*, or squid; *tako*, or octopus; and *muru-gai*, or mussels. There was sliced lotus root stuffed with minced meat, deep-fried chunks of pork, spears of asparagus. A third tray offered batter-fried shrimp, slices of shiitake mushrooms and skewers of *yakatori* and *unagi*, or eel.

The waiter, a young man in black pants and a gleaming white shirt, also set a tray of sauces in white porcelain bowls on the table. Tanaka-san explained the contents: a greenish sauce made of salt and tea leaves whose name I didn't catch; another of sour vinegar called *ponzu*, and a garlicky sauce known as *ninniku*. There was also a brass cup of chopped zucchini and cabbage and slivers of raw onion bathed in a tangy sauce. Of course, we washed down the meal with large bottles of ice-cold Kirin beer.

Tanaka-san's lesson in Japanese aesthetics made the meal even more enjoyable. Looking at the food in front of me, I tried to *see* it as a Japanese would. There were four morsels of eel side by side on a small, rectangular ceramic plate, the dark texture of the seafood enhanced by the white background of the plate. White slices of lotus root formed an upside-down crescent on a blue circular plate. They reminded me of the green fronds of a bamboo tree silhouetted against the sky. The dark green of the asparagus spears was made more vivid by the gleaming background of the red lacquer tray. I thought of the forests I had walked through on my pilgrimage.

"*Wakarimasu*," I said, looking at Tanaka-san and Suji. "I see." And I did: I was looking at Shinto on a tray.

My companions smiled, gratified. "*Saa, tabemashō*," said Tanaka-san. "Well, let's eat."

Shinto is Japan's indigenous religious, pre-dating the arrival of Buddhism from China. One of Shinto's core concepts is the notion of purity, which, as scholar and photographer Fosco Maraini writes, is "one of the principal inner forces of Japanese civilization." This principle, while rooted in religion, has gone from shrine to home. You can see it in the Japanese insistence on cleanliness, particularly the tradition of meticulous ablutions at the temples or in the home. But the principle of purity was also evident in the Nisiya Restaurant. As Maraini puts it: "Japanese cuisine manifests a delicate and poetic respect for the gifts of field, mountain and water as they are presented to man by nature … A Japanese meal is a communion with nature."[4]

Tanaka-san's lesson stuck with me over the next week. I tried to look at everything with conscious intention. Sometimes when I did so, everything stood out sharp and distinct from the surrounding background. Ordinary things – a child's tricycle in a driveway, three oranges in a roadside shrine, wind ripples on a flooded rice field, green spring wheat – resonated with an aura of significance, a corona of importance. But it wasn't only my sense of sight that was acute. The crunch of gravel, the whiff of a barnyard, the smoothness of a bamboo trunk: my senses vibrated like wires humming with electricity.

In *seeing* with such intensity I was enjoying the psychological benefits of pilgrimage. After seven weeks of walking, I had reached a kind of psychic plateau that left me feeling both deeply contented and, at the same time, buzzing with excitement. It was as if my body and my mind had finally decided to co-operate in attending to the world, as if some radio station in my head had tuned into a static-free frequency. I walked fully involved in the walking, and in what I was seeing and hearing and smelling. I didn't think about other places or people or fret about whether the bills back home were paid or daydream about the future. For one of the few times in my life, I was fully and completely in the moment.

The walk out of Imabari the next day exemplified this state of mind. Everything was sharp and clear and intense, as though I was seeing the world with fresh eyes. In the morning we traipsed beyond the suburbs of Imabari, praying at the small temples of Taisanji and Eifukuji, Temples 56 and 57, in Koizumi and Tamagawa. We stopped at a convenience store at about 11 o'clock to buy food, intending to have lunch at Senyuji, Temple 58. Besides the usual bottles of water and Pocari Sweat, I bought a *bentō* lunch box. Then we walked for another hour to Senyuji.

The path to the temple climbed through a narrow gorge with moss-covered walls looming overhead. A canopy of cedar trees turned the sun green. Every few feet there were shrines set into alcoves in the rock face. A stream tumbled down on the right, splashing and gurgling. The air was cool and damp and fragrant. My senses feasted on the world: The scent of cherry trees along a suburban street; nodding rhododendrons in a garden behind a wall; a grinning gargoyle on the corner of a tiled roof; a caterpillar crawling across the road; a circling hawk; the sparkle of water drops on the filaments of a cobweb on a trailside shrine; the hot diesel smell of a passing farm tractor. I was alive to the ordinary.

After we reached the temple and performed our pilgrim rituals, we found a table beneath a white-draped statue of Kannon, the goddess of compassion, where we could enjoy our lunch while admiring the valley below and the gleaming spread of the Inland Sea. It was Tanaka-san's influence, of course, that made me pause before picking up the chopsticks. *Bentō* is basically an all-in-one square box with compartments for different morsels of food – everything from rice and vegetables to *sashimi* and *tempura*. You buy it at corner kiosks, railway stations and convenience stores. Mine had four compartments. One contained rolls of rice wrapped with bands of dried seaweed. Another held slices of *sashimi*: *maguro* and *shimesaba*, or tuna and mackerel, along with a green dab of *wasabi*, the hot Japanese horseradish. A third was reserved for vegetable *tempura*. Finally, a fourth section held *takemoko* and a piece of *tomago* – bamboo shoots and sweetened omelet – and a couple of slices of *kamaboko*, a fish-paste roll.

I tried to eat first with my eyes, tried to see the landscape of my lunch, gazing down before I lifted my chopsticks. And for a moment, I had it. I was looking down from a great height on the Japanese landscape: vegetables from valley farms, rice from the terrace paddies, slices of bamboo from the mountain slopes, raw fish from the surrounding seas; all packed into the confines of four squares. I ate slowly, savouring the flavours – the melt-in-your-mouth *maguro*, the crunch of bamboo, the sinus-clearing *wasabi*.

"*Wakarimasu*," I said, turning to Tanaka-san. "I see."

"*Guddo*," he said. "We make you Japanese someday."

Western psychologists sometimes refer to the experience of direct perception; that is, an experience in which the normally self-absorbed ego is quiescent and doesn't immediately try to judge and analyze everything we do. In direct perception there is, in theory, no distance, no gap, between the experience and the perception of the experience. The Japanese concept of *yoin* gets at the same thing, but better captures the feeling and quality of such experiences. *Yoin* literally refers to the reverberation or resonance of a struck bell. More figuratively, *yoin* is the "reverberation" that ripples through you after some extraordinary stimulus, illumination or learning, when you intuitively understand something without having to articulate, rationalize or otherwise explain it. In a moment of *yoin*, you experience insight or deep feeling without reflection or articulation. It is instantaneous. A silent smile between husband and wife, the immediate communication between lovers reunited after an absence, a parent's wordless caress of a sleeping child; such situations embody *yoin*. But *yoin* is also evident in moments where the ordinary turns extraordinary and you find yourself on the threshold of transcendence. In a modest way, my *bentō* benediction was such an occasion. In that brief moment I *saw* Japan the way Tanaka-san wanted me to see it. I don't mean I suddenly acquired some deep knowledge of the Japanese soul, or that I'd gained a profound insight into the Japanese character. It was simply that suddenly I perceived something important about Japan that I hadn't previously grasped. The only way I can explain it is to say I suddenly *felt* my two months in Japan resonate in me like, well, the aftermath of a struck bell.

Of course, that moment of seeing was unique to me – and could only be important to me – because no one else could possess those particular circumstances and my particular psychic state that would allow them to see what I saw in exactly the same way. As I pointed out in an earlier essay, moments of vision are highly subjective and intensely personal. What's meaningful to one person is insignificant to another. But that does not mean others cannot experience similar moments of *yoin* (or direct perception or, if you prefer, simultaneous perception) based on their situation and state of mind. The experiences I've described in these essays have one thing in common: They are connected to ordinary situations and everyday objects. For me that day at Senyuji, it was a small box of *sushi* and *sashimi*. For Proust it was a *madeleine*. For Rupert Brooke, sunlight on a bare wall. For Van Gogh, well, everything, it seems. In other words, moments of transcendence are to be had in the here and now, in the everyday and the ordinary.

In making this claim, I am following the admonishments of one of the twentieth century's great theologians, Karl Rahner, who spoke of the "mysticism of everyday life."[5] Rahner held that a sense of transcendence is not limited to religious adepts. "In his seemingly secular weekday existence the human being experiences that even his daily life is borne along and carried by God."[6] I fall short of Rahner's theological certainty, but my own experience tells me that everyday mysticism of one sort or another is possible, and essential. I hope I have more than demonstrated through these essays the possibility that our everyday experiences can foster a greater sense of meaning and purpose in our lives. But why are such meaningful experiences essential?

To address that question, I need to consider both the notion of the everyday and exactly what kind of mysticism I am talking about.

****

Philosopher Charles Taylor argues that one of the more extraordinary aspects of the modern era is its "affirmation of ordinary life." The Judeo-Christian tradition has always elevated the ordinary life of birth and marriage and nurturing above anything the more stoical Greeks imagined. But it was only with the arrival of the Reformation and on through to the Romantics that everyday life took on the importance it has for us now. For Taylor, this is one of the great paradoxes of modern philosophy. Modern science, while ostensibly devoted to the improvement of the human condition, also calls for a radical disengagement from ordinary experience.

Scientism effectively diminishes the human in interpreting humans themselves as "objects" or "things" that can be "known" for what they most essentially are when detached from the social and natural worlds in which they live. Yet, at the same time, the modern demands for self-responsible freedom and self-exploration, in awakening notions of dignity and authenticity, require a deeper engagement with our ordinary individual lives. On this point, we do well to remember that the Greek philosophers distinguished between life and the good life, with the former being a necessary (if insufficient) condition of the latter. For the Greeks, you left the life of the household, the realm of economics and reproduction, for the greater good of public life, the realm of politics and philosophy. With the arrival of modernity, however, 'ordinary life' – family, marriage, work and other 'economic' matters – became a fundamental value. Work and family, production and reproduction are no longer regarded as lesser achievements than public honour or philosophic contemplation; indeed, in the Christian tradition they are held up as even higher ideals. As Taylor says, "the fullness of Christian existence was to be found within the [ordinary] activities of this life, in one's calling and in marriage and the family."[7]

By 'ordinary life,' Taylor means "those aspects of human life concerned with production and reproduction, that is, labour, the making of things needed for life, and our life as sexual beings, including marriage and the family." This affirmation of ordinary life had its origins not in Romanticism, but in religion. However, while the affirmation of ordinary life originates in Judeo-Christian spirituality, its modern impetus came first from the Protestant Reformation and its rejection of the mediating role of the Catholic Church and its understanding of the sacred. The Protestant rejections of a priestly elite that renounces profane life in order to mediate the presence of the divine reflects the notion that ordinary life gives everyone equal access to the divine. This rejection of the sacred and of mediation resulted in "an enhanced status for (what had formerly been described as) profane life." The consequences were immense: By denying the Church and the priesthood as the "privileged locus of the sacred," the Reformation effectively denied the distinction between the sacred and the profane, between higher and lower spheres of life. And this denial of Catholic hierarchy amounted to "an affirmation of ordinary life as more than profane, as itself hallowed and in no way second class."[8]

At the same time as the Reformation was challenging the Church, modern science was lending its support to the new emphasis on ordinary life. The new science was dedicated to the betterment of ordinary life, improving the human condition. It was not the elite activity of a few with the leisure for rational contemplation. Citing Francis Bacon, the father of the scientific method, Taylor writes that for early moderns, "science is not a higher activity which ordinary life should subserve; on the contrary, science shall benefit ordinary life."[9] And as the Cartesian-Newtonian understanding of the world took hold of the Western mind, the emphasis on the empirical, the observable and the measurable – that is, ordinary everyday things – became more and more pronounced. In effect, Taylor says, science's "instrumental stance towards the world [was] given a new and important spiritual meaning ... Instrumentalizing things is the spiritually essential step."[10] Thus, science and religion went their separate ways. Mastery of the profane world was next to godliness, as far moderns were concerned.

But is there not a danger that the modern effort to master the world might lead to attempts to master ordinary life by means of technological intervention? Taylor claims that this has in fact taken place, because modern instrumental science denies its own spiritual sources and its original moral purposes. Scientism, with its devotion to instrumental reason, the mastery of nature and a rigid paradigm of knowledge, has lost the original purposes of science's affirmations of the ordinary. It was the Romantics such as Rousseau and Wordsworth who sought to restore this affirmation. Since I have already discussed both of these Romantics (among others) in previous chapters, it is perhaps sufficient here to simply reiterate the point that it was Romantics such as Wordsworth who showed the spiritual significance of ordinary things.[11] As scholar Don Fisher puts it, "It is through a re-visioning of the 'ordinary' that Wordsworth sees the greatest hope for authentic connection with the divine."[12]

This search for the divine in the ordinary was evident in other Romantic poets, too, including Coleridge, Keats and Shelley, as well as in the neo-Romanticism of the nineteenth-century American Transcendentalists, especially Henry David Thoreau and Ralph Waldo Emerson, both of whom emphasized the "extraordinary of the ordinary."[13] Prose writers, too, turned to the ordinary, whether or not they related it to the divine. Daniel Dafoe, Samuel Richardson, Henry Fielding, Jane Austen, Charlotte Brontë, Charles Dickens: each of these eighteenth- and nineteenth-century novelists was devoted to the affirmation of ordinary life, writing as they did about everyday matters of home, love, loss, marriage, children and death. Even their way of writing revealed their attachment to the ordinary: "The very form of narration, relating the – sometimes minute – particulars of life, puts all events and lives on the same stylistic footing."[14]

This artistic turn to the ordinary may well possess religious or spiritual significance. Morris Beja, whom I drew on in discussing the concept of wonder, suggests that as moderns found themselves less able to hold on to the truths and absolutes of the past, they increasingly looked to the "trivia of existence" for a sense of meaning. However, this regard for "trivia" was far from trivial. Moderns, says Beja, "sought meaning in what they could see, all around them, in the apparently inconsequential objects and events of everyday life."[15] This point suggests that we should understand the affirmation of the ordinary as an attempt, in its origins, to deify the ordinary, to find the divine in the everyday.[16] Taylor makes a similar point, arguing that the emphasis the Romantics placed on everyday epiphanies reflected their aspiration to recover contact with moral and spiritual sources, whether divine or mundane, spiritual or psychological. This aspiration, he says, "is usually made more urgent by the sense that our modern fragmented, instrumentalist society has narrowed and impoverished our lives."[17]

But it wasn't only the Romantics who sought to evoke the sacred in the mundane. You can see this attempt to recover the "divine" in the ordinary in many contemporary writers, including John Updike, Flannery O'Connor, Graham Greene and J.D. Salinger. As literary scholar William Closson James says, a great deal of contemporary fiction "relocates the sacred from its older abode beyond the earth to some place or other within ordinary experience."[18] A prime example of this relocation of the sacred, according to literary scholar Don Fisher, is the work of Alice Munro, the well-known short story writer. Munro's work may not be explicitly religious in the manner of Catholic writers such as Greene and O'Connor, but she nonetheless reveals a consistent concern for the *mystery* residing at core of the religious and the spiritual.[19]

In making this claim, it is well to bear in mind the argument I made in the introduction regarding the word "spirit." This term, from the Greek word *psyche*, refers to the principle that gives meaning and purpose to life. Religion, on the other hand, comes from the Latin *religare*, meaning to "bind fast," "contain" or "tie back." Religion is "a means of relating the individual to what is taken to be the ultimate nature of reality."[20] A person is being religious when he or she struggles to bind or contain or express their spiritual experience.

You see this struggle in many of Munro's characters, Fisher says. They often reveal their religious nature when they try to express, acknowledge or approach the mystery of their lives. In this light, Munro should be seen as a religious writer, albeit in a non-traditional sense. "Munro's writing is religious to the extent that it attempts to 'bind' aspects of 'ordinary experience' – 'the details of our lives in this world' – 'so precisely, so intensely' that it helps to reveal that which is 'luminous' as well as that which is 'dark' in ways that 'recognize and approach' the divine – that which 'some people name God'." And central to religious *cum* spiritual vision is "a pronounced focus on 'ordinary' life."[21]

A couple of examples from Munro's stories reinforce the point. For instance, there is a major epiphany in the short story "Walker Brothers Cowboy, " which some critics regard as a microcosm of Munro's work. The main character, a youthful Del Jordan, experiences an epiphany while taking an ordinary walk along a town street with her father, Ben Jordan, to the shore of Lake Huron. Set in the Depression years of the 1930s, the story is filled with detailed descriptions of ordinary things – a wooden sidewalk that becomes a sandy path, "the washing noise of stones on the beach," a "pavilion, full of farmers and their wives, in stiff good clothes, on Sundays" – leading up to Del's first epiphanic moment, when, after her father explains about the geological age of the Canadian Shield, she suddenly realizes her father's mortality, and her own.

> The tiny share we have of time appals me, though my father seems to regard it with tranquility. Even my

father, who sometimes seems to me to have been at home in the world as long as it has lasted, has really lived on this earth only a little longer than I have, in terms of all the time there has been to live in … I will be barely alive – old, old – when it ends. I do not like to think of it.

But Del's penultimate epiphany comes when she is driving with her father as he returns home after they'd visited a woman "friend" from his past. Suddenly Del's father is a mystery to her because she realizes that he has a history that precedes her own existence, which only reinforces her sense of her mortality. Maybe all humans are a mystery; maybe we are all unknown and unknowable.

So my father drives and my brother watches the road for rabbits and I feel my father's life flowing back from our car in the last of the afternoon, darkening and turning strange, like a landscape that has an enchantment on it, making it kindly, ordinary and familiar while you are looking at it, but changing it once your back is turned, into something you will never know, with all kinds of weather and distances you cannot imagine.[22]

Another Munro narrator, in the story "Miles City, Montana," experiences a similar epiphany after the near drowning of one of her two daughters. As the woman, her husband and the two girls drive out of Miles City, she remembers as a child attending the funeral of a friend who had drowned.

When I stood apart from my parents at Steve Gauley's funeral and watched them, and had this new, unpleasant feeling about them, I thought that I was understanding something about them for the first time. It was a deadly serious thing. I was understanding that they were implicated. Their big, stiff, dressed-up bodies did not stand between me and sudden death, or any kind of death. They gave consent. So it seemed.[23]

What you see in these and other stories, Fisher argues, is a focus on ordinary life so intense and precise that "this experience occasionally takes on religious/spiritual significance." Munro has intimated as much in remarks about her writing. In a 1974 essay she writes that "the ordinary place is sufficient, everything here is touchable and mysterious."[24] It is an interesting choice of words, implying that the material world, all that is touchable (or, presumably, seeable, taste-able, smell-able or hear-able), is somehow mysterious, possessing some hint of the ineffable and the divine. Munro's characters often experience this ineffable presence in epiphanic moments that on the surface seem utterly commonplace. These "queer, bright moments," as Munro calls them, form the very core of her "implicit spiritual/religious vision."[25]

Interestingly, as Fisher points out, the presence of epiphanic moments in Munro's fiction is in line with what has happened in twentieth century literature and art. And that suggests epiphanic experiences have come to fulfill a crucial function in Western culture after two centuries of decline in traditional religious faith. The modern epiphany is a response to a world that has become increasingly secular, analyzable and disenchanted. Modern writers have found in epiphanic experience a means for re-enchanting the world and finding spiritual significance in everyday life. These 'modern' epiphanies seldom emerge out of extraordinarily dramatic moments – say, Paul's conversionary experience or Moses' confrontation with the burning bush. Nor do they result from the kind of deliberate contemplation of nature or metaphysical speculation you find in the Romantic poets.[26] Such situations are simply not realistic to our post-

Darwinian, secular sensibility. Nonetheless, the epiphanic moments in contemporary literature – Joyce, Woolf, Munro, and others – are extraordinary in their own way, as Morris Beja explains:

> Despite the general disillusion with religion in the past few generations a continuing need – perhaps even an intensified one – had been felt for meaningful, unifying, "spiritual" emotions or experiences that could provide men with answers to some of their burning questions. No longer confident, however, of a divine answer, men have wanted their own; no longer willing to wait for Truth until God calls them to it, they have sought for it today, on earth, here and now. There has been a general secularization of what once was inevitably regarded – and, of course, *still often is* – as the *divinely inspired moment* of new knowledge.[27]

Charles Taylor goes a little further in heightening the importance – and the possible source – of these epiphanic moments when he describes the modern resort to everyday epiphanies as a form of "achieving contact with something where this contact either fosters and/or itself constitutes a spiritually significant fulfillment of wholeness." Taylor does not explain the nature of this contact beyond referring to it as a "moral source." But he does observe that modern artists have emphasized these "privileged moments," as Virginia Woolf called them, because traditional expressions of spirituality are no longer readily available in a culture dominated by scientific epistemology and secular morality. The epiphanic experience, he argues, is "genuinely mysterious and it possibly contains the key – or a key – to what it means to be human."[28] To the degree this applies to Munro's characters, what you see in many of her stories is how the ordinary, everyday world can be the place where the human and the divine meet. As it happens, this is exactly the argument made by Karl Rahner.

*****

Rahner follows the teachings of Ignatius Loyola, the founder of the Jesuit order to which Rahner belonged, in maintaining that God, the divine, is present in all things. "We always, even in the midst of everyday life, extend beyond ourselves and the specific thing with which we are now concerned. We might say that mysticism occurs in the midst of everyday life, but it is hidden and undeclared."[29] What kind of mysticism is Rahner talking about? In the popular imagination, the mystic is someone who doesn't worry about making mortgage payments, changing diapers, shovelling snow or even indulging in the occasional Scotch and cigar on Saturday evening. Somehow, he (or she) lives in splendid self-sufficiency, preoccupied with the ineffable and detached from the get-and-spend world. This is not Rahner's mystic.

Mysticism's Greek etymological root is *mystikōs*, referring to the possession of secrets, and *mystes*, meaning one initiated into those secrets. These words are, in turn, linked to *myein*, meaning to shut one's eyes, in the sense that initiates are able to see the *mysterion*, the secret rites or doctrines.[30] It's not hard to see how such an etymological history could produce the idea that mystics are those who have knowledge of great mysteries. And, indeed, Rahner understands mysticism as the experience of mystery. But his view of what constitutes a mystery or the mystic life is not necessarily esoteric or exotic. Indeed, rather than pursuing esoteric cults, chasing after exotic gurus or seeking other-worldly visions (in drugs or hypnotic ritual), Rahner's mystic is one who dwells in the Mystery through participation in the everyday world of work and worship, friendship and joy, love and death.

The Mystery Rahner wants us to experience is one that he believes we encounter in our daily lives even if we are unaware of it: talking to our spouses in the kitchen at the end of the day, taking an evening walk around the block, spending quiet moments in the backyard, sharing a meal with friends, and finding pleasure (and gratitude) in the achievements of our children. Our inability to see the mystery of these everyday events, our repression of the wonder of the ordinary, highlights the spiritual poverty of the mechanistic and utilitarian worldview that dominates Western consciousness. An orientation toward the divine is inherent in human consciousness, says Rahner. You can suppress it, but not destroy it. "There is something like an anonymous, unthematic, perhaps repressed, basic experience of being oriented to God, which is constitutive of man in his concrete make up, which can be repressed but not destroyed, which is mystical or (if you prefer a more cautious terminology) has its climax in what the older teachers called infused contemplation." [31]

This makes everyone a potential mystic, since everybody has the potential to experience God's grace, according to Rahner. The encounter with the divine is not reserved for a saintly few or an institutional elite, but is available to anyone willing to make the effort to watch and listen, to reflect, and contemplate. Such efforts allow for the possibility of discerning the divine. To achieve this state, to reclaim a divine presence in our everyday life, makes life more intelligible. The everyday mystic unmasks false idols of the modern world and learns to see the enchantments that he or she had previously overlooked or ignored.[32] Given our evident devotion to diversion, unconscious or otherwise, we clearly need everyday mysticism more than ever. As one Rahner interpreter, Annemarie Kidder, states: "Mysticism is especially needed when people have the impression that

God can no longer be discovered, that a secularized, self-sufficient, technological and scientific age with its laws has pre-empted the need to search for a God who lends purpose and meaning to humanity, world history and the evolutionary cosmic principle."[33]

What sustains Rahner's commitment to everyday mysticism is his confidence that God-as-Mystery resides at the core of human consciousness; the Logos speaks in the deepest recesses of the human spirit, whether we hear it or not. God is the atmosphere in which we live in the same way that water is the medium in which fish have their being. We can deny, repress, overlook or ignore this "basal spiritual metabolism," but, admit it or not, when it comes to the presence of the divine in our lives, we are "like sponges in water. We take the water for granted."[34] Mystical experience is thus to be found in personal experience. As theologian Harvey Egan explains, "the essence of mysticism can be found in every person's primordial, albeit anonymous, experience of God. For Rahner, the human person is *homo mysticus* – one who experiences God because of an orientation to God rooted in the way God has made humans. Strictly speaking, therefore, everyone is at least an anonymous mystic."[35]

This view of mysticism coincides with the views of the early Church Fathers, who did not make a serious distinction between the seemingly weak experiences of God (everyday mysticism, as it were) and the more ecstatic, visionary experiences of, say, Paul on the road to Damascus. While Christian mystics often experienced God in a decidedly dramatic fashion, Rahner insists that "an 'ordinary' Christian's life of faith, hope, and love contains a mystical dimension, an experience of God."[36] We exist in a world infused with divine presence and work out our ultimate destiny in our humdrum ways. This "mysticism of the everyday" takes into account the most humble of our daily routines, including a home life engaged in everything from working, eating and sleeping to such seemingly banal activities as walking, sitting and standing.

Rahner offers a meditation on walking that calls attention to the way in which this everyday activity can, when rightly perceived, express the essence of human freedom and truth-seeking. Walking may be one of the most common activities of daily life, but we only have to lose that ability through confinement or a crippling illness to realize that walking is something of a miracle. In walking, says Rahner, "we experience ourselves as changing, as those who are searching, as those who have yet to arrive. We realize that we are the ones walking toward a goal and not simply drifting toward nothingness." He sees processions, parades and pilgrimages as symbolic walks that demonstrate how our lives express a fundamental human experience such as walking in a sacramental manner. The single act of walking symbolizes the whole of human existence in its assertion of freedom and purpose. Walking says we are here.[37]

Rahner sees equal significance in simple sitting. Only it is not that simple; there is a theology of place involved in sitting. "Who has not experienced sitting down with gratitude and gladness after some exhausting work or a hiking trip? Who does not have the wish, in spite of restless longings, to finally settle down?" To sit in Rahner's sense implies that we long for roots, that we need a place where we can be ourselves at our best, that all our movement, all our walking, is pointed to some place we can call home, where we feel fulfilled.

However, Rahner goes beyond this physical appreciation of "sitting" to seeing the activity as a spiritual challenge. The physical side of sitting does not capture the "peace of fulfillment," of finding the place where our deepest response to the world is experienced. This experience is possible in moments of stillness when we no longer divert ourselves with restless and shallow activity, when we are sufficient in our solitude to hear the inner voice. Like Pascal, Rahner suspects that at least one of the causes of unhappiness for men and women is their unwillingness to sit quietly with their own thoughts. He questions whether we have the courage and discipline to be inactive, to sit down long enough to hear the approach of God. Too often we throw ourselves into activities – *divertissements?* – because we cannot endure the quiet or the solitude, or ourselves. "We need to learn that inactivity can be and ultimately is a higher form of activity, namely that of the heart, which serves the person as a whole." Only in being at one "with the infinite mystery we call God can one arrive in such a way that one does not have to go any further."[38]

I imagine that few us think of walking or sitting (or most daily activities) in such a reflective manner. But that is Rahner's point (and mine, too): The significance of such activities, their spiritual import, becomes apparent only when properly perceived. We need to pay attention to our everyday life – home and place, solitude and walking – if we are to experience life's mystical potential. This potential, if achieved, opens us to a more joyful life. The mysticism of the everyday opens us to a fuller appreciation of "the many good and lovely experiences that punctuate even the most banal lives." And this is as it should be, according to Rahner. Everyday mysticism distinguishes between the empty *divertissements* by which we try to avoid the existential conditions of our lives and those authentic responses to the world that implicitly reflect the presence of God in those experiences that fulfill us spiritually. The good things of life re-create us, filling us with joy and hope.[39] For Rahner, it is the everyday things that are the source of our constant re-creation.

The Bible illustrates Rahner's argument that everyday mysticism is, or can be, a source of joy and hope. In the New Testament, we find Jesus attending wedding feasts and banquets, providing food, offering wine (including wine from water). By all accounts, he enjoyed the good things of the world. "Jesus marvelled at the birds of the air, the flowers of the field, and rejoiced in the many joys found in ordinary life."[40] The Old Testament, too, is full of joyful people. To be sure, dour prophets warn about false gods, plenty of people get smited, sons are lost or sacrificed and Jehovah is often full of wrath. Yet, amidst all their trials and tribulations the ancient Hebrews were joy-filled. Indeed, the Old Testament celebrates feasting and rejoicing. Everybody, it seems, danced and sang to the harps and tambourines. And almost any "ordinary" event – the birth of a child, the presence of a beloved husband or wife, a long life, an abundant harvest – was cause for celebration. This joy is beautifully captured in the Book of Proverbs: "Rejoice in the wife of your youth ... Let her affection fill you at all times with delight, be infatuated always with her love" (5:19).

Such experience of joy in the everyday is "a spontaneous and complete joy involving the whole man – body and spirit, interior and exterior," says biblical scholar Pietro Dacquino. The ancients' joy reveals a unitary quality to their lives. They possessed undivided psyches. And that makes them different from us. "Modern man either neurotically represses his innate desire for joy or lets it loose in the world in the most capricious and irrational manner." (Think of all our technological and entertainment diversions.) Only rarely do moderns experience the kind of deep joy that simultaneously expresses physical, psychological and spiritual well-being, "the joy which is the fruit of full human maturity," as Dacquino puts it. Certainly, the ancients had their share of death and despair. You can imagine the desolation of spirit that would prompt the author of Ecclesiastes to declare human existence a worthless vanity. But as Dacquino observes, "the biblical pages exude the clear and genuine profound aspiration for joy and complete happiness which essentially distinguishes men of all ages."[41]

You can say something similar about hope. It, too, is rooted in our everyday experience. The Jews and Christians of the ancient world knew this. In the Bible, hope is a matter of trusting God to complete His divine plan. Christian theologians such as Augustine and Thomas Aquinas reinforced this idea of God as both the source and aim of hope. Augustine regards hope as a kind of spiritual courage that enables people to endure the sufferings of this life. Aquinas writes in the *Summa Theologica* that the proper purpose or end of hope is eternal happiness, which is impossible without faith in God. Our salvation is therefore linked to hope because "hope makes us adhere to God, as the source whence we derive perfect goodness."[42]

In modern times, the philosopher Immanuel Kant held that there are three things the rational human being asks: What can I know? What ought I to do? and What may I hope? People seek meaning in their lives, says Kant, and we are motivated in our search for meaning by the ends toward which our actions aim.[43] Thus, our capacity for reason implies an inherent moral sensibility. However, we often need incentives to ensure that our actions remain morally worthy. Hope provides that incentive, helping us to maintain our ideals despite our flaws and failures. Hope is the source of moral strength and courage in the face of everyday adversity and disappointment.

Nowadays, though, we often seem to feel hopeless. Is it because we feel trapped in a dull, mechanistic process – Max Weber's "disenchanted world"? (Unless, of course, you count the numbness of drugs and the diversions of entertainment as genuine modes of enchantment.) Gabriel Marcel, a twentieth-century French existentialist philosopher, suggests this view in considering Kant's third question. Marcel traces the source of modern nihilism and ennui to the modern way of thinking. Our technologically minded worldview tends to regard the world as a "problem" in need of a solution rather than as a "mystery" to be encountered and lived with courageously. The world-as-problem attitude reflects the mode of thinking and paradigm of knowledge found in science, mathematics and technology. Marcel calls this way of thinking "primary reflection." We "know" nature, including human nature, when we analyze it by means of empirical evidence, and understand its worth according to its biological or social functions. We are our functions, as it were, and our value depends on whether we function efficiently.[44]

Marcel acknowledges the necessity of the problem-solving mind. It cures disease, feeds billions and puts men on the moon. Nonetheless, it is too narrow a way of knowing the world because it tends to dismiss other, more experiential, ways of knowledge as less legitimate. "We have become so fascinated with technical knowledge that we have let our sense of wonder atrophy. And while we can scientifically accomplish any task we set before ourselves we no longer have the wisdom to know what projects are worth doing. We no longer know who we really are, nor do we know the value and purpose of life."[45] For Marcel, hope is one of those experiences that, like love, fidelity and faith – "concrete approaches," as he calls them – can restore our sense of the "mystery of being." These concrete experiences are mysterious because they involve us so intimately that we can't fully comprehend their meaning when we attempt to "scientifically" detach ourselves and understand them through abstract conceptual reasoning.

Like Rahner, Marcel uses "mystery" in a specific way. "A mystery is something in which I am myself involved, and it can therefore only be thought of as a sphere where the distinction between what is in me and what is before me loses its meaning and its initial validity."[46] Our lives are a fundamental mystery because no one can stand outside their life to achieve an objective position that allows them to know its meaning as a whole. There is no empirically verifiable scientific method, no objective perspective, that can be adopted to answer many fundamental questions – Why are we here? What is the meaning of life? – because we are unable to detach ourselves from our embeddedness in the existential circumstances that prompts us to ask such questions. Like fish in water, we cannot remove ourselves from the environment in which we live to ask the deepest questions about that environment. To do so would be to die.

For Marcel, it is this inability to step outside our human condition that should awaken us to the mystery of our lives. Our search for meaning and purpose must always begin with the exploration of personal experience in order to decide whether it possesses any hints (rumours?) of a reality that stands as a bulwark against the corrosions of disenchantment and nihilism. This isn't to suggest that the meaning of life is solely a matter of personal feelings or subjectivist self-regard – "if it feels good, it's meaningful," as the contemporary sophists might say. Nor does it mean abandoning science for superstition. It simply acknowledges that problem-solving modes of thought – all that abstract, scientistic conceptual theorizing – don't necessarily comprehend the full panoply of human *being*, or that all human experience is empirically verifiable. We look to science and technology for certitude and safety (it doesn't work, but foolishly we keep thinking it should). But to expect verifiable answers to every question is to regard life as a sickness in need of a cure and not a mystery to be comprehended in all its uncertainty. As psychologist Sam Keen observes, "Life which is psychologically and philo-sophically" – and, I would argue, theologically – "healthy always ventures beyond certainty, lived meaning is never wholly verifiable."[47]

This is Marcel's point. He looks to everyday experiences – what he calls "ontic" states – to provide "concrete approaches" to the mystery of our lives, including our experience of love, our sense of responsibility, or fidelity, to others, moments of joy, and the experience of hope. Hope is not calculation or prediction, but openness to possibility, which is, by its very nature, unverifiable. The opposite of hope is despair. And despair, in Marcel's view, is the inevitable result of thinking that only experiences you can measure, calculate and verify by scientistic thought are truly legitimate. The functional view of the world reduces the mystery of human existence, dilutes everyday experiences of love and joy, pain and death to mechanisms of biochemical cause and effect. This denial of mystery disenchants the world and corrodes the sense of wonder. You can investigate everything in this functional world, but the result is inevitably a disenchanted world. A life viewed strictly from the perspective of instrumental reason is without enchantment, wonder and, ultimately, deep inter-est. To paraphrase Keen, when the giant mechanism is fully explained, does anyone feel awe or gratitude at its being? You might admire the handiwork, and feel curious about its workings, but there is no wonder. Sooner or later boredom sets in, with all its attendant pathologies.[48]

Hope, on the other hand, is an attitude of openness to the endless mystery. "A mystery," says Marcel, "consists in asserting that there is at the heart of being, beyond all data, beyond all inventories and all calculations, a mysterious prin-ciple which is in connivance with me."[49] Thus, our lives, if they are to be lived and not "solved," require our courageous and joyful participation in the mystery. That, obviously, requires openness to the world, a measure of hopefulness. You can't approach *being* directly as a concept in need of understanding, but as a lived reality to be experienced prior to conceptual thought. We live, and then we think. Or, to borrow philosopher Paul Ricoeur's wonderful line, "Man is the Joy of Yes in the sadness of the finite."[50]

Ludwig Wittgenstein, in one of his more trenchant expressions of dissatisfaction with the modern tendency to disenchant the world through conceptualization, once said, "It is not *how* things are in the world that is mystical, but *that* it exists." "Don't think, but look," he advised.[51] To look in the sense that Wittgenstein means is, of course, inherently hopeful. Thus, our everyday lives, all those humdrum, repetitious actions of ordinariness, take on a quality of everyday mysticism – if we attend to them properly.

****

How might we do this? It's all very well to consider everyday mysticism from the high ground of philosophy and theology, but the task at hand is learning "how extraordinary the ordinary is when we rediscover it by way of the mystical."[52] How do we foster this attitude in the quotidian realities of our lives, particularly in our aggressively secular society? How, in other words, do we experience all those "concrete approaches" to the mystery in the humdrum here-and-now? I have already offered the examples of experiences of Munro's fictional characters, and elsewhere I have pointed to the epiphanic evidence of poets and novelists, philosophers and theologians. Perhaps, though, a few examples of people experiencing "moments of being" would be worthwhile.

I'm rather fond of the example of Rev. Mark Roberts, a Lutheran minister in Texas. Roberts recounts how he was waiting in a long line at Costco, and as he stood there he could feel his blood pressure rising. "The more I waited, the more frustrated I became. Words I never say (well, almost never say) filled my mind," he writes. "Then, all of a sudden, it dawned on me. I had one of those moments of grace, in which God managed to slip a word into my consciousness. As I stood in line at Costco, I was waiting. Waiting! I was doing exactly what Advent is all about. Of course, I wasn't waiting for God to save me or anything momentous … But, nevertheless, I was waiting. I was forced to experience something that's at the very heart of Advent."[53]

Roberts' epiphany is not particularly profound. I'm sure he would agree that as epiphanies go, it was a modest one. Nonetheless, it qualifies as an epiphanic moment in the sense that he gained a modicum of self-knowledge and, for a brief moment, transcended the ethos of instant gratification that prevails in our society. You might call this a moral epiphany. In any case, his experience also demonstrates another aspect to the practice of everyday mysticism: You become attentive by deliberate acts of attention. That is, our capacity for everyday mystical experience is, to some degree at least, a matter of education in the Aristotelian sense of habituation. In the same way that we become "educated" golfers or learn to swim by attending to the skills necessary to being good at those practices, so, too, we become skilled at the practice of everyday mysticism by paying attention, by looking instead of thinking, as Wittgenstein might say.

Theologian Mary Reuter offers a couple of examples on this score. She describes how she once asked friends and acquaintances if they had ever had any mystical experiences. Most immediately denied any such thing, as though it would have been embarrassing to step outside the corral of secularism. But on second thought, a few shyly came forward to admit to moments that might qualify as mystical.

I recall one event that I might describe as "mystical," I was walking in the woods in late fall. I was shuffling through the dead leaves, not thinking anything in particular. Suddenly my foot felt held back from making the next step. Ahead of me was a single violet – regal ... rich in color – standing elegantly in a two-inch square of clear space in the midst of brittle maple and oak leaves. In an instance I knew something of the experience of death and resurrection. Both were a reality at my feet. This event occurred about ten years ago, but it still remains new to me. It is an event I recall often and each time that I dwell with it for a few moments, I know again.

Here's another experience Reuter received:

Maybe mysticism is like the time I was thinking about a close friend and our relationship when suddenly I knew what love is. I cannot logically explain it, but I know it in a way that I'll never *not* know again. Sometimes I try to recall and reconstruct and experience my original event, but I cannot do so. But I still know deep in my heart what I learned.[54]

Both these examples meet Rahner's idea of everyday mysticism, and Reuter's point in offering them is similar to his: Mystical experience is not something rare or exotic. Mystical experiences can be a feature of everyday life, if we are attentive to their possibility in our daily activities. As Reuter says, "We are stopped, often within the usual sequence of incidents of the day, often suddenly as if by an outside force or person. Any reality of life can cause the interruption." But however it comes, "insight comes quickly and deftly, leaving us in the freedom of truth that cannot be denied."[55]

That was certainly Thomas Merton's experience. The monk, whose desire for solitude I discussed in Chapter Four, was visiting Ceylon (or Sri Lanka, as it is called today) in late 1968. A few days before his death in Bangkok, he visited the garden of Buddhas at Polonnaruwa. At the entrance to a cave there was a large, seated Buddha on the left, and a reclining Buddha on the right. As he approached barefoot and alone, he noticed the wet grass and the sand and the silence. He stopped before those "extraordinary faces" and their great smiles. And suddenly he knew the beauty of the world. "Looking at these figures I was suddenly, almost forcibly jerked clean out of the habitual, half-tied vision of things, and an inner clearness, as if exploding from the rocks themselves, became evident and obvious ... I don't know when in my life I have ever had such a sense of beauty and spiritual validity running together in one aesthetic illumination."[56]

Merton, of course, was an adept at spiritual exercises and highly sensitive to those things that might foster epiphanic moments. But what I find fascinating is the similarity between what Merton felt as a man, and what Reuter's uncertain acquaintances felt. While the form and intensity of the experience was different in each case, the emotional substance – the sense of wonder or awe or insight – was similar. And that goes to my point: Mysticism is not particularly esoteric, otherworldly or irrational. Nor is it irrelevant to our everyday lives. No doubt, there are cloistered monks sitting on mountaintops meditating away, and no doubt they have profound visions. But all the examples I've offered here and elsewhere, whether literary or personal, underscore the notion that we should stop thinking of mysticism as something otherworldly.

Mysticism is essentially a way of *seeing* the world. I realize that sounds simplistic, but it is perhaps one of the most difficult things to learn about mysticism, at least the kind I'm talking about. The difficulty is not intellectual in the sense of applying logic and reason. Nor is it a matter of empirical

329

investigation. Because mysticism is a matter of seeing, the problem is one of acquiring another way of looking at the world, of occasionally removing the blinkers of functional reasoning. The seeing is the knowing in everyday mysticism. This might sound rather convenient, a nifty duck-and-run obfuscation to avoid having to justify my claim. It might even seem conveniently elitist. Those who see as the mystic sees know what he's talking about; those who don't see as he sees, don't. But the fact is that not everything we experience is amenable to logical reasoning and available for sharing with others through our normal means of communication. Just because you can't prove an experience by scientific-rational-objective-empirical means does not mean it wasn't real, or that you can dismiss it as touchy-feely romantic irrationalism. Try proving empirically that you love your spouse and that all those gifts you give aren't a form of self-aggrandizement and control. As philosophers Charles and Jean Cox put it, "One cannot change the way one sees the world by logical argument, nor can one perform some ritual for bringing about such a change ... This change of vision is like falling in love: such things happen to one, they are not subject to will or reason." They compare the experience of changed vision to what happens when you suddenly understand a problem that you had previously been unable to solve despite your best rational efforts: "Suddenly, usually with surprise and pleasure or even amazement, one comes to see in a new way. The difference between the mystic's way of seeing and our ordinary way of seeing is like the difference between one who sees unity and harmony in a work of art and one who sees only a jumble of lines or words."[57]

The mystical moment is that moment when something clicks. What had been a jumble of incomprehension suddenly and surprisingly becomes harmonious and comprehensible. How can you explain that experience, or prove it, to someone who continues to see only a jumble of lines and words? You see or you don't see. Something clicks or it doesn't. The fact is, everyone experiences *being in* the world every day, but it is the mystic that sees everyday *being* as a wonder. Such experience, while eluding adequate description or even logical, rational explanation, can be transformative. For a few moments you let go of the functionalist and calculative approach to life and see it as a mystery, and, perhaps, as a gift.

Here, for example, is how Richard Bucke, a late-nineteenth-century Canadian psychiatrist living in Montreal, described one his mystical epiphanies. Coming home in a carriage after delivering a lecture, he suddenly felt overwhelmed by "immense joyousness accompanied or immediately followed by an illumination quite impossible to describe." The experience lasted no more than a few moments, but it was enough for Bucke that he "saw and knew" that "the Cosmos is not dead matter but a living Presence, that the soul of man is immortal, that the universe is so built and ordered that without any peradventure all things work together for the good of each and all."[58] Then there is the example of Sir Francis Younghusband, an eminent British geographer who, while walking in the hills outside Lhasa, the capital of Tibet, experienced a mystical moment that stayed with him for many years. It was, he said, a moment of "deep inner-soul satisfaction" that left him, like Bucke, with "a curious sense of being literally in love with the world."[59]

No doubt, most anyone would be inspired in Tibet. But the point I've been trying to make in these essays is that such experiences are open to most anyone in any place, so long as they are willing and able to make the effort. With imagination and empathy it is possible to approach the mystical experience at an intellectual level and, perhaps, lay the groundwork for your own moments of being. And you don't need to trek to Tibet or Spain or Japan to do it.

You can do it in your own backyard. As Virginia Woolf says, "Let us not take it for granted that life exists more fully in what is commonly thought big than in what is commonly thought small."[60]

These essays are an attempt to address certain "small" everyday experiences – home, place, solitude, etc. – that, as it seems to me, provide the conditions or circumstances for epiphanic moments. Through reflection, sensory awareness, periods of silence, and focused attention on our immediate world, we make it possible to better realize the mystical potential of ordinary, everyday life. Zen tradition tells how the fifteenth-century master Ikkyu was once asked by a visitor to write a maxim of the "highest wisdom." Ikkyu wrote only one word: "Attention." The visitor was displeased. "Is that all?" Ikkyu obliged. He wrote two words: "Attention. Attention."[61]

I hope this doesn't sound smugly ambiguous, but that's all there is to it: We need only pay attention. But attention is not easy to achieve. As Merton's experience in the garden of Buddhas suggests, it can take a lifetime of discipline to achieve a moment of proper attention, and even then there is no guarantee you'll get the results you seek. You can't buy mystical experience in the supermarket. There is a poem by the ancient Zen master Ch'ing-yuan that sums up the conundrum: "Before I studied Zen I saw mountains as mountains, and waters as waters. When I learned something of Zen, the mountains were no longer mountains, waters no longer waters. But now that I understand Zen, I am at peace with myself, seeing mountains as mountains, waters as waters."

I figure I'm somewhere low down on the second level. A child still sees the wonder because worldly diversions have yet to completely take over its mind – at least that was the case before the invention of television and the Internet – but, like most adults, I long ago lost my childhood sense

[handwritten margin note: This is Gurdjieff]

of wonder. It has taken years to discover what I need to recover. Indeed, it has taken me the better part of a lifetime to learn that I should see mountains as mountains, both intellectually and experientially, and even now I still struggle against the diversions of the modern world that would have me *see* otherwise. At times I think I would be content to spend the rest of my life *seeing* landscapes and paintings and poetry. But that is unlikely. There are bills to pay, duties to perform and a job to do. Even mystics still have to eat and find shelter. Besides, release from the get-and-spend world is no guarantee of inner stillness. The conscious mind, with its constant chatter, categorizing concepts and fretful regard for past and future, does not readily relinquish the mind to stillness and inactivity. Still, I try. I take whatever moments I can and whatever methods are available to me to slip – or try to slip – into a mystical mind. My preferred method for achieving such a state of mind is, obviously, walking: to wander in solitude until the mental chatter quiets down sufficiently to make wonder possible.

Where might all that wandering and wondering lead? That is the ultimate question, of course. Theologian Adrian Van Kaam teaches that our lives are journeys in search of the "epiphany at the root of our privacy." We are, he says, "enfleshed spirits," embodied in this world with all its vital, sensate and imperious requirements for ambition and self-assertion. Such worldly requirements are, of necessity, distractions. But they also conceal the "unique epiphany" in the depths of our being, luring us into illusions as we "search for the sacred source that calls us forth."[62] It is dangerous, he says, to journey without competent guides. I like to think these essays have offered some guidance. I have drawn on artists, poets, philosophers and theologians to suggest that certain experiences, including that of aesthetic appreciation, particularly in relation to nature, constitute a spiritual experience that can lead to religious experience. Those experiences, those moments of everyday mysticism, arise from ordinary things like sunlight on a wall or immobility at the edge of a mud puddle. Such moments are, in Van Kaam's phrase, "epiphanic intimations" of the all-forming mystery, "feeble pointers to the ineffable they symbolize."[63] Religious belief may not result from attending to the mystery of being, but rumours of God are more likely heard in such enchanted moments.

****

I'm sometimes tempted to think that was the case when I had lunch with a lizard on my last day on the Shikoku Henro. I walked alone most of my last day, leaving the Ryokan Ishiya in Shido, where I'd spent the night, just after 7 a.m. It was cool and overcast, perfect walking weather. I started with my pilgrimage companions, Syuji, Jun and Tanaka-san, but we separated as we settled into our particular rhythm of walking. I had only two temples left – Nagaoji, Temple 87, and Okuboji, Temple 88 – to finish my pilgrimage. The hike to Nagaoji was boring. The path paralleled a highway for the first five kilometres and there wasn't much to see except passing cars and trucks. The longer hike – eighteen kilometres – to Okuboji turned out much better.

Five kilometres beyond the town of Nagao, just before the Maeyama Dam, the pilgrim route turned off the road and ran along the edge of a reservoir below the dam until it entered the forests of Mount Nyōtai. I strolled happily along a narrow earthen path through the cedar forest. Sunlight splashed through gaps in the trees, falling like paint splotches on the leaf-padded path. The damp earth was pungent. A rush of water from a narrow creek gurgled beside the trail. Here and there the path twisted through copses of bamboo. I was careful to duck under the rain-jewelled cobwebs that spanned the narrower portions of the trail between the bamboo trees. Butterflies looped around my head.

I stopped for lunch at a trailside shrine surrounded by *sakura*, or cherry trees. I set my *bentō* box on a wobbly picnic table patchy with moss and speckled with the petals of pink blossoms. I ate with my eyes before savouring the *sashimi*. As I ate, I spotted a line of ants trooping across the tabletop. I was in a generous mood, so I shredded pieces of the rice ball and laid out a few grains for them. Then I had another luncheon guest. A lizard, black with silver stripes, poked its head over the edge of the tabletop. I remained still as he crept forward on the table. He must have seen me, but he didn't seem to be afraid as he waggled his way up the length of the table, his silvery head swaying back and forth, tail flicking.

I watched as he ate a larger piece of the rice ball. I reached out slowly with one of the chopsticks and pushed another piece across the table. He took that one, too. Staring at him, I remembered my other lizard encounter from years ago, the green lizard I had plucked from a fountain on the Camino de Santiago. I felt the hair rise on the back of my neck, although there is no rational reason why I should see any connection between this lizard in front of me on a mountainside picnic table in Japan and one at a fountain years before in Spain. One lizard reminds me of another. No big deal. Yet, there was a moment when my encounters with lizards seemed to be more than mere coincidence. I shook away the thought, of course. Still, the crazy notion crossed my mind that maybe I was lunching with a *kami*, one of the spirit-gods that tradition says occupy the mountains and forests of Japan. After two months walking through Shikoku's haunting landscape, I appreciated why the ancient Japanese believed the world enchanted by spirits. And so, I continued to watch my latest lizard companion, happy to share my rice ball with him.

I don't know how long I sat there before I noticed how quiet it was. I couldn't even hear any birds. I looked up at the sky through the trees. There was no breeze, nothing to rustle the leaves or sway the treetops. I looked back down. The lizard was still there. And I thought, "Let time stop here, now. Let this moment last. This is the real world, this table, this food, this creature, this silent forest – everything else is unreal." I felt a strange sense of weightedness. It wasn't heavy or oppressive. I *knew* I was supposed to remain at that moss-flecked table forever, immobile, while plants grew up around me, entwining me in their roots and branches until I became part of the forest. I had a vision of myself turning into a moss-covered trail marker, planted in this place forever like Jizõ, greeting passing pilgrims across the ages.

Then the wind blew through the trees and petals from the cherry blossoms rained down and my moment of *yoin* wafted away on a breeze. I looked up as the petals fell on my head and when I looked down I saw my lizard companion streaking across the table and jumping to the forest floor to disappear into the foliage. Plucking blossoms from my hair, I started to laugh. I felt immensely happy, like a child who has been given a marvellous gift. Maybe I had. On impulse, I pulled a notebook from my waist pouch and wrote my first poem in more than thirty years, trying to follow the five-seven-five syllable pattern of traditional haiku:

Wind shakes blossoms
from Nyotai's cherry trees.
Spring snow greets henro.

Haiku, I remembered from my long-ago literature classes, attempts to capture moments of intense awareness of the world. My poem certainly wasn't up there with Bashõ's verse, but the juxtaposition of "spring" and "snow" was a reasonable metaphor for the paradox of that moment. I put away the notebook and cleared the table. I was reluctant to leave, but I had three hours of walking ahead of me to reach Okuboji, the Temple of Completion. I left the remains of my *onigiri* at the foot of the shrine's Jizō statue, thanking him for the poem. If the god didn't want the rice ball, it was there for my *kami* companion.

NOTES

In order to reduce the number of endnotes – and to save space – I have followed *The Chicago Manual of Style*'s guidance and sometimes grouped several citations in a paragraph, or even several paragraphs, in a single note. In these instances, the specific citations are separated by semi-colons and follow the same order as the material in the text to which they refer.

Chapter One

1 Blaise Pascal, *Pensées* (Harmondsworth: Penguin, 1966), #427, 156.

2 Quoted by May Sarton, *Journal of a Solitude* (New York: W.W. Norton & Company, 1973), 99.

3 William James, *The Varieties of Religious Experience* (New York: New American Library, 1958), 292–94.

4 I owe this point to James Horgan, *Rational Mysticism: Dispatches from the Border Between Science and Spirituality* (Boston: Houghton Mifflin, 2003), 6–7.

5 Andrew Greeley, *Ecstasy: A Way of Knowing* (Englewood, NJ: Prentice-Hall, 1974). Here's the full quotation: "The mystical experience is a natural form of knowledge in the sense that one need postulate no special intervention of the deity to explain it. Nevertheless, in the mystic experience, the person makes contact with the Way Things Are." Quoted by James H. Austin, *Zen and the Brain: Toward an Understanding of Meditation and Consciousness* (Cambridge, MA: MIT Press, 1999), 19.

6 James, *The Varieties of Religious Experience*, 294.

7 Readers will notice a difference between this version of Bashō's haiku and the one I quote in Chapter Six. It's a matter of translators, I presume.

8 Austin cites studies showing that as many as thirty per cent of adults acknowledge having a "sudden or dramatic religious or mystical experience sometime in their lives." He points to another survey that indicated between thirty-three and forty-three per cent of people over twenty have had a mystical experience that "conforms to the definition of 'being very close to a powerful spiritual force that seemed to lift you out of yourself.'" Austin also cites a study by the psychologist Abraham Maslow, who found that many people were afraid to admit having had such experiences. See *Zen and the Brain*, 20.

9 Max Weber, "Science as a Vocation," in *From Max Weber: Essays in Sociology* (Oxford: Oxford University Press, 1946), 155.

10 Ibid., 139.

11 Morris Berman, *The Re-enchantment of the World* (Ithaca, NY: Cornell University Press, 1981), 2.

12 Hent De Vries, *Philosophy and the Turn to Religion* (Baltimore: The Johns Hopkins University Press, 1999), 2–3.

13 Paul Brockelman, *Cosmology and Creation: The Spiritual Significance of Contemporary Cosmology.* (Oxford: Oxford University Press, 1999), 82; 91.

14 Robert Bartlett, "Souls Without Longing," *Public Interest* (Winter 2003), 108–09.

15 Ibid., 109.

16 Eugene Rose, *Nihilism: The Root of the Revolution of the Modern Age*, 2nd ed. (Platina, CA: St. Herman of Alaska Brotherhood, 2001), 7.

17 Friedrich Nietzsche, *The Gay Science*, translated, with commentary by Walter Kaufmann (New York: Random House, 1974), 181.

18 Friedrich Nietzsche, *The Will to Power*, translated by Walter Kaufmann and R.J. Hollingdate, ed. Walter Kaufmann (New York: Random House, 1967), 3.

19 Quoted in Mark Richard Barna, "Dostoyevsky and Holy Russia," *World and I*, Vol. 13, Issue 9 (September, 1998), 321ff.

20 Ibid., I have also taken the quotations from Dostoyevsky from Barna.

21 David B. Hart, "Believe It or Not," *First Things* (May, 2010), n.p. Hart is always worth quoting when he challenges the vapid thoughts of the New Atheists: "In their moral contentment, their ease of conscience, [Nietzsche] sees an essential oafishness; they do not dread the death of God because they do not grasp that humanity's heroic and insane act of repudiation has sponged away the horizon, torn down the heavens, left us with only the uncertain resources of our will with which to combat the infinity of meaninglessness that the universe now threatens to become ... He understood also that the death of God beyond us is the death of the human as such within us." http://www.firstthings.com/article/2010/04/believe-it-or-not. Accessed June 12, 2010.

22 Jacques Barzun, *From Dawn to Decadence: 500 Years of Western Cultural Life* (New York: HarperCollins, 2000), 798.

23 W.L. Reese, *Dictionary of Philosophy and Religion: Eastern and Western Thought* (New Jersey: Humanitarian Press, 1980), 488; 547.

24 Charles Taylor, *Reconciling the Solitudes: Essays on Canadian Federalism and Nationalism* (Montreal and Kingston: McGill-Queen's University Press, 1993), 59.

25 Susan Shell, "No Angst and All Play: Postmodernism and the Humanities," *Perspectives on Political Science*, 24, 2 (1995), 84–86.

26 Barzun, *From Dawn to Decadence*, 11.

27 Eric Cohen, "To Wonder Again," *First Things* (May, 2000), 23–29. I have taken the pop culture references from Cohen. http://www.firstthings.com/article/2007/01/to-wonder-again-19. Accessed April 20, 2010.

28 Cohen, "To Wonder Again," 23ff.

29 Bartlett, "Souls Without Longing," 101–03.

30 Ibid., 110.

31 Nietzsche, *The Birth of Tragedy*, translated, with commentary by Walter Kaufmann (New York: Vintage Books, 1967), 52.

32 Leslie Paul Thiele, "Postmodernity and the Routinization of Novelty: Heidegger on Boredom and Technology," *Polity* (June, 1997), 489+.

33 Ibid.

34 Francis Fukuyama, *The End of History and the Last Man* (New York: Free Press, 1992), 330. At the same time, though, Fukuyama was also doubtful that mankind could live without struggle. Some men, he said, "will struggle ... out of a certain boredom: for they cannot imagine living in a world without struggle. Indeed, even if the better part of the world is a peaceful, prosperous liberal democracy, these men will struggle against all of that so as not to be bored."

35 I owe the preceding argument to Patrick Sherry, "Disenchantment, Re-enchantment and Enchantment," *Modern Theology*, 25: 3 (July, 2009), 377–78.

36 Alistair McGrath, *The Re-enchantment of Nature: The Denial of Religion and the Ecological Crisis* (New York: Doubleday/Galilee, 2003), 184–86.

37 David Brown, *God and Enchantment of Place: Reclaiming Human Experience* (Oxford: Oxford University Press, 2004), 17–18; 21.

38 Ibid., 21–22; 30; 36.

39 Andrew Greeley, *The Catholic Imagination* (Berkeley: University of California Press, 2000), 1–2.

40 Ibid.

41 On this topic, see especially Christopher H. Partridge, *The Re-enchantment of the West: Alternative Spiritualities, Sacralization, Popular Culture, and Occulture*, Vols. 1 and 2 (London: T & T Clark, 2004, 2005).

42 Eric Michael Mazur and Kate McCarthy, eds. *God in the Details: American Religion in Popular Culture* (New York: Routledge, 2001), 4–6. Cited in Craig A. Baron, "Christian Theology and the Re-enchantment of the World," *Cross Currents*, 56, 4 (Winter 2007), 112ff.

43 Partridge, "Alternative Spiritualities, New Religions, and the Re-enchantment of the West," *The Oxford Handbook of New Religious Movements* (Oxford: Oxford University Press, 2004), 60.

44 Partridge, *The Re-enchantment of the West, Vol.* 2, 169. Cited by Sherry, "Disenchantment, Re-enchantment and Enchantment," 376.

45 Cohen, "To Wonder Again."

46 Rachel Carson, *The Sense of Wonder* (New York: Harper & Row, [1956] 1965), 42–43; 52.

47 Geddes McGregor, *Dictionary of Religion and Philosophy* (New York: Paragon House, 1989), 61.

48 Robert C. Fuller, *Wonder: From Emotion to Spirituality* (Chapel Hill, NC: University of North Carolina Press, 2006), 13.

49 Brown, *God and Enchantment of Place*, 153; 163.

50 Peter Berger, *A Rumor of Angels: Modern Society and the Rediscovery of the Supernatural* (Garden City, NY: Doubleday, 1969), 120.

51 Ibid.

52 Charles Taylor, *Sources of the Self: The Making of the Modern Identity* (Cambridge, MA: Cambridge University Press, 1989), 469; 425.

53 I must emphasize that my purposes are contemplative rather than active. I have no political or social program for restoring Western spiritual life. Indeed, the notion that you can "fix" the world through political, social or bureaucratic techniques is part of the spiritual crisis. Surely the twentieth century demonstrated that when the longing for a better world is not moderated by a prudent awareness of and acceptance of the limitations of human nature, ideologically driven attempts to create utopian societies inevitably lead to horror and destruction. That is why my "prescriptions" are individualistic in orientation. They address individual spiritual concerns: How do you live a meaning-filled life in a world that, as it seems, denies the possibility of meaning or purpose to life, or, worse, is indifferent to the desire for such meaning? How can the individual retain or reclaim a spiritual sensibility in a hyper-secular age of decadence, disenchantment and nihilism? Obviously, society will benefit if the individuals who compose it achieve greater spiritual self-awareness, but that is ancillary to my primary concerns.

54 Berger, *A Rumor of Angels*, 120.

55 Nancy Frey, *Pilgrim Stories: On and Off the Road to Santiago* (Berkeley, CA: University of California, 1998), 82–83.

56 Richard Niebuhr, "Pioneers and Pilgrims," *Parabola*, IX: 3 (Fall, 1984), 7.

Chapter Two

1 William Goyen, *The House of Breath* (New York: Random House, 1950), 40–41.

2 I recall the titles so readily simply because the books were from my father's boyhood collection, which came to me early in my own reading career. I still have them on my bookshelves, and hope to pass them on some day to my grandchildren, assuming children in the future read books.

3 G.I. Gurdjieff, *Views from the Real World: Talks of Gurdjieff as Recollected by His Pupils*, foreword by Jeanne De Salzmann (New York: Dutton, 1973), 79–80.

4 I later discovered my memory of that interview was faulty. Nevertheless, it still serves my point. See Bob Thompson, "The Hand of Time: For Kurt Vonnegut, the Past Is Ever Present and the Future, Well ...," *Washington Post*, Oct. 12, 2005. http://www.washingtonpost.com/wpdyn/content/article/2005/10/11/AR2005101101844.html. Accessed September 8, 2010.

5 Carl Jung, *Memories, Dreams, Reflections* (New York: Vintage Books, 1965), rev. ed., 32–33.

6 Clare Cooper Marcus, *House as a Mirror of Self: Exploring the Deeper Meaning of Home* (Berkeley: University of California Press, 1995). I have drawn my commentary on childhood from Marcus' splendid book, and recommend it highly. Marcus, a landscape architect who specializes in the psychological and social aspects of architecture and land use design, was much influenced by Carl Jung.

7 Ibid., 4.

8 Edward Relph, *Place and Placelessness* (London: Routledge Kegan and Paul, 1975), 40.

9 Vincent Vycinus, *Earth and Gods: An Introduction to the Philosophy of Martin Heidegger* (The Hague: Martinus Nijhoff, 1961), 84.

10 Relph, *Place and Placelessness*, 39–41. Relph points out that it may be difficult to experience this deep attachment to home in the contemporary globalized world, with its emphasis on mobility and distance-spanning communications. Yet it would be too sweeping to dismiss the significance of home in our psychic lives.

11 Leonard Woolf, *Beginning Again: An Autobiography of the Years 1911 to 1918* (UK: The Hogarth Press, 1964). Cited in Jean Moorcroft Wilson, *Virginia Woolf: Life and London* (London: Cecil Woolf, 1987), 17.

12 J. Douglas Porteous, "Home: The Territorial Core," *Geographical Review*, 66, 4 (Oct. 1976), 384.

13 Jung, *Memories, Dreams, and Reflections*," 158–60. Jung interpreted his dream, saying, "It was plain to me that the house represented a kind of image of the psyche – that is to say, of my then state of consciousness, with hitherto unconscious additions ...."

14 Ibid., 225. Jung writes, "From the beginning I felt the Tower as in some way a place of maturation – a maternal womb or a maternal figure in which I could become what I was, what I am and will be. It gave me a feeling as if I were being reborn in stone."

15 Janet Carsten and Stephen Hugh-Jones, "Introduction," In *About the House: Lévi Strauss and Beyond*, edited by Janet Carsten and Stephen Hugh-Jones (Cambridge: Cambridge University Press, 1995), 2. Cited by Kathy Mezei and Chiara Briganti, "Reading the House: A Literary Perspective," *Signs*, 273, 3 (Spring, 2002), 841–42.

16 Porteous, "Home: The Territorial Core," 385–86.

17 Ibid., 387.

18 Joan Kron, *Home-Psych: The Social Psychology of Home and Decoration* (New York: Clarkson N. Potter, 1983), 22. My remarks on the movie's message are adapted from her entertaining book.

19 Quoted by Mezei and Briganti, "Reading the House: A Literary Perspective," 843.

20 Rita Eng, *Ruthie: A Novel* (New York: Simon & Schuster, 1960), 69. Cited in Mezei and Briganti, "Reading the House: A Literary Perspective," 843.

21 Marilynne Robinson, *Housekeeping* (New York: Farrar Straus Giroux, 1980), 90.

22 John Hollander, "It All Depends," *Home: A Place in the World*, edited by Arien Mack (New York: New York University Press, 1993), 27–29.

23 Ibid., 41–42.

24 Mezei and Briganti, "Reading the House: A Literary Perspective," 843. They cite contemporary novels by authors such as Anita Brookner, Margaret Drabble, Fay Weldon and Doris Lessing as examples of how the home can also be a psychological trap for both men and women. They also offer this scene from Vita Sackville-West's 1931 novel, *All Passion Spent*, in which an elderly character, Lady Slade, recalls her youthful marriage and the resulting smothering of her artistic dreams through a poignant description of the household objects that were part of her trousseau: "table-cloths, dinner napkins, towels (hand and bath), tea-cloths, kitchen rubbers, pantry cloths, dusters and, of course, sheets … After that she was lost."

25 Cited by Porteous, "Home: The Territorial Core," 387.

26 Aiping Zhang, *Enchanted Places: The Use of Setting in F. Scott Fitzgerald's Fiction* (Westport, CT: Greenwood Press, 1997), 16. The references to Poe and Hawthorne are also taken from Zhang. In regard to Fitzgerald, he writes, "A difference in living places usually shows differences in characters and, in some cases, differences in various states of one character's life."

27 Emily Carr, *The Book of Small* (Toronto: Oxford University Press, 1942), 74, 81. Cited in Porteous, "Home: The Territorial Core," 387.

28 Graham Greene, *A Burnt-Out Case* (London: Heinemann, 1961), 25–26, 33. Cited in Porteous, "Home: The Territorial Core," 387–88.

29 Cited in Porteous, "Home: The Territorial Core," 388.

30 Quoted by John Hollander, "It All Depends," 35.

31 Huston Smith, "The Long Way Home," *Parabola* (Winter, 2006), 40: 36–41.

32 Porteous, "Home: The Territorial Core," 390. I have leaned heavily on Porteous' work in this section of my essay, in large part because he is one of the few theorists to deal specifically with the concept of home in a philosophical manner (as distinct from a sociological, psychological or literary historical manner).

33 Mark Zandi, *Financial Shock: A 360° Look at the Subprime Mortgage Implosion, and How to Avoid the Next Financial Crisis* (Upper Saddle River, NJ: FT Press, 2008), 45. Zandi reinforces the point with subsequent lines: "Most of us define financial success by the size and quality of our home. The pecuniary and psychological benefits we attach to home ownership are unique: no other country values health and home more highly." He's referring to the United States, but the sentiment is widely applicable throughout the Western world.

34 On this point, I recommend Nicolas Retsinas and Eric Belsky, *Low-Income Homeownership: Examining the Unexamined Goal* (Washington, DC: Brookings Institute Press, 2002), esp. 1–11.

35 I have largely drawn my brief "history of home" from cultural historian Witold Rybczynski's marvellous book *Home: A Short History of an Idea* (New York: Viking Penguin, 1986), esp. Chapter Two, 15–49.

36 Philippe Ariès, *Centuries of Childhood: A Social History of Family Life*, translated by Robert Baldick (New York: Vintage Books, 1962), 394.

37 Rybczynski, *Home*, 26–30. See also Ariès, *Centuries of Childhood*, 390–98.

38 The quotation is taken from Rybczynski, *Home*, 31.

39 Ibid., 32–33.

40 John Lukacs, "The Bourgeois Interior," in *The Passing of the Modern Age* (New York: Harper & Row, 1970), 191–207. Lukacs identifies modernity with the development of bourgeois consciousness, with its praiseworthy emphasis on "certain rights and privileges, certain aspirations, a certain way of thinking even more than living." Indeed, he points out that scientific thinking ("the mathematicability of reality"), the insistence on reason, the promotion of liberalism, the contractual basis of state-individual relations, constitutionalism, nationalism and even individualism – these were all bourgeois ideas, not aristocratic ideas, much less the fruit of working-class thinking. Given this, Lukacs suggests that "instead of the Modern Age we *could* speak of the Bourgeois Age." See 194–95.

41 Quoted by Rybczynski, *Home*, 36.

42 Ibid., 48.

43 Lukacs, "The Bourgeois Interior," 198–99. Rybczynski, drawing on Lukacs, makes a similar point in *Home*, 35.

44 Tamara Hareven, "The Home and Family in Historical Perspective," in *Home: A Place in the World*, edited by Adrian Mack (New York: New York University Press, 1992), 232–33.

45 Rybczynski, *Home*, 35–36.

46 Ibid., 48–49.

47 Ibid., 77.

48 Ibid.

49 Ibid., 107–108.

50 Jane Austen, *Mansfield Park*, http://www.gutenberg.org/etext/141 (1814), 80–81. Accessed September 8, 2010.

51 Virginia Woolf, *To the Lighthouse* (Oxford: Oxford University Press, 1992), 7.

52 Ibid., 152–53.

53 Alfred Kazin, *A Walker in the City* (New York: Harcourt, Brace and World, 1951), 65–66.

54 Marilyn Chandler, *Dwelling in the Text: Houses in American Fiction* (Berkeley, CA: University of California Press, 1991), 1. Cited in Mezei and Briganti, "Reading the House: A Literary Perspective," 840.

55 Earl Rovit, "The American Concept of Home," *The American Scholar*, 29 (Autumn, 1960), 521–22. Home, he writes, is "one of the major structuring forces of the human psyche, basic not only to the individual's search for and sense of identity, but fundamental, as well, to the group's collective attempt to achieve a cohesive image of itself."

56 Derek A. Kelly, "Home as a Philosophical Problem," *The Modern Schoolman*, 52 (January, 1975), 151. He writes: "Modern man is caught between two unknowns: on the one hand he feels himself tossed to and fro without anchor or sail in a universe not of his own making, with a life not of his own asking. He feels homeless, forlorn, and naked before the powers, human or cosmic."

57 The great Jewish philosopher Martin Buber expressed the existential aspect of home this way: "In the history of the human spirit I distinguish between epochs of habitation and epochs of homelessness. In the former man lives in the world as in a house, as in a home. In the latter, man lives in the world as in an open field and at times does not even have four pegs with which to set up a tent." Quoted in Kelly, "Home as a Philosophical Problem," 151.

58 Kelly, "Home as a Philosophical Problem," 151–52. Kelly makes the worthwhile point that our sense of involvement in the world, our lived experience, needs to be clarified conceptually in order to more fully understand, and thereby more fully appreciate, that experience.

59 Martin Heidegger, "Building Dwelling Thinking," in *Basic Writings* (New York: Harper & Row, 1977), 323–39.

60 Kelly, "Home as a Philosophical Problem," 166–67. I have relied on Kelly's interpretation in setting forth Heidegger's views.

61 Ibid., 163. It is worth quoting Kelly more fully on this point: "By moving from a manipulative to a non-manipulative relationship to the world we can come to be at home in the world and thus see the world-as-home."

62 Ibid., 167.

63 Marcus, *House as a Mirror of Self*, 10.

64 Ibid., 40. Marcus writes, "If we start to consider the messages from the unconscious made manifest through our dreams, we have even more striking evidence of the house-as-self symbol."

65 Gaston Bachelard, *The Poetics of Space* (Boston: Beacon Press, [1964] 1994), xxvii.

66 Patrick McGreevy, "Place in the American Christmas," *Geographical Review* (January, 1990), 32.

67 Ibid., 33.

68 Ivor Debenham Spencer, "Christmas, the Upstart," *The New England Quarterly*, Vol. 8, No. 4 (December, 1935), 498–517.

69 McGreevy, "Place in the American Christmas," 39.

70 Lukacs, "The Bourgeois Interior," 204.

71 G.K. Chesterton wrote "The Spirit of Christmas," *The Thing: Why I Am a Catholic*, in *The Collected Works of G.K. Chesterton*, Vol. 3 (San Francisco: Ignatius Press, 1986), 333.

72 Ibid., 335.

73 I've taken the phrase from Walker Percy, *Lost in the Cosmos: The Last Self-Help Book* (New York: Picador, 2000).

74 Václav Havel, *Summer Meditations*, translated by Paul Wilson (New York: Knopf, 1992), 31. Also quoted by Aviezer Tucker, "In Search of Home," *Journal of Applied Philosophy*, Vol. 11, No. 2 (1994), 182: 181–87.

75 Kathryn Allen Rabuzzi, in *The Encyclopedia of Religion*, Vol. 6, edited by Mircea Eliade (New York: Macmillan, 1987). Cited in Rabuzzi, "In My Father's House Are Many Mansions," *Parabola* (Winter, 2006), 12–13.

76 Robert Rakoff, "Ideology in Everyday Life: The Meaning of the House," *Politics & Society*, 7 (1977), 86.

77 Ibid., 102–103. Rakoff's research conclusion is worth noting: "[M]ost of my subjects had not achieved the fulfilling synthesis they sought through homeownership. At the end of nearly every conversation, people turned to non-home metaphors – for example, the open road, going back to the land, a new religious commitment – to

express their desire for a more fulfilling, freer future and to judge the failure, for them, of the promises of the American Dream."

78   Quoted in Zhang, *Enchanted Places*, 15.

79   Tracy Cochran, "At Home in …," *Parabola* (Winter, 2006), 11: 6–11.

80   Quoted in Mezei and Briganti, "Reading the House: A Literary Perspective," 842–43.

81   Kathryn Allen Rabuzzi, *The Sacred and the Feminine: Toward a Theology of Housework* (New York: Seabury, 1982), 96.

82   Ibid., 88.

83   Ann Romines, *The Home Plot: Women, Writing & Domestic Ritual* (Amherst, MA: University of Massachusetts Press, 1992), 6.

84   Bachelard, *The Poetics of Space*, xxxv–vi. He writes, for example, "the house image would appear to have become the topography of our intimate being." And elsewhere, he says, "A house that has been experienced is not an inert box. Inhabited space transcends geometrical space" (47).

85   Caroline Joan S. Picart, "Metaphysics in Gaston Bachelard's *Reveries*," *Human Studies*, Vol. 20, No. 1 (January, 1997), 66: 59–73. The adjective "oneiric" comes from the ancient Greek word *oneiros*, referring to dreams. Thus, Bachelard is speaking of our deepest experience of home as a "dream house." However, it should be noted that in speaking of daydreaming, Bachelard does not mean idle narcissistic fantasies of self-aggrandizement, but rather the constructive daydreams of poetry, painting, craftsmanship and even philosophic reflection. He is referring to creative daydreaming, or a kind of deep reverie. To Bachelard, as Picart notes, the capacity for reverie is part of a healthy psyche. See Picart, 67.

86   Bachelard, *The Poetics of Space*, xxxvii.

87   Ibid., 5–6.

88   Picart, "Metaphysics in Gaston Bachelard's *Reveries*," 59.

89   Bachelard, *The Poetics of Space*, xxxvi. He refers, for instance, to the possibility of a house as a "hostile space," a "space of hatred." Yet, he also insists, "with the house we are in possession of a veritable principle of psychological integration."

90   For a useful overview of Bachelard's thought, see Roch C. Smith, *Gaston Bachelard* (Boston: Twayne Publishers, 1982), especially Chapter Seven, 116–39.

91   Bachelard, *The Poetics of Space*, 4.

Chapter Three

1   Edward Abbey, *Desert Solitaire: A Season in the Wilderness* (New York: Simon & Schuster, 1968), 1.

2   Paul Horgan, *Whitewater* (New York: Farrar Straus Giroux, 1970), 4.

3   Hoffer described the symptoms of the medical condition as a "sad mood originating from the desire to return to one's native land." If you suffer nostalgia you are detached from present reality and feel indifferent to your surroundings. You might even confuse past and present and hear voices. You could take on a lifeless and haggard appearance. On the topic of nostalgia, see Svetlana Boym, *The Future of Nostalgia* (New York: Basic Books), 2002.

4   Edward Relph, *Place and Placelessness*, 43.

5   Tony Hiss, *The Experience of Place* (New York: Knopf, 1990), xi–xii.

6   Yi-Fu Tuan, *Topophilia: A Study of Environmental Perception, Attitudes, and Values* (Englewood Cliffs, NJ: Prentice-Hall, 1974), 4.

7   Ibid., 4; 93.

8   Yi-Fu Tuan, "Place: An Experiential Perspective," *Geographical Review*, 65, 2 (April, 1975), 152–53; 165.

9   Philip Sheldrake, *Spaces for the Sacred: Place, Memory and Identity* (Baltimore: SCM Press, 2001), 8.

10 Quoted by Tim Cresswell, *Place: A Short Introduction* (Oxford: Blackwell Publishing, 2004), 20.

11 Yi-Fu Tuan, "A View of Geography," *Geographical Review*, 81 (1991), 102; 105. Cited in Cresswell, *Place*, 109.

12 Yi-Fu Tuan, *Space and Place: The Perspective of Experience* (Minneapolis: University of Minnesota Press, 1977), 144. Tuan quotes Wright Morris' novel, *The Home Place* (New York: Charles Scribner's Sons, 1948), 138–39.

13 Ibid., 142; 149. Tuan quotes Updike's story, "Packed Dirt, Churchgoing, A Dying Cat, A Traded Car," in *Pigeon Feathers and Other Stories* (New York: Fawcett World Library, 1962),168–89.

14 Jeff Malpas, a prominent scholar of Heidegger's thought, writes, "Heidegger's work provides us with perhaps the most important sustained inquiry into place to be found in the history of Western thought." See *Heidegger's Topology: Being, Place, World* (Cambridge, MA: MIT Press, 2006), 3.

15 Martin Heidegger, "Building Dwelling Thinking," in *Basic Writings*, 327; 338. Heidegger's emphasis.

16 Relph, *Place and Placelessness*, 38–39.

17 Heidegger, "Building Dwelling Thinking," 338. Heidegger's emphasis.

18 Quoted by Relph, *Place and Placelessness*, 28.

19 Cresswell, *Place*, 22. I am indebted to Cresswell's book for its excellent overview of Heidegger's concept of place.

20 Relph, *Place and Placelessness*, 6.

21 Genesis 1:1-2, in *The Holy Bible: Revised Standard Version* (New York: Nelson, 1953), 1.

22 Edward S. Casey, *The Fate of Place: A Philosophical History* (Berkeley: University of California Press, 1997), 13.

23 Ibid., 4; 344. Casey cites Simplicius, *Aristoles Categorias Commentarium*, in *The Concept of Place in Late Neoplatonism*, translated, in part, by Shmuel Sambursky, editor (Jerusalem: Israel Academy of Sciences and Humanities, 1982), 37.

24 Michael S. Northcott, "A Place of Our Own?" in *God in the City: Essays and Reflections from the Archbishop's Urban Theology Group* (London: Mowbray, 1995), 120; 119–138. I must acknowledge my debt to Northcott's essay, from which I have partially drawn my discussion on the historical connection between religion and place.

25 John Inge, *A Christian Theology of Place* (Aldershot: Ashgate Publishing, 2003), 92. Inge's emphasis.

26 Casey, *The Fate of Place*, 107.

27 Inge, *A Christian Theology of Place*, 6. Inge is taking his arguments largely from Casey.

28 Casey, *The Fate of Place*, 107.

29 Casey, *Getting Back into Place: Toward a Renewed Understanding of the Place-World* (Bloomington: Indiana University Press, 1993), xiv. Cited by Inge, *A Christian Theology of Place*, 11.

30 Inge, *A Christian Theology of Place*, 12. Inge's emphasis.

31 Anne Buttimer, "Home, Reach and the Sense of Place," in Anne Buttimer and David Seamon, editors, *The Human Experience of Space and Place* (London: Croom Helm, 1980), 174. Quoted by Sheldrake, *Spaces for the Sacred*, 8.

32 Sheldrake, *Spaces for the Sacred*, 8.

33 Ibid., 8–9.

34 Simone Weil, *The Need for Roots: Prelude to a Declaration of Duties Towards Mankind* (New York: Routledge, 2001), 40.

35 Christian Norberg-Schulz, *Existence, Space and Architecture* (New York: Praeger, 1971), 19. Quoted by Relph, *Place and Placelessness*, 42.

36 Relph, *Place and Placeslessness*, 43. Relph's emphasis.

37 Ibid., 143–45.

38 Gertrude Stein, *Everybody's Autobiography* (New York: Random House, 1937), 289. The full quotation is "The trouble with Oakland is that when you get there, there isn't any there there."

39 Heidegger, "Letter on Humanism," in *Basic Writings*, 219.

40 Tony Hiss, "Experiencing Places, Part I," *The New Yorker* (June 22, 1987), 45. The essays were later published as a book, *The Experience of Place* (New York: Knopf, 1991).

41 Ibid., 59.

42 Ibid.

43 Lisa Kadonga, "Strange Countries and Secret worlds in Ruth Rendell's Crime Novels," *The Geographical Review*, 88, 3 (July, 1998), 417.

44 William R. Siebenschuh, "Hardy and the Imagery of Place," *Studies in English Literature, 1500–1900*, 39, 4 (Autumn, 1999), 775: 773–89.

45 Thomas Hardy, *Jude the Obscure* (Harmondsworth: Penguin, [1896] 1978), 53.

46 Albert Camus, *Notebooks: 1935–1942* (New York: Alfred A. Knopf, 1963), 8.

47 William James, *The Varieties of Religious Experience* (New York: New American Library, 1958), 218. Cited by Tuan, *Topophilia*, 98.

48 Quoted by Tuan, *Topophilia*, 99.

49 Woolf, *To the Lighthouse*, 192.

50 Ernest Hemingway, *A Moveable Feast: Sketches of the Author's Life in Paris in the Twenties* (New York: Charles Scribner's Sons, 1964), 11.

51 Robert Lance Snyder, "Elbowing Vacancy: Philip Larkin's Non-Places," in *Papers on Language and Literature*, 43, 2 (Spring, 2007), 115–45.

52 Philip Larkin, *Collected Poems* (London: Faber and Faber, 1988), 136–37. I have drawn my "critique" of Larkin from Snyder, "Elbowing Vacancy"; James Booth, "From Here to Bogland: Larkin, Heaney and the Poetry of Place," in *New Larkins for Old: Critical Essays* (Houndmills: Macmillan Press, 1999), 190–212; M.W. Rowe, "The Transcendental Larkin," *English: The Journal of the English Association*, 38, 161 (1989), 143–52; and J.R. Watson, "The Other Larkin," *Critical Quarterly*, 17 (1975), 347–60.

53 Ian Almond, "Larkin and the Mundane: Mystic Without a Mystery," in *New Larkins for Old*, 188: 182–89.

54 Watson, "The Other Larkin," 352; 354.

55 Larkin, *Collected Poems*, 97–98.

56 Almond, "Larkin and the Mundane," 189. Another critic, Andrew McKeown, refers to Larkin as a "mystic with no God to believe in." See McKeown, "Ambiguity and Religion in Philip Larkin's Poems," *Imaginaires: Revue du Centre de Recherche sur l'Imaginaire dans les Littératures de Langue Anglaise*, 8 (2002), 182: 173–83.

57 Edmund Husserl, the father of the phenomenological school of philosophy, argued that we cannot act or think except in terms of something. Thus, all consciousness is intentional in the sense that all consciousness is consciousness of something. See Husserl, *Ideas: General Introduction to Pure Phenomenology* (London: George Allen & Unwin, [1913] 1967), 119–20.

58 T.S. Eliot, "Little Gidding," *Four Quartets* (London: Faber and Faber, 1959), 59.

59 Tuan, *Space and Place*, 154.

60 Guy Debord, "Introduction to a Critique of Urban Geography," *Internationale Situationiste*, 1 (June, 1958), n.p. Available at http://library.nothingness.org/articles/4/en/display/2. Accessed May 10, 2010. Also quoted by John Davies, "Walking with the psycho-geographers," n.p. http://www.johndavies.org/sermons/talk-gb-08-08-25.html. Accessed May 10, 2010.

61 Not too much, though. After a breakfast visit with Mrs. By, Frances Ramsay Simpson, the newlywed eighteen-year-old wife of Hudson's Bay Company governor George Simpson, wrote in her diary on May 4, 1830: "The house which stands in a good garden overlooks one of the most beautiful spots I have seen in this Country ... It commands an extensive view of the river, on the opposite side of which is the little village of Hull ... From the upper storey are to be seen the fine and romantic Kettle Falls, and beneath runs the Rideau Canal."

62 Casey, *The Fate of Place*, ix.

63 Ibid., xii.

64 Inge, *A Christian Theology of Place*, 14.

65 David Brown, *God and Enchantment of Place* (Oxford: Oxford University Press, 2004), 21–22.

66 Frazim Kohak, *The Embers and the Stars: A Philosophical Inquiry into the Moral Sense of Nature* (Chicago: University of Chicago Press, 1984), 6–7. It is worth quoting Kohak further on this point: "In a real, though not a customary sense, it is what we mislabel 'poetic imagination' that is, 'objective,' a spontaneous experiential given. It is our image of nature as dead and mechanical – an image of the human as either a robot or a rebel – that is 'subjective,' a product of the subject's active imagination rather than a given of lived experience – and actually quite counterintuitive."

67 Ibid., 7. Kohak's emphasis.

68 Brown, *God and Enchantment of Place*, 6.

69 Ibid., 160.

70 Ibid., 22.

71 I refer the reader to note #3 in Chapter Two.

72 Stephen and Rachel Kaplan, *Cognition and Environment: Functioning in an Uncertain World* (New York: Praeger Publishers, 1982), 84–85; 93. I owe the reference to this book to Hiss, "Experiencing Places – 1," 63.

73 Quoted by Relph, *Place and Placelessness*, 43.

Chapter Four

1 Thomas Merton, *The Wisdom of the Desert: Sayings from the Desert Fathers of the Fourth Century* (New York: New Directions, 1960), 23.

2 A 28-year-old Quebec man, Jean-François Pagé, was mauled to death by a grizzly bear in April 2006. Like me, he had been working for a mining exploration company, staking claims in the bush near Ross River, a small community about 200 kilometers northeast of Whitehorse, Yukon. http://www.cbc.ca/canada/north/story/2007/05/07/yk-bear.html#ixzz0j9KeyXy4. Accessed September 8, 2010.

3 Loren Eiseley, *All the Strange Hours*, 146.

4 Ibid., 245; 249.

5 Richard Wentz, "The American Spirituality of Loren Eiseley," *Christian Century* (April 25, 1984), 430.

6 Peter Suedfeld, "Aloneness as a Healing Experience," *Loneliness: A Sourcebook of Current Theory, Research and Therapy*, edited by Letitia Anne Peplau and Daniel Perlman (New York: John Wiley & Sons, 1982), 54–67.

7 Helen Waddell, *The Desert Fathers* (London: Constable, [1936] 1960). Cited in Suedfeld, "Aloneness as a Healing Experience," 59.

8 Anthony Storr, *Solitude* (London: HarperCollins, 1997), ix. I have greatly benefited from Storr's study, and willingly acknowledge my debt to what is perhaps the best single overview on the subject of solitude. It is certainly one of the most cited sources by those who've studied the concept. I must thank my one-time teacher Leon Logie for giving me a copy of Storr's book.

9 Christopher Long and James Averill, "Solitude: An Exploration of Benefits of Being Alone," *Journal for the Theory of Social Behaviour*, 33, 1 (2003), 22.

10 Ester Buchholz, *The Call of Solitude* (New York: Simon & Schuster, 1999), 18.

11 Blaise Pascal, *Pensées* (Harmondsworth: Penguin, [1966] 1988), 66–68. I owe this reference to *divertissement* to Edward T. Oakes' essay "The First Modern Christian," *First Things: A Monthly Journal of Religion and Public Life* (August–September, 1999), 41–48.

12 Buchholz, *The Call of Solitude*, 183.

13 Ibid., 182. Buchholz's emphasis.

14 Ibid., 30; 146; 278. Buchholz points out that in religious terminology, "solitude" once meant the experience of oneness with God.

15 Suedfeld, "Aloneness as a Healing Experience," 64–65.

16 Ibid., 55–56; 65.

17 One of the best books I've read on the psychological aspects of the pilgrimage experience is that of anthropologist Nancy Frey, *Pilgrim Stories: On and Off the Road to Santiago* (Berkeley, CA: University of California Press, 1998), especially 117–25.

18 Buchholz, *The Call of Solitude*, 9.

19 Suedfeld, "Aloneness as a Healing Experience," 59.

20 Ibid., 61.

21 Buchholz, *The Call of Solitude*, 239.

22 John Barbour, for instance, refers to "physical distance from others and mental disengagement." See *The Value of Solitude*, 1. Long and Averill, "Solitude," draw on the *Oxford English Dictionary* to conceive of solitude as "compatible with 'being or living alone,' 'seclusion,' or 'solitariness,'" and basically reduce solitude to a matter of "time alone," 22.

23 Philip Koch, *Solitude: A Philosophical Encounter* (Chicago: Open Court Publishing Company, 1994), 15; 49; 57. My discussion of solitude has largely been shaped by Koch's work, along with that of Barbour, Storr, Buchholz and Suedfeld.

24 Long and Averill, "Solitude," 23. However, they note that "aloneness is not a necessary condition for solitude: A person can experience solitude while in the presence of others, as when 'alone' in the company of strangers or when an intimate couple seeks solitude for togetherness." Nonetheless, they take solitude primarily as a condition of "being alone."

25 Koch, *Solitude*, 57. Throughout his book, Koch adds nuances to his definition of solitude. For example: "Solitude is consciousness disengaged from other people, the mind wandering along its pathways alone." Solitude is not necessarily framed by the presence of others, but neither is it necessarily structured by an explicit sense of the absence of others. "Disengagement from people does not entail awareness of being disengaged, for one can be totally absorbed in the small waves raised by the evening wind over the pond, the stony shore, the scampering in the woods" (49).

26 Barbour, *The Value of Solitude*, 2.

27 Ibid., 3.

28 Koch, *Solitude*, 45.

29 Barbour, *The Value of Solitude*, 3; 5. Barbour's statements regarding the moral purpose of solitude are worth quoting more fully: "Solitude allows a person to focus on certain experiences and dimensions of reality with a fuller attention, a more complete concentration, than is possible when one must also attend to the reactions of other people ... A return to solitude may allow one to recover the deep springs of personal identity, those memories, feelings, bodily experiences, and other aspects of one's being that are not always expressed in social roles ... Sometimes a person can only recover integrity, wholeness, and centeredness of character by establishing some healthy distance in relationships with others."

30 Alfred North Whitehead, *Religion in the Making* (New York: New American Library, [1960] 1974), 16.

31 Paul Tillich, *The Eternal Now* (New York: Charles Scribner's Sons, 1963), 23. Tillich also writes about the consequences of solitude: "In these moments of solitude something is done to us. The center of our being, the innermost self that is the ground of our aloneness, is elevated to the divine center, and taken into it. Therein we can rest without losing ourselves" (24).

32 Peter France, *Hermits: The Insights of Solitude* (New York: Random House, 1996), 21; 26.

33 Waddell, *The Desert Fathers*, 29. Quoted by France, *Hermits*, 24.

34 Richard E. Byrd, *Alone* (New York: G.P. Putnam's Sons, 1938), 4.

35 Ibid., 57.

36 Ibid., 154–55.

37 Ibid., 93–94.

38 Ibid., 171; 178.

39 Ibid., 84–85.

40 Ibid., 85.

41 Storr, *Solitude*, 37.

42 Sigmund Freud, *Civilization and Its Discontents*, translated by Joan Riviere, revised and edited by James Strachey (London: The Hogarth Press, 1979), 9. See also Storr, *Solitude*, 38.

43 See William B. Parsons, *The Enigma of the Oceanic Feeling: Revisioning the Psychoanalytic Theory of Mysticism* (New York: Oxford University Press, 1999), 3–4; 19–20 and, especially, 35–37. The emphasis is Rolland's. I shall return to the subject of mystical experience in Chapter Seven.

44 Storr, *Solitude*, 38–39.

45 Freud acknowledged having no such "oceanic" experiences himself, which, he admitted, mitigated his judgment against them. See *Civilization and Its Discontents*, 2.

46 Byrd, *Alone*, 295–96.

47 Carl Jung, *Memories, Dreams, Reflections*, rev. ed., (New York: Vintage Books, 1965), 226.

48 Bertrand Russell, *A History of Western Philosophy* (New York: Simon & Schuster, 1960). Cited by Buchholz, *The Call of Solitude*, 68.

49 Clark Moustakas, *Loneliness* (New York: Prentice-Hall, 1961), 65.

50 William Wordsworth, "I Wandered Lonely as a Cloud," *The Selected Prose and Poetry of Wordsworth* (New York: New American Library, 1970), 157–58.

51 William Wordsworth, "The Prelude" (Book Four, lines 354–57), *The Prelude and Selected Poems and Sonnets*, edited and with an introduction by Geoffrey H. Hartman (New York: New American Library, [1948] 1966), 266.

52 Cited by Storr, *Solitude*, 198.

53 Wordsworth, "The Recluse" (lines 755–60), *The Selected Prose and Poetry of Wordsworth*, 199.

54 Ibid., "The Prelude" (Book Two, lines 343–60), 232–33.

55 George Watson, "The Bliss of Solitude," *Sewanee Review*, Vol. 101, Issue 3 (Summer, 1993), 343–44. My emphasis. Watson makes the interesting point that our pleasure in solitude – "hedonistic solitude," as he calls it – is of recent vintage, being "an extreme rarity before the nineteenth century." Before that, solitude was conceived of as a largely melancholic condition. As he writes, "It is only in the past century or two, and then only in the prosperous lands of the Western world, that mankind has had much choice of solitude in his daily life – a room of one's own, even a house of one's own – and that earlier ages cannot have cherished or cultivated what they did not know" (342).

56 Quoted by Watson, "The Bliss of Solitude," 341; 343; 344.

57 W.B. Yeats, "The Lake Isle of Innisfree," *The Poems*, edited by Daniel Albright (London: J.M. Dent, 1994), 60.

58 Quoted by Watson, "The Bliss of Solitude," 341.

59 Ibid., 349.

60 Storr, *Solitude*, 21. Barbour makes this point, too. See *The Call of Solitude*, 147.

61 Ibid., 122.

62 On this point, see Storr, *Solitude*, 32–33, and Koch, *Solitude*, 101–03.

63 Suedfeld, "Aloneness as a Healing Experience," 64.

64 May Sarton, *Journal of a Solitude* (New York: W.W. Norton, 1973), 12.

65 Ibid., 26.

66 Ibid., 119.

67 Ibid., 145.

68 Ibid., 207–08.

69 Barbour, *The Value of Solitude*, 149–50.

70 Virginia Woolf, *A Room of One's Own* and *Three Guineas* (Oxford: Oxford University Press, 1992), 4; 53.

71 Virginia Woolf, *To the Lighthouse*, 85.

72 Ray Monk, *Ludwig Wittgenstein* (London: Cape, 1990), 93–94.

73 Ibid., 94.

74 Jan Estep, "Showing the way out of the fly bottle: searching for Wittgenstein in Norway," *Cultural Geographies*, 15, 2 (2008), 256: 255–260.

75 Monk, *Ludwig Wittgenstein*, 94.

76 Arnold H. Modell, *The Private Self* (Cambridge, MA: Harvard University Press, 1993), 128–29.

77 A recent example of this capacity to create a 'private space' under appalling conditions is Maziar Bahari, the Iranian-Canadian journalist who was imprisoned and harshly interrogated for four months in 2009 in Iran's notorious Evin prison. In an interview with the Canadian Broadcasting Corporation after his release, Bahari recounted how, in the midst of a beating, he was able to imagine himself elsewhere, creating, as he put it, "a parallel universe that he [the interrogator] could not penetrate." http://www.cbc.ca/world/story/2009/11/23/f-rfa-durham. html#ixzz0h3kIGJkp. Accessed March 3, 2010.

78 Koch, *Solitude*, 15; 44–45.

79 Hemingway, *A Moveable Feast*, 5–6.

80 France, *Hermits*, 163. France notes that Merton published more than thirty-seven books and 300 articles, including a bestselling autobiography, *The Seven Storey Mountain*.

81 Thomas Merton, "Notes for a Philosophy of Solitude," in *Disputed Questions* (New York: Farrar, Strauss and Cudahy, 1960), 178. I am indebted to Meng-hu, the proprietor of a website devoted to solitude – http://www.hermitary.com/solitude/merton_notes.html – for drawing my attention to this essay. But I must also acknowledge having benefited greatly from the material on solitude available at this site.

82 Ibid., 182–83. It is worth quoting Merton on the limitations of society in terms of self-transcendence: Societies "tend to lift a man above himself only far enough to make him a useful and submissive instrument in whom the aspirations, lusts and needs of the group can function unhindered by too delicate a personal conscience. Social life tends to form and educate a man, but generally at the price of a simultaneous deformation and perversion."

83 Ibid., 179.

84 The commentator is Meng-hu. http://www.hermitary.com/solitude/merton_notes. html. Accessed September 8, 2010.

85 Merton, "Notes for a Philosophy of Solitude," 184. See Meng-hu on this argument also. http://www.hermitary.com/solitude/merton_notes.html.

86 Tillich, *The Eternal Now*, 21.

87 Ibid., 21.

88 Psychologist James Howard describes our 'ontological' circumstance this way: "No matter how closely we make contact with another person, we do not occupy a single skin, share a nervous system, or achieve identity in [bodily] structure, function, or [physiological] sensation ... Each of us exists within his unique epidermal envelope as a separate *thing*. No other person can enter that envelope, nor can any of us escape from it. We were born in that enclosure, exist within it, and will wear it as our funeral shroud." *The Flesh-Colored Cage* (New York: Hawthorn, 1975). Quoted in Ben Lazare Mijuskovic, *Loneliness in Philosophy, Psychology, and Literatures* (Assen, The Netherlands: Van Gorcom and Company, 1979), 81. Mijuskovic's emphasis. It is also worth noting that this idea of bifurcated consciousnesses is reflected in some of the oldest stories of Western civilization. In Plato's *Symposium*, for example, the playwright Aristophanes tells the story of how humans were once a hermaphroditic race, men and women living in one body. The gods were jealous of the happiness of these humans and split them in two. Ever since, men and women have yearned to become one again. Similarly, in the Bible story of Genesis, we read, "Then the Lord God said, 'It is not good that man should be alone.'" Thus, he created Eve out of Adam's rib. In other words, at one time "Adam" contained both male and

female elements. After Eve's creation they recognize each other as "the flesh of my flesh and the bone of my bone," and long to come together as one.

89 Ilham Dilman, *Love and Human Separateness* (Oxford: Basil Blackwell, 1987), 105–06. Quoted by Koch, *Solitude*, 181–83.

90 Koch, *Solitude*, 296–97.

91 Quoted by France, *Hermits*, 165–66. For this last section on Merton's thoughts on solitude, I have drawn on France's *Hermits*, 163–91, and Barbour, *The Value of Solitude*, 160–84.

92 France, *Hermits*, 166. France is worth quoting more fully on this matter because he points to the limitations of rationalism when it comes to comprehending the gamut of human experience. "An insistent inner voice urging a specific course of action leading to faith is not granted to most of us. Our inner promptings tend to be vague and often connected with anxieties about our situation or the satisfaction of our appetites. Most agnostics would say that they would happily listen to the voice of God if he would only speak to them and they take his silence to indicate either that he isn't interested or that he doesn't exist. The unanswered cry for a sign is as old as religion itself. But the voice that speaks unambiguously and with authority takes away free will and is rarely heard." In other words, we refuse to quiet the ego and, thus, are unable to hear the divinity that we deny.

93 Quoted by France, *Hermits*, 171.

94 Merton, *The Wisdom of the Desert* (New York: New Directions, 1960), 23.

95 Richard Anthony Cashen, *Solitude in the Thought of Thomas Merton* (Kalamazoo, MI: Cistercian Publications, 1981), 173. On this point, Cashen, 171, cites Raymond Bailey, *Thomas Merton on Mysticism* (New York: Doubleday, 1975), 12; 206.

96 Ibid., 241–43, 267–68. Merton also observes: "The immature person, when forced to be silent, tends to experience his inauthenticity, and has no escape from it. Communications with others, even about nothing, at least offers some diversion" (78).

97 France, *Hermits*, 187.

98 Ibid., 164.

99 Merton, "Notes for a Philosophy of Solitude," 192.

100 Ibid., 181–82; 188.

101 Ibid., 178; 188; 194.

102 Ibid., 206–07. Merton's emphasis.

103 Merton, *Contemplation in a World of Action*, 157–58.

104 Merton, *A Vow of Conversation: Journals, 1964–1965* (New York: Farrar Straus Giroux, 1988), 207–08.

105 Ibid.

Chapter Five

1 Thomas Carlyle, *Sartor Resartus; On Heroes and Hero Worship* (London: J.M Dent, 1908), 50.

2 G.K. Chesterton, *Orthodoxy* (Garden City, NY: Image Books, 1959), 11.

3 Polly the Parrot was for many years the most famous resident of Carcross. He became a fixture at the hotel in 1918, when a certain Captain James Alexander asked the then owners to care for him while Alexander and his wife took a trip south. The couple never returned; they died along with more than 300 others when the *Princess Sophia* sank in late October of 1918 near Juneau, Alaska. Polly died in 1972 – reputedly at the age of 126 – after gaining a reputation for his

capacity to drink, sing opera and utter the bluest profanities. He is buried in the local cemetery, his grave marked with a fine bronze sculpture. I found a lovely little story about "Carcross Polly" in, of all places, the Bowling Green, Kentucky, *Daily News*, of Monday, Oct. 23, 1972. http://news.google.com/newspapers?nid=1696 &dat=19721023&id=cccdAAAAIBAJ&sjid=m0YEAAAAIBAJ&pg=7297,4064175. Accessed April 11, 2010

4   In researching the topic of wonder I came across some scholarly support for my experience in an essay by philosopher Mark Kingwell. "What is wonderful," he writes, "is not simply the oak leaf I look at, making me wonder why there is not nothing ... *What is also wonderful is this experience of wondering itself, and myself as the person in whom astonishment before the world is felt.*" See "Husserl's Sense of Wonder," *Philosophical Forum*, Vol. XXXI, No. 1 (Spring, 2009), 89: 85–107. Kingwell's emphasis.

5   According to some cultures, the full meaning of a visionary experience can take a lifetime to play out. See Lee Irwin, *The Dream Seekers: Native American Visionary Traditions of the Great Plains* (Oklahoma: University of Oklahoma Press, 1994), 170. In reference to the Native American tradition of "dream visions," he writes, "The dream cannot be interpreted or understood in any 'finished' way; it is part of an ongoing process of interaction, dialogue, reflection, and insight unfolding over the years."

6   Morris Beja, *Epiphany in the Modern Novel* (Seattle: Owen, 1971), 13. The book is long out of print, but I still have my copy. An Internet search of the University of Victoria reveals that the book is listed in the McPherson Library catalogue. I have no idea if it is the same book I borrowed so long ago, but learning that a copy still sits on the shelf had me remembering – a modest epiphany – my late-night wanderings among the stacks, plucking books whose titles caught my eye and skimming a few pages to see if I wanted to read more. I can't say that's how I found Beja's book, but I hazard a guess that the title caught my eye in light of my Emerald Lake experience. Maybe there is something to Carl Jung's notion of synchronicity, or, as the phenomenologists might say, to the intentionality of consciousness.

7   Beja, *Epiphany in the Modern Novel*, 24–26. In referring to epiphanies as "one type of moment of illumination," Beja traces the main tradition for these moments to Paul's conversionary experience on the road to Damascus, arguing that in the West, "the moment of vision is a Christian phenomenon." However, he also points out that epiphanies are not necessarily mystical. Many of those who have undergone epiphanic experiences – Augustine, John Bunyan, Thomas Carlyle – cannot be legitimately called mystics.

8   Kelly Bulkeley, *The Wondering Brain: Thinking About Religion with and Beyond Cognitive Neuroscience* (New York: Routledge, 2005), 4; 42; 198. Bulkeley's emphasis. He also makes the point that the "clearest indication" that your "visionary power is alive and well" is "the frequency with which [you] experience moments of wonder."

9   Robert C. Fuller, *Wonder: From Emotion to Spirituality* (Chapel Hill, NC: University of North Carolina Press, 2006), 101–02.

10   Rachel Carson, *Silent Spring* (Boston: Houghton Mifflin, 1962), 249. Quoted in Fuller, *Wonder*, 104.

11   Carson, *The Sense of Wonder*, 52; 66.

12   Carson, *The Edge of the Sea* (Toronto: The New American Library, [1955] 1963), 15; 216.

13   Kenneth L. Schmitz, *The Recovery of Wonder: The New Freedom and the Asceticism of Power* (Montreal and Kingston: McGill-Queen's University Press, 2005), xii–xiii.

14 Ibid., 3–4; 11.

15 Everyone, it seems, makes this point in one form or another. See Beja, *Epiphany in the Modern Novel*, 17–18; Schmitz, *The Recovery of Wonder*, 11; and Bulkeley, *The Wondering Brain*, 199.

16 Beja, *Epiphany in the Modern Novel*, 14–15.

17 Quoted by Dennis Quinn, *Iris Exiled: A Synoptic History of Wonder* (Lanham, MD: University Press of America, 2002), 32.

18 Ibid., 36.

19 Plato, *Theatetus*, 155d, Vol. IV, *The Dialogues of Plato*, translated by Benjamin Jowett (Oxford: Oxford University Press, 1875), 301–02.

20 Aristotle, *Metaphysics*, 982b12, translated by W.D. Ross, in *The Basic Works of Aristotle*, edited by Richard Mckeon (New York: Random House, [1941] 1966), 692.

21 The whole debate about mind-body relationship that preoccupies cognitive neuroscience is far beyond the scope of my discussions. Bulkeley, however, offers an overview of the subject. See *The Wondering Brain*, 17–35. I shall rely on his judgment as my excuse for sidestepping the body-versus-mind, nature-versus-spirit debate. He writes, "Do feelings of revelation and mystical ecstasy derive entirely from chemical and electrical activities inside the brain, or do such feelings connect people *through* their brains and bodies to transcendent powers and cosmic patterns of relatedness? ... I leave the question open, while strongly endorsing efforts to explore that latter possibility" (199).

22 Juan De Pasquale. "A Wonder Full Life," *Notre Dame Magazine* (Spring, 2003), n.p. http://magazine.nd.edu/news/11305/. Accessed April 11, 2010. De Pasquale's short essay makes an eloquent personal statement about the meaning of wonder in one man's life.

23 Fuller, *Wonder*, 158.

24 Austin Farrer, *Reflective Faith*, edited by Charles C. Conti (London: SPCK, 1972), 39. Farrer's emphasis. He also writes, "We go about most of our time with our eyes glued to the floor, or looking up only to take in the dull façade of things, unable to penetrate and seize the living being in which the Creator himself is expressed" (31).

25 Ibid., 37–38.

26 Fuller, *Wonder*, 9.

27 John Ayto, *Bloomsbury Dictionary of Word Origins* (London: Bloomsbury Publishing, 1990), 576. See also Robert K. Barnhart, editor, *The Barnhart Dictionary of Etymology* (New York: H.W. Wilson, 1988), 1243.

28 Alfred North Whitehead, *Modes of Thought* (Cambridge: Cambridge University Press, 1938), 232.

29 Jerome S. Miller, "Wonder and Hinge," *International Philosophical Quarterly*, Vol. XXIX, 113 (Winter, 2007), 62: 53–66.

30 Gabriel Marcel, *The Existential Background of Human Dignity* (Cambridge, MA: Harvard University Press, 1963), 12.

31 Lorraine Daston and Katherine Park, *Wonders and the Order of Nature, 1150 to 1750* (New York: Zone Books, 2001), 14.

32 Quinn, *Iris Exiled*, 159. I have benefited from Quinn's overview of "wonder," and, indeed, his entire book. He offers the best historical survey of the topic of which I am aware.

33 René Descartes, *Discourse on Method*, part 2, part 4, translated by John Veitch (London: Dent & Dutton/Everyman, 1937), 12; 26. He wrote, "As for the opinions which up to that time I had embraced, I thought that I could not do better than resolve at once to sweep them wholly away," and "I thought that ... I ought to reject as absolutely false all opinions in regard to which I could suppose the least grounds for doubt."

34 Descartes, *The Passions of the Soul*, translated by Stephen Voss (Indianapolis: Hackett, [1642] 1989), 56. Quoted by Daston and Park, *Wonders and the Order of Nature*, 13.

35 Ibid., *The Passions of the Soul*, 307. Quoted by Fuller, *Wonder*, 9–10.

36 Bulkeley, *The Wondering Brain*, 196.

37 Quinn, *Iris Exiled*, 184–85.

38 Ibid., 232.

39 Alfred North Whitehead, *Science and the Modern World* (New York: New American Library, [1925] 1948), 55.

40 Quinn, *Iris Exiled*, 185. Again, I acknowledge leaning on Quinn for my description of Cartesian ideas. He, in turn, relied on the insights of philosopher Josef Pieper, particularly his philosophic study of leisure.

41 Josef Pieper, *Leisure: the Basis of Culture* (London: Faber and Faber, 1952), 32.

42 Ibid., 33.

43 Ibid., 33–34.

44 Ibid., 92.

45 Ibid., 93.

46 Ibid., 31.

47 Ibid., 35.

48 Daston and Park, *Wonders and the Order of Nature*, 14–15.

49 Quinn, *Iris Exiled*, 191.

50 Wolfgang Mommsen, *The Age of Bureaucracy: Perspectives on the Political Sociology of Max Weber* (New York: Harper and Row, 1974), 37.

51 On this topic, see Christopher Partridge, "The Disenchantment and Re-enchantment of the West: The Religio-Cultural Context of Contemporary Western Christianity," *The Evangelical Quarterly*, 74, 3 (2002), 235–56. See also Joshua Landy and Michael Saler, "Introduction," *The Re-enchantment of the World: Secular Magic in a Rational Age* (Stanford: Stanford University Press, 2009), 1–14; Michael Saler, "Modernity and Enchantment: A Historiographic Review," *American Historical Review* (June, 2006), 692–716; and Sherry, "Disenchantment, Re-enchantment and Enchantment," 369–85

52 Charles Taylor, *A Secular Age* (Cambridge: Belknap Press, 2007), 25–27; 32–34.

53 Ibid., 12.

54 Taylor, *Modern Social Imaginaries* (Durham: Duke University Press, 2004), 18. He writes, "Individualism and mutual benefit are the evident residual ideas that remain after you have sloughed off the older religions and metaphysics."

55 Taylor, *A Secular Age*, 717.

56 Virginia Woolf, *The Waves* (London: Penguin, [1931] 1992), 83.

57 Ibid., 83–85.

58 William Wordsworth, *The Selected Prose and Poetry of Wordsworth*, 172.

59 Philip Larkin, *Collected Poems* (London: Faber and Faber, 1988), 114–16.

60   I have taken my aesthetic standard from Philip Larkin, who once wrote that the duty of a writer is to the "original experience." "It seems as if you've seen this sight, felt this feeling, had this vision, and have got to find a combination of words that will preserve it by setting it off in other people." See Larkin, *Required Writing: Miscellaneous Pieces, 1955–1982* (London: Faber and Faber, 1983), 58.

61   The observation is that of philosopher Karl Jaspers. Cited by Michael Tucker, *Dreaming with Open Eyes: The Shamanic Spirit in Twentieth Century Art and Culture* (London: Harper Collins, 1992), 114. Jaspers wrote: "He [Van Gogh] simply wants to paint present actuality, in return he conceives this presence as a mythos; by emphasizing the reality he sees it transcendentally."

62   Quoted in David Sweetman, *The Love of Many Things: The Life of Vincent Van Gogh* (London: Hodder and Stoughton, 1990), 92.

63   Thomas Traherne, *Centuries of Meditations* (London: The Editor, 1908). Quoted by Quinn, *Iris Exiled*, 30.

64   The poem is available on many websites. I used http://www.poemhunter.com/ poem/wonder/. Accessed September 8, 2010.

65   I owe this point to Quinn, *Iris Exiled*, 43. He writes: "All the devices of poetry are efforts to get at the mystery of what things are … Thus in poetry we never emerge from wonder; the poet immerses us in his own wonder at the mystery he sees, and in the process the poem itself participates in the mystery and itself becomes a dark reflection of dim shadow."

66   William Wordsworth, "I Wandered Lonely as a Cloud," *The Selected Prose and Poetry of Wordsworth*, 157.

67   William Wordsworth, "The World Is Too Much with Us," *The Selected Prose and Poetry of Wordsworth*, 172.

68   Ashton Nichols, *The Poetics of Epiphany: Nineteenth-Century Origins of the Modern Literary Moment* (Tuscaloosa, AL: University of Alabama Press, 1987), xi.

69   W.B. Yeats, "The Lake Isle of Innisfree," *The Poems* (London: J.M. Dent, 1994), 60.

70   Ibid., "Vacillation," 299.

71   Rupert Brooke, *The Collected Poems of Rupert Brooke: With a Memoir* (London: Sidgwick and Jackson, 1919), liii–liv.

72   Quoted in Nicols, *The Poetics of Epiphany*, 209; 212.

73   Mark Twain, *Life on the Mississippi* (London: Chatto and Windus, 1883), 92–93.

74   Quinn makes a similar point in *Iris Exiled*, 38–39. He writes: "Even though he [Twain] says the river's beauty ceased to impress him, he is still able to recall and retell vividly his experience of that beauty."

75   Tony Tanner, *The Reign of Wonder: Naivety and Reality in American Literature* (Cambridge: Cambridge University Press, 1965), 229. I first read Tanner's book during my undergraduate years, when I wrote an essay on Hemingway for an American literature course. Tanner reinforced my instinctive admiration for Hemingway's writing at a time when he was increasingly out of favour among literary scholars parading their new feminist sensitivities. I sought out Tanner's book as I worked on this chapter; reading it again after all these years was a minor epiphany in itself. I willingly acknowledge my debt to Tanner in drawing on his work.

76   Ernest Hemingway, *The Snows of Kilimanjaro and Other Stories* (New York: Charles Scribner's Sons, 1927), 18–19.

77   Tanner, *The Reign of Wonder*, 230.

78   Hemingway, *The Sun Also Rises* (New York: Charles Scribner's Sons, 1926), 93.

79   Tanner, *The Reign of Wonder*, 247.

80 Hemingway, *For Whom the Bell Tolls* (New York: Charles Scribner's Sons, 1940), 471.

81 Tanner, *The Reign of Wonder*, 238.

82 The phrase is Gertrude Stein's, according to Tanner, *The Reign of Wonder*, 235.

83 Marcel Proust, *Remembrance of Things Past*, Vol. 1, *Swann's Way. Within a Budding Grove* (New York: Random House, 1981), 48.

84 Ibid., 49–51.

85 Beja, *Epiphany in the Modern Novel*, 46.

86 Ibid., 50.

87 It is worth noting the refrain of weary hedonism with which Peggy Lee answers her own question: "Is that all there is, is that all there is/ If that's all there is, my friends, then let's keep dancing/ Let's break out the booze and have a ball/ If that's all there is." Much as I love the song, I prefer my methods of enchantment.

88 Virginia Woolf, *Moments of Being* (London: Mariner Books, 1985), 78–79.

89 Ibid., 64–65. My emphasis.

90 I owe this discussion to Beja, *Epiphany in the Modern Novel*, 115.

91 Virginia Woolf, *A Room of One's Own* and *Three Guineas*, 142–43. The emphasis is mine.

92 Woolf, "Moments of Vision," *Times Literary Supplement*, 853 (May 23, 1918), 243.

93 Ibid., *To the Lighthouse*, 88–89.

Chapter Six

1 Søren Kierkegaard, *Letters and Documents*, translated by Henrik Rosenmeier, with introduction and notes (Princeton, NJ: Princeton University Press, 1978): 214–15. My thanks to Cathie Brettschneider for tipping me off to Kierkegaard's remark.

2 Quoted by Chris Arthur, "Walking Meditation," in *Irish Nocturnes* (Aurora, CO: Davies George Publishers, 1999), 224.

3 Rebecca Solnit, *Wanderlust: A History of Walking* (New York: Viking, 2000), 3. I have certainly benefited from Solnit's work and have drawn on it where it covers the ground that interests me.

4 Jean-Jacques Rousseau, *The Confessions*, translated by J.M. Cohen (Harmondsworth: Penguin, 1953), 113; 382.

5 Solnit makes this point in *Wanderlust*, 14–16.

6 *The Republic of Plato*, translated by Allan Bloom (New York: Basic Books, 1968), 327a; and *Phaedrus and Letters VII and VIII*, translated by Walter Hamilton (Harmondsworth: Penguin, 1973), 25; 43; paragraphs 230, 242.

7 Arnold Haultain, *Of Walks and Walking Tours: An Attempt to Find a Philosophy and a Creed* (London: T. Werner Laurie, 1914), 9.

8 I obtained the information regarding Christ's walking from a brief website article entitled "How Far Did Jesus Walk?" by Cari Haus, who, it seems, likes to walk and read the Scriptures. I am indebted to Haus' knowledge of the Bible, and for doing all those calculations. http://iluvwalking.com/blog/2009/02/28/how-far-did-jesus-walk. Accessed May 13, 2010.

9 John Milton, "Paradise Lost," Book Ten. http://www.literature.org/authors/milton-john/paradise-lost/chapter-10.html. Accessed May 20, 2010.

10 Solnit, *Wanderlust*, 76–78.

11 Ibid., 77.

12 Philip Larkin, *Required Writing*, 79. He is worth quoting on this point: "I write poems to preserve things I have seen/ thought/ felt (if I may so indicate a composite and complex experience) both for myself and for others, though I feel that my prime responsibility is to the experience itself, which I am trying to keep from oblivion for its own sake. Why I should do this I have no idea, but I think the impulse to preserve lies at the bottom of all art."

13 Quotes taken from Joseph H. Lane, Jr., and Rebecca R. Clark, "The Solitary Walker in the Political World: The Paradoxes of Rousseau and Deep Ecology," *Political Theory*, 34, 1 (February, 2006), 63–64; 62–94. I have drawn from this excellent essay to buttress my claim for Rousseau's status as a walker.

14 Jean-Jacques Rousseau, *The First and Second Discourses*, edited and translated by Roger D. Masters and Judith R. Masters (New York: St. Martin's Press, 1964), 201–02.

15 Jean-Jacques Rousseau, *On the Social Contract*, edited and translated by Roger D. Masters and Judith R. Masters (New York: St. Martin's Press, 1978), 46.

16 Solnit, *Wanderlust*, 18.

17 Rousseau, *The Confessions*, 64.

18 Ibid., 157–58.

19 Solnit, *Wanderlust*, 21.

20 Rousseau, *Reveries of a Solitary Walker*, translated and introduced by Peter Frances (Harmondsworth: Penguin, 1980), 27; 31; 35; 50. Solnit provides a tidy summary of *Reveries* in *Wanderlust*, 20–21.

21 Rousseau, *Reveries*, 81–82.

22 Ibid., 88.

23 Ibid., 88–89; 114.

24 Kierkegaard, *Letters and Documents*, 214–15. Kierkegaard's emphasis. There is something odd about this advice, considering that Henriette Kierkegaard was crippled and would have had difficulty doing what her brother-in-law urged.

25 Joakim Garff, *Kierkegaard: A Biography* (Princeton, NJ: Princeton University Press, 2000), 308–10.

26 Ibid., 309; 314–15.

27 *Søren Kierkegaard's Journals and Papers*, edited and translated by Howard V. Hong and Edna H. Hong (Bloomington: Indiana University Press, 1978), 5: 271 (1849–1851), and 5:177 (1841).

28 Garff, *Kierkegaard*, 314.

29 Ibid., 315–17.

30 Quoted by Garff, *Kierkegaard*, 317–18.

31 Ibid., 312. The street was also where Kierkegaard's life came to an end. He collapsed while out walking on October 2, 1855. A month later, on November 11, 1855, he died in hospital. He was forty-two years old.

32 Solnit, *Wanderlust*, 26.

33 Edmund Husserl, "The World of the Living Present and the Constitution of the Surrounding World External to the Organism," in *Husserl: Shorter Works*, translated by F.A. Elliston and Lenore Langsdorf, and edited by F.A. Elliston and P. McCormick (Notre Dame: Notre Dame University Press, 1981), 248. Cited by Casey, *The Fate of Place*,, 224.

34 Casey, *The Fate of Place*, 224.

35 Wallace Stevens, "Tea at the Palaz of Hoon," in *Poems by Wallace Stevens*, selected and with an introduction by Samuel French Morse (New York: Vintage Books, 1959), 23–24.

36 Guy Debord, "Theory of the Dérive," *Internationale Situationiste*, 2 (1958), n.p. http://library.nothingness.org/articles/SI/en/display/314. Accessed May 18, 2010. See also Geoff Nicholson, *The Lost Art of Walking: The History, Science, Philosophy, and Literature of Pedestrianism* (New York: Riverhead Books, 2008), 151. Nicholson writes: The *dérive* involves "abandoning your usual walking habits and letting the environment draw you in, letting your feet take you where they will and where the city dictates."

37 Will Self, *Psychogeography: Disentangling the Modern Conundrum of Psyche and Place* (London: Bloomsbury, 2007), 11. See also http://www.worldhum.com/qanda/item/will_self_on_psychogeography_and_the_places_that_choose_you_20071217. Accessed May 18, 2010.

38 http://www.johndavies.org/sermons/talk-gb-08-08-25.html. Accessed September 8, 2010.

39 Frey, *Pilgrim Stories*, 45.

40 Steven D. Carter, "Bashō and the Mastery of Poetic Space in *Oku No Hosomichi*," *Journal of the American Oriental Society*, 120, 1 (April–June, 2000), 190: 190–98.

41 Carter, "On a Bare Branch: Bashō and the *haikai* profession," *Journal of the American Oriental Society*, 117, 1 (January–March, 1997), 64: 57–69.

42 Sam Hamill, "Translator's Introduction," *Narrow Road to the Interior and Other Writings*, Shambala Publications (Boston, 2000), xx; xxxi. I have generally relied on Hamill's translation of Bashō's work, although I have also drawn on the translations of others when it suited my purposes.

43 Thomas Heyd, "Bashō and the Aesthetics of Wandering: Recuperating Space, Recognizing Place and Following the Ways of the Universe," *Philosophy East and West*, 53, 3 (July, 2003), 291–93: 291–307.

44 Bashō, *Narrow Road to the Interior*, 3.

45 Ibid., 4.

46 Carter, "Bashō and the Mastery of Poetic Space," 192–93.

47 Quoted by Carter, "Bashō and the Mastery of Poetic Space," 193.

48 Ibid.

49 Steven Carter, *Traditional Japanese Poetry: An Anthology* (Stanford: Stanford University Press, 1991), 356–57. Cited in Carter, "Bashō and the Mastery of Poetic Space," 193.

50 Carter, "Bashō and the Mastery of Poetic Space," 194.

51 Ibid., 195–96.

52 Ibid., 196.

53 Quoted by Heyd, "Bashō and the Aesthetics of Wandering," 299.

54 Ibid., 293.

55 Quoted by Carter, "On a Bare Branch: Bashō and the *haikai* profession," 67.

56 Heyd, "Bashō and the Aesthetics of Wandering," 295.

57 Hamill, *Narrow Road to the Interior and Other Writings*, 20.

58 Heyd, "Bashō and the Aesthetics of Wandering," 295.

59 Ibid., 299. Heyd cites one of Bashō's disciples, Doho, on this linkage of subject and object.

60 Ibid., 296.

61 Ibid., 295.

62 Ibid., 293.

63 Carter, "Bashō and the Mastery of Poetic Space," 196.

64 *Narrow Road to the Interior and Other Writings*, 50.

65 I've seen this quotation attributed to Bashō in several places, but I don't know the original source.
66 See Ian Reader, *Religion in Contemporary Japan* (Honolulu: University of Hawaii Press, 1991).
67 Robert Rhodes, "The Kaihōgyō Practice of Mt. Hiei," *Japanese Journal of Religious Studies*, 14, 2–3 (1987), 185–202. See also John Stevens, *Marathon Men of Mount Hiei* (Boston: Shambala, 1988).
68 Ibid., 194; 197.

Chapter Seven

1   Virginia Woolf, *To the Lighthouse*, 218.
2   G.K. Chesterton, *Orthodoxy* (Garden City, NY: Prentice-Hall, 1959), 28. The quotation goes on: "As long as you have mystery you have health; when you destroy mystery you create morbidity. The ordinary man has always been sane because the ordinary man has always been a mystic. He has permitted the twilight. He has always had one foot in earth and the other in fairyland."
3   Kenji Ekuan, *The Aesthetics of the Japanese Lunchbox* (Cambridge, MA: MIT Press, 2000), 1–9. I discovered this book a few months after Tanaka-san's lesson, and incorporated it into my pilgrimage account. Ekuan writes, "It is poor manners to start eating the instant you remove the lid of the lunchbox. You must allow your eyes time to peruse and enjoy the food before moving on to gratify your taste buds ... The habit of enjoying things first with the eyes is an integral part of the Japanese lifestyle" (1; 4).
4   Fosco Maraini, *Japan: Patterns of Continuity* (Tokyo: Kodansha, 1975), 26.
5   Robert Kress, *A Rahner Handbook* (Atlanta: John Knox Press, 1982), 55.
6   Ibid., 55.
7   Taylor, *Sources of the Self*, 218.
8   Ibid., 215–18.
9   Ibid., 211–13.
10 Ibid., 232.
11 Ibid., 426.
12 Don Fisher, "The Ordinary and the Epiphanic/Death and Eros: Religious and Spiritual Question in the fictions of Alice Munro." Ph.D. Thesis (Edmonton, 2004), 15.
13 Ibid., 16. I owe the observation on Thoreau and Emerson, as well as the quotation, to Fisher. He, in turn, drew on Stanley Cavell, *In Quest of the Ordinary: Lines of Skepticism and Romanticism* (Chicago: University of Chicago Press, 1988), 9.
14 Taylor, *Sources of the Self*, 287.
15 Morris Beja, *Epiphany in the Modern Novel*, 17.
16 Fisher, "The Ordinary and the Epiphanic," 15.
17 Taylor, *Sources of the Self*, 490.
18 William Closson James, *Locations of the Sacred: Essays on Religion, Literature and Canadian Culture* (Waterloo, ON: Wilfrid Laurier University Press, 1998), ix.
19 Fisher, "The Ordinary and the Epiphanic," 8.
20 Reese, *Dictionary of Philosophy and Religion*, 547. Quoted in Fisher, "The Ordinary and the Epiphanic," 5–8.
21 Fisher, "The Ordinary and the Epiphanic," 12; 21.

22 Alice Munro, "Walker Brothers Cowboy," in *Dance of the Happy Shades* (Toronto: Penguin, [1968] 1997), 3; 18.

23 Munro, "Miles City, Montana," in *The Progress of Love* (Toronto: McClelland & Stewart, 1987), 140. Quoted in Fisher, "The Ordinary and the Epiphanic," 221–23. I must acknowledge my indebtedness to Fisher's dissertation for its penetrating analysis of and commentary on the many "queer, bright moments" in Munro's fiction.

24 Quoted by Fisher, "The Ordinary and the Epiphanic," 17–18. He is referring to Munro's essay "Everything Here Is Touchable and Mysterious," in *Weekend Magazine, The Globe and Mail* (May 11, 1974), 33.

25 Fisher, "The Ordinary and the Epiphanic," 192.

26 Ibid., 202.

27 Beja, *Epiphany in the Modern Novel*, 21. My emphasis.

28 Taylor, *Sources of the Self*, 425; 481.

29 Karl Rahner, *The Practice of Faith: A Handbook of Contemporary Spirituality* (New York: Crossroads, 1986). http://www.seescapes.com/SG_Rahner. Accessed June 5, 2010.

30 Barnhart, *The Barnhart Dictionary of Etymology*, 690–91.

31 Rahner, *Opportunities for Faith: Elements of Modern Spirituality*, translated by Edward Quinn (New York: Seabury Press, 1974), 125.

32 Annemarie S. Kidder, "Introduction," in Karl Rahner, *The Mystical Way in Everyday Life*, edited and translated by Annemarie S. Kidder, with a foreword by Cardinal Karl Lehman (Maryknoll, NY: Orbis, 2010), xv. Kidder adds that everyday mysticism "involves understanding and practising right seeing and right praying, at theology and application."

33 Kidder, "Introduction," xvii.

34 Harvey D. Egan, "The Mysticism of Everyday Life," *Studies in Formative Spirituality* (February, 1989), 8.

35 Ibid., 8.

36 Ibid., 9. Egan cites Karl Rahner, "The 'Spiritual Sense' according to Origen," *Theological Investigations* XVI, translated by David Morland (New York: Seabury, 1979), 81–103; and "Mysticism," *Encyclopedia of Theology* (New York: Seabury, 1975), 1010–11.

37 Rahner, *The Mystical Way in Everyday Life*, 175–77.

38 Ibid., 177–78.

39 Egan, "The Mysticism of Everyday Life," 10–11.

40 Ibid., 10.

41 Pietro Dacquino, "Human Joy and the Hereafter in the Biblical Books," *Concilium*, Vol. 39 (1968), 17–31.

42 Quoted in Patrick Shade, *Habits of Hope: A Pragmatic Theory* (Nashville, TN: Vanderbilt University Press, 2001), 179.

43 Curtis H. Peters, *Kant's Philosophy of Hope* (New York: Peter Lang, 1993).

44 Among Gabriel Marcel's works, I recommend *Being and Having: An Existentialist Diary* (New York: Citadel Press, [1935] 1965); *The Mystery of Being*, Vol. 1 (London: Harvill, 1951); *Homo Viator: Introduction to a Metaphysic of Hope* (London: Gollancz, 1962); and *The Philosophy of Existentialism* (New York: Citadel Press, 1956).

45 Katherine Hanley, "Cultural Diversity and a Path Toward Wisdom: Perspectives of Gabriel Marcel," in *The Humanization of Technology and Chinese Culture*, edited by Tomonbu Imamachi et al. (Washington, DC: The Council for Research in Values and Philosophy, 1998), 157: 157–64.

46 Marcel, *Being and Having*, 117.

47 Sam Keen, *Gabriel Marcel* (Richmond, VA: John Knox Press, 1967), 47.

48 Ibid., 10.

49 Gabriel Marcel, *Position et approches concrètes du mystère ontologique* (Paris, J.-M. Place, 1977). Quoted by Rosa Slegers, "Reflections on a Broken World: Gabriel Marcel and Williams James on Despair, Hope, and Desire," in *Hope: Probing the Boundaries*, edited by Rochelle Green and Janet Horrigan (Freeland, UK: The Inter-Disciplinary Press, 2006), 145–46. See http://www.inter-disciplinary.net/publishing/id-press/ebooks/hope-probing-the-boundaries. Accessed September 8, 2010.

50 Paul Ricoeur, *Fallible Man*, revised edition, revised translation by Charles A. Kelbley, with an introduction by Walter J. Lower (New York: Fordham University Press, [1960] 1986), 140.

51 The first quote comes from Ludwig Wittgenstein, *Tractatus Logico-Philosophicus* (London: Routledge and Kegan Paul, [1921] 1961), #6.44, 73. Wittgenstein's emphasis. He goes on (in #6.45) to say, "Feeling the world as a limited whole – it is this that is mystical." The second quotation is from *Philosophical Investigations* (London: Basil Blackwell, [1953] 1978), # 66, 31.

52 James P. Carse, *Breakfast at the Victory: The Mysticism of Ordinary Experience* (New York: HarperOne, 1995), xi.

53 Mark D. Roberts, "My Greatest Advent Discovery," *Advent and the Christian Year* (2005). http://www.markdroberts.com/htmfiles/resources/advent.htm#dec205. Accessed June 6, 2010.

54 Mary Reuter, "A Second Look: Mysticism in Everyday Life," *Studies in Formative Spirituality* (February, 1984), 81: 81–93.

55 Ibid., 85.

56 Thomas Merton, *The Asian Journals of Thomas Merton*, edited from his original notebooks by Naomi Burton et al. (New York: New Directions, 1973), 233–34. This vision was in early December of 1968. A few days later in Bangkok, on December 10, Merton died of electrocution in a hotel room.

57 Charles H. Cox and Jean W. Cox, "The Mystical Experience: With an Emphasis on Wittgenstein and Zen," *Religious Studies*, 12, 4 (December, 1976), 483–84: 483–91.

58 Quoted by John Horgan, *Rational Mysticism: Dispatches from the Border Between Science and Spirituality* (Boston: Houghton Mifflin, 2003), 6. Horgan is quoting Bucke's most famous work, *Cosmic Consciousness*.

59 Quoted by David Matless, "Nature, the Modern and the Mystic: Tales from Early Twentieth Century Geography," *Transactions of the Institute of British Geographers*, New Series, 16, 3 (1991), 275. Matless is quoting Younghusband's 1921 book, *The Heart of Nature*.

60 Virginia Woolf, "Modern Fiction," in *The Common Reader: First and Second* (New York: Harcourt, Brace and Company, 1948), 213.

61 I owe the reference to Horgan, *Rational Mysticism*, 226.

62 Adrian Van Kaam, *Formation of the Human Heart: Formative Spirituality*, Vol. 3 (New York: Crossroads Publishing, 1986), 208–09.

63 Ibid., 210.

SELECTED BIBLIOGRAPHY

Bachelard, Gaston. *The Poetics of Space*. Translated by Maria Jolas, with a foreword by John R. Stilgoe. Boston: Beacon Press, [1964] 1994.

Barbour, John D. *The Value of Solitude: The Ethics and Spirituality of Aloneness in Autobiography*. Charlottesville, VA: University of Virginia Press, 2004.

Bartlett, Robert. "Souls Without Longing." *The Public Interest* (Winter 2003): 101–14.

Bashō. *Narrow Road to the Interior and Other Writings*. Translated and with an introduction by Sam Hamill. Boston: Shambala Publications, 2000.

Beja, Morris. *Epiphany in the Modern Novel*. Seattle: University of Washington Press, 1971.

Brown, David. *God and Enchantment of Place: Reclaiming Human Experience*. Oxford: Oxford University Press, 2004.

Buchholz, Ester Schaler. *The Call of Solitude: Alonetime in a World of Attachment*. New York: Simon & Schuster, 1999.

Bulkeley, Kelly. *The Wondering Brain: Thinking About Religion with and Beyond Cognitive Neuroscience*. New York: Routledge Publishers, 2005.

Byrd, Richard E. *Alone*. New York: G.P. Putnam's Sons, 1938.

Camus, Albert. *Notebooks: 1935–1942*. New York: Alfred A. Knopf, 1963.

Carson, Rachel. *The Sense of Wonder*. New York: Harper & Row, [1956] 1965.

Casey, Edward S. *The Fate of Place: A Philosophical History*. Berkeley: University of California Press, 1997.

———. *Getting Back into Place: Toward a Renewed Understanding of the Place-World*. Bloomington: Indiana University Press, 1993.

Cohen, Eric S. "To Wonder Again." *First Things*, 103 (May, 2000): 23–29. http://www.firstthings.com/article/2007/01/to-wonder-again-19

Daston, Lorraine and Katherin Park. *Wonders and the Order of Nature, 1150 to 1750*. New York: Zone Books, 2001.

Debord, Guy. "Introduction to a Critique of Urban Geography." *Internationale Situationiste*, 1, (June 1958), n.p. http://library. nothingness.org/articles/4/en/display/2.

Egan, Harvey D. "The Mysticism of Everyday Life." *Studies in Formative Spirituality*, Vol. 10, (February 1989): 7–26.

Eiseley, Loren. *All the Strange Hours: The Excavation of a Life*. New York: Charles Scribner's Sons, 1975.

Fisher, Don. "The Ordinary and the Epiphanic/Death and Eros: Religious and Spiritual Questions in the fictions of Alice Munro." Ph.D. Thesis. Edmonton: University of Alberta, 2004.

France, Peter. *Hermits: The Insights of Solitude*. New York: St. Martin's Griffin, 1996.

Fuller, Robert C. *Wonder: From Emotion to Spirituality*. Chapel Hill, NC: University of North Carolina Press, 2006.

Heidegger, Martin. "Building Dwelling Thinking." *Basic Writings*. Edited by David Farrell Krell. New York: Harper & Row, 1977.

Hemingway, Ernest. *A Moveable Feast: Sketches of the Author's Life in Paris in the Twenties*. New York: Charles Scribner's Sons, 1964.

———. *For Whom the Bell Tolls*. New York: Charles Scribner's Sons, 1940.

———. *The Snows of Kilimanjaro and Other Stories*. New York: Charles Scribner's Sons, 1927.

———. *The Sun Also Rises*. New York: Charles Scribner's Sons, 1926.

Hiss, Tony. "Experiencing Places, Parts I and II." *The New Yorker* (June 22 and 29, 1987): 45–68 and 73–86.

Hollander, John. "It All Depends." *Home: A Place in the World*. Edited by Arien Mack. New York: New York University Press, 1993, 27–45.

James, William. *The Varieties of Religious Experience*. New York: New American Library, 1958.

Jung, Carl. *Memories, Dreams, Reflections*. Revised edition. Recorded and edited by Aniela Jaffé, and translated by Richard and Clara Winston. New York: Vintage Books, 1965.

Kelly, Derek A. "Home as a Philosophical Problem." *The Modern Schoolman*, 52 (January 1975): 151–68.

Koch, Philip. *Solitude: A Philosophical Encounter*. Chicago: Open Court Publishing, 1994.

Kohak, Erazim. *The Embers and the Stars: A Philosophical Inquiry into the Moral Sense of Nature*. Chicago: University of Chicago Press, 1984.

Larkin, Philip. *Collected Poems*. London: Marvell Press and Faber and Faber, 1988.

Long, Christopher and James Averill. "Solitude: An Exploration of Benefits of Being Alone." *Journal for the Theory of Social Behaviour*, 33, 1 (2003): 21–44.

Lukacs, John. *The Passing of the Modern Age*. New York: Harper & Row, 1970.

Marcus, Clare Cooper. *House as a Mirror of Self: Exploring the Deeper Meaning of Home*. Berkeley, CA: Conari Press, 1995.

McGreevy, Patrick. "Place in the American Christmas." *Geographical Review*, January, 1990: 32–42.

Merton, Thomas. "Notes for a Philosophy of Solitude." *Disputed Questions*. New York: Farrar, Straus and Cudahy, 1960, 177–207.

———. *Contemplation in a World of Action*. Introduction by Jean Leclercq. New York: Doubleday & Company, 1971.

———. *A Vow of Conversation: Journals, 1964–1965*. Edited and with a Preface by Naomi Burton Stone. New York: Farrar Straus and Giroux, 1988.

Mezei, Kathy and Chiara Briganti. "Reading the House: A Literary Perspective." *Signs*, Vol. 273, No. 3 (Spring 2002): 837–46.

Munro, Alice. *The Progress of Love*. Toronto: McClelland & Stewart, 1987.

———. *Dance of the Happy Shades*. Toronto: Penguin, [1968] 1997.

Nichols, Ashton. *The Poetics of Epiphany: Nineteenth-Century Origins of the Modern Literary Moment*. Tuscaloosa, AL: The University of Alabama Press, 1987.

Parsons, William B. *The Enigma of the Oceanic Feeling: Revisioning the Psychoanalytic Theory of Mysticism*. New York. Oxford University Press, 1999.

Partridge, Christopher. "Alternative Spiritualities, New Religions, and the Re-enchantment of the West." In *The Oxford Handbook of New Religious Movements*. Edited by James R. Lewis. Oxford: Oxford University Press, 2004, 39–67.

———. "The Disenchantment and Re-enchantment of the West: The Religio-Cultural Context of Contemporary Western Christianity." *The Evangelical Quarterly*, 74, 3 (2002): 235–56.

Pascal, Blaise. *Pensées*. Translated with an introduction by A.J. Krailsheimer. Harmondsworth, UK: Penguin Books, 1966.

Pieper, Josef. *Leisure: The Basis of Culture*. Translated from the German by Alexander Dru, with an introduction by T.S. Eliot. London: Faber and Faber, 1952.

Porteous, J. Douglas. "Home: The Territorial Core." *Geographical Review*, 66, 4 (Oct. 1976): 383–90.

Proust, Marcel. *Remembrance of Things Past*, Vol. 1, *Swann's Way/ Within a Budding Grove*. New York: Random House, 1981.

Quinn, Dennis. *Iris Exiled: A Synoptic History of Wonder*. Lanham: University Press of America, 2002.

Rakoff, Robert. "Ideology in Everyday Life: The Meaning of the House." *Politics & Society*, 7 (1977): 85–104.

Rahner, Karl. *The Mystical Way in Everyday Life*. Edited and translated by Annemarie S. Kidder, with a foreword by Cardinal Karl Lehman. New York: Orbis Books, 2010.

Relph, Edward. *Place and Placelessness*. London: Pion Limited, 1976.

Rybczynski, Witold. *Home: A Short History of an Idea*. New York: Viking Penguin, 1986.

Sarton, May. *Journal of a Solitude*. New York: W.W. Norton & Company, 1973.

Sheldrake, Philip. *Spaces for the Sacred: Place, Memory and Identity*. Baltimore: Johns Hopkins University Press, 2001.

Sherry, Patrick. "Disenchantment, Re-enchantment and Enchantment." *Modern Theology*, 25: 3 (July 2009): 369–86.

Solnit, Rebecca. *Wanderlust: A History of Walking*. New York: Penguin, 2000.

Storr, Anthony. *Solitude*. London: HarperCollins, 1997.

Tanner, Tony. *The Reign of Wonder: Naivety and Reality in American Literature*. Cambridge: Cambridge University Press, 1965.

Taylor, Charles. *A Secular Age*. Cambridge: Harvard University Press, 2007.

———. *Sources of the Self: The Making of the Modern Identity*. Cambridge: Harvard University Press, 1989.

Thiele, Leslie Paul. "Postmodernity and the routinization of novelty: Heidegger on boredom and technology." *Polity* (June 1997): 489ff.

Tuan, Yi-Fu. "A View of Geography." *Geographical Review*, 81 (1991): 99–107.

———. *Space and Place: The Perspective of Experience*. Minneapolis: University of Minnesota Press, 1977.

———. "Place: An Experiential Perspective." *Geographical Review*, 65, 2 (April 1975): 151–65.

———. *Topophilia: A Study of Environmental Perception, Attitudes, and Values*. Englewood Cliffs, NJ: Prentice-Hall, 1974.

Waddell, Helen. *The Desert Fathers*. London: Constable, [1936] 1960.

Weber, Max. "Science as a Vocation." In *From Max Weber: Essays in Sociology*. Edited and translated by H.H. Gerth and C. Wright Mills. Oxford: Oxford University Press, 1946, 129–56.

Wittgenstein, Ludwig. *Philosophical Investigations*. Translated by G.E.M. Anscombe. London: Basil Blackwell, [1953] 1978.

———. *Tractatus Logico-Philosophicus*. Translated by D.F. Pears and B.F. McGuinness, with the Introduction by Bertrand Russell. London: Routledge & Kegan Paul, [1921] 1961.

Woolf, Virginia. *A Room of One's Own* and *Three Guineas*. Edited and with an introduction by Morag Shiach. Oxford: Oxford University Press, [1929] 1992.

———. *Mrs. Dalloway*. With an introduction and notes by Elaine Showalter. London: Penguin Books, [1925] 1992.

———. *To the Lighthouse*. Edited with an introduction by Margaret Drabble. Oxford: Oxford University Press, [1927] 1992.

———. *The Waves*. Edited and with an introduction and notes by Kate Flint. London: Penguin Books, [1931] 1992.

———. *Moments of Being*. Second edition. Edited and with an introduction and notes by Jeanne Schulkind. London: The Hogarth Press, [1976] 1985.

———. *The Common Reader: First and Second Series Combined in One Volume*. New York: Harcourt, Brace and Company, 1948.

SELECTIVE INDEX*

---

* I have confined this index to those people, concepts and places I mention most often or draw on most heavily.

Transcontinental
PRINTING
IMPRIMERIE GAGNÉ

PRINTED IN CANADA